Living in VIENNA

Bev Bachmayer
Editor

American Women's Association of Vienna

All proceeds received by the American Women's Association of Vienna from the sale of *Living in Vienna* will be donated to the charitable activities of the AWA.

This publication was created to provide practical information for the international English-speaking community living in Vienna. Information was gathered in good faith and was accurate to the best of our knowledge at the time of publication. However, laws and regulations change, as do telephone numbers. Prices inevitably go up. We regret any inconvenience this may cause our readers; however, the organization, editors, contributors, advertisers or printer shall not assume liability for any loss or damage caused directly or indirectly by the content contained herein.

Editor-in-Chief Bev Bachmayer

Editor for Design and Layout Anett Zahradnik

Design and Layout Associate Angela French

Printer Druckerei Peter Dorner

Advertising Manager Pamela Musselmann

Business Manager Anett Zahradnik

Distribution Manager Billie Ann Lopez

Marketing Manager Laura Dorrans

Illustrations Jilly Ringwood

Cover Artwork Gerhard Bachmayer

Cover Photo © www.viennaslide.com

Title Page Artwork Christine Sauermann

ACKNOWLEDGEMENTS

WRITERS

Gerhard Excel, Elizabeth Gerlitz, Andrea Kopecek, Billie Ann Lopez,
Silvia McDonald, Anett Zahradnik

COPY EDITORS

Ria Anderl, Janel Bedell, Carol Camacho, Mary L. Cooper,
Elizabeth Dobie-Sarsam, Martin Filtzmaier, Angela French,
Dawn Rae Gartlehner, Ngaire Jehle, Irene Jenkins,
Annika Johansson, Sue Liebetrau, Billie Ann Lopez, Judith Mueller,
Dinah Owen, Christina Rachler, Jane Ried, Amanda Seidel,
Lisa Shandalov, Ami Starnegg, Cristina Tallent,
Kathy Turk, Cathy Warley, Ruth Webster, Anett Zahradnik

CONTRIBUTORS

Gerhard Bachmayer, Connie Bremer, Mary L. Cooper
Liz Cow, Suzanne Gassner, Ute Kraushaar, Kit Leung,
Judith Mueller, James D. Pettt, Margaret Mary Richards,
Judy Roberts, Libby Slovenkay, Becky Still, Margaret Talbot,
Bonnie Toepfer, Mary Wagener

SPECIAL ACNOWLEDGEMENT

Maggie Lee Huckabee

OTHERS

There are a number of people in Vienna's international community, in embassies,
consulates, Austrian government offices and private businesses, who spent a
significant amount of time either on the phone or in person with us to ensure that
information we have is comprehensive, accurate and understandable. To all of
them, we offer our thanks. Hopefully, the time they spent with us will be time they
don't have to spend with others asking the same questions!

From The U.S. AMBASSADOR TO AUSTRIA

As American Ambassador to Austria and as Honorary President of the AWA, I am very happy to welcome you to Vienna – a city rich in tradition and history, but also a vibrant center for younger people with eyes towards the future.

LIVING IN VIENNA has itself become a tradition, helping thousands of our fellow Americans and other English-speaking newcomers to settle in and adapt to a new culture. During the years that my husband, children and I have lived in Vienna, we have all been repeatedly impressed with the authenticity of the tips and experiences offered by AWA old timers to the recently arrived. The editors definitely know what information will make life more comfortable and the adjustment easier in this beautiful city.

The transatlantic ties between the U.S. and Austria are deep, enduring, and dynamic, and Vienna is in the center of this lively exchange. I wish you great pleasure in using this guidebook to get around Vienna and sample its delights. And, I hope that all of you will feel as welcome in Vienna as my family and I always have.

Kathryn Walt Hall

FROM THE MAYOR OF VIENNA

As Mayor and Governor of Vienna I would like to welcome you to the capital of Austria and hope that you feel very much at home here.

Vienna is a city of many faces and facets. As a former imperial city it boasts many treasures of art and magnificent architectural monuments which call to mind the reign of the Habsburg emperors. It is also a stronghold of culture and in particular of music, for it was here that the great composers of the Vienna classical period wrote and performed their works, which today live on in Vienna's music institutions. It is the third official headquarters of the United Nations, along with New York and Geneva, home of numerous organizations and one of the two most popular conference venues in the world - a meeting place of nations and international communication.

Beyond that Vienna is also the vibrant center of the Austrian economy, one of the most prosperous regions in Europe, a pivot of East-West trade, which has become even more attractive as a business location since Austria's accession to the European Union. Today's Vienna is a modern, cosmopolitan city at the heart of Central Europe, drawing energy from its rich tradition and long history.

Above all, however, Vienna is a place of high living standards, a city sparkling with life and exuberance: reveling in the waltzes of the Opera Ball or the New Year's Concert, spending a night out with friends at the *Heurigen*, relishing breakfast in one of the coffee houses, stepping out into spring in the Vienna Woods or taking in the open air opera performances at the summer film festival in front of the City Hall - there are endless ways of turning a long sojourn in Vienna into an eventful and memorable experience.

Thus I would like to thank the American Women's Association of Vienna for its commitment and its laudable endeavors for the welfare of this city and its people. May this latest edition of *Living in Vienna* find many happy readers and may they feel at home and well-looked-after in this city.

Dr. Michael Häupl
Mayor and Governor of Vienna

FROM THE AWA PRESIDENT

Living in Vienna – the words bring to mind a new experience and hopefully a pleasant time spent in the beautiful capital city of Austria. The American Women's Association (AWA) has been a vital part of life in Vienna for many years. We are pleased to share the collected knowledge and wisdom about our current hometown with you, whether your stay in Vienna will be measured in days, months or years.

This is the tenth edition of *Living in Vienna* that has been revised and updated by the editor in chief, Bev Bachmayer and her team of wonderful volunteers. Everyone who worked on this book is a valuable part of what makes living in Vienna such a positive experience – the willingness of AWA members to share their knowledge and the commitment of the organization to help newcomers adapt to life in this city. Without the support of our volunteers and sponsors, this book would not have become a reality. To the volunteers and sponsors, please accept my thanks on behalf of all who will use this book and those who will benefit from the proceeds of the sale of the book.

The purpose of the AWA is to bring together women living in the international community to assist them in making friends, broadening their horizons and learning more about our current home, Austria. We are truly an international group where women who have lived in Vienna only a short time and women who have lived in Vienna their entire life may come together to learn, have fun and give back to our community. Your purchase of *Living in Vienna* assists the AWA in supporting a variety of charities that touch the lives of those in need. We thank you for your help.

I hope that the information contained in *Living in Vienna* will answer your questions about life in Vienna. No matter how long you have lived here, there is always new information found and shared by the women who have prepared this book. Enjoy!

JoAnn Martin
President (2000 - 2001)

FROM THE EDITOR

Last autumn I received a request to help out the group that was working on *Living In Vienna*. They just needed me to edit a few chapters, verify telephone numbers and such. I agreed and believed that with my current full-time work that this was the most of what I could do to help with the Millennium Edition of *Living In Vienna*. As Christmas drew near and the previous LIV Editor, Maggie Lee Huckabee's time in Vienna was coming to a close, she asked me to take over the Editor position. The one thing that she stressed is that you could be Editor and hold down a full-time job. My comment to her now is that yes, it is true, you can act as Editor of LIV and work full-time, but you had better have a very dedicated team to back you up. With that said, I want to thank everyone who helped with this revision of *Living In Vienna*.

My first thanks goes to Pamela Musselman. Pamela launched a very successful effort to sell advertisements to support the printing costs for the book. In addition to the advertising effort, Pamela gave me moral support and was always available for brainstorming of ideas. Pamela never hesitated to help out in any way she could. Pamela's efforts helped me realize the massive task and effort that was necessary for the overall production of the book.

I also want to thank Angela French for her determination and effort in working with PageMaker. Through minor and major technical difficulties she continued to fight the incompatibilities of PageMaker and Windows 98. She discovered and overcame the reasons for the crashes and edited over half the book.

Finally, I cannot thank enough, Anett Zahradnik for her unbelievable efforts over the last few months. She has jumped in and really wrapped up the final draft, she has coordinated, edited and completed the final layout. Without Anett's efforts this book would not be in existence today. Her business capability and computer skills are unsurpassed. I am very glad that she agreed to help out on the book, but even more I am very glad that she is my friend.

Additionally, I want to thank the scores of people that helped with the final edits and organization, Sue Liebetrau, Billie Ann Lopez, Jane Ried, Cris Tallent, Mary Wagener and all the others who helped in all those last-minute updates.

Beverly Bachmayer

Bev Bachmayer

ESSENTIALS

1

AUSTRIA

37

TRANSPORTATION

63

DRIVING

83

COMMUNICATIONS

101

COMPUTER

121

BANKING

131

Contents

Essentials

I f you've never been to Europe before—let alone Austria—you may be in for a few surprises. You can, however, minimize the risk of moving here unprepared if you read the following chapter before you come. It has sections with things you should know before you come, information you may need before you have time to read the whole book, explanations of documents and formalities you may encounter once you are here, suggestions for finding housing and getting through relocation, information about working here and basics about customs/duty as you enter and leave the country with purchases.

BEFORE YOU COME

Advice from those who have been through the experience of moving to Vienna is often valuable. Try to talk to future coworkers and friends already here to find out what you will need to do, buy or arrange before you leave your home country. After you get over the initial culture shock, you'll discover that Vienna has its own unique attributes, products and lifestyle. We polled our membership to compose this list of suggestions:

THINGS TO DO BEFORE YOU MOVE

- **Apply for or renew passports.** Make sure that every family member's passport is up-to-date and photocopy each one, leaving copies with a reliable person in your home country and keeping another set for yourself in case any are lost or stolen.

- **Sign up for a cultural adaptation program.** If one isn't available, read up on Austria and Vienna (see Books appendix) and talk to friends who have visited or lived there as well as to future coworkers

- **Get medical checkups.** Make appointments for complete medical, dental and eye examinations. Tell your doctors that you'll be out of the country for an extended period of time and need to stock up on medical prescriptions for as long as possible. Also, ask for a written generic-drug prescription to take with you. Be sure to stock up on contact lenses and an extra pair of glasses (or at least bring the prescriptions).

- **Apply for an international driver's license.** If you plan to drive here, you will need an international driver's license, although you can also apply in Vienna. Ask your country's embassy for more information (see Driving chapter).

- **Inform magazines and catalogs of your address change.** If you don't have an address in Vienna yet, at least change your address to that of a trusted family member or friend in the meantime. You may also want to order some other magazines and catalogs to stay connected to your home country.

ESSENTIAL THINGS TO BRING

- **Important documents.** In your carry on luggage, you should bring passports (and photocopies), birth certificates (originals or notarized copies), a certified marriage certificate, medical, legal and financial records.

- **Enough cash and/or traveler's checks.** Many places in Vienna do not accept credit cards, and it may take some time to set up an Austrian bank account, so bring enough cash to cover your start-up expenses. (See Banking chapter.)

- **Things special to your family.** You many want to bring some family mementos to make your new house or apartment in Vienna feel like home (e.g., holiday decorations, photos and home videos).

THINGS THAT MAY NOT BE READILY AVAILABLE IN VIENNA

- **Bedding.** Beds and pillows may be different sizes from your home country (they are different from U. S. sizes), so you may not be able to find sheets, comforters and pillowcases that fit.

- **Food items.** If you don't have legal access to the United Nations or U.S. Embassy commissaries and there are foods you absolutely can't live without or require for dietary reasons, you should bring at least these hard- or impossible-to-find products: Brown sugar, canned pumpkin, chocolate chips, cream of tartar, jellied cranberry sauce, diet food items (each grocery has a diet/diabetic section, but until you get used to the labeling, you may want to have products you know), graham crackers, Karo syrup, macaroni-and-cheese mix, marshmallows, pancake mix, canned roasted onion rings and unusual spices and condiments.

- **Games.** If you enjoy certain board games (e.g., Trivial Pursuit, Monopoly), you should bring them.

- **Household items.** Spare ironing-board covers are a must (European sizes are different). Consider bringing freestanding and mountable towel racks and toilet-paper holders because most apartments don't have them (and they're expensive to buy here). If you use seam binding when sewing, bring it (bias tape is available).

- **Kitchen supplies.** You will have trouble finding Ziploc bags, waxed paper and plastic wrap that clings. You definitely won't find American measuring cups and spoons because Austria uses the metric system. Don't forget your cookbooks!

THINGS THAT MAY BE DIFFERENT IN STYLE (or more expensive) IN VIENNA

- **Adapter plugs and converters.** Austrian plugs have two round prongs and run on 220 volts. Lamps need only a converter plug and a European lightbulb to function here (although American halogen lamps won't work and bayonet-style bulbs for British lamps are not available). For small appliances (e.g., food processor, mixer, rice cooker), buy adapter and converter plugs, which are available at luggage or travel stores (and at Radio Shack in the United States).

- **Transformers (for those coming from countries with 110-volt AC).** These are available in Vienna but are much cheaper in the United States. For example, you can buy a 1,000-watt transformer for about $100 there, while it can cost $300 in Vienna.

If your transformers are fused, buy extra fuses. You can often buy used transformers from people moving back to the United States. (Lists are posted at international schools, the American Women's Association (AWA) office and embassy and U.N. bulletin boards.)

- **Area rugs and carpets.** Most apartments have wooden floors, so if you want to cover them, bring rugs. You may also want to bring bathroom and kitchen rugs with nonslip backings because rugs available in Vienna are usually reversible.

- **Books.** You can get English-language books in Vienna; however, they are much more expensive and best sellers take longer to arrive. A good German/English dictionary (more expensive in Vienna though they come from Germany) and a German verb book (e.g., *501 German Verbs*) are essential for those planning to communicate with the natives. Guidebooks, cookbooks, craft books and your favorite fiction are also good to bring.

- **Office supplies.** Most stationery stores (*Papierhandlungen*) here are still small and expensive, so stock up on your favorite pens, folders and files (be aware of size differences: Europe uses A4-size paper), staples, etc. Rollerball pens are expensive because most Austrians prefer ballpoint or fountain pens. Austrians use shiny cellophane tape rather than invisible tape.

- **Card table and chairs.** Believe it or not, these are in high demand here and hard to find, so you may want to bring them.

- **CDs, DVDs, and videos.** American movies hit the theaters here about the same time they're released on video in the United States, plus, video rentals can cost $5 for one night. You can buy a multisystem VCR in your home country or Vienna so you can watch both American and European videos. Many expatriates borrow one another's tapes as well. (A note on compatibility: Video formats vary. The United States and Japan use NTSC, Europe uses PAL, except France and Spain, which use SECAM. See the Television section of the Communications chapter.) Compact discs are more expensive here and the music selection may not be the same, so you may want to stock up on your favorites. (If your favorites happen to be classical, disregard the stock-up advice, as Vienna has an incredibly good selection.) DVDs in Europe are coded for the region and cannot be used in another region's player. Europe is generally code 2, whereas The US is code 1. However, players are available that are dual-coded.

 A good source to order media online is www.amazon.co.uk (in English) or www.amazon.de (in German). The shipping fees are minor and the prices are comprarable to those in the US.

- **Cloth or mesh shopping bags.** You usually have to pay for plastic and paper shopping bags at supermarkets, so buy sturdy reusable ones to save money and the environment.

- **Clothing.** European proportions and sizes differ from American and Asian sizes, so it's better to bring all your clothes and then determine whether you can find a comparable size here.

- **Computer hardware and software.** Programs here are in German, so you'll probably want to bring your computer and all its software. First, be sure to ask your local dealer if your computer is dual voltage. Also, subscribe to computer catalogs from your home country. If you're an avid e-mailer, ask your carrier whether your account will transfer (see Computers chapter and Internet section of Communications chapter).

- **Curtains.** If you know the size of your windows, it would probably be cheaper to buy curtains or fabric to make them before coming to Vienna.

- **Fabric.** Cotton prices begin at about ATS 100 a meter, and some dress fabric can cost ATS 1.000, so consider buying enough fabric for future projects, such as making curtains.

- **Furniture.** Don't leave furniture behind thinking that you can buy new things upon arrival. Affordable furniture stores tend to stock modern Scandinavian styles.

- **Greeting cards and wrapping paper.** Cards can cost more than $5 each, with sentiments in, of course, German, so stock up on greeting and Christmas cards. Wrapping paper is beautiful but may be pricey. Gift bag selection is limited, but beautiful boxes are a specialty.

- **Health and beauty products.** You should buy enough of your favorite products so they last until you find equivalents here. Name-brand makeup, such as Estée Lauder and Clinique, is available but more expensive and may be formulated differently here (some women have complained of allergic reactions). Contact-lens solution can cost $20 a bottle and is only available through optometrists, while canned preservative-free saline solution doesn't exist in Vienna—so stock up until your next trip back home. Also, you may want to buy birth-control items.

- **Kitchenware and dishes.** You should bring any unusual-sized or unique items (e.g., American muffin pans and pie pans, Asian teacups, rice bowls, rice cooker, fajita skillet).

- **Plasticware.** Plastic is not as prevalent here, and is more expensive, so bring food-storage containers, microwave-cooking containers, clothing-storage containers, wastebaskets, buckets, laundry baskets and utensils.

- **Over-the-counter drugs.** The drugs will be different—if not more expensive—here, so stock up on products such as aspirin, Advil, Tylenol, acne medicine, cough syrup and drops, cold and allergy medicine, hydrocortisone cream, Ace bandages, Band Aids, Mycatracin, etc.

- **Sewing machine and supplies.** If you plan to do a lot of sewing and don't want to buy a machine here, be sure you have the appropriate transformer.

- **Silk flowers and plants.** The ones here are not as realistic-looking as those available in the United States and are much more expensive.

- **Sporting equipment.** If you like to play sports such as baseball, softball, basketball, American football or golf, you should buy the necessary equipment in your home country because it may be hard to find or more expensive here.

- **Storage containers.** Because most apartments in Vienna don't have much closet or storage space, you should consider buying containers and organizers for under the bed and in drawers and closets.

- **Tools.** If you like to fix things around the house or have a green thumb, you should bring your tools because they are much more expensive here.

THINGS NOT TO BRING

- **Anything huge.** Storage space in most apartments is extremely limited. Consider the access route to your apartment (i.e., the size of your elevator, width of stairs).

- **Appliances with heating units.** These may require massive and expensive transformers to run them. There are companies in the United States that sell 220-volt appliances at prices lower than here. One such company is:

APPLIANCES OVERSEAS
276 Fifth Avenue, Suite 407
New York, NY 10001-4509
☎ (212) 545-8001
Fax (212) 545-8005

- **Clock radios.** Even with a transformer, they tend to run faster. Converted cassette tape recorders will play tapes accurately but won't record properly.

- **Oversized cookware and utensils.** Ovens, stoves and refrigerators are smaller than in the United States, so standard American cookie sheets, roasting pans, pitchers and food-storage containers don't fit. Even two nine-inch cake pans often don't fit on one shelf in the oven (and many ovens here have only one shelf).

- **School and office supplies.** Don't stock up on school supplies because even the English-speaking schools use A4-size paper, report covers, notebooks and computer paper. Be aware that American-letter-sized paper and other stationery don't match or fit conveniently with A4 size.

THINGS TO BUY IN VIENNA

- **Coffeemaker.** If you plan to use one every day, it's better to buy a 220-volt model here.

- **Iron.** An appliance using this much power should be wired for it, so it's safer and easier to buy one here.

- **Telephone and answering machine.** Because the phone system and electricity are different, it's better to buy them here.

- **Vacuum.** Most apartments here have wood floors, so you'll find a mobile 220-volt vacuum handier than an upright that requires a weighty transformer.

- **Washer and dryer.** Many apartments have a place for a small washer. You can buy a drying rack and/or a dryer.

APARTMENT/HOUSE-HUNTING TIPS

If you make a trip to Vienna before you move, **bring a tape measure** for measuring windows, rooms, doors, cupboards and ovens to make sure your existing items fit. It's wise to **note room and window sizes** for later reference (when buying rugs, curtains). Also, try to **visit a drugstore** (*Drogerie*) to see what health and beauty products are available and which ones you should bring (e.g., makeup, feminine-hygiene products, first aid, contact-lens solution).

KEYS TO THE CITY

There are some important things you need to know right away before you have time to read this whole book. Glance through this section to discover some important facts about living in Vienna.

BICYCLES

There are many bicycle paths sharing pavement with pedestrian sidewalks, so avoid lanes with bicycle symbols. Be especially careful of speedy riders when crossing these lanes.

CHIMNEY SWEEPS

Chimney sweeps have an absolute right to enter your house or apartment. This is a safety measure. Usually the day and approximate time of their arrival is posted (in apartment buildings) or mailed to you (houses) ahead of time. Someone must be there to admit them, or you can pre-arrange an alternate time.

COAT CHECK

Garderobe means coat check. There is often a posted charge that's paid when leaving your coat. If no amount is stipulated, ATS 10 per coat is usually an appropriate tip (depending on the location).

CREDIT CARDS

Be aware that many restaurants and stores do not accept credit cards.

The districts of Vienna spiral out from the central first district.

STADTBEZIRKE   URBAN DISTRICTS

1. Innere Stadt	7. Neubau	13. Hietzing	18. Währing
2. Leopoldstadt	8. Josefstadt	14. Penzing	19. Döbling
3. Landstraße	9. Alsergrund	15. Rudolfsheim-	20. Brigittenau
4. Wieden	10. Favoriten	Fünfhaus	21. Floridsdorf
5. Margareten	11. Simmering	16. Ottakring	22. Donaustadt
6. Mariahilf	12. Meidling	17. Hernals	23. Liesing

DISTRICTS

Vienna is divided into 23 districts (*Bezirke*). Addresses are given by district. Many streets run through more than one district, so it's always important not only to know the name of the street but also which district. The district can be a Roman numeral (e.g., I, V, XIX), an ordinal (e.g., first, third, 22nd) or indicated as a part of postal code (e.g., **101**0 Wien is the first district, **120**0 is the 20th district). An ordinal number is indicated by a period after the number (e.g., 1.= first, 19. = nineteenth district). For details on how to write or decipher an address, see the Post section of the Communications chapter.

District numbers are posted on street signs before the street name.

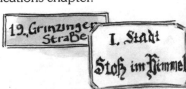

ELEVATORS/LIFTS

Elevators/lifts with unlit buttons have no programmed memories. You must wait until the door shuts to press a floor button. If another button is pressed by a second person, only the first will register. The second person's choice must be pushed after the first exits (which may mean coordinating who is getting off first). Some older elevators will go up, but cannot be called to carry people down.

The ground floor is the *Erdgeschoss* (E on elevator buttons). The next floor is often, but not always, the *Mezzanin*. Then comes the first floor (1. *Stock*). Therefore, a person living on the 1. *Stock* would be on the American sixth floor.

EMERGENCY ALARMS

Occasionally Vienna's disaster-alert system is tested. Of course the population is notified ahead of time via TV, newspaper and radio, but if you're unable to understand these announcements, the event can be rather disconcerting. If a real emergency occurs, Vienna's population is warned in two ways:

- Via loudspeakers installed at public-transportation stops, emitting continuous three-minute signals
- Via mobile sirens installed on both police and municipal cars, emitting a continuous signal of unchanging pitch.

If you're in the open when such a warning is given, go to the nearest public building and wait there for further instructions issued by the city authorities on the radio.

If you're at home, turn on your TV or radio. The authorities will give further instructions (on all channels).

In addition, the city will organize a "disaster hotline" (☎ 402 08 08), which is only operated in such emergency situations. As soon as the potential danger is over, an all-clear message will be announced on the radio.

FALLING SNOW

Dachlawine (literally "roof avalanche") signs attached to red-and-white-striped poles leaned against buildings in winter warn of the possibility of falling snow. Melting and freezing snow sliding down high, steep roofs make walking in these marked areas hazardous.

GERMAN WORDS

Umlaut vowels come after the normal corresponding letter (e.g., "*Boz* . . . " would come before "*Böb* . . . ") in German-language alphabetical listings (e.g., the telephone directory), but are mixed in German-English dictionaries.

Language authorities from the Austrian and German governments decided in the mid-1990s to streamline and simplify spellings. This affects the **ß** (a sharp s sound), which is sometimes "ss." You will find both in use and may use them interchangably. Still under discussion (and heated debate) is the capitalization of nouns.

 To avoid being misunderstood (or not understood at all), write down German words so you can at least show people what you're trying to say. (All vowels and some consonants are pronounced differently in German—a good reason to take a German class!)

IDENTIFICATION

You must carry a photo identification with you at all times. Austrians have an *Ausweis*. A driver's license with a photo is adequate, but if asked by any Austrian authorities, you may have to produce a passport within 24 hours. An identification card for foreigners (*Ausweis für Ausländer*) is available by applying at your head district police office (*Bezirkspolizeikommissariat*). Look in the telephone directory's white pages under *"Bezirkspolizei."*

 Usually when giving your name, the Austrians expect only your last/family name/surname (*Name, Familienname, Nachname*). Giving your first/given name (*Vorname*) confuses the process.

JAYWALKING

You can be ticketed for jaywalking (i.e., crossing the street somewhere other than a crosswalk or at a corner).

LOCKED OUT

When locked out, call an *Aufsperrdienst*, listed in the yellow pages, to unlock your door (see Keys & Locksmiths in Home chapter).

MEASUREMENTS

Europe (except the United Kingdom) uses the metric system. See the Measurements appendix for conversions.

PAYING AT STORES

In some stores, a clerk must write a receipt for goods you want to purchase before you give them to the cashier *Kassa*. In some department stores, however, you must present your selected goods to a clerk, who then writes a ticket for you. You present this ticket to a *Kassa* and pay, then return with your receipt to pick up your ready-packed goods from the original clerk.

If you're just browsing in a store, you can say, *"Ich schaue nur, danke"* ("I'm just looking, thanks").

PHOTOS

Many official forms and identification cards, such as an Austrian ID card (*Ausweis*), year's public-transportation pass (*Jahreskarte*) and driver's license, require a passport-sized photo. You can get these taken at many one-hour photo shops here or at automatic-photo booths found in many *U-Bahn* stations. You may also consider getting photos taken in your home country (and get multiple copies), as they can be quite expensive at Vienna photo shops.

SPELLING

The Austrian telephone authorities suggest using the following code to facilitate spelling (especially when you have to give your name over the phone):

A = Anton	**I** = Ida	**R** = Richard
Ä = Ärger	**J** = Julius	**S** = Siegfried
B = Berta	**K** = Konrad	**T** = Theodor
C = Cäsar	**L** = Ludwig	**U** = Ulrich
Ch = Christine	**M** = Martha	**Ü** = Übel
D = Dora	**N** = Norbert	**V** = Victor
E = Emil	**O** = Otto	**W** = Wilhelm
F = Friedrich	**Ö** = Österreich	**X** = Xavier
G = Gustav	**P** = Paula	**Y** = Ypsilon
H = Heinrich	**Q** = Quelle	**Z** = Zacharias

For example, if your name is Smith, you would say, "**S**iegfried, **M**artha, **I**da, **T**heodor, **H**einrich."

STREETS

Street numbers often do not correlate from one side of the street to the other. For example, you could stand in front of house 82 and look across the street at 53. Street numbers either begin at the end of the street nearest the center of the city or progress in a clockwise direction. Street numbers are indicated in tiny print at intervals on maps and in map books (*Buchpläne*). They can help you decide which public-transportation stop to use.

Compound words take on a new meaning here. One of the most daunting aspects of the German language is the length of words. When you first arrive, even street names appear to be longer than even the best memory can accommodate. Therefore, try to mentally separate *strasse* (street), *gasse* (alley/street) and *platz* (place) to make the locations more manageable.

SURVIVAL VOCABULARY

Cancel *Abbruch*

Closed *geschlossen*

Confirmation *Bestätigung*

Correction *Korrektur*

Danger *Gefahr*

Entrance *Eingang*

Exit *Ausgang*

Info *Auskunft*

No vacancies/full *Besetzt*

Open *geöffnet*

Out of order/not working *ausser Betrieb*

Please/you're welcome/ excuse me (when you didn't hear what someone said) *bitte*

Pull *ziehen*

Push *drücken, stossen*

Signature *Unterschrift*

Thanks *danke*

Toilets *Toiletten, WC*

Working *in Betrieb*

Zero 0 *Null*

TIME

Military time is generally used. For example 5 PM = 1700. Variations of this may be 17 U or 17.00 or 17 h.

Times (especially in movie and theater listings) are distinctly Austrian:

$$^1/_4\ 4 = 3:15 \qquad ^1/_2\ 4 = 3:30 \qquad ^3/_4\ 4 = 3:45$$

TRAMS

A tram (*Strassenbahn*) is never at fault in an accident, so be careful when driving near one as it can make turns and have nowhere to go to avoid you (see Driving chapter).

TAX STAMPS

For those unfamiliar with the tradition, tax stamps (*Stempelmarken*) are required on many official documents, such as residence permits and contracts. You can buy them at any tobacconist/newsstand (*Tabak-Trafik*). Tax stamps are bing eliminated. You can now pay directly in the government office or electronically on the internet

OFFICIAL DOCUMENTS

Regardless of how long your stay in Austria will be, whether you are working or studying or retired, it is important to remember that you are a guest here and have an obligation to follow the laws of your host country. Some documents authorizing your stay must be obtained prior to departing from your home country, while others must be acquired as soon as you arrive.

Austria requires foreigners to have the following permits or authorizations to establish residence here:

- Visa (*Sichtvermerk*) or residence permit (*Aufenthaltsbewilligung*)
- Police registration (*Meldezettel*)
- Work permit (*Arbeitsgenehmigung*)

The legal procedures described in this chapter are often subject to change. The information given is only intended to give you a general idea of what to expect. Contact the Austrian Embassy or Consulate in your home country prior to your departure for detailed information about procedures relevant to your situation. General information is also available from the Austrian government web site online at: www.austria.org/govsite.htm.

DOCUMENTS TO BRING FROM HOME

Bring originals or notarized copies of all official documents for yourself and all family members. You should leave notarized copies of these documents with a reliable person (e.g., relative, lawyer) in case of loss. The following are required documents:

- **Passport (*Reisepass*)** Make sure your passport is valid for the duration of your stay. If it expires while you're here, your consulate may issue either a temporary or a new passport. Ask your consulate for details. Note that the validity of visas or residency permits (*Aufenthaltsbewilligung*) is not typically granted for a period exceeding the expiration date of the passport.
- **Birth certificate (*Geburtsurkunde*)**
- **Marriage/Divorcecertificate**
  (*Heiratsurkunde/Scheidungsurkunde*)
- **Children's school records** (*Zeugnisse*)
- **Driver's licence** (*Führerschein*)
- **Diplomas, degrees, certificates of education** (*Diplom, Zeugnisse*)
- **Proof of health insurance** valid in Austria (accident and health insurance is *Unfall- und Krankenversicherungsnachweis*)
- **Vaccination Record** (*Impfzeugnis*)

RESIDING IN AUSTRIA

The documents required to enter Austria and remain here legally depend on your nationality, the purpose of your trip (e.g., business, tourism, personal) and the duration of your planned stay. Consult the Austrian Embassy or Consulate in your home country prior to your departure.

EU CITIZEN

Austria joined the European Union on January 1, 1995. Citizens of EU-member states enjoy privileges similar to those of Austrian citizens: They have the right to enter Austria and remain here for an indefinite period of time. However, if you don't intend to work here, you must demonstrate to authorities that you have a regular source of income exceeding the amount at which you would be entitled to welfare in your home country. You meet this condition, of course, if your spouse earns the family income.

EU COUNTRIES (as of mid-1997)	EEA COUNTRIES (as of mid-1997)
Austria, Belgium, Denmark, Finland, France, Germany, Great Britain, Greece, Ireland, Italy, Luxembourg, the Netherlands, Portugal, Spain and Sweden	The European Economic Area (*Europäischer Wirtschaftsraum* or *EWR*) consists of the above-mentioned EU countries with the addition of Liechtenstein, Norway and Iceland

RESIDENCE PERMIT FOR EEA CITIZENS

If you establish residency in Austria as a national of a European Economic Area member state, a permit, known as *Lichtbildausweis für EWR Bürger*, is required. To apply for this identification, you need to take the original and one copy of each of the following documents to your district police station (look in the telephone directory's white pages under *"Polizei"*):

- Passport (*Reisepass*)
- Copy of your police registration (*Meldezettel*)
- Proof of sufficient means of financial support (*Einkommensbestätigung*)
- Proof of health insurance valid in Austria (accident and health insurance is *Unfall- und Krankenversicherungsnachweis*)
- Two official passport-sized photos (*Passfotos*)
- Document tax stamps (*Stempelmarken*)

VISA & RESIDENCE REQUIREMENTS FOR U.S. CITIZENS

A visa is not required for U.S. citizens who wish to stay in Austria for up to two three-month periods during one calendar year. At the conclusion of the six-month stay, you must leave the country. The exception is if you have already submitted and received the residence permit (*Aufenthaltsbewilligung*).

Be aware that the fact that you've submitted the application for the *Aufenthaltsbewilligung* does not grant or imply the right to remain in Austria beyond the six-month period. If you haven't received the *Aufenthaltsbewilligung* within that time, you must leave the country until the permit is issued.

Even short-term residents are required to register with the police or municipal authorities (*Meldeamt/Meldebehörde*) within three days of their arrival.

RESIDENCE PERMIT FOR U.S. CITIZENS (first-time applications)

U.S. citizens wishing to establish residency for a period exceeding six months per calendar year, or for the purpose of gainful employment, need to apply for a residence permit (*Aufenthaltsbewilligung*). To do this, you must be able to provide proof of health insurance, housing and financial means of support.

Applications for a residence permit can be made either from outside of Austria, at any Austrian Embassy or Consulate, or at the local magistrate (*Magistrat/Magistratisches*), district office (*Bezirksamt*) or regional district office (*Bezirkshauptmannschaft*) in Austria. Applicants must complete the forms in German identifying the purpose of stay (e.g., seeking gainful employment, joining dependents residing in Austria, retiring or studying). The application must be submitted for each family member, including all key documents as listed below. The residence permit will then be issued locally within the limits of quota regulations.

First-time applicants need to bring the following documents with notarized German translations:

- Birth certificate (*Geburtsurkunde*)
- Passport (*Reisepass*)
- Proof of accommodation (lease or rental agreement) (*Mietvertrag*)
- Proof of sufficient means of support (*Einkommensbestätigung*)
- Proof of health insurance valid in Austria (accident and health insurance is *Unfall- und Krankenversicherungsnachweis*)
- Police record certificate not more than three months old*
- Students need appropriate university acceptance papers (*Zulassungsbescheid*).
- Persons seeking gainful employment need to obtain through their prospective employer the necessary working papers *(Arbeitsgenehmigung)* issued by the Labor Office (*Arbeitsmarktservice*).

* In lieu of a U.S. police certificate, a sworn statement attesting that the applicant has no police record in the United States may be made before a consular officer.

SPECIAL VISA RULES

Third-Country Dependents of Austrian Nationals *Angehörige von Österreichern, Die Staatsangehörige eines Drittstaates Sind*

Third-country (i.e., non-Austrian, non-EEA citizen) spouses and children under the age of 18 of Austrian nationals are eligible for a visa (*Aufenthaltsgenehmigung*), meaning that they are exempt from the quota regulations. Couples must have been married for at least six months at the time of application to fall within this provision.

Third-Country Dependents of Nationals of the European Economic Area (EEA) *Angehörige von EWR-Bürgern, Die Staatsangehörige eines Drittstaates Sind*

Third-country dependents (i.e., spouses and minor children) of resident EEA nationals are entitled to a special visa (*Sichtvermerk*), which is not subject to quota restrictions. The validity of this visa will conform to that of the ID card issued to the EEA national (*Lichtbildausweis für EWR-Bürger*). You must apply for the *Sichtvermerk* at the foreign police (*Fremdenpolizei*) in your district. Look under the telephone directory's white pages under *"Polizei,"* then *"Bezirkspolizeikommissariate."* Call the *Fremdenpolizeiliches Büro* first to ask for a list of necessary documents (☎ 313 44-0).

PERSONS WITH DIPLOMATIC STATUS

Diplomats and their families, which includes United Nations and foreign-embassy and consulate employees, do not need a residence permit (*Aufenthaltsbewilligung*). Instead, an identity card (*Legitimationskarte*) is issued to these individuals.

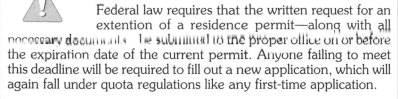

Extending Residence Permits

Federal law requires that the written request for an extention of a residence permit—along with all necessary documents—be submitted to the proper office on or before the expiration date of the current permit. Anyone failing to meet this deadline will be required to fill out a new application, which will again fall under quota regulations like any first-time application.

In most cases, you submit the application for the extension of the residence permit to the district office of the magistrate (*Magistratischer Bezirksamt*) where you reside. Look under *"Bezirksämter, Magistratische"* in the telephone directory's white pages. You should visit the magistrate's office prior to the date of submitting an extension in order to obtain the necessary forms (*Antrag auf Erteilung einer Bewilligung nach dem Aufenthaltsgesetz-Verlängerungsantrag*) and verify the documents you must provide (*Merkblatt für Antragsteller*).

PERMANENT VISA *UNBEFRISTETE BEWILLIGUNG*

After a minimum stay of five years, you can apply for a permanent visa, the issuance of which is solely at the discretion of the Austrian government.

OBTAINING AUSTRIAN CITIZENSHIP

If you reside in Vienna and want information on how to obtain Austrian citizenship, contact City Hall, Magistrate Department 61 (*1080, Rathaus, Magistratsabteilung* 61) ☎ 40 00 61. If you're a resident of one of the other Austrian provinces, contact the citizenship department (*Staatsbürgerschaftsabteilung*) of the respective provincial government (*Amt der Landesregierung*).

POLICE REGISTRATION *Meldepflicht*

Anyone staying in Austria in a private house or apartment (not a hotel, hostel, etc.) is required to register with the police (*Bundespolizeikommissariat/Meldeamt*) or the municipal authorities (*Gemeindeamt*) within three days of arrival. The registration slip (*Meldezettel*) can be purchased at a *Tabak-Trafik*. It must be completed, signed by the person registering *and* the landlord and submitted to the police station or municipal office in the district of residence. A passport will serve as proof of identification.

The registration office must also be notified in case of change of address within Austria (*Ummeldung*) or permanent departure from Austria (*Abmeldung*). Again, notification must take place within three days.

Tourists staying at a hotel or hostel temporarily (up to 60 days) are asked to provide their personal information for the guest book (*Gästebuch/Gästeblatt*). Longer-term guests (i.e., beyond 60 days) need to register with the police or municipal authorities (*Meldezettel*).

The *Meldezettel* is valid for an unlimited period of time as long as your residence and name remain the same.

 Persons with diplomatic status are exempt from the requirements of a *Meldezettel*. You can get information in your home country, or at your local embassy or consulate, or the Ministry of Foreign Affairs (*Bundesministerium für Auswärtige Angelegenheiten*).

 A *Meldezettel* is not the same as a visa or a residence permit. Each member of the family—even your children—needs a *Meldezettel*.

Registration Procedure

Complete a registration form (*Meldezettel*) as follows and take it with a passport (one for each person's *Meldezettel*) to your district police station:

- **Buy a *Meldezettel* for each family member from any *Tabak-Trafik* for a nominal fee.**

- **Fill out each *Meldezettel* and sign each one.** Use a ball-point pen and press firmly because all five copies must be legible.

- **If you rent or lease, the landlord must sign the *Meldezettel* as the accommodation provider (*Unterkunftgeber*).** If you own your home, then you must sign.

- **File the registration at the registration office (*Meldeamt*) of the main police station in your district.** Check the telephone directory's white pages under "Polizei" in the bold-print section "Bezirkspolizeikommissariate und Wachzimmer." Each district is sublettered, so the first address is the one you want. Police stations are open Mon - Fri, 8 AM - 1 PM. Children who are minors do not need to be present.

- **The *Meldezettel* and its copies will be stamped.** Two of the copies will be returned to you. Keep them in a safe place because you need to present them if you move, leave the country, change your name, register your car, obtain a driver's licence, apply for a library card, etc. If you lose the Meldezettel, you can obtain a duplicate for a nominal fee from the Meldeamt where you're registered.

- **A change of address requires a cancellation of the existing registration and then an application for new registration, which can be done in the *Meldeamt* in the new district of residence.** You'll need two copies of the existing Meldezettel, as well as a set of new forms. A legal change of first or last name also requires cancellation of existing registration and application for new registration. Be sure to take documentary evidence of the legal change of name.

Meldezettel

FAMILIENNAME (in Blockschrift), AKAD. GRAD (abgekürzt) ①	Geschlecht ② männ. weiblich	Religionsbekenntnis ③
VORNAMEN lt. Geburtsurkunde (bei Fremden laut Reisedokument) ④		STAATSANGEHÖRIGKEIT ☐ Österreich ☐ anderer Staat (Name) ⑤
Familienname vor der e r s t e n Eheschließung ⑥		

GEBURTSDATUM ⑦ GEBURTSORT laut Reisedokument (bei österr. Staatsbürgerschaft auch laut Geburtsurkunde); Bundesland bzw. Staat (Ausland) ⑧

REISEDOKUMENT bei Fremden (Art, z.B. Reisepaß, Personalausweis; Nummer; Ausstellungsdatum; ausstellende Behörde) ⑨

UNTERKUNFT ⑩	Straße (Platz) bzw. Ort ohne Straßennamen ⑪	Haus-Nr. ⑫	Stiege ⑬	Tür-Nr. ⑭
HAUPTWOHNSITZ ☐ ja ☐ nein	Postleitzahl ⑮ Ortsgemeinde ⑯			
Wenn ja, BISHERIGER HAUPTWOHNSITZ ⑰	Straße (Platz) bzw. Ort ohne Straßennamen	Haus-Nr.	Stiege	Tür-Nr.
	Postleitzahl Ortsgemeinde	Staat, falls Ausland		
Allfällige weitere Wohn ⑱	Postleitzahl, Ortsgemeinde, Bundesland bzw. Staat (Ausland)			

VERZOGEN NACH (Ortsgemeinde, Bundesland bzw. Staat, falls Ausland) ⑲

Unterkunftgeber (Name in Blockschrift, Unterschrift) ⑳	Raum für behördliche Vermerke ㉒	
	ANGEMELDET am (Amtsstampiglie, Unterschrift) ㉓	ABGEMELDET am (Amtsstampiglie, Unterschrift) ㉔
Unterschrift des Meldepflichtigen (Bestätigung der Richtigkeit der Meldedaten) ㉑		

REGISTRATION FORM *Meldezettel*

1. *Familienname*
Family name

2. *Geschlecht* Gender
Männlich Male
Weiblich Female

3. *Religionsbekenntnis*
Religious Denomination

4. *Vornamen lt. Geburtsurkunde (bei Fremden laut Reisedokument)*
First name according to birth certificate (for foreigners, according to travel document)

5. *Staatsangehörigkeit*
Nationality
anderer Staat (Name)
Other country (name)

6. *Familienname vor der ersten Eheschliessung*
Maiden name

7. *Geburtsdatum* Date of birth

8. *Geburtsort laut Reisedokument* Place of birth according to travel document

9. *Reisedokument bei Fremden (Art, zB. Reisepass, Personalausweiß, Nummer, Ausstellungsdatum, ausstellende Behörde)* Travel document for foreigners (type: e.g. passport. pesonal ID card, number, date of issuance, issuing authority)

0. Unterkunft
Accommodation

Hauptwohnsitz
Primary residence
Ja Yes   **Nein** No

1. Strasse (Platz) bzw. Ort ohne Strassennamen
Street (Place/Square) or town name if without street name

2. Haus Nr. (Haus Nummer) House number

3. Stiege
Apartment block, stairway

4. Tür Nr. (Tür Nummer)
Door/apartment number

5. Postleitzahl
ZIP code

6. Ortsgemeinde
City or township

7. Wenn ja, bisheriger Hauptwohnsitz
If yes, last previous primary residence

18. Allfällige weitere Wohnsitze
Other places of residence

19. Verzogen nach
Moved to city, state, country

20. Unterkunftgeber (Name in Blockschrift, Unterschrift)
Landlord (name in capital letters, signature)

21. Unterschrift des Meldepflichtigen (Bestätigung der Richtigkeit der Meldedaten)
Signature of person responsible for registration (confirmation of correctness of information contained therein)

22. Raum für behördliche Vermerke Place for official remarks ("for official use only")

23. Angemeldet am (Amtsstampiglie, Unterschrift)
Registration of arrival on (date), (stamp and signature of official)

24. Abgemeldet am (Amtsstampiglie, Unterschrift)
Registration of departure on (date), (stamp and signature of official)

 Failure to comply with the registration regulations may result in a fine of up to ATS 3.000 or two weeks in prison, imposed by the police magistrate.

You should bring these documents for each new registration (e.g., change of address or name). In fact, you should bring these documents whenever you need to complete an official task, known in German as an *Amtsweg*.

Prior to a permanent departure from Austria, cancellation at the registration office is required. Bring your existing *Meldezettel* (see *Auf Wiedersehen* chapter).

WORKING IN AUSTRIA

Finding a job in Austria is as challenging, competitive, complex and time-consuming as it is anywhere else in the world. The added hurdles may include required fluency in German or other languages important for Austria's markets and the fact that you're a foreigner and subject to quotas. You'll need a work permit (*Arbeitsgenehmigung*) in order to be employed in Austria, unless you're specifically exempt according to the Law Governing the Employment of Foreigners (*Ausländer-beschäftigungsgesetz*). Your embassy or consulate, as well as the Austrian Ministry of Labor and Social Affairs (*Bundesministerium für Arbeit und Soziales*; ☎ 711 10-0), can provide updated information and assistance concerning the requirements.

EEA CITIZEN *EWR Staatsbürger*

Citizens of the European Economic Area are exempt from the requirements of a specific work permit in accordance with the Austrian Law Governing Employment of Foreigners (*Ausländerbeschäftigungsgesetz*).

Third-Country Dependents of Austrian Nationals *Angehörige von Österreichern, Die Staatsangehörige eines Drittstaates Sind*

Third-country (i.e., non-Austrian, non-EEA citizen) spouses and minor children of Austrian nationals are exempt from the requirements of a work permit. However, you must have a residence permit (*Aufenthalts-bewilligung*). In addition, prior to starting work in Austria, you will need written confirmation from the regional Labor Office (*Arbeitsmarkt-service*), which certifies your work-permit exemption. For the office near you, look in the telephone directory's white pages under *"Arbeitsmarktservice."*

Third-Country Dependents of Nationals of the European Economic Area (EEA) *Angehörige von EWR-Bürgern, Die Staatsangehörige eines Drittstaates Sind*

Third-country dependents (i.e., spouses, minor children) of residing employed EEA nationals are exempt from specific-work-permit requirements. For more information, call or visit the *Arbeitsmarkt-service* in your area.

FINDING A JOB

LABOR OFFICE *Arbeitsmarktservice*

Provided you have an *Aufenthaltsbewilligung* or similar authorization to remain in Austria, you can register at the Labor Office (*Arbeitsmarktservice*), which is the main public facility for everything related to employment. It has job and information centers. Check the telephone directory's white pages under *"Arbeitsmarktservice"* to find the one nearest you.

CAREER SERVICES FOR ENGLISH SPEAKERS

If you're determined to pursue your career here, the following are a few resources that may be able to help you:

INTERNATIONAL HOUSE VIENNA
1010, Schwedenplatz 2/6
☎ 535 57 46-0
Fax 535 57 46-17
This institute helps native English speakers study to attain the Cambridge University–approved and internationally recognized qualification Certificate in English Language Teaching to Adults (CETLA). Courses are taught biannually. The CETLA qualification is valuable in acquiring employment as an English teacher in Austria. (See Education chapter.)

McCOLLUM BUSINESS SERVICES

1010, Weihburggasse 29
☎ 513 10 23
Fax 513 10 25
eMail 106350.2061@compuserve.com

Carl McCollum, a former U.S. Consul General in Vienna, offers personalized assistance and shared use of office space in the Marriott Hotel on a one-time, part-time or full-time basis. The following services are available: Virtual Office (use of address, work space, communications, computer, printing and copying equipment, secretarial and general advisory and support services, translating). Shared use keeps overhead costs low. This service is especially useful for those starting their own businesses.

WOMEN'S CAREER NETWORK

c/o American Women's Association
1190, Sieveringer Strasse 22A/1
☎ 320 14 95
Fax 318 25 34

The Women's Career Network, affiliated with the American Women's Association, acts as a resource and support network for women seeking to develop and expand their career opportunities. It is an international group of well-educated professional women living and working primarily in Vienna. Monthly meetings at the Marriott Hotel include programs of interest to professional women. A newsletter, the Career Counseling Club, Entrepreneurs' Club and member directory are benefits of membership. The group has written a book entitled *American Women and Work in Austria*, which is revised regularly. It addresses the legalities of working here, as well as specific employment prospects. Call the above number for details.

PUBLIC NOTARY *Öffentlicher Notar*

Look in the yellow pages under "*Notare.*" In advertisements, "*gerichtlich beeidete*" (abbreviated as "*beeid.*") means they have made an oath before the court (i.e., they are responsible and certified).

HOUSING

Finding a place to live in Vienna, while dealing with both an unfamiliar language and a new system, can be daunting. Whether you tackle the job alone, work with a real-estate agent (*Immobilienmakler*) or use a relocation service, the following information should help make the process a little easier (or at least more understandable).

RELOCATION SERVICE ERIKA STROHMAYER
2320 Schwechat, Am Concorde Park 1/B6
☎ 701 324-40
Mobile 0664 100 40 38
Fax 701 324-41
eMail: reloserv@netway.at

This service provides information before you move and helps you find housing here. It coordinates your move, completes all necessary documents for a visa, work permit and car import, and even helps with settling in (e.g., children's schools, utility connection, shopping). It can also help you leave Austria by coordinating your move, deregistering you with Austrian authorities and exporting your car.

TEMPORARY HOUSING

APARTMENT HOTELS *Appartement-Hotels*

Finding a new home may take a few weeks, and regular hotels can be expensive, so staying at an apartment hotel is both practical (especially for families) and more affordable. The following apartment hotels have reasonable rates, kitchens, laundry facilities and pleasant English-speaking staff. Some have one- or two-bedroom apartments. You can usually make arrangements to get a key if you plan to arrive when no one is on duty at the front desk.

APPARTEMENTHAUS SINGERSTRASSE
1010, Singerstrasse 21-25
☎ 514 49-0   Fax 513 16 17
Mon - Fri 8 AM - 8 PM

APPARTEMENT-PENSION RIEMERGASSE
1010, Riemergasse 8
☎ 512 72 20   Fax 513 77 78
Mon - Fri 9 AM - 9 PM

PENSION SACHER
1010, Rotenturmstrasse 1/7. Stock (7th floor)
☎ 533 32 38 or ☎ 480 03 20
Mon - Sat 7:30 AM - 1 PM

MONDIAL APPARTMENT HOTEL
1090, Alserbachstrasse (entrance at Pfluggasse 1)
☎ 310 71 80   Fax 310 31 83
Daily 24 hours (at night, ring bell)

KAISER FRANZ JOSEPH APPARTEMENT-RESIDENZ
1190, Sieveringer Strasse 4
☎ 329 00-0   Fax 320 73 55
Daily 24 hours

COUNTRY INN & SUITES
1220, Wagramerstrasse 16-16A (near Vienna International Center)
☎ 269 40-0
Daily 24 hours

These are additional suggestions:

Astron Suite Hotel
   1070, Mariahilfer Strasse 32-34 (main entrance at
   Lindengasse 9)
   ☎ 521 72-0
   Daily 24 hours

Rothensteiner Appartements Pension
   1070, Neustiftgasse 66
   ☎ 523 96 43-0
   Daily 8 AM - 9 PM

Appartements in der Josefstadt
   1080, Alser Strasse 29 (entrance at Kochgasse 36)
   ☎ 406 46 10
   Mon - Fri 8:30 AM - 12:30 PM

PERMANENT HOUSING

RENTAL PROPERTY & COSTS

Housing in Austria is described in terms of area. Prices are calculated according to square meters (*Quadratmeter*), noted as m^2. As a point of reference, Austrians spend an average of 30 percent of their net income on housing. Some factors affecting housing prices are universal location (district and neighborhood) and the condition of the premises. The regulations governing leases in Austria are complex. Rental rates and duration of leases depend on things such as the age of the building, historical significance, parking facilities, etc. If acting alone, you should consider consulting a consumer or tenant organization or a lawyer before signing a rental contract.

Unfurnished accommodations are generally easier to find than furnished ones. Be aware that in Europe, an unfurnished apartment or house may have no lighting fixtures, kitchen appliances (such as refrigerators or dishwashers) or cupboards and usually no closets of any kind. So look for *"teil mobliert"* ("partially furnished") in advertisements. If you opt for a fully furnished apartment, but then choose later not to use any or all of the furnishings, you—not the landlord—may be responsible for storing the unused items.

FINDING PLACES FOR RENT *zu Vermieten*

You can find real-estate ads in the *"zu Vermieten"* section of the Thursday and Saturday issues of the Viennese newspaper *Kurier* or the special Wednesday edition of *Bazar*, a classifieds paper. Real-estate agents also offer their services for a fee, and their connections are valuable because Austria has no central listing service.

Breaking Down the Rent

The rental price of a unit has several components. The net rent (*Nettomiete*) is the base price. To calculate the gross rent (*Bruttomiete*), add the *Nettomiete* plus the maintenance charges (*Betriebskosten*), which usually average between ATS 15 to ATS 20 per m^2, plus the value-added tax (*Mehrwertssteuer*, often abbreviated as *MwSt*), which is 10 percent for an apartment and 20 percent for a garage.

Betriebskosten cover such diverse services as chimney sweeping, snow shoveling and trash removal. In the case of an apartment, it might also include the cost of cleaning the building's public areas, elevator maintenance costs, superintendent (*Hausbesorger*) services and your share of the repair fund (*Reparaturreserve*).

 Do not make a verbal agreement to take an apartment or house before you're absolutely sure you want it because the owner can rightfully take that to be as good as a written agreement.

RENTAL CONTRACTS

Many foreigners find housing on an initial trip before actually moving to Vienna. If the time between that trip and the date you actually take up residence is short, you would just sign a rental contract. If, however, the period is extended, you might be asked to sign an offer (*Anbot*), which states under what conditions and at what price you're willing to rent. Countersignature by the landlord means an agreement has been reached, leading to a rental contract. The *Anbot* is binding, so if you withdraw from the offer, you'll be expected to pay approximately three months' gross rent as a cancellation fee.

All rental contracts must be registered with the government. The fee is one percent of the gross rent (*Bruttomiete*) for the length of the contract, or for three years. If you're working with a real-estate agent or relocation service, the agent will file for you. If you rent on your own, either you or your landlord must send a copy to the following address:

FINANZAMT FÜR GEBÜHREN UND VERKEHRSSTEUERN
Vordere Zollamtsstrasse 5
1030 Wien
☎ 711 35 34-19

This office will then send a bill that must be paid within a short period.

Contracts either have fixed periods or are indefinite. Landlords have defined termination periods, during which they can cancel the contract (unless you fail to pay your rent, go bankrupt, sublet or abuse the premises). The tenant, however, isn't bound by the termination period. With a diplomatic clause in your contract, you can terminate by giving three months' notice. If you want the contract translated in English, you must bear the costs. You may choose to have a lawyer, someone in your firm or the real-estate agent approve the terms.

RENTAL DEPOSIT *Mietenvoramszahlung*

A deposit, which is usually three times the gross rent, is required. If you rent deluxe accommodations, you may pay significantly more because the purpose of the deposit is to cover potential damages or nonpayment of rent. The money is kept as equity in a bank savings account (*Sparbuch*) or as a bank guarantee (you pay your bank a one-time fee and it agrees to guarantee the deposit). Unless otherwise specified, you have the right to receive the interest (*Eckzinssatz*), which is calculated according to the minimum interest rate.

REAL-ESTATE AGENT'S COMMISSION

Real-estate agents (*Immobilienmakler*) work on commission, and, according to one Viennese newspaper, agent commissions in Vienna are among the highest in the world. The maximum commissions permitted are as follows:

- For an apartment rental of up to two years, the commission is one month's gross rent.

- For two to three years rental, it is two months' gross rent.

- For leases of more than three years, the commission is three months' gross rent.

You must then add the 20 percent value-added tax (*MwSt*) to that amount, which is paid in full when the contract is signed. If you'd like more information about renting in Vienna, you can get a brochure (in German) called *"Wohnen"* from the Consumer Information Association (*Verein für Konsumenteninformation*; see Info Offices appendix).

RENTAL INSPECTION

It's customary to conduct a joint inspection with the landlord or real-estate agent when assuming occupancy of the rental property. At that time, you should check and note on an inventory sheet the condition of all furnishings (e.g., toilets, faucets, windows, appliances). You'll be responsible for repairs to damages not noted at this time.

TENANT'S RESPONSIBILITIES

During occupancy, you're expected to take care of all minor repairs (e.g., leaky faucets, burnt-out lightbulbs). The landlord handles major repairs (e.g., the heating system). Whether you have to repaint the unit when moving out should be stipulated in your lease, though custom is leaning toward leaving the property in the same condition you found it. If you want to paint or decorate while living there, get written permission from the owner.

You, as a tenant, are expected to arrange and pay for one heating system check per year. You're also required to admit the chimney sweep (*Rauchfangkehrer*) when he comes to clean and check the building's chimneys (if it has any). A notice of the date and approximate times of his work will be posted in a common area of the apartment building or mailed to your house. You're expected to be there or to arrange for him to be admitted. You must also admit meter readers if the meters are inside (most are not). This usually occurs once a year, and you can ask to see proper identification.

UTILITIES

FORMER TENANT'S BILLS

Be sure all former utility and phone bills have been paid by the previous tenant. Your real-estate agent will do this for you. If you're on your own, however, ask to see receipts or check with the following offices (where generally only German is spoken):

WIENER STADTWERKE/WIEN STROM (ELECTRICITY)
1090, Spitalgasse 5-9
☎ 313 69-0

WIENER STADTWERKE/WIEN GAS (GAS)
1080, Josefstädter Strasse 10-12
☎ 401 28-0

POST UND TELEKOM AUSTRIA/TELEKOM RECHNUNGSSTELLE (TELEPHONE)
1010, Dr.-Karl-Lueger-Platz 5
☎ 515 00-0

PAYING UTILITY BILLS

Gas and electricity bills are issued five times per year. Fees are based on the previous year's usage. Discrepancies are adjusted in January, at which time you may be shocked to find out that you owe an additional ATS 10.000 to ATS 20.000. This can happen when the previous tenants were Austrian (they knew utility costs, so they turned off lights more often and avoided using the clothes dryer). You should know that your dishwasher and washing machine heat their own water electrically. The utility company can arrange monthly budget billing if you request it.

Although no longer common, you may occasionally find an apartment with a central-oil heating system. The heating costs could be included in your *Betriebskosten*, charged proportionately by square meters occupied or metered by apartment.

RADIO & TELEVISION REGISTRATION

Electronic media in Austria are government-financed via user taxes. The law requires that you register your televisions and radios at your local post office. It's possible that someone might appear at your door to question your radio or TV use if you haven't registered these appliances. If this happens, you must let the person in.

You can arrange for automatic withdrawal from your current bank account (see Banking chapter), or you can pay when you receive the bimonthly payment form (*Zahlschein*) in the mail.

For information about arranging for and registering cable TV, contact the following office (where English is spoken):

TELEKABEL WIEN
1100, Erlachgasse 116
☎ 17 01 71

Before leaving your current address, all registration must be canceled (*Verzichtserklärung*). There are specific times when this can be done, so you should plan ahead. Go to your local post office before the fifth day of an *even* month, because the cancellation takes effect on the first of the following *uneven* month.

CUSTOMS *ZOLL*

There are restrictions on what you can bring into Austria from other countries. Depending on the products involved, the limits may be a general monetary limit per person or they may be a quantity limit on individual products. The customs guidelines also depend on whether you're coming from another EU-member state or from a non-EU country. Because Austria is bordered by some non-EU-member countries, the means of transportation is yet another factor in determining duty-free limits.

The current guidelines for importing certain products to Austria are listed below. These only serve to give you a basic idea, so you should verify this information before or during your travels as they're subject to periodic change. Consult the pamphlet *"Zoll-Info Tips für Auslandsreisende"* ("Customs Info Tips for Foreign Travelers"), which is issued by the Federal Ministry of Finance (*Bundesministerium für Finanzen*) at 1010, Himmelpfortgasse 4-8, ☎ 514 33-0. You can also pick up the "Travel Information" (*"Reise Informationen"*) brochure, which is in English, from the airport.

TRAVELING WITHIN THE EUROPEAN UNION

Regardless of the mode of transportation, you can bring the following items from any EU-member state into Austria duty-free, provided that you paid taxes on them in that country and that you are personally transporting them for your own use:

Tobaccco

- 800 cigarettes
- 400 cigarillos
- 200 cigars
- 1 kilogram of smoking tobacco

Alcohol

- 10 liters of spirits
- 20 liters of alcoholic beverages other than beer, sparkling wine or wine with an alcohol content of no more than 22-percent volume
- 90 liters of wine (maximum 60 liters sparkling wine)
- 110 liters of beer

DUTY-FREE PURCHASES IN AUSTRIA

If you travel by air from Austria to another EU country, you can purchase the following items in Austria duty-free:

Tobaccco

200 cigarettes

or 100 cigarillos (cigars with a maximum unit weight of three grams)

or 50 cigars

or 250 grams smoking tobacco

or Any proportional combination of the above

Alcohol (per person above the age of 17)

2 liters nonsparkling wine

and 1 liter distilled drinks and spirits with an alcohol content exceeding 22-percent volume or consumable ethyl alcohol with an alcohol content of 80-percent volume or more

or 2 liters distilled drinks, spirits and aperitives, sake or similar drinks with an alcohol content less than 22-percent volume

or 2 liters champagne, sparkling wine or liqueur wine

or Any proportional combination of the above

and 50 grams perfume

and 250 milliliters Eau de Toilette

and 500 grams coffee or 200 grams coffee extract or essence

and 100 grams tea or 40 grams tea extract or essence

 ## VAT Refunds

Nonresidents traveling directly to a non-EU country can be refunded the value-added tax (VAT) on purchases exceeding ATS 1.000. You can get the necessary form from stores where items are purchased. Look for the tax-free sign in shop windows.

DUTY-FREE LIMITS ON PRODUCTS PURCHASED/ ACQUIRED IN NON-EU COUNTRIES

The limits are the same — except for coffee and tea — for bringing duty-free products into Austria from a non-EU country, provided they're for your own use and you're personally transporting them. You must declare other gifts exceeding ATS 2.400 (ECU 175). You are not allowed to share total customs-free limits with other passengers (i.e., the value of one item cannot be declared by two people). There are restrictions on ivory, certain leather goods, potted plants and flower bulbs, potatoes and salt. You can bring medications for personal use in quantities needed during travel. The free customs limits apply to one calendar day per person.

 If, however, goods enter Austria from the bordering countries of the Czech Republic, Hungary, Slovakia or Slovenia, other than by air travel, the total value of other products and articles is reduced to 75 ECU, or ATS 1.000. You can travel duty-free with other items for your personal use (e.g., sport articles, professional equipment, camera, laptop computer). However, if you purchased an item shortly before your trip, you should carry the receipt with you to avoid any unnecessary customs inquiries.

You are not allowed to combine total customs-free limits with other travelers (i.e., the value of one item cannot be declared by two people each donating the 175 ECU maximum limit toward the total). In addition the "free" limits listed may not exceed once per calendar day.

For health, safety and veterinary reasons, the import of certain foodstuffs is also limited by quantity as follows:
- Milk, cream, whipped cream and other dairy products in dairy packaging: total one liter or one kilogram per person
- Poultry, eggs (including hard-boiled): one kilogram per person
- Meat and meat products (including raw meat and raw-meat products): total one kilogram per person
- Fish and fish products: total one kilgram per person
- Shellfish and other crustaceans: total one kilogram per person
- Honey and other products from bees: total one kilogram per person
- Fruit: 15 kilograms per person.

An outbreak of a contagious animal disease (such as hoof and mouth disease or swine fever) may cause an import embargo whereby the products identified cannot be brought into the country. In such an event, a multilingual notice is posted at border stations.

Austria

This chapter is meant to help you bridge the gap between your native culture and the one you encounter here. The first section deals with ways to adjust to any new culture. The second deals specifically with assimilating to life in Vienna. The next gives dates and explanations of Austrian holidays so that you won't be caught off guard when shops are closed and people are celebrating. Once you understand what is happening around you, you can make it a point to watch for, or to join in, the festivities. Because you may want to know more about the country itself, the last section has a bit about Austria's history, government, politics and economics, as well as some general information concerning its people and geography.

BRIDGING
THE CULTURAL GAP

If nine blind men were asked to describe an elephant, they would give nine different descriptions, depending on whether they touch the tail, tusk or ear. Similarly, your perspective on living in Vienna will also be unique, depending on what you experience. Initially, you're sure to encounter some obstacles—some easier to surmount than others. The information in this section comes from dozens of people—Austrians, Americans married to Austrians, long-term foreign residents and newcomers. We're grateful for all their time and thoughtful input. When, however, we received contradictory information, we tried to form a general consensus. Of course, half the fun of living in a new country is making your own observations.

CHANGING CULTURES

When you move to a new country, the adjustment process will be easier if you keep certain things in mind. Although our examples are tailored to Americans (remember that this book was produced by the American Women's Association), many of the suggestions hold true for anyone who moves to a new place.

First, consider what it means to be American, Japanese, Arab or whatever your nationality. What culture do you come from? What do others think about your country? Will they have inaccurate stereo-types about you? Are the traits you value equally important to people in Austria? Many Americans believe in such ideas as the Puritan work ethic, the efficient use of time and that change is always for the better. They like being busy and productive, taking charge and solving problems. They stress equality. They feel comfortable with a casual atmosphere of friendliness and camaraderie. But Americans are often seen by others as acting too superior and self-assured and of appearing to have all the answers—or being unbelievably naive. Some see Americans as insisting that others do everything the "American" way— which, Americans assume, is the most logical. Americans seem to have no respect for hierarchy or class. They seem not to know how to enjoy life and appear to be too rushed, aggressive and overly concerned about being liked.

Americans must understand that their rugged, independent natures and present mobile lifestyles make them different from most of the world. They often make friends faster and in a more casual fashion.

Europeans have generations of family and friends surrounding them and don't always feel the need to seek out new friends. Americans expect established neighbors to greet newcomers, but in most places outside the United States, the newcomer must take the initiative. We, as the newcomers, are the ones doing things differently. We are the ones who must adjust and adapt. We should not waste our time and energy expecting the new culture to adjust to us.

PERSONAL INFLUENCES

Consider what else is happening in your life at the time of your move. Are you leaving behind elderly parents or children in college? Are your children leaving behind their friends? Are you leaving behind your friends? Are you bringing marriage, health or other personal problems with you? Problems cross borders without passports. A child experiencing the "terrible twos" will now learn how to say "No!" in two languages. The teenager will still be rebellious. Try to separate life problems from those associated with moving to a new culture. When you left your home, you left behind many relationships, situations and commitments. Many will be missed, but some will not. Try to remember those you don't miss whenever you feel sad about leaving home.

It's exciting to remember that in the course of adapting to a new culture, you will acquire new skills and a new outlook on life and the world. Today, a person's job is no longer permanent, so new skills acquired here can also prepare you for future career opportunities.

ADAPTING TO A NEW CULTURE

Plan Ahead

If possible, you should begin the adjustment process before leaving home. Start to learn about Austria. Call the Austrian Embassy or Consulate in your country for information and talk to people who've lived there. Read about Austria's history and culture. Give yourself a head start by taking a German course or at least buy some tapes to familiarize yourself with the language. Prepare your children for the move by involving them in the process. Give them time to say goodbye to friends and encourage them to keep in touch with them. Remind your kids that they'll be making new friends, too. Remember that everyone in the family may not be equally excited about making this big change. The wife leaving her career or the teenagers leaving behind their friends might have a much harder time adjusting than the husband headed for his promotion.

Settle In

Once you arrive, try to get your environment (i.e., new home) settled, and then get on with living. Realize that your house in Vienna will not be just like the one you left. Most of us have to compromise on space, location, layout and appearance. Get the children's rooms settled first. Take breaks from unpacking by going out and exploring—the boxes will still be there when you get back. Maybe even get away for a weekend excursion before you're completely settled.

Talk to Someone

Try to find someone from your own culture you can talk to. If you're lucky, this will be someone who can keep you positive about your new situation. If not, find someone who can. Once you've found your niche with people from your own country, then reach out to other cultures. It's particularly nice to find an Austrian friend to help you understand your new home and its people better.

Get Involved

Church, school, the American Women's Association (AWA), the United Nations Women's Guild and Contact are some of the groups available to English speakers (for details and for more opportunities, see the Organizations, Religion and Education chapters). The easiest way to make new friends is to see them regularly in some shared activity. The AWA, for instance, has many smaller groups catering to every age and interest.

Volunteer

Most spouses aren't able to pursue their careers overseas. There are, however, many volunteer activities. Try to be selective—in addition to helping others, the activity will be more satisfying if it enhances your life or your family's. You will also be a more effective volunteer if you enjoy what you're doing. Volunteering can help develop new skills and increase your self-confidence.

Tours & Language Classes

Tours get you out meeting other people. While you learn about a country's history and culture, you'll discover that many are in the same boat as you (and you'll get some exercise). Enrolling in a language class is even more important, because learning German will make life so much easier and more enjoyable for you. For those who feel they're not good at learning a foreign language or prefer spending time on other interests, consider that even an introductory class can be useful—it will give you basic phrases to get around as well as help you understand the culture. So decide how much of the language you want to learn, then do it and move on.

Cultural Transition

Something happens when you go from your own culture to a different one. At first, it can be confusing and stressful. You feel disoriented and tired. Things you did routinely and automatically now require extensive conscious thought. All your circuits go into overload.

The adjustment cycle has many phases. It has been said that the four H's of adjusting are: honeymoon, hostility, humor and home. Although these stages are different for each of us, we all go through them in one form or another. Just be sure to take it easy and be kind to yourself and your family. Keep an open-minded curiosity and a sense of humor. Avoid finding fault with or blaming Austria or Austrians for everything that is less than perfect in your life. Try not to make comparisons. Things are not better or worse, they're just different. Try to bloom where you are planted, even if it wasn't your choice to be planted there!

AUSTRIAN & VIENNESE CUSTOMS

The following section deals more with living in Vienna than in Austria. As is true all over the world, the capital city is very different from the provinces. Vienna has even more distinct differences because of its long, rich and unique heritage as the capital of a multinational empire. All of the past is reflected in the way Viennese conduct themselves today. It helps to understand Vienna's history—the Roman period, the Turkish invasion attempts, Maria Theresia, the Biedermeier period, Franz Josef, the *fin de siècle* period and the two World Wars—in order to understand why Vienna and the Viennese are what they are today (see A Glimpse of Austria section of this chapter for more information and the Books appendix for reading suggestions).

MEETING & GREETING

The many ways of greeting in Vienna may seem elaborate and involved. And to complicate matters, they vary by generation, social class and individual style.

Verbal Greetings

A common greeting is *"Grüss Gott,"* which, roughly translated, means "God's greetings/blessings." *"Guten Tag"* ("Good day") and *"Guten Morgen"* ("Good morning") are also used. The greeting is used when entering small shops, whether you know the clerks or not. In the city, it's never used with passers-by or strangers on the street (but when hiking, it is polite to greet your fellow walkers in response to their greetings). *"Auf Wiedersehen"* ("See you again") is used when leaving. When a man meets a woman he knows, he should greet her first. While greeting fellow hikers on mountain trails, you can use the *"du"* form with them as long as you're actually walking on a trail. You must revert back to *"Sie"* once you're in a restaurant, rest hut (*Schutzhut*) or in some form of transportation.

Shaking Hands

Austrians shake hands whenever they greet or leave acquaintances; this is done with everyone in a group. A woman offers her hand first to the man, and the older person to the younger. Handshakes are firm with direct eye contact. It's considered rude to have your hands in your pockets while being introduced or while talking to anyone.

Kissing

Close friends (women with women and women with men, but not men with men) kiss each other on the cheeks as a greeting. Both cheeks are kissed, right then left. The trick is to know when. When you enter a group, it may be a bit confusing because some shake hands and others kiss. For the non-Viennese, it's best to let the Austrians decide if you're now on close enough terms to greet with a kiss!

Kiss the Hand *Küss die Hand*

In certain circles, European men may still kiss a woman's hand (or the air above her hand). He may also simply bow his head, gently raise her hand and say, *"Küss die Hand."* Don't be disappointed if it never happens, but also don't be caught off guard if it does. American men should never attempt this feat because they'll probably look silly.

Introductions

Austrians would prefer to have the host at a function introduce them to the other guests rather than introduce themselves. When Austrians do introduce themselves, they usually just give their family name. First names may or may not come later in a relationship. Although first names are used immediately in social situations in the United States, with many employees calling their bosses by their first names, this is not so in Vienna. There are, of course, exceptions, particularly among the younger generation. Take your cues from the people around you.

Titles

Titles here are more prevalent and considered more important than in the United States. With some groups, the rules aren't as rigid as in the past. People with academic, government or diplomatic titles, such as doctor, professor, engineer or ambassador, are addressed as such (e.g., "Herr—or Frau—Doktor"). It's no longer necessary to call the wife of a doctor "Frau Doktor." But when in doubt, you can't go wrong by using a title.

Visiting

Viennese tend to entertain at new-wine taverns (Heurigen), restaurants or coffeehouses, rather than in their own homes. Often foreigners must take the initiative to invite Austrians to their homes. If Austrians do invite you to their home, consider it an honor. They will go to a lot of trouble to make the occasion special for you. Be punctual and take a small gift—something from your home country, flowers, candy or a special wine. If you bring flowers, unwrap them before presenting them, unless they are covered with clear cellophane wrap and a bow. A small seasonal plant is also appropriate. Offer to remove your shoes when entering the home. Often your host will have several pairs of slippers near the door, or you could take your own. Men should always stand the first time a woman enters or leaves a room, but not each time thereafter. It's always nice to call the next morning to thank your host.

If you're in doubt about what to wear, ask the host. If, for some reason, you can't ask, it's better to err on the side of overdressing. Women usually wear a simple dress or suit—rarely slacks. Men should wear a suit (or at least a blazer) with a tie.

Don't ever drop in on an Austrian friend or neighbor unannounced. Always call beforehand.

When inviting Austrians to your home or for dinner in a restaurant, you should cover all the costs and prepare all the food. If you say you would like to "invite" someone, it means you are paying. If you have been invited, don't argue about paying and simply thank your gracious host.

EATING

Both hands are kept above the table because it's impolite to have your hands in your lap. Rest your wrists or forearms on the table, but not your elbows. Elbows should be kept close to your body. Austrians eat Continental style with the fork in the left hand and the knife (used for cutting or pushing) in the right hand. Dumplings, potatoes, pancakes and fish should be sectioned with a fork, or in the case of fish, with a special knife. Don't use the knife if the fork will cut, because using the knife is a sign that you think the food is too tough. When you're finished eating, place the knife and fork together at an angle on the plate, top left to bottom right. If you want to take a second helping, knife and fork should be crossed. During the meal, while pausing to take a drink or to talk, lay your silverware on both sides of the plate, face down. Don't eat or drink until the host begins. Toasting is done by looking each person at the table in the eye, giving a slight nod, then drinking. Clinking glasses together is only done on special occasions and only with alcoholic beverages.

At a restaurant, the host will have a small sample of wine poured into his glass first. He takes a sip, and if it's to his liking, he nods. The waiter then fills the other glasses at the table, finishing with the host. A white-wine glass is held by the stem, not the bowl. After eating, it's considered rude to apply lipstick at the table, unless it's done very discreetly.

CLOTHING

Like elsewhere in the world, what you wear in Vienna depends on your age, occupation, income and the occasion, as well as individual style. You can see everything in Vienna—from ripped jeans and leather jackets at Karlsplatz to traditional *Loden* garments at Michaelerplatz. Once again, you should observe the people around you to make your own decisions about what to wear. However, most people reading this book will find that the Austrians they meet dress in a rather classic, neat and more formal style than you find in the United States. Although some Americans feel comfortable in jeans, sweatsuits/jogging attire and tennis shoes, many Austrians only wear these when participating in sports. Especially in the first district, you'll receive better service if you're dressed nicely.

Layering is not only a style here, it's a way of life. Beautiful old buildings are difficult and expensive to heat in the winter. In the summer, often the only cooling system a shop, office or home has is an open door or windows. Therefore, in any season, you should be prepared to put on or take off layers of clothing to maintain a comfortable body temperature.

SHOPPING

The details of shopping are discussed in the Food, Home and Appearance chapters, so here we'll discuss the common courtesies of shopping. Especially in small shops, you should not touch, smell or shake anything. Watch your children. You normally ask for assistance by saying *"Bitte . . . "* ("Please . . . "). If you try on something, don't feel pressured to buy it—just smile and decline politely—because many stores here have a no return or exchange policy. If you prefer to just look, say, *"Ich schaue, danke."*

Bagging Groceries

Only occasionally do you find supermarkets that provide shopping bags for free (normally you have to buy them for a few Schillings), so take your own basket or bags. Even in large grocery stores, you have to bag your own groceries. Try not to panic or get frustrated. Just put your purchases back into the shopping cart and move away from the counter. There's usually a bagging section (a counter) to the side where you can take your time cramming too many purchases into the too few bags you have. Eventually, you'll get the hang of this.

Waiting in Line

The absence of orderly lines at deli, meat, cheese and bread counters can sometimes make it unclear who is next. At some places, you take a number (but you need to know German because you have to hear your number being called). If this system doesn't exist, you just have to watch carefully so that when your turn comes, you'll be prepared to step in with your order before someone jumps in ahead of you (and they will if you hesitate). It's okay to say, *"Ich bin die Nächste"* ("I'm next").

Dogs and children are expected to be well-behaved and relatively quiet on public transportation and in stores and restaurants (yes, dogs are allowed in restaurants).

MAKING A TELEPHONE CALL

When you call an Austrian, give your family/last name, then ask to speak with the person (e.g., "My name is Smith. May I speak with Frau Schmidt?"). When you have the person on the line, exchange a few pleasantries before getting down to business. Nine in the morning seems to be the most acceptable time to call in Austria. End a telephone conversation by saying *"Auf Wiederhören"* ("Hear from you again").

GENERAL RULES OF BEHAVIOR

- Remember—especially when you're in public areas (e.g., restaurants, public transportation, on the street, in stores)—that most Austrians speak some English. Thoughtless or inappropriate remarks will probably be understood.

- Backslapping, excessive touching or proximity and exaggerated physical behavior should be avoided because Austrians consider these to be too familiar and intrusive. Loud, overly effusive, frenetic speech is also frowned upon.

- Avoid chewing gum in public; if you must, then do it discreetly.

- In diplomatic and business circles, business/calling cards (*Visitenkarten*) are exchanged regularly. Even some nonprofessionals exchange cards (with name, address and phone number) for social purposes.

- Austrians consider it rude to interrupt a sentence in progress.

- "Quiet hours" are not only a custom, but also the law. Weekdays from 10 PM to 6 AM and weekends from Saturday 2 PM to Monday 6 AM, you are not allowed to make noises that can be heard outside your premises. So hang your pictures, run your washing machine and mow your lawn outside of those times!

- In environmentally conscientious Austria, car washing is usually done at a car wash, where the soap and oil are filtered from the wastewater before it enters the sewage system.

- Stand to the right on escalators to allow others to pass by.

- Knock before entering an office.

- Use whatever German you know whenever you can because Austrians appreciate it—and it may prompt them to use whatever English they know.

FUNERALS

Death has its own rituals, and, usually in a time of grief, they become very important to all concerned. In Austria, the official funeral announcement (*Parte*) is usually a black-bordered sheet of paper giving details of the memorial service. It is delivered to friends and family before they find out from another source. Services usually occur at both the cemetery (*Friedhof*) and the church (*Kirche*). Although it's acceptable to attend either one or the other, you show the greatest amount of respect for the deceased if you attend both. When greeting and consoling the mourning family, shake hands and say, *"Mein Beileid"* ("My condolences"). Follow the lead of other mourners, but take three roses (usually red) with you, even if the *Parte* specifies that flowers not be given. These are to be cast, along with a scoop of dirt, onto the coffin after it has been lowered into the grave. (This scoop will be handed to you by an attendant, who will murmur his thanks for the ATS 10 you discreetly offer him.) These days, a *Parte* may suggest a contribution to a favorite charity of the deceased in lieu of flowers. If you take the *Parte* to your local bank, it will see to it that proper payment is made in the amount you request, which is usually a minimum of ATS 500.

SMOKING

Unlike in the United States, where nonsmokers are the clear majority, they're the minority in Europe, and Austria is no exception. Europe is beginning to institute some restrictions, but among certain groups (e.g., women and teens), smoking is on the rise. Nonsmoking sections are available in very few restaurants (see Dining chapter). Although smoking is banned on public transportation and in elevators, don't be surprised to see no-smoking signs blatantly ignored. Austrians will usually ask permission to smoke if they're aware you're a nonsmoker, but don't hold your breath (or perhaps you should). This is simply a courtesy— they expect you to grant their request.

TIPPING

Although there are no laws about this, there are some customs that may differ from yours. Hotels and restaurants include a 10- to 15- percent service charge in their bills. However, in restaurants, it's customary to round up the total when paying—don't leave the tip on the table (see Dining chapter). Taxi drivers normally receive an extra 10 percent over the metered fare. ATS 10 per bag is typical for porters and bellhops.

Here, daily encounters also often call for tipping. For example, you might give a repairman ATS 20 as he leaves. A postal carrier who has climbed the stairs or taken time to deliver a package to your door might get ÖS 10. The chimney sweep gets ATS 20. Movers usually get ATS 100 per mover per day, which is given to the on-site supervisor to distribute. Since you may have different workers on different days, offer it at the end of each day for a multiple-day move. Not giving a tip won't detract from the service you receive, but it is an acknowledgment of the care they took with your precious possessions.

The Christmas season is also the tipping season for many service people. Of course, this is not obligatory, but you ignore this tradition at your own risk! If you live in a house, you should give the waste collectors each ATS 20 when they come ringing a bell. Other people you probably want to "remember" are: your cleaning lady, postal carrier, building superintendent (*Hausbesorger*), hairstylist, a regular gas-station attendant—in short, anyone who routinely provides a service to you.

HOLIDAYS & FESTIVALS

Austria is a Roman Catholic country, so many of its holidays are related to the church calendar. For a newcomer here, the frequency of "days off" can be a source of both joy and frustration. The secret for coping is investing in an Austrian calendar. To help you avoid being caught without essentials because stores are officially closed, the following is a list (with explanations) of Austrian public holidays. Once you're forewarned and prepared, you can begin enjoying the celebrations as much as the Viennese!

January 1: NEW YEAR'S DAY *Neujahr*

Everything is closed. The traditional Vienna Philharmonic Concert, featuring the music of the Strausses, begins at 11 AM. If you want to attend, you must order tickets from a ticket agency at least a year in advance, or you can stay home and watch the live worldwide TV broadcast as you recover from the previous night's celebrating. Another tradition is to attend a performance of Beethoven's "Ninth Symphony" at the *Konzerthaus* (see Music section of Entertainment chapter).

January 6: EPIPHANY *Heilige Drei Könige*

Everything is closed. On Epiphany and preceding days, young people dressed as the Three Wise Men with a star bearer go from house to house to bring good tidings and news of Christ's birth. On behalf of local Roman Catholic parishes, they collect monetary donations for underdeveloped countries (but appreciate a small gift of cookies or chocolate). Usually they'll write C(aspar), B(althasar), M(elchior) and the year in chalk over the entrance of Roman Catholic homes.

CARNIVAL *Fasching*

Fasching in Austria is one long season of merrymaking, which begins on the 11th hour of the 11th day of the 11th month, the moment the new (*Heuriger*) wine becomes old (*alt*), and ends with Ash Wednesday (*Aschermittwoch*). Girls might find ball gowns under the tree at Christmas. Vienna becomes a little-girl's-dream-come-true each year when the city's sumptuous palaces and hotels become the venues for throngs of beautifully dressed couples waltzing the night away. The ball season starts with the New Year's Eve Imperial Ball (*Kaiserball*) at the *Hofburg* and officially lasts until Ash Wednesday (*Aschermittwoch*). But in reality, you may attend a ball as early as November and as late as June. Almost every group or profession has one: *Kaffeehaus* owners, pastry chefs (*Zuckerbäcker*), lawyers, florists, doctors, criminal investigators and hunters. Even schools and *Kindergartens* have balls. Dress codes are strictly enforced, with evening dress (*Abendkleid*) meaning floor-length gowns (you won't be admitted with anything shorter). At some balls, the national dress (*Trachten*) is an option, at others, men must wear tuxedos with tails (*Frack*) or a military uniform. Balls are opened with a formal entry processional (*Polonaise*), usually done by debutantes in white ball gowns and their tuxedo-clad escorts. People go to see and be seen. The Opera Ball in February is the pinnacle of the Vienna ball season, so tickets are at a premium, both in availability and price. A complete brochure listing all of Vienna's balls is available in mid-November at the Vienna Tourist Information Office (see Info Offices appendix). Make your reservations early and get ready to dance until dawn!

Opera Ball Rehearsal

The Opera Ball rehearsal, which is on the night before the ball, is open to the public. For the price of a ticket (about ATS 200, but buy well in advance), you can watch the 400 or more young people achieve the precision necessary for all of them to make the same moves at the same time, as well as preview the ballet and musical entertainment, all from preassigned box seats.

Fasching festivities quiet down during Advent, but then get rolling again on New Year's Eve (*Silvester*) and peak the week before Shrove Tuesday (*Faschingsdienstag*), when many people dress up in lovely or outrageous costumes and make merry. On the last Saturday of *Fasching*, children come to school dressed as fairies, animals or whatever their imaginations (and parents) allow. The neighborhood butcher may also get into the spirit by disguising himself as a clown, and your friendly bartender may be dressed as a dragon. And someone will be elected "witch of the year." Before Ash Wednesday, the witch will confess her sins and be burned in effigy, and, for a while, the city will take on a different mood. Some will promise to give up one vice, at least for the 40 days of Lent (*Fastenzeit*). Then one final celebration remains before the more somber days preceding the Easter weekend: the herring feast (*Heringsschmaus*), which can be found throughout Austria on Ash Wednesday (*Aschermittwoch*). Roman Catholics, not allowed to dance or eat meat during Lent, dine on an abundance of fish set out in gorgeous buffets.

LENT *Fastenzeit*

Though neither Maundy Thursday (*Gründonnerstag*) nor Good Friday (*Karfreitag*) are public holidays, stores and offices may close early. The root of the word *Gründonnerstag* comes from an old German word for "weeping." But people sometimes eat spinach on that day, so there is also a connection with the other definition of *grün* (green). *Rosenmontag* is really more a German holiday than Austrian, but you may see store clerks wearing funny hats. Good Friday is a serious day of fasting for most Roman Catholics. During the last two weeks of the Lenten (*Fastenzeit*) season, Easter markets (*Ostermärkte*) appear in many districts throughout the city (see Holiday Markets section of Food chapter). You will find a huge variety of hand-blown decorated eggs, wooden toys and other handicrafts. On Palm Sunday, priests bless decorated pussy willow branches (*Palmkatzerl, Palmkätzchen*), symbols of rebirth and renewal, which are placed in special corners of people's homes.

EASTER *Ostern*

Easter is observed both Sunday and Monday in Austria. Beautiful music is performed in the churches. Many stores and offices are closed from mid-afternoon Good Friday until the following Tuesday, though these customs are changing. Austrian schools are closed Monday and Tuesday.

May 1: LABOR DAY *Tag der Arbeit*

Everything is closed. Public transportation does not run until midday. Political rallies and soapbox speeches abound. There are parades at the Rathausplatz and Ringstrasse, which is closed to traffic. In the countryside, you may see a Maypole (*Maibaum*). In some areas, it is customary for older boys to decorate them. Sometimes they grease them with soap or oil and try to impress the girls with their ability to shinny up and grab hanging sausages. Pranksters may also steal the Maypole of a neighboring village.

ASCENSION *Christi Himmelfahrt*

Everything is closed. *Christi Himmelfahrt* is always on a Thursday and nine days prior to Pentecost/Whitsun.

MOTHER'S DAY *Muttertag*

This always occurs on the second Sunday in May. Reserve early for a restaurant!

PENTECOST/WHITSUN *Pfingsten*

This holiday is 50 days after Easter. Stores close Monday. Austrian schools are also closed Tuesday. On Whitmonday, the Whitsun Kings in Arbesthal, southeast of Vienna, wear hazelnut branches in homage to spring.

CORPUS CHRISTI *Fronleichnam*

This is the second Thursday after Whitsunday. Everything is closed. The procession on the Ringstrasse in the center of Vienna is famous. The emperor used to march behind the bishop and the Host, which was encased in a precious shrine called a monstrance and carried to the Graben. This memento of the more ornate pageantry of the past can now be seen in the Treasury. For a long time, this celebration and sharing of the Host with the people was also an opportunity for political demonstration. After World War II, the Church wanted to get away from that association. Processions are held in every church, churchyard or lake in every parish from St. Stephan's Cathedral (*Stephansdom*) to the tiny chapel in Salmannsdorf.

FATHER'S DAY *Vatertag*

This is on the second Sunday in June.

August 15: ASSUMPTION DAY/ASCENSION *Mariähimmelfahrt*

This day is in commemoration of the Virgin Mary's ascension into Heaven. Everything is closed.

October 26:
AUSTRIAN NATIONAL DAY
Nationalfeiertag

Everything is closed. This holiday commemorates the day in 1955 when the National Council passed the Law of Neutrality of the Republic of Austria. It has become a patriotic "fitness day," as many people all over Austria take long walks. There are many speeches, but fireworks are not part of this holiday. The *Parlament* building and all national museums are open and visits are free to the public. (Busloads of people from Austria and neighboring countries take advantage of this opportunity, so museums are packed!)

November 1 & 2:
ALL SAINTS' DAY & ALL SOULS' DAY
Allerheiligen und Allerseelen

All stores and schools are closed; on the second, only schools are closed. Austrians visit the graves of loved ones to light candles and lay wreaths or dried-flower arrangements. Additional public-transportation routes are provided to the cemeteries.

November 11:
ST. MARTIN'S DAY *Martinstag*

This is not a public holiday. It is the beginning of *Fasching*, when traditional meals of roast goose (*Martinigansl*) are eaten. Children may make paper or wood lanterns, parade with them and sing.

November 15:
DAY OF THE PATRON SAINT OF LOWER AUSTRIA
Leopoldustag

This is a day of festivities in Klosterneuburg and a regional holiday in Lower Austria (*Niederösterreich*), where schools are closed. It honors the Babenberg ruler and founder of the abbey, Leopold III.

ADVENT

Advent begins on the fourth Sunday before Christmas. The rich Austrian Advent traditions include the special magic of the Advent Markets (*Christkindlmärkte*), which may open as early as the middle of November. While the large and colorful market at City Hall (*Rathaus*) is the best known, other markets are also well worth a visit (see Holiday Markets section of Food chapter). For a complete list and more information about Advent markets in Vienna, ask for the annual *"Wiener Adventzauber"* pamphlet (in English and German) at the Vienna Tourist Information Office (see Info Offices appendix) or check local newspapers. Also be sure to see the annual nativity scene/*crèche* (*Krippen*) display at St. Peter's Church (*Peterskirche*), just off the Graben. Each year more than 150 families lend their handmade *Krippen* for the exhibit. Go early. The display ends December 15, when the *Krippen* are returned to the families.

December 4:
ST. BARBARA'S DAY *Barbaratag*

This is not a public holiday. Branches of cherry and apple trees are cut and placed in water to bloom by Christmas. This custom originated from a story about St. Barbara, who brought sustenance to the poor against her father's wishes. One day he caught her leaving home with an apronful of food, but when he asked her to show him what she was hiding, she discovered her burden had turned into cherry blossoms. Today, the blossoms are a symbol of the hope and the sense of anticipation associated with Christmas.

December 6:
ST. NIKOLAUS DAY *Nikolaustag*

This is not an official holiday, but the day when white-robed *St. Nikolaus* and his mischievous evil-spirit companion, *Krampus*, wander the streets. They usually reward Austrian children for the previous year's behavior. In some families, *Nikolaus* rewards the good children, and *Krampus* punishes the naughty ones by leaving coal or switches. Parents, *Kindergartens* and churches often "ask" *St. Nikolaus* to come (you can hire one), and he usually arrives alone carrying a golden book praising children for their good deeds and chastising them for their not-so-good ones. Children respond with a poem or sweets for *Nikolaus*. Sometimes children put their shoes on the windowsills to find them filled the next morning with small treats from *Nikolaus*.

December 8:
IMMACULATE CONCEPTION
Mariä Empfängnis

Everything is usually closed, though this custom is changing.

December 24:
CHRISTMAS EVE
Heiliger Abend

Stores close in the afternoon and don't reopen until December 27. During the Advent season, some stores may stay open a little later. Try to get your shopping done early. Christmas is celebrated with a festive meal and distribution of presents provided by the Christ child (*Christkind*). While Santa Claus (*Weihnachtsmann*) has taken over as gift giver in some homes, many families maintain the old tradition. Theaters, cinemas and concert halls are closed, but there is a Christmas concert at City Hall (*Rathaus*) in the early afternoon. Roman Catholics celebrate the day with midnight Mass, the culmination of which is the singing of "Silent Night" (*"Stille Nacht"*).

December 25:
CHRISTMAS DAY *Christtag*

Everything is closed. This is a holy day for resting, going to church and visiting family. Traditionally, friends and relatives are invited to eat roast goose.

December 26:
ST. STEPHEN'S DAY *Stefanitag*

Everything is closed. Family and friends visit one another.

December 31:
NEW YEAR'S EVE *Silvester*

Most stores close early in the afternoon. The heartiest of Viennese celebrants gather at *Stephansplatz* and wait for the church bell to ring. (Watch out for people opening shaken champagne bottles and tossing them, or firecrackers, or placing firecrackers in loose garments.) Fireworks are traditional and may be bought by anyone over 18. Also part of the festivities are performances of *"Die Fledermaus"* at the opera houses. (If you are interested in attending, order tickets very early. Sometimes a few may be found at the last minute, but, as is always the case, at extraordinary prices.) The *Kaiserball* is held at the *Hofburg* palace. Outside on the streets is a bigger party with snacks, drinks, music and cabaret under festive tents throughout the city. It is customary to give relatives and friends good-luck charms for the New Year, which are usually marzipan pigs, clovers, chimney sweeps and mushrooms sold at stands at the New Year's markets that appear a day or so before at the *Rathaus*, *Schottenkirche* and *Stephansplatz*.

If you want to have dinner at a restaurant on New Year's Eve, make a reservation well in advance. Keep in mind that some places will only have fixed menus.

SEASONAL EVENTS

The following events occur at approximately the same time each year:

Spring

- **Mozart Week (March):** Concerts
- **IFABO (early spring):** Vienna's largest electronics/computer exhibition at the *Messegelände*
- **Wiener Frülingsfest (second week of April - mid-May):** Classical-music performances in the *Musikverein* and *Konzerthaus*
- **Vienna Spring Marathon (April or May):** *Schönbrunn* to *Rathaus*
- **Freyung Ostermarkt (two weeks before Easter):** See the Holiday Markets section of the Food chapter.
- **Waltz and Operetta Concerts (April - Oct):** Concerts at the *Hofburg* and *Konzerthaus*
- **Spanish Riding School Performances (May - June):** See the Spanish Riding School section of the Entertainment chapter.
- **Jazzfrühling (May):** Jazz concerts at the *Konzerthaus*

Summer

- **Vienna Music Film Festival (June - Sept):** *Rathausplatz* opera and ballet films (see Music section of Entertainment chapter)
- **Wiener Festwochen (May - June):** Music, theater, exhibitions and dance
- **Danube Island Festival (June):** See the Holidays & Festivities section of the Entertainment chapter.
- **Klangbogen in Wien (June - Sept):** Vienna's summer of music at the *Musikverein*, *Schloss Schönbrunn*, *Augustinerkirche* and *Konzerthaus*

- *Neuberg an der Mürz* **(August):** Music students take lessons from famous musicians. Concerts every evening in the 14th-century monastery.

Fall

- **Vienna Trade Fairs (Sept - Nov)**
- **Vienna Film Festival (Oct)**
- **Viennale Film Festival (Oct):** Asian films
- **Jewish Film Week (Oct)**
- *Jeunesse Musicale Festival* **(Oct):** *Musikverein, Konzerthaus*
- **International Antiques Fair (Nov)**
- **International Children's Film Festival (Nov)**
- **Spanish Riding School performances (Sept - Nov)**
- *Wien Modern* **Festival (Oct - Nov):**
  Modern-music festival at *Konzerthaus* or *Musikverein*
- **Vienna Boys' Choir Mass (Sept - Dec):**
  See the Music section of the Entertainment chapter.
- *Perchtoldsdorf* **(Nov, Sun after St. Leopold's Day):**
  Annual procession of vineyard guardians, a tradition dating back to 1683

Winter

- **Advent Markets** *Christkindlmärkte* **(end Nov - Dec 24):**
  See the Holiday Markets section of the Food chapter.
- **Imperial (*Kaiser*) Ball at the *Hofburg* (Dec 31)**
- **New Year's Day Concert of the Vienna Philharmonic (Dec 31 - Jan 1)**
- **Vienna's Ball Season (New Year's Eve - *Fasching*)**
- **Vienna Boys' Choir Mass (Jan - June)**
- **Vienna Trade Fairs (Jan - Feb)**
- **Opera Ball (last Tues of *Fasching* season)**

A GLIMPSE OF AUSTRIA

GEOGRAPHY

Austria is a predominantly mountainous, landlocked Central European country, with an area of 32,378 mi²/83,855 km², a size somewhat larger than the U.S. state of Maine. Austria borders eight other countries: Italy, Switzerland, the Principality of Liechtenstein, Germany, the Czech Republic, Slovakia, Hungary and Slovenia (former Yugoslavia). The capital, Vienna, lies on the Danube (*Donau*) River, partly surrounded by the hills of the Vienna Woods (*Wienerwald*).

Austria is divided into nine federal provinces
(Bundesländer):

Vienna	**Wien**
Lower Austria	**Niederösterreich**
Upper Austria	**Oberösterreich**
Salzburg	**Salzburg**
Carinthia	**Kärnten**
Tyrol	**Tirol**
Vorarlberg	**Vorarlberg**
Styria	**Steiermark**
Burgenland	**Burgenland**

POPULATION

Austria's population is eight million, with about 1.6 million people, approximately 20 percent of the total population, living in Vienna (on one half of one percent of the country's area). Ninety-two percent of Austrians are German-speaking and the country has a diverse ethnic mix, which includes six officially recognized ethnic groups: Croats, Czechs, Hungarians, Roma/Sinti, Slovaks and Slovenes. Austria also has a significant number of immigrants from other countries, many of them refugees from the former Yugoslavia. Although about 78 percent of the population is Roman Catholic, there are 11 other officially recognized religions in Austria.

CLIMATE

Austria enjoys a Central European climate that varies considerably from the Alpine region to the eastern plain. Summers can be hot, humid and long; cold winters bring snow and ice. The average annual precipitation ranges from 700 mm–2,000 mm, depending on altitude and location. Snow on the mountains in spring and autumn is not uncommon, and Vienna itself can be quite windy at any time of year.

HISTORY IN A NUTSHELL

- Excavations show that there was human habitation in the region of present-day Austria beginning in the Paleolithic period.

- In the first century A.D., Vindobona was founded on the present site of Vienna as part of Roman fortifications along the Danube valley.

- During the fourth and fifth centuries A.D., Roman frontiers broke down. The area of present-day Austria was overrun by many different tribes and peoples during the next three centuries.

- At the end of the 10th century, the Babenberg dynasty settled many parts of this country, established important trade routes and then ruled for 270 years.

- After a short time of uncertainty and chaos, the country came under the rule of the Habsburg family in the last quarter of the 13th century. The Habsburg rulers enlarged their land holdings through acquisitions and through shrewd marital choices. During the 640 years of their reign, the Habsburgs became one of the most important dynasties in the development of Europe. Friedrich

III, already crowned German King, was crowned Emperor in Rome in 1452. He was the first Austrian ruler to wear the Imperial Crown of the Holy Roman Empire. It remained with the House of Austria—only leaving once, from 1742 - 1745, until the end of the Holy Roman Empire in 1806.

- In the 16th to 17th centuries, Vienna, then the seat of the Austrian line of the Habsburgs, was under constant threat from the Ottoman Empire, repeatedly afflicted by the Plague and shaken by the conflict between Protestantism and Catholicism. With the help of allies and the brilliant Prince Eugene of Savoy, the Turks were, after many skirmishes and battles, finally and decisively beaten. The victory over the Turks and the emphasis on the Roman Catholic Church led to an enormous building boom in Vienna and other parts of Austria. Splendid mansions, churches and abbeys are testimonies to the ensuing period, referred to as the era of Austrian Baroque.

- Music and art were cherished at the Habsburg court and many members of the family were skilled musicians; some were also composers. This appreciation, together with support from the rest of the aristocracy, made Vienna a focal point of music in Europe. Many Habsburgs were also knowledgable collectors of art. Their coin, mineral, gem and various art collections can be enjoyed in many museums today.

- With the rise of the Bourbon family in France and the extinction of the Spanish line of the Habsburg dynasty in 1700, a fierce battle over the hegemony in Europe had broken out between Austria and France. The Habsburgs lost their Spanish possessions but maintained rule over their holdings in Italy and the Netherlands.

- In the second half of the 18th century under Maria Theresia (and later her son Joseph II), a vast reform program was introduced. It was implemented by a large Vienna-based central administration.

- The ideas of the French revolution and the activities of Napoleon Bonaparte changed the political landscape of Europe; after the Congress of Vienna in 1815, Austria reverted to autocratic rule. Austria became somewhat of a police state under the powerful influence of Chancellor Metternich. The general population retreated into the safety of domestic and artistic pursuits during that period, which we now call the *Biedermeier* era.

- In the middle of the 19th century, Vienna was shaken by two revolutions, which were ruthlesssly crushed by the military and which brought 18-year-old Franz Josef I to the throne. With the help of the military, he quickly established an absolute monarchy, hereby again excluding the people from political decisions. In the late 1850s, the emperor ordered the outdated fortifications of Vienna to be demolished and replaced by a grand boulevard. This monumental construction project reshaped Vienna in the following decades; the Ringstrasse as we know it today was the outcome. The suburbs and villages outside the city were incorporated into Vienna. This and the consequences of the rapid rise in industrialization resulted in an enormous increase in population with all the ensuing social problems.

- Strong nationalistic tendencies emerged in the multinational empire, resulting in the formation of the Austro-Hungarian Monarchy—and ultimately the disintegration of the Habsburg Empire. It was also a period of liberalization that saw the beginning of a parliamentary system as well as an explosion of new ideas in many aspects of life, preceding the horrors of World War I.

- In 1918 to 1919, the Habsburg Empire of more than 50 million people, composed of 11 recognized national groups, collapsed. In the Treaty of St. Germain, the Republic of Austria was legally endorsed as a new state with about 6.5 million people.

- Under a new constitution, a federal state was created in 1920 with a bicameral legislature and democratic suffrage. The new Austria faced enormous economical and political problems and in 1933 became an authoritarian state.

- In March 1938, Austria ceased to exist as an independent country and became part of Hitler's Germany.

- At the end of WWII, Soviet troops liberated Vienna (April 1945). Soon afterward, a provisional Austrian government was formed by the Socialist Karl Renner. For the next 10 years, the country was occupied by the four Allied powers.

- Austria's economy was in ruins after WWII. However, with the help of direct grants from the European Recovery Program initiated by U.S. Secretary of State G. C. Marshall, the establishment of a social partnership between government, industry and the work force, and the institution of a strict hard-currency policy, the country became one of the wealthiest nations in Europe.

- In May 1955, Austria was again restored as a free and sovereign state. It became a member of the United Nations in December 1955.

- In 1979 the Vienna International Centre (VIC) was opened and now houses several United Nations organizations.
- At the beginning of 1995, Austria obtained full membership in the European Union. Since the opening of Eastern Europe, the country has again become a passageway between east and west and has taken the lead in investing in Eastern European ventures.

ECONOMY

Austria's economy is based on a combination of private and public enterprise and has a well-developed industry with a large and highly skilled service sector. The GDP in 1995—expressed in percentages and compiled by the Austrian Chamber of Commerce in June 1996—was composed of the following: (a) primary sector (agriculture, forestry and mining), 3.2 percent; (b) secondary sector (industry, commerce, power production and construction), 39.5 percent; and (c) tertiary sector (trade, hospitality, transportation and communication, administration of estates and other private services, public services, banking services and import duties), 57.3 percent. The main trading partners are the other EU countries, especially Germany. The United States and Japan lead the list of other countries. As in several other European countries, unemployment has increased in recent years but is still less than 10 percent.

In Austria, environmental protection and conservation are of great importance with significant economic implications and responsibilities for the public at large. Particular emphasis is given to the quality of water, biological treatment of waste, control of air pollution and the conservation of forests. In 1985, a Federal Environmental Office was set up to analyze, evaluate, monitor and document environmental pollution.

GOVERNMENT & POLITICS

Austria is a democratic, federal republic governed under the constitution of 1920 and subsequent reform and amendments thereof, which provide a clear division of power among the legislative, executive and judicial branches of government.

The legislative power rests with the Austrian Parliament that consists of the National Council (*Nationalrat*) with 183 members elected by popular vote according to proportional representation for a four-year term, the Federal Council (*Bundesrat*) with, at present, 64 members chosen by the provincial legislature (*Landtag*) in proportion to the population of each province, and the Federal Assembly (*Bundesversammlung*), made up of both councils.

Executive power is exercised by the federal president (*Bundespräsident*), who is elected every six years by popular vote, and by the government, which is headed by the federal chancellor (*Bundeskanzler*), the vice chancellor (*Vizekanzler*) and the council of ministers (*Ministerrat*).

The judicial system is composed of three supreme courts: the Supreme Constitutional Court (*Oberster Verfassungsgerichtshof*), the Supreme Administrative Court (*Oberster Verwaltungsgerichtshof*) and the Supreme Judicial Court (*Oberster Gerichtshof*).

There are five main political parties in Austria. These are often referred to by their acronyms and party colors. As a result of the elections in October 1999, they are represented in the National Assembly (*Nationalrat*) as follows:

SPÖ   *Sozialdemokratische Partei Österreichs*
                (Social Democratic Party of Austria, red)   65 seats

ÖVP   *Österreichische Volkspartei*
                (Austrian People's Party, black)   52 seats

FPÖ   *Freiheitliche Partei Österreichs*
                (Freedom Party of Austria, blue)   52 seats

LIF   *Liberales Forum*
                (Liberal Forum, yellow)   0 seats

Die Grünen   (Green Party, green)   14 seats

More information is available in a 200-page book published by the Austrian Federal Press Service entitled *Austria: Facts and Figures*. Updated yearly, it addresses the topics mentioned above in detail, as well as education, science, research, culture, social services, sports and media. Ask the Austrian Consulate in your home country for a copy. You can also check the Austrian government website, which is in both English and German, at www.austria.gv.at.

Vienna, like many major European cities, has an excellent public-transportation system with reliable, clean and convenient service. Moreover, taking public transportation into and within the city is a lot less stressful than dealing with Vienna's numerous one-way streets, constant traffic, oncoming trams, extensive pedestrian areas and expensive parking garages.

VIENNA'S PUBLIC TRANSPORTATION

The Eastern Region Transportation Association (*Verkehrsverbund Ost-Region* or *VOR*) is a network of eight zones covering a huge area that includes Vienna and surrounding towns. The city itself is Zone 100, or the core zone (*Kernzone*), where you can travel on one ticket. When traveling in one direction in Zone 100 within one hour, you can transfer from the subway/underground (*U-Bahn*) to tram (*Strassenbahn*) or bus (*Autobus*) or local train without buying another ticket. When you travel from Vienna to outlying regions within the *VOR* area, the fare depends on the number of zones you travel through.

VOR PUBLIC TRANSPORTATION

Bus	*Autobus* (including *Nightline*), *Regionale Autobusse*
Local train	*Schnellbahn* (*S-Bahn*), *Regionalbahn* (*R-Bahn*), *Badner Bahn*
Subway/underground	*U-Bahn* (*Untergrundbahn*)
Tram/streetcar	*Strassenbahn*

STATION SIGNS

Eingang
Entrance

Ausgang
Exit

Schnellbahn
Fast train/
local train

U-Bahn
Subway/underground

Strassenbahn
Tram/streetcar

BASIC TRANSPORTATION TIPS

1. **Get a good (not tourist) map of the city.** A map book (*Buchplan*) has all the public-transportation stops marked and has a street index, yet fits in a purse or briefcase.

2. **Use the map to plan your route.** Which direction (designated by the end station for that line) will you go? What is the name of your stop? It also helps to listen for the stop ahead of yours.

3. **Buy your ticket.** Check the section in this chapter on types of tickets and where to buy them.

4. **Validate your ticket in a blue canceling machine (*Entwerter*).** This is located inside *Strassenbahnen*, in the center of buses, at the entrance of *U-Bahn* platforms and on *Schnellbahn* platforms.

5. **Get on board.** Let everyone exit before you try to enter. If no one gets out and you need to open the door, press the button beside the door, or where there's only a handle, give it a sharp sideways pull. When nearing your destination or transfer point, press the button inside the *Strassenbahn* or bus to signal that you want to exit at the next stop (in an *U-Bahn*, you just wait near the door because it stops at all stations). Be at the door, ready to exit when the vehicle stops.

MAPS & TIMETABLES

You can buy the following maps and timetable books at any *U-Bahn* ticket office. Also, information offices in major *U-Bahn* stations provide helpful pamphlets about tickets and ways to reach a destination, as well as a pamphlet in English explaining Vienna's public-transportation system (see Info Offices appendix).

• *Verkehrslinienplan Wien* (map of Vienna's public-transportation system)

• *Verkehrslinienplan Ost-Region* (map of VOR lines)

• *VOR-Fahrpläne* (timetables of all public transportation)

Bus lines are identified by numbers ending with an "A" (e.g., 1A, 39A) or by three-digit numbers (e.g., 149, 234).

Strassenbahn line numbers or letters stand alone (e.g., 2, 18, J, D).

U-Bahn lines are numbered 1 to 4 and 6, and are preceded by "U" (e.g., U1, U2).

WHERE TO BUY
PUBLIC-TRANSPORTATION TICKETS
Fahrscheine

Vienna relies on the honor system for use of its public transportation— you are simply expected to have a valid ticket. In Zone 100, as mentioned earlier, you can use one validated ticket to take all forms of public transportation between your starting point and destination (within one hour). You can purchase tickets from presale-ticket windows (*Vorverkaufsstellen*) or ticket machines (*Automaten*) at most *U-Bahn* stations, or from a tobacconist/newsstand (*Tabak-Trafik*).

If you can't buy a ticket ahead of time, you can get one from a machine inside a *Strassenbahn* or *Autobus* (but not on the *U-Bahn*). It will cost a little more and you must have exact change. If you don't, ask other passengers for change (*"Können Sie mir, bitte, wechseln?"* or *"Haben Sie Wechselgeld, bitte?"*). And if you plan to buy a ticket on a *Strassenbahn*, be sure to board the first car, where the ticket machine is usually located directly behind the driver.

To use an *Automat* in a station, you must have change or ATS 100 bills.

Full-Price Tickets *Fahrscheine* and
Half-Price Tickets *Fahrscheine zum Halbpreis*

Fahrscheine	For adults
Fahrscheine zum Halbpreis	For children, dogs and bicycles
Kurzstrecke	For short-distance riders

Children up to the age of six can travel free year-round, and children up to the age of 15 can travel free on Sundays, public holidays and Austrian school holidays. (Wallet-sized calendars with these holidays are available from most *Vorverkaufsstellen*.) Children must carry their student ID cards (*Schülerausweis*) at all times.

Senior citizens (women from 60 years, men from 65) can travel with senior-citizen tickets (*Seniorenfahrscheinen*), which can be bought in advance in sets of two and are valid only in Zone 100 (see Seniors chapter)

STRIP TICKETS
Streifenkarten

One *Streifenkarte* is valid for four or eight trips, which can be used by one person four or eight times or by a group of two to eight people (who must be traveling together). Half-price strip tickets (*Streifenkarten zum Halbpreis*) are also available for those eligible.

SHORT-DISTANCE TICKETS
Kurzstreckenkarten

For rides of one to four stops, there is a *Kurzstreckenkarte*, which is cheaper than a regular ticket. The predetermined boundaries (*Kurzstreckengrenzen*) are announced and shown as alternating black-and-white stripes on route signs on *Strassenbahnen* and *Autobusse*. On the *U-Bahn* and *Schnellbahn*, two stops is the limit even if you change trains.

TIME TICKETS *Zeitkarten*

Zeitkarten are less expensive and more convenient for the frequent user of public transportation. The following three must be time-stamped in order to be valid.

- The Vienna Shopping Ticket (***Wiener Einkaufskarte***) is valid in Zone 100 one calendar day 8 AM - 8 PM.

- The Vienna 24-hour or 72-hour ticket (***Netzkarte 24- or 72-Stunden Wien***) is valid in Zone 100 for 24 or 72 hours after it has been punched.

- An "eight-day" network strip ticket (***"8-Tage" Umwelt-Streifennetzkarte***) is valid for unlimited travel within Zone 100 for any eight (calendar) days, not necessarily in succession, and is transferable (i.e., can be used by different people). It can be shared in two ways: Different people can use it (e.g., one uses it in the morning and another in the afternoon); or more than one person can each punch a strip for the day (but they must stay together in order not to be caught without a ticket). There are directions in English on the back of the ticket.

WEEKLY, MONTHLY & YEARLY PASSES
Wochenkarten, Monatskarten und Jahreskarten

Wochenkarten and *Monatskarten* are weekly and monthly passes, which can be purchased from some ticket machines at *U-Bahn* stations, at presale-ticket windows (*Vorverkaufsstellen*) at major *U-Bahn* stations or at a *Tabak-Trafik*. The yearly pass (*Jahreskarte*) requires a passport-sized photograph and a completed form (with bank-account information), which is only available at *Vorverkaufs-stellen*. *Jahreskarte* holders can use their passes as *Familienkarten* Sat, noon - end of service, which allows two children up to the age of 15 free Zone 100 travel when accompanied by the holder.

 Many rental-car companies offer discounts to *Jahreskarte* holders. (You'll receive information in the mail, or you can ask someone at the ticket office about other discounts associated with the pass.)

STUDENT COMMUTER PASSES
Schülerstreckenkarten

You can get a *Schülerstreckenkarte* for your child by getting the appropriate form from his or her school and taking it, with two small student photos, to the following address:

WIENER VERKEHRSBETRIEBE
  1031, Erdbergstrasse 202
  Schülerkartenauskünfte
  ☎ 7909-120
  Mon - Fri, 8 AM - 3 PM

With the *Schülerstreckenkarte*, students can travel between their homes and school Mon - Sat during the school year, Sept - June. The afternoon education ticket (*Nachmittags-Bildungskarte*), offered for a small additional fee per month during the school year, allows unlimited travel Mon - Sat after 1 PM and all day Sunday and on holidays. The student needs a valid school ID card (*Schülerausweis*) and a passport-sized photo. More monthly tickets (*Nachmittags-Bildungskarten*) can be purchased from any *Vorverkaufsstelle* and attached to the existing card.

CANCELING/STAMPING/VALIDATING TICKETS

Tickets not already validated (e.g., presold tickets, *Streifenkarten* and *Zeitkarten*) must be punched in a blue ticket-canceling machine (*Entwerter*) upon boarding a *Strassenbahn* or *Autobus*, or before reaching an *U-Bahn* or on a local-train platform. One-time-use tickets bought from a machine on board a *Strassenbahn* or *Autobus*,

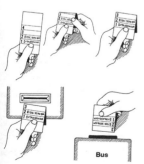

or from an *Automat* in an *U-Bahn* station, do not require punching as they are already time-stamped. Any multiple-use ticket must be stamped for each day of use and for each person using it. Be sure you fold the ticket so it's stamped in numerical order. If you cancel out of order, the ticket becomes invalid.

Bus

USING PUBLIC TRANSPORTATION

Plan your route before you leave home, using a transportation map (*Verkehrslinienplan Wien*) or a map of the city (*Stadtplan* or *Buchplan*). You need to know which direction you're headed so that you choose the *U-Bahn*, *Strassenbahn* or *Autobus* with the correct terminal or last stop (e.g., to travel to the Vienna International Centre from the city center, you would take the U1 in the direction of Kagran).

Strassenbahnen have all stops listed on white placards on one of the windows inside. Stops are also announced by name, with corresponding connecting lines (*"Umsteigen zu den Linien U1, U4, Strassenbahnen 1, 2, N…"*). Buses have announcements for each stop; some also have a digital display at the front of the bus indicating the next stop. *U-Bahnen* announce stops. However, it's possible for these announcements to be out of sync, so watch for station signs to verify your location.

All *U-Bahn* routes are color-coded on maps (U1 is **red**, U2 is **purple**, U3 is **orange**, U4 is **green** and U6 is **brown**) with all station signs in the same colors.

At *Autobus* and *Strassenbahn* stops, a *"Doppelhaltestelle"* sign means the stop serves two or more lines, so one may park right behind the other. The second vehicle will not pull up and stop again, so if you need to take it, go back to where it's parked to board. Most *Autobus* and *Strassenbahn* lines stop running around midnight, while the *U-Bahnen* start their last run then, and the *Lokalbahnen* finish their last run by midnight.

ENTERING & EXITING PUBLIC TRANSPORTATION

To enter or exit a *Strassenbahn*, *Autobus* or local train, press the button next to the doors. To open the doors of an *U-Bahn*, pull the door handle sharply when it stops or push the lighted button. Regardless of the mode of public transportation, be ready to exit quickly. Entering passengers should wait to the sides while those leaving exit through the middle. Also, when you're taking an escalator in an *U-Bahn* station, be sure to stand to the right so others can pass on the left.

DESIGNATED SEATS
FOR THE DISABLED & ELDERLY

You will notice that on all public transportation, seats closest to the doors are designated for the disabled, elderly, pregnant women and passengers with babies. The disabled often wear yellow armbands with black dots so others will know to act accordingly. You should avoid sitting in a designated seat, or at least get up when someone who needs it boards.

BABY STROLLERS & SHOPPING CARTS

None of Vienna's public transportation (especially the *Strassenbahn*) is conducive to strollers and carts being rolled on, so people with them appreciate help getting on and off an *Autobus* or *Strassenbahn*. You can either offer to help (*"Kann ich helfen?"*) or someone may ask you for help when boarding or exiting. There are designated areas near the doors for strollers, as well as orange straps to hold them in place.

SHORT U-BAHN TRAINS
Kurzzüge

During weekends, holidays and evening hours, you may see the word *Kurzzug* on the digital display above the platform, which means the train will have fewer cars than usual. In order to board, you should stand at the designated end of the platform, usually indicated by signs above the track as well as by a drawing of solid and outlined cars. Go in the direction of the solid (white) cars.

ILLEGAL/BLACK RIDER
Schwarzfahrer

A *Schwarzfahrer* is someone without a ticket. Plainclothes public-transportation officers (*Fahrscheinkontrolle*) regularly check passengers, with the fine being ATS 500 plus ATS 20 (for the cost of a ticket). If you're caught and don't have enough money, you will be given a payment form (*Zahlschein*) upon showing a photo ID. If you don't have one, you may be taken to the police station to sign a sworn statement. Either way, you must pay the fine within three days, or else it is increased to ATS 1.000.

BICYCLES ON THE U-BAHN & SCHNELLBAHN

You must be older than 12 or accompanied by an adult to take a bike on an *U-Bahn* or *Schnellbahn* car marked with a bicycle symbol. You also must have an additional half-price ticket for the bike and must keep it in the marked area of the car. Only two baby strollers or bikes are allowed per car, so if you see the area already occupied, move to the next available car. Keep in mind that strollers take precedence over bikes. Bicycles are allowed on all *U-Bahn* (except U6) and *Schnellbahn* lines at the following times: Mon - Fri 9 AM - 3 PM, 6:30 PM - end of service, Sat 9 AM - end of service and Sunday and holidays all day.

NIGHTLINE

From 12:30 AM - 5 AM, night buses (N) run at half-hour intervals on 22 lines, with Schwedenplatz as the hub. Regular late-night (*Nightline*) bus tickets can be bought on the bus or at a *Vorverkaufsstelle*. These buses require a ticket other than the ones described earlier. However, you can buy a discounted ticket if you already have a *Jahreskarte*, *Monatskarte*, *Hochschüler-Semester-karte/Monatsnetzkarte* or other validated multiple ticket. You can also buy a book of 10 tickets for the price of nine at any ticket office. A *Nightline* brochure, available from any *U-Bahn* information office (see Info Offices appendix), gives details and routes.

SPECIAL HOLIDAY SCHEDULES

On some holidays, Vienna's public-transportation system operates on a different schedule. For example, on May 1, all *U-Bahnen*, *Strassenbahnen* and *Autobusse* do not run until around 2 PM; and on New Year's Eve (*Silvester*), some lines operate throughout the night. Signs posting holiday times are located at each stop.

LOCAL TRAINS & TRAIN TO BADEN
Schnellbahnen und Badner Bahn

The *Schnellbahn* travels within and outside of Vienna. The *Badner Bahn* connects Vienna and the town of Baden, which was a vacation spot for Austrian aristocrats in the 19th century. The casino and curative swimming pools (*Kuren*) are now the main attractions. The *Badner Bahn* leaves from opposite the Hotel Bristol on Kärntner Ring and goes to Josefplatz in the center of Baden, which takes about an hour. It also stops at Shopping City Süd.

If you take the *Schnellbahn* or *Badner Bahn* within Vienna, you can use a Zone 100 ticket. If you travel beyond Zone 100, you need to buy a ticket for the number of zones through which you're traveling. Look on the colored bull's-eye-like zone map (*Zonenkarte*) posted in all stations to determine that number. You can buy a ticket at any ticket window or *Automat*. If you're using a presale ticket, you have to cancel it before getting on the train because a conductor usually comes around to check. If you already have a weekly, monthly or yearly pass, you only need to buy a ticket for the number of zones beyond Zone 100.

BUS TO IKEA AT SHOPPING CITY SÜD

A special yellow-and-blue bus offers free rides from Opernring (across from the State Opera House) to IKEA (see All-Purpose Stores section of Home chapter). However, for a ride back, you must buy a ATS 20 ticket at the information counter in the store's main entrance (*Eingangsinformation*). You then give the ticket to the bus driver when you board. The bus, which takes about 20 minutes each way, operates Mon - Fri 10 AM - 5:30 PM and Sat 8:30 AM - 4 PM at one-and-a-half-hour intervals. Check the sign for return times or pick up a schedule inside the bus.

REGIONAL BUSES
Regionale Autobusse

To take a bus to the *Weinviertel* or *Waldviertel*, call Bus Information at ☎ 711 01 (Mon - Fri 7 AM - 7 PM), which can tell you if service is available. *Regionale Autobusse* lines with three-digit numbers (e.g., 243, 443) go to the suburbs. Check the map and timetable for further details.

TAXIS

In Vienna, taxis are plentiful and relatively reasonably priced. However, they won't respond if you try to hail them on the street; instead, they can be found at clearly marked taxi stands (*Taxistandplätze*), usually located near *U-Bahn*, *Strassenbahn* and *Autobus* stations and busy intersections. A list of *Taxistandplätze* can be found on the inside front cover of the A–H telephone book.

There is a basic rate on weekdays plus a per-kilometer charge and a small transportation fee. On Sundays, public holidays and at night (11 PM - 6 AM), both the basic fare and the per-kilometer rate go up. There is also a waiting charge. Luggage placed in the trunk has two rates: one for up to 20 kg and one for more than 20 kg and up to 60 kg. Be aware that trips out of the city are double in order to cover the driver's trip back, though you may be able to negotiate a flat rate beforehand. Trips into the city are usually a flat rate.

When calling for a taxi from home, state your district and house address. If you're at a phone booth, state the cross streets. Also, specify if you need a station wagon (*Kombiwagen*). Generally, you will be put on hold while the dispatcher tries to locate a taxi in your vicinity. You may have to try another company if the first one can't find a nearby cab. You will then be given the number of the taxi as well as your waiting time. Most services also offer smoke-free taxis or taxis with female drivers (for women who are more comfortable with another woman).

- Most taxis don't take credit cards.
- A receipt (*Rechnung*) is available upon request.

TAXI PHONE NUMBERS

To call a cab, look under *"Taxi"* in the yellow pages (*Gelbe Seiten*), or call one of the following phone numbers:

☎ 31 300	☎ 81 400
☎ 40 100	☎ 91 091
☎ 60 160	

AUSTRIAN NATIONAL RAILWAY Österreichische Bundesbahnen/ÖBB

Austria has an excellent railway network throughout the country and to neighboring countries (see Excursions chapter). The following are terminal stations in Vienna:

- **Westbahnhof**   To the west, such as Salzburg, Frankfurt, London and Paris

- **Südbahnhof**   Mainly to the south and east, such as Bratislava, Budapest, Prague, Venice and Rome

- **Franz-Josefs-Bahnhof**   To northwestern Austria and Prague

- **Wien Nord**   To nearby areas and northern Austria

- **Wien Mitte**   To nearby areas

You can pick up free train-timetable sheets (*Fahrplanauszüge*) from the information office at any train station or purchase a yearly Austrian train schedule book (*Fahrpläne Bahn Österreich*) in May at a ticket counter or any bookstore. Timetables of domestic (*Inland*) lines are updated every year and timetables for international (*Ausland*) lines (e.g., EuroCity/EC, EuroNight/EN and InterCity/IC) are updated in the summer and winter. For information about train schedules, connections, accommodations or prices, call ☎ 1717 (24 hours), where English may be spoken.

BUYING TRAIN TICKETS

You can buy tickets and also reserve seats at the train station or at the Austrian Travel Agency (*Österreichisches Verkehrsbüro*). You can call the ticket office, but if you're new to the process, you should go in person to familiarize yourself and also to get travel information and brochures.

Finding a Train Seat

If you haven't reserved a seat, simply look for *"Nicht Reserviert"* signs. Non-smoking sections (*Nichtraucher*) are also available.

Free Passenger Pick-Up Service
Abholservice

In cooperation with the Austrian Tourist Association, *ÖBB* offers a pick-up service to its customers with confirmed reservations. In 117 communities, a reserved taxi or hotel representative meets you at the train station and takes you to your accommodations, occasionally free of charge (though you should tip the driver). Make arrangements when you buy your train tickets. You can also pick up the brochure *"Abholservice"* at train stations and travel agencies where train tickets are sold.

Luggage Pick-Up Service
Haus-Haus-Gepäck

Within Austria, *Haus-Haus-Gepäck* will pick up your bags (for a reasonable fee) from your house or hotel and deliver them to accommodations at your destination. This service allows you to take public transportation without your heavy luggage or without having to call a taxi. Ask for more details when you buy your ticket.

Sleeper-Car Trains
Autoreisezüge

There are 15 domestic and international lines of *Autoreisezüge* that only stop at major stations and offer second-class (with four to six couchettes) and first class (private beds) compartments. You can find a brochure at any train station information office.

Discount Train Tickets

Frequent Austrian railway travelers may want to buy an Advantage Card (*VORTEILScard*), which provides about a 50-percent discount off Austrian train fares as well as some hotel rates and car-rental fees. You can get the *VORTEILScard* at any train station or participating travel agency. Discount fares also may be available for senior citizens, students and groups.

InterRail Passes

If you plan to travel extensively through Europe, you could buy an InterRail pass, which allows European residents of at least six months to receive about 50 percent off all regular train fares within your country of origin. Travelers older than 26 are also eligible for the InterRail 26+, which is good for travel in Austria, Bulgaria, Croatia, the Czech Republic, Denmark, Finland, Germany, Greece, Hungary, Ireland, Luxembourg, the Netherlands, Norway, Poland, Romania, Slovakia, Sweden and Turkey, as well as 50 percent off DDSG services (see Ships section) from Vienna to Budapest. InterRail passes are available for 15 days or one month. For more information, go to any train station information office.

LOST & FOUND

If you lose something on a *Strassenbahn* or *Autobus*, within three days call the General Information office at ☎ 7909 43 500. For items lost on Austrian trains, call *Südbahnhof* Mon - Fri, 7 AM - 5 PM at ☎ 5800 356 56. Each *Autobus* and *Strassenbahn* has a station where found articles are taken. After one week, however, everything is stored to the central police lost-and-found office at the following location:

ZENTRALES FUNDAMT
 1090, Wasagasse 22
 ☎ 313 44 92-11 (no English spoken)
 Mon - Fri, 8 AM - noon

It is better to go in person.

VIENNA INTERNATIONAL AIRPORT (VIA) AT SCHWECHAT
Flughafen Wien

TRANSPORTATION TO & FROM VIA

Buses and trains take about 20 minutes to go to and from VIA. Buses operate three routes: between City Air Terminal (*Station Wien Mitte*) at the Vienna Hilton and VIA; between the Vienna International Centre and VIA; and between Vienna's *Westbahnhof*, via *Südbahnhof*, and VIA. The fare covers one passenger and up to three pieces of luggage. You pay the bus driver as you board. Buses run about every half hour, but at odd times. For more information, call Vienna Airport Lines at ☎ 93000 23 00 (Mon - Fri 4 AM - 8:30 PM) or pick up a schedule on the bus, at the airport or at destination stops. Vienna Airport Lines also offers a charter-bus service for groups traveling to and from VIA. For information, call ☎ 93000 344 08. Trains to the airport include the *Schnellbahn* 7 between *Wien Nord*, via *Wien Mitte*, and VIA (*Flughafen Wien Schwechat*). For more information or a prospectus in English, call ☎ 93000 353 98, where English is spoken.

AIRLINE & AIRPORT INFORMATION

Vienna is the gateway to Eastern Europe. For individual airlines, look under *"Fluggesellschafen"* in the yellow pages (*Gelbe Seiten*). For flight information at Vienna International Airport at Schwechat (*Flughafen Wien Schwechat*), visit them online at www.viennaairport.com, or call one of the following numbers, where there are English speakers:

GENERAL FLIGHT INFORMATION
  ☎ 7007 22 31 or 22 32 or 22 33

ARRIVAL INFORMATION
  ☎ 7007 21 97

DEPARTURE INFORMATION
  ☎ 7007 21 84

You can find the information booklets *"Services am Airport"* (which is in both English and German) and *"Wo ist was am Airport"* in the airport concourse. These provide information about the airport and its facilities and services, which include porters, luggage storage, lost and found, post office, medical center, pharmacy, chapel, VIP Business Center, lounges and the World Trade Center. There are also lists of airport hotels, passenger services (e.g., travel agents, hotel reservations, tour operators, taxi and limousine companies) and important airport-related phone numbers.

AIRPORT TAXIS

When going to the airport, it is cheaper to take an airport taxi (*Flughafen Taxi*) than a normal city cab because airport taxis charge flat rates (call for exact fares). The following are two companies where English is spoken.

AIRPORT SERVICE MAZUR
☎ 7007 64 22 or
☎ 7007 64 91
Fax 7007 63 93

This company has limousines, small and large vans and buses (handy for families with lots of luggage), but you should reserve these before your arrival or departure date.

C & K AIRPORT-SERVICE
☎ 1731

This company has taxis that can hold large baggage.

For other companies, look under *"Taxi"* in the yellow pages. At the airport, there is a taxi service counter just outside the luggage-claim exit, where someone will call a cab and collect the fare. If you take a taxi from the taxi stand, you may be charged the standard per-kilometer rate.

REFUNDS FOR LATE OR CANCELED FLIGHTS

An EU regulation allows travelers to file a claim if an airline flight is delayed or canceled (without having to prove damages), depending on the delay and distance involved. If your flight is canceled, you can claim ATS 2.000 (Euro 150) for a booked distance of up to 3,500 km (ATS 4.000 for flights more than 3,500 km) on a regularly scheduled flight. If the airline offers a substitute flight that arrives no more than two hours later than the original scheduled arrival time for flights up to 3,500 km (four hours later for more than 3,500 km), you can only file for a 50-percent refund.

REFUNDS FROM TRAVEL AGENTS

Another EU provision allows you to file for a refund when claims by a travel agent are not honored (e.g., your guaranteed ocean-view room turns out to be a brick-wall view). Go to the Austrian Consumer Information Association (*Verein für Konsumenteninformation*; see Info Offices appendix) for a brochure called *"Reise"* with more details.

LIMITS ON IMPORTED GOODS

There are limits on certain goods, such as alcohol and tobacco, that are brought into Austria from other EU countries. There are no limits on personal-use items bought in other EU countries, regardless of your citizenship. Random checks (*Kontrollen*) are made to prevent the import of illegal or regulated items (e.g., illegal drugs, guns, uranium). There is a limit of ATS 1.000 per person for purchases made outside the EU. (See the Customs section of the Essentials chapter.)

SHIPS *Schiffe*

Although Austria is landlocked, Vienna lies on the Danube River (*Donau*), one of the continent's major waterways where ships travel both up- and downstream for business and pleasure. Go to a Vienna Tourist Information Office for tour and travel information (see Info Offices appendix and Excursions chapter).

DDSG BLUE DANUBE SCHIFFAHRT
    1010, Friedrichstrasse 7
    ☎ 588 80
    Fax 588 80 440

This company offers hydrofoil trips to Bratislava or Budapest and special holiday (e.g., *Oktoberfest*, New Year's and Advent) excursions.

TRAVEL FOR THE DISABLED

While it's not impossible to get around Vienna in a wheelchair, it's not always easy. The *Strassenbahn* has no wheelchair lift and the *U-Bahn* may take you from one accessible station to an inaccessible one. Many places with one or two steps are listed as accessible because the assumption is that people in wheelchairs will either travel accompanied (*mit Begleitperson*) or ask for help. (Also note that Vienna's public-transportation workers have no obligation to help anyone.)

U-Bahn

To get information on *U-Bahn* use by the blind, call the *Wiener Verkehrsbetriebe* at ☎ 7909 100. Ask for the *"U-Bahnpläne in Blindenschrift"* (*"U-Bahn* Plans in Braille"), which has directions (such as from which side to exit the train9 in Braille and on audio tape. There are four notebooks with audiocassettes, at ATS 100 for each notebook (in German).

Taxis

Several companies in Vienna have vehicles equipped to transport passengers in wheelchairs. Call *Eiseler & Löffler GmbH*, one of the largest and most well-known firms, Mon - Fri 7 AM - 5 PM, Sat - Sun 8 AM - 5 PM at ☎ 258 58 80 or ☎ 258 58 20 for flat rates to destinations within Vienna and to the airport.

Österreichische Bundesbahnen (ÖBB)

If you are planning to travel by *ÖBB*, get a copy of the *"Behindertenführer der ÖBB."* (This may not be published under the same name every year, call ☎ 93000-335 77 for help or to order it—ask for Herr Kollner.) It describes everything from wheelchair-accessible parking and toilets to tracks. Or you can pick one up at most train stations. The *ÖBB* also recommends that passengers in wheelchairs call their departure station several days in advance to make arrangements to find help with inaccessible facilities.

Designated Parking Spaces

You must have a pass registered to your car's license-plate number in order to park in spaces designated for the disabled. Short-term parking zones (*Kurzparkzonen*) are free for such cars. If you have a foreign car with a pass from your home country, it will generally be honored, though the pass cannot be transferred to a car registered here. A car without a pass, however, can pull into a designated space to drop off a disabled passenger. If you want to obtain a pass (*Behindertenausweis*), call *MA 46* (in German) at ☎ 811 14-926.

General Accessibility Information

Call City Information (*Stadtinformation*) for a guide to public accessibility in Vienna (e.g., from accessible pay-phone locations to restaurants and museums) at ☎ 525 50-0. "Vienna for Guests with Handicaps" (*"Wien für Gäste mit Handicaps"*), which is in English and German, is available at the Vienna Tourist Information Office (see Info Offices appendix). Information may not be totally accurate, so we suggest you call establishments to confirm their accessibility.

U nlike North American cities, most European cities were well established before the advent of the automobile, so city streets are not built to accommodate today's motorized traffic. Narrow, winding streets are part of what gives Vienna its charm, but can also be a driver's headache. One way streets, names that change even though you're on the same street, dark blue street signs attached high on the corners of buildings that are hard to read while driving, and *Strassenbahn* tracks can make navigating the inner city a challenge. Be alert when driving, and use city maps to research your route before starting off. While public transportation is generally a faster, more economical and stress-free way to get around Vienna, there are times when driving a car is necessary or preferable. The following pages will explain some of the basics you need to know to be a well-prepared Viennese driver. Most of all, keep your sense of humor, and don't get discouraged. You'll get used to it!

GETTING A DRIVER'S LICENSE

The legal minimum driving age in Austria is 18. Foreigners above that age holding a valid national or state driver's license, along with an international driver's license, can drive in Austria for up to six months. After that, only an Austrian driver's license legally entitles you to drive here.

You should begin your application for an Austrian driver's license immediately upon your arrival in Austria, as the process can take 2-3 months. Citizens of many countries and some U.S. states can have their driver's licenses "conveyed," which means they can be issued an Austrian driver's license without passing a full or partial examination (see box on opposite page). Application for driver's license conveyance (*Führerscheinumschreibung*) must be made with the federal police after taking up residence (i.e., filing your *Meldezettel*; see Essentials chapter), but remember, the process MUST BE COMPLETED WITHIN SIX MONTHS. It's illegal to drive without an Austrian driver's license after this date, and the fact that you've applied for one doesn't count. Your insurance, however, will cover you, if the license has been applied for by six months' residency, but you don't yet have it because of Austrian "red tape" holding up the process.

VIENNA TRANSPORTATION OFFICE OF THE FEDERAL POLICE DEPARTMENT (*Verkehrsamt der Bundespolizeidirektion Wien*)
  1090, Liechtenwerder Platz 5
  ☎ 31 34 50
  Mon - Fri 8 AM - 12:30 PM

Doors open at 8 AM, but you should be there by 7:30 AM, particularly in the summer. Go to the third floor, room 3128, and wait. The clerks may decide to use a number system, so if you don't get a number, you need to come back the next day and start over.

DOCUMENTS NEEDED

- Application (available at *Verkehrsamt*), completed and signed
- Current driver's license + 2 copies
- German translation of your driver's license (can be obtained from the ÖAMTC; see Automobile Clubs section) Free for members or ATS 100 for non-members.
- Passport and visas (if any) + 2 copies each
- Police registration form (*Meldezettel*) + 1 copy
- Two identical passport-sized photos

- Proof of at least one year's driving experience (e.g., a letter in German from your company or a friend verifying that you've driven a car for one year prior to this application)
- Medical check (obtainable at the *Verkehrsamt*, or from a doctor on the approved list). If you wear glasses, you will need a copy of your prescription *Brillenpass* (free of charge from an optician), and if you wear contact lenses, you will need a certificate from the optometrist

If you need to pass a practical test of your driving you will also need:

- Car registration + 1 copy
- A recent automobile inspection (*Pickerl*) + 1 copy, or if it is a new car (up to 1 year old), a *Typenschein* * 1 copy
- If you drive a company car, you will need a letter from the company authorizing you to drive this car

Once your application has been accepted, you'll be notified by mail as to when and where you need to take your test or be examined. (If you don't speak German, take a translator with you.) If this isn't required, you'll be notified about when to collect your license and how much you have to pay. Allow two to three months for this process.

COUNTRIES THAT ALLOW DRIVER'S LICENSE CONVEYANCE

ALL CLASSES

Andorra

Geurnsey

Isle of Man

Hungary

Japan

Jersey

Malta

Monaco

San Marino

Switzerland

CLASS B

(Motor vehicles carrying no more than 8 people and no more than 3,500 kg)

Israel

Canada

Poland

Slovenia

Slovakia
(if issued before 1.1.1993)

Republic of South Africa

Republic of South Korea
(if issued after 1.1.1997)

Czech Republic

United States of America

If your license can't be conveyed, you'll need to attend a driving school (*Fahrschule*) here. Many teachers speak English, and the driving school will help you obtain your license once you've passed its course. Here is one driving school in Vienna where you can find English-speaking instructors:

FAHRSCHULE NON-STOP
   1090, Sobieskigasse 1a
   ☎317 44 05
   Fax 319 93 36
   Mon - Thurs 8 AM - 7 PM, Fri 8 AM - 6 PM

THINGS TO HAVE WITH YOU IN THE CAR

(*Never* leave important or official papers in the car)

- Driver's license (see "Getting a Driver's License" section)
- Car registration (*Zulassungsschein*)
- Valid automobile-inspection sticker (*Pickerl*) plus document showing that the test has been performed. (A thorough inspection must be conducted annually.)
- Insurance papers
- Radio registration (if applicable). See Radio section of Communications chapter)
- First-aid kit and red reflective warning triangle (*Pannendreieck*)
- Snow tires (required during winter and earlier at higher elevations where snow and ice are possible). Radio stations broadcast warnings to remind motorists.
- Fog lights (extremely useful, especially in the Danube Valley area, where thick fogs can occur). Fog lights can only be turned on in reduced visibility, so when visibility improves, turn them off or risk paying a fine.
- Country identification sticker (*Internationales Autokennzeichen*)
- Road-tax sticker (*Vignette*) must be obtained and displayed when driving on any expressways/freeways (*Autobahnen*). Don't forget that there are even *Autobahnen* within the city.

 Don't Leave Your Auto Licensing Booklet (*Einzelgenehmigung*) in the Car

The *Einzelgenehmigung* should not be left in the car's glove compartment/box because if your car is stolen containing it, not only can thieves register your car, but your insurance company may invalidate your claim. It's often a condition of your policy to carry the papers separately. Also, parked cars must be locked in order for insurance to be valid.

CAR INSURANCE *Autoversicherung*

All owners of vehicles registered in Austria, as well as temporarily imported vehicles, must have recognized third-party or liability insurance. All EU countries have the same requirement, so these cars don't need insurance green cards (*Grüne Karte*), although Italy does still expect one. All drivers traveling outside the EU are expected to present the green card (valid for one year from the issue date) at the border.

In addition to basic liability insurance, you can also buy partial comprehensive insurance (*Teilkaskoversicherung*), which covers fire, theft and natural disasters (e.g., storms, hail, floods and avalanches), for up to ATS 5.000 for personal effects and damage to parked cars (*Parkschaden*), or full comprehensive insurance (*Vollkaskoversicherung*), which adds collision and vandalism damages to the *Teilkasko* coverage. A letter from your previous insurance company stating that you've had no recent liability claims can earn you up to 50 percent off your premium.

One of Austria's largest insurance companies is Wiener Städtische, which has an English-speaking agent experienced in dealing with international customers. If you have a license that can be conveyed, she, or her assistant, can help you with this procedure for a fee of about ATS 1.500. Contact her at the following:

WIENER STÄDTISCHE
   Mrs. Trixie Schuba
   1030, Landstrasser Hauptstrasse 97-101
   ☎ 715 56 83-37

You can also insure your car in the United States if it will be in Europe for one year or less and will be keeping U.S. license plates. For information, contact the following:

 AIU NORTH AMERICA, INC.

505 Carr Road
Mail Drop R23-7A
Wilmington, DE 19809, U.S.A.
☎ 001 (302) 761-3000 or ☎ 001 (800) 343-5761
Fax 001 (302) 761-3302

This company writes policies for expatriates and third-country nationals in foreign countries, as well as furloughing U.S. expatriates. You can pay with a credit card.

GENERAL DRIVING TIPS

- Safety belts must be worn at all times by all passengers. If you're in an accident and found not wearing a seat belt, you will be held at least partially responsible for your injuries.

- Children younger than 12, or shorter than 1.5 m, are not allowed to sit in the front seat (with the exception of school carpools). Infant car seats are mandatory for newborns to nine-month-olds. These must be put in the back seat, as passenger-side air bags pose a potential danger to babies and small children. (ÖAMTC rents infant seats to members; see Automobile Clubs section of this chapter and Children chapter.)

- Buses and trams have no insurance, and they ALWAYS have the right of way. When passing a bus, always use your turn signal. Buses usually use their blinkers when starting up after discharging passengers, but don't depend on it. You MUST yield to a bus leaving a bus stop. Be especially aware of trams because they're silent, heavy and have nowhere to go to avoid hitting you. Tracks cross car lanes and the middle of some streets. Cars must stop when a tram has stopped for passengers to get on and off.

- Pedestrians about to enter or who have entered crosswalks (marked with zebra stripes) have the right of way. So don't stop in crosswalks and be careful not to turn into crossing pedestrians.

- Unless otherwise indicated, traffic coming from the right has the right of way, even on roundabouts or traffic circles (unless posted otherwise). Don't ever forget this rule because it's probably the biggest cause of accidents among non-European drivers.

- You cannot enter an intersection until it's clear, even if you have the right of way and the light is green. No matter what, don't block intersections.

- You're not allowed to honk your horn (except in necessary situations) in Vienna (though that doesn't deter frustrated drivers).

- The red-and-white "lollipop" sign held up by police on the street or in cars means "Stop."

- Even though gas stations may look familiar (e.g., Shell, Mobil, Texaco), many still only accept cash and not gas-station or credit cards. With Austria now part of the European Union, however, this policy is beginning to change.

TRAFFIC REGULATIONS
Verkehrsregeln

Failure to adhere to any Austrian traffic regulation can result in a stiff fine, often payable on the spot. Ignorance of the law is no excuse. Therefore, it's a good idea to enroll in a driving school for a few lessons, even if you can have your license conveyed (see Getting a Driver's License section). Until you're able to do this, however, read the following section, which addresses Austria's major traffic laws.

SPEED LIMITS
Geschwindigkeitsbeschränkungen

Unless otherwise indicated, the following are the legal speed limits in Austria:

30 km per hour (20 mph) In residential areas
50 km per hour (30 mph) In developed areas
100 km per hour (60 mph) On country roads
100 km per hour (60 mph) On priority roads with
crossroads (Autostrasse)
130 km per hour (80 mph) On expressways/freeways
(Autobahnen)

A speed-limit sign with the word "Zone" written underneath designates the speed for an area, not just that street. That limit is valid until you see the sign again with a slash mark across it. Remember, even when you turn onto another street, the limit is still valid.

RIGHT OF WAY Vorrang

Vehicles coming from the right have the right of way. Austrian law and insurance companies won't dispute this, regardless of the apparent fault of a driver to your right in an accident, so pay attention! The following are exceptions:

- Steadily moving traffic has priority.
- Vehicles leaving parking places, gas stations or buildings don't have the right of way.
- Trams or emergency vehicles *always* have the right of way.
- Drivers to the right can forfeit their right of way by clearly indicating so.

TRAFFIC LIGHTS *Verkehrsampeln*

Before changing to yellow, a green light blinks four times. During this time, you can enter the intersection. When the light turns yellow, you must stop short of the intersection if you're able to do so safely; if you're already in it, you can proceed. When the light shines yellow before it turns green, you cannot enter the intersection. As in most countries, if you find yourself in a lane with an arrow signal, you must turn in that direction, regardless of your original intention.

ROAD SIGNS *Verkehrszeichen*

Traffic signs are classified into the following six categories:

Warning Signs *Warntafeln*

Red-bordered triangles warn of actual or potential hazards ahead (e.g., intersection of a nonpriority road)

Road Narrows Signs

The law requires that drivers merge every other vehicle.

Prohibitory Signs *Verbotstafeln*

Red-bordered circles prohibit specific behavior for all or some drivers. Details may be found on a rectangular sign located immediately below (e.g., a "no entry" sign with "EXCEPT BICYCLES" below).

Mandatory Signs *Gebotstafeln*

Blue circles indicate a driving requirement (e.g., traffic is permitted only in the direction of the arrow).

Priority Sign *Vorrangtafel*

This white diamond with a yellow center indicates that you have the right of way.

Information Signs *Hinweistafeln*

Rectangular signs can tell you how far a city or *Autobahn* is, explain a warning sign or call attention to something (e.g., hospital, parking, monument).

SHORT-TERM PARKING ZONES
Kurzparkzonen

Several districts (e.g., first, fourth, sixth to ninth—with more possible, so ask) are called blue zones (*Blauzone*) because their streets may be bordered with blue lines. These are designated short-term parking zones (*Kurzparkzonen*), which means there's a same-place one-and-a-half-hour parking limit in the first district Mon - Fri 9 AM - 7 PM, Saturday as marked, and a same-place two-hour limit in the second to ninth, and parts of the twentieth districts Mon - Fri 9 AM - 8 PM and Saturday as marked. Residents of these districts can buy a parking sticker that allows them to park anywhere in their district during the restricted hours. In addition, you may find posted short-term parking zones in other areas of the city. Hours are listed under signs designating the beginning (*Anfang*) of the permissible parking area.

PARKING VOUCHERS *Parkscheine*

Except on Saturday evening, Sunday and holidays, you must display appropriately marked parking vouchers (*Parkscheine*) on your dashboard. These can be purchased at a *Tabak-Trafik*, post office or *ÖAMTC* in three durations. Ten-minute parking ones are free, while others are for a half hour, one hour and one-and-a-half hours, which can be combined up to the legal limit. Fill in the year (*Jahr*) and use an X to cross off the date, arrival time (month – *Monat*, day = *Tag*, hour = *Stunde*) and upcoming quarter hour (e.g., if you park at 10:05 AM, you can mark 10:15). When using two *Parkscheine* together (e.g., one for one hour and one for a half hour to total one-and-a-half hours), mark the same hour on both. Remember to use military time. Failure to display these results in two fines: one for not having a *Parkschein* and one for illegal parking.

You must always have a *Parkschein* displayed when parking at any train station because there is no free parking. These rules, however, don't apply to disabled people, who, when displaying the disability disk, can park for any length of time. For posted *Kurzparkzonen* in provinces, you can use a parking disk, available at a *Tabak-Trafik* or bank. Set the pointer to the exact time of your arrival (within a 10-minute limit).

NO-PARKING ZONES

- Pedestrian zones (*Fussgängerzonen*)
- Loading area (*Ladezone*)
- Sidewalk (*Gehsteig*)
- Vehicle entrance/exit (*Einfahrt/Ausfahrt*) to buildings
- Bus stop (*Autobus-Haltestelle*)
- Tram stop (*Strassenbahn-Haltestelle*)
- Airport loading and unloading zones

Cars hindering traffic will be towed immediately. If your car has been towed, ask the nearest police station where it has been taken. Chances are, you'll need to go to the car-impound area at 1100, Eibesbrunnergasse 9. (Every taxi driver in Vienna knows the way.) Paying for the towing and impounding is the responsibility of the registered owner or license holder.

P PUBLIC PARKING LOTS & GARAGES

You can find public parking by looking for a large blue square sign with the letter P. Under this sign may be an arrow or the distance in meters to the actual parking site. If you took a ticket to enter, before exiting, you pay at the cashier (*Kassa*) or a machine. Insert your ticket, and the machine will tell you how much you owe. Then insert the amount. Many parking lots now take credit cards, which can be used at the *Kassa*, the machine or sometimes directly at the ticket-reading machine when you exit. Simply insert your ticket, then your credit card, and both will be returned with the proper amount charged.

BE ADVISED

- Spot road checks are normal in Austria, and so is the sobriety test (i.e., alcohol breath test). Stiff penalties apply if you're caught driving with a blood-alcohol level exceeding .08 (though there's discussion about lowering it to .05). So if you drink, don't drive. Either take public transportation, call a taxi or have a designated driver (someone who is not drinking) to take you home.

- Police can issue you a ticket for a moving violation even when they haven't stopped you personally. A civilian or a police officer you haven't seen may have reported you. The ticket will come in the mail along with the bank payment form (*Zahlschein*). You must pay the fine, unless you have compelling evidence to challenge it.

- In some areas, such as radar-monitored zones or at certain intersections, cameras photograph license plates of cars that have exceeded the speed limit or done something else illegal. Tickets are mailed to car owners.

- Just before and after school, there are often police officers or crossing guards (who have the same authority as police at these times) at crosswalks frequented by school children.

- Be prepared! If you don't speak German, have the telephone number handy of someone who can help you if you're in an accident. Police reports will be done in German and signed by you. While you may be able to communicate with the police, it's unnerving to sign something you can't read, so you should at least have it translated by someone you know.

- The legal number of seats (*Sitzplätze*) and passengers for your car is noted on the yellow form (*Zulassungsschein*) among your automobile papers. A child younger than 12 counts as half a person. The following are terms you should know:

Gesamt	Total
Ohne Lenker	Without (not counting) driver
2. Reihe	Back seat (literally, "second row")

 If You're Involved in a Traffic Accident

- Stop your car immediately, turn on your hazard lights and set up your red warning triangle to prevent further accidents.
- Administer basic first aid or call an ambulance if necessary (☎ 144 for ambulance, ☎ 133 for police). If there are no injuries or major damage, you don't have to call the police.
- Establish the circumstances of the accident, but don't automatically claim responsibility (this could be used against you later).
- Call your insurance company.

 Large cities have *Polizei* and other areas have *Gendarmerie*, which are the same thing and have the same emergency number (☎ 133). Look in the telephone directory's white pages under both *"Polizei"* and *"Gendarmerie."*

WHEN YOU ARE INVOLVED IN AN ACCIDENT

Fill out the accident form (*Europäischer Unfallbericht*) provided by your insurance company. This is available in English from British insurance companies (see following example). Private settlement is not advised, so be sure to check with your insurance company before you sign anything other than the accident form. In some instances you'll need a lawyer to defend your case or fight for your rights. In this event, it's helpful to have legal-defense insurance (*Rechtsschutzversicherung*). Ask your agent for details.

Exchange:
- Names (including passengers)
- Addresses
- Telephone numbers

Take note of details:
- Make and model of car(s)
- License-plate number(s)
- Driver's license number(s)
- Name of insurance company(s) and policy number(s)

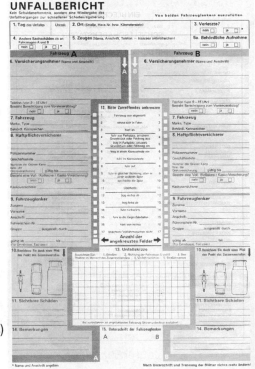

EUROPEAN ACCIDENT STATEMENT

agreed statement of facts on motor vehicle accident

Does NOT constitute an admission of liability, but a summary of identities
and of the facts which will speed up the settlement of claims.

Must be signed by BOTH drivers

1. **date** of accident	time	2. **place** (exact location of accident)	3. **injuries** even if slight
			no ☐ yes ☐ *

4. **property damage** other than to the vehicles A and B	5. **witnesses** names, addresses and tel. nos. (to be underlined if it relates to passenger in A or B)
no ☐ yes ☐ *	

vehicle A

6. insured policyholder (see insurance cert.)

Name _____
(capital letters)
First name _____
Address _____

Tel. No. (from 9 hrs. to 17 hrs.) _____
Can the Insured recover the Value Added Tax
on the vehicle?   no ☐   yes ☐

7. vehicle
Make, type _____
Registration No. (or engine No.) _____

8. insurance company _____

Policy No. _____
Agent (or broker) _____

Green Card No.
(if issued) _____
Ins. Cert. or } valid until _____
Green card }
Is damage to the vehicle insured?
  no ☐   yes ☐

9. driver (see driving licence)

Name _____
(capital letters)
First name _____
Address _____
Driving licence No. _____
Groups   issued by _____

valid from _____ to _____

10. Indicate by an arrow the point of initial impact

11. visible damage

14. remarks

12. circumstances
Put a cross (X) In each of the relevant spaces to help explain the plan.

A			B
☐	1	parked (at the roadside)	1 ☐
☐	2	leaving a parking place (at the roadside)	2 ☐
☐	3	entering a parking place (at the roadside)	3 ☐
☐	4	emerging from a car park, from private grounds, from a track	4 ☐
☐	5	entering a car park, private grounds, a track	5 ☐
☐	6	entering a roundabout (or similar traffic system)	6 ☐
☐	7	circulating in a roundabout etc.	7 ☐
☐	8	striking the rear of the other vehicle while going in the same direction and in the same lane	8 ☐
☐	9	going in the same direction but in a different lane	9 ☐
☐	10	changing lanes	10 ☐
☐	11	overtaking	11 ☐
☐	12	turning to the right	12 ☐
☐	13	turning to the left	13 ☐
☐	14	reversing	14 ☐
☐	15	encroaching in the opposite traffic lane	15 ☐
☐	16	coming from the right (at road junctions)	16 ☐
☐	17	not observing a right of way sign	17 ☐

← State TOTAL number of spaces marked with a cross →

13. plan of the accident
Indicate: 1. the layout of the road - 2. by arrows the direction of the vehicles A, B - 3. their position at the time of impact - 4. the road signs - 5. names of the streets or roads

15. signatures of the drivers
A   **B**

vehicle B

6. insured policyholder (see insurance cert.)

Name _____
(capital letters)
First name _____
Address _____

Tel. No. (from 9 hrs. to 17 hrs.) _____
Can the Insured recover the Value Added Tax
on the vehicle?   no ☐   yes ☐

7. vehicle
Make, type _____
Registration No. (or engine No.) _____

8. insurance company _____

Policy No. _____
Agent (or broker) _____

Green Card No.
(if issued) _____
Ins. Cert. or } valid until _____
Green card }
Is damage to the vehicle insured?
  no ☐   yes ☐

9. driver (see driving licence)

Name _____
(capital letters)
First name _____
Address _____
Driving licence No. _____
Groups   issued by _____

valid from _____ to _____

10. Indicate by an arrow the point of initial impact

11. visible damage

14. remarks

*In the event of injuries or in the event of damage to property other than to the vehicles A and B, give information overleaf.

Do not alter anything in the statement after signature and the separation of the copies for the two drivers.

For Insured's accident report see back →

DC 15.513

LPO 445

KEEP THIS FORM (AND A BALLPOINT PEN) IN YOUR CAR.

IMPORTANT—PLEASE READ THIS CAREFULLY

Directions for use of the European Accident Statement

GENERAL NOTES

THE OBJECT OF THIS FORM IS TO GET A STATEMENT OF THE FACTS OF THE ACCIDENT AGREED BY EACH DRIVER.

The Continental driver will also have a similar form in his own language and it does not matter which one is completed, **BUT you must ensure that you keep either the original or the copy of the completed form to send to your insurer.**
(e.g., an Austrian may fill in his part of his own form in German, leaving you to complete your part of his form in English—you will know what the questions mean by looking at your own form.)

INSTRUCTIONS

AT THE SCENE OF THE ACCIDENT

1. Get details of all witnesses before they leave. Complete question 5.
2. Preferably using a ballpoint pen, complete fully either the blue or the yellow part of the Agreed Statement of Facts (you will need to refer to your insurance certificate, green card and driving license).
3. When you are satisfied with the accuracy of the statement, sign it and have it signed by the other driver (15).
4. Don't forget to—
   (a) mark clearly under (10) the point of initial impact.
   (b) put a cross (X) in each appropriate square on your side of (12) and state the total number of spaces marked with a cross.
   (c) draw a plan of the accident location (13) showing all the information indicated.

UNDER NO CIRCUMSTANCES ALTER ANYTHING ON THE AGREED STATEMENT OF FACTS AFTER COMPLETION

WHEN YOU RETURN HOME

1. FULLY COMPLETE the Motor Accident Report on the back of the English version of the Agreed Statement of Facts.
2. Send the completed Agreed Statement of Facts and Motor Accident Report immediately to your insurer.

SPECIAL NOTE

This form may be used even if no other vehicle is involved, for example: own damage, theft, fire, injury to pedestrian, etc.

AUTOMOBILE CLUBS

The following are two automobile associations you can join. Members receive free roadside service and towing, but even if you aren't a member you can call for help and pay the membership fee to join on the spot.

AUSTRIAN AUTOMOBILE, MOTORCYCLE AND TOURING CLUB (*Österreichischer Automobil-, Motorrad- und Touring Club /ÖAMTC*)

    1010, Schubertring 3

    ☎ 7299-0 (information)

    ☎ 120 (24-hour roadside service)

    ☎ 982 13 04 (*Euronotruf*)

For an additional yearly fee, members have access to European Emergency Call (*Euronotruf*), which provides roadside assistance anywhere in Europe.

AUSTRIAN AUTO, MOTOR AND BICYCLE LEAGUE (*Auto-, Motor- Und Radfahrerbund Österreichs/ARBÖ*)

    1150, Mariahilfer Strasse 180

    ☎ 891 21-0 (information)

    ☎ 123 (24-hour roadside service)

IMPORTING A CAR

Although the process of importing a car from outside the EU can be quite daunting, it can be done. You must request a permission form beforehand and file all forms and receive necessary inspections within a short time after arriving in Austria. Your car must meet Austria's environmental standards or be altered to do so (a costly and time-consuming process). The car must have been in the owner's possession and have been driven at least six months in the home country in order to be imported duty-free. Check with your embassy or consulate for details.

BUYING A CAR

Because importing a car can be very frustrating, many people prefer to buy one in Austria. There are two different categories of car buyers: those who pay Austrian taxes and those who don't. Those who have diplomatic status can buy a car for eventual export on a tax-free basis. Those who pay taxes here don't have that privilege and won't receive money back from such a purchase. If in doubt, check with your embassy or consulate. Each country differs in its diplomatic-status qualifications and privileges. The following dealerships have English-speaking sales representatives to help you. They can also guide you through the complexities of buying and registering a car in Austria.

AUDI, VOLKSWAGEN (SCHWANDL)
Mr. Walter Mensik
1220, Wagramer Strasse 14
☎ 260 66-0

BMW DENZEL
Mr. Friedrich Glatz
1010, Parkring 12
☎ 515 53-1701

BMW WIEN
Mr. Christoph Svoboda
1190, Heiligenstädter Lände 27
☎ 360 61 19

CHRYSLER/JEEP (AC AUSTRO CAR)
Mr. Martin Gottlieb
1211, Felmayergasse 2
☎ 250 50-0

FORD (KÖNIGER)
Mr. Matthäus Schmutz
1210, Brünner Strasse 66
☎ 277 80 48

HONDA (HAVELKA)
Mr. Anton Horill
1180, Sternwarte-strasse 20-22
☎ 476 99 14

MAZDA (BAUMKIRCHNER UND COLLOREDO)
Mr. Klima
1020, Handelskai 344
☎ 727 86-0

MERCEDES-BENZ WIESENTHAL & CO.
Mr. Wolfgang Kraft
1010, Opernring 4
☎ 514 12 27
Fax 513 75 37

RENAULT ÖSTERREICH AUTOMOBILVERTRIEB
Mr. Werner Rannert
1100, Laaer-Berg-Strasse 66
☎ 680 20
Fax 680 20-628

SAAB TARBUK
Mr. Fritz Kleisch
1100, Davidgasse 90
☎ 601 80-333

TOYOTA (FREY AUSTRIA)
Mr. Paul Cserna
1040, Wiedner Gürtel 2
☎ 610 04-601

VOLVO AUSTRIA
Mr. Peter Nesuta
1110, Erdbergstrasse 189
☎ 740 50 42-50

USED CARS

If you want to buy a used car, you can call:

MR. HORST MADER
1400, Vienna International Centre A0766
☎ 20 60 21 158 (Mon - Fri 2 PM - 4 PM, or leave a message)

Or pick up a *Bazar* at your local tabacco shop (*Tabak*). It is filled with private used cars for sale.

REPAIRING A CAR

Look in the yellow pages under *"Autoreparatur."*

PEUGEOT REICHL & PFIEL FIX-ALL (KFZ-WERKSTÄTTE)
   1140, Pfadenhauergasse 10
   ☎ 982 02 93-0
   Mon - Thurs 7:30 AM - noon, 1 PM - 5 PM, Fri 7:30 AM - noon

This repair shop specializes in service for Peugeots, but all cars can be repaired and serviced here.

DISTANCE CONVERSIONS

1 kilometer (km)	=	0.62 miles
1 mile	=	1.6 km
1 meter (m)	=	1.09 yards
1 yard	=	0.91 m

Communications

In order to communicate with people back home—wherever that may be — you'll need to use Austria's postal and telecommunications services. With some perseverance, and a bit of luck, you'll soon become adept at maneuvering through the intricacies of the Austrian system. The following is some basic information about *Post und Telekom Austria* and other private communications companies. You will also find information on Radio, Television and translators — the many aspects of modern and traditional communications.

TELEPHONE *Telefon*

Telecommunication services are reliable in Austria. The phone system is fully automated and direct dialing is available to most European countries and to North America at varying international rates.

APPLYING FOR TELEPHONE SERVICE

You can apply for telephone service at the telecommunications service counter (*Fernmeldedienst*) of your local post office or by calling Telekom's toll-free number 0800 100 100 (ask for an English-speaking representative). It takes 1-2 weeks to have a new line installed and a one-time installation fee of about ATS 2.000. It's faster to take over the phone number of the previous tenant and, assuming there are no outstanding bills, cheaper. Some owners of apartments/flats or houses provide telephones or you can purchase one from an electronics store.

TELEPHONE FEES

As in many large cities, a fee is levied whenever you make a call. Receiving calls costs nothing. If cost is a serious consideration, for a one-time rental fee and a monthly service fee, you can have a telephone meter (*Gebührenrechner* or *Zähleranschluss*) installed on your phone. Pick it up in person (bring a photo ID) from:

Telecommunications Information Office
(*Fernmeldeberatungsstelle*)
    1010, Fleischmarkt 19   ☎ 535 38 03
    1030, Erdberger Lände 36-48 ☎ 715 25 12
    1230, Baumgartnerstrasse 121 ☎ 662 90 99
    Mon - Fri, 8 AM - 5 PM

For about ATS 1.000, you can install the meter yourself or arrange for someone to do it for you . You can also now buy telephones that already have a meter installed.

Once you have your telephone connected, you may want to choose another service provider than Telekom. The telephone market has been deregulated and there are companies charging fees that are more reasonable. A price war is taking place and prices are being adjusted almost weekly. To sign up with any of these companies, you must fill out an application form (by eMail, fax or mail). An access code will be given to you to dial via this company, thus circumventing Telekom. make sure to choose a company that has no sign-up, monthly or minimum fees. The following are a few names and numbers:

ECONO PHONE
1180, Gustav-Tschermak Gasse 10
☎ 478 20 00

Also issues international calling cards for travel abroad.

M.I.T.
☎ 0800 1066 1066

MULITKOM
☎ 963 10 03

UTA
☎ 0800 882 882

TELEPHONE BILLING

Billing is done bimonthly, with charges for local and long-distance calls listed separately on the bill, without any itemized-call information. An itemized bill can be obtained by calling ☎ 0800 100 180 for a service fee. Note that the last 3 digits of the numbers you called will not be revealed due to privacy protection.

PUBLIC TELEPHONES

You can make long-distance calls from any post office. Simply go to the telephone-call (*Telefongespräche*) counter, and you'll be directed to a telephone booth where you can make your call. When you're finished, return to the counter to pay the charges. Public telephone booths are also conveniently located throughout the city, usually on busier streets as well as in *U-Bahn* and train stations and public buildings. Pictures on the telephone show you how to use it. You also can reach an information operator at ☎ 11811. Usually, you'll find two booths back-to-back: one that accepts coins and another that only takes a telephone value card *Telefonwertkarte*, which is a telephone debit card valued at ATS 50 (at a cost of ATS 48) or ATS 100 (at a cost of ATS 95). The public telephone will show a digital reading of the amount being deducted for your call. You can get *Telefonwertkarten* from post offices and some *Tabak-Trafiks*.

**Emergency calls for police, fire department
and ambulance are free
(numbers are listed on the telephone).**

DIRECT LONG-DISTANCE DIALING

To make a direct call outside Austria, first dial the country code, then the area code and finally the phone number. International country codes are listed in the front pages of Vienna's A–H telephone book. Naturally, the country name is in German. Area codes for major cities within specific countries are also listed. Country codes are in dark type, area codes in light type. This list also provides the time difference *(Zeitunterschied)* given in the number of hours between Austria and the country. For credit card calls dial ☎ 0802 34 56 or ☎ 0800 287 874 21 (toll-free). For long-distance information call ☎ 11811 Austria, ☎ 11813 Europe (except Germany), ☎ 11812 Germany, and ☎ 11814 Outside Europe.

CALL-BACK LONG-DISTANCE SERVICES

There are also "call-back" long-distance carriers that offer reasonably-priced calls to the United States. They are known as "call-back" services because you call a phone number, hang up and wait for it to call back, which then connects you to an open U.S. phone line. One such company is:

TELEGROUP, INC.
1010, Franz-Josefs-Kai 49/15
☎ 535 81 46
Fax 533 38 86
www.spinnst.co.at/Robin
eMail d.robin@magnet.at
Mon - Fri, 9 AM - 6 PM

CALLING CARDS

Pre-paid phone cards are available at tobacco stores (Tabak) and post offices.

INTERNET CALLING

A new option with long-distance calling is free internet phone service. By using a company like the one listed below, you can make long distance calls to anyone in the U.S. There's no special software to download or install. With an internet connection, a sound card and microphone, you can go to the website and make free, unlimited, long-distance calls. Keep in mind that the faster your internet connection, the better this service will work.

Dialpad   **PhoneFree**
www.dialpad.com   www.phonefree.com

INTERNATIONAL COUNTRY CODES

Australia	*Australien*	0061
India	*Indien*	0091
Ireland	*Irland*	00353
Japan	*Japan*	0081
New Zealand	*Neuseeland*	0064
South Africa	*Südafrika*	0027
United Kingdom	*Grossbritannien und Nordirland*	0044
U.S.A. & Canada	*Vereinigte Staaten von Amerika und Kanada*	001

TELEPHONE NUMBERS & AREA CODES

Austria's country code is 43. All telephone numbers in Austria have prefixes, usually printed in parentheses. Vienna's prefix is 1 for calling from outside both Vienna and Austria. In order to call Vienna from elsewhere in Austria, you would press 0, 1 and the phone number. With the exception of a few Vienna suburbs, calling a number with a different prefix means you're making a long-distance call. Most of Vienna's phone numbers have seven digits, but provincial numbers may have as few as four. Numbers for various information and for large companies often only have four to five digits. Mobile phone can have very long numbers.

A phone number with parentheses in the middle means that the inserted number is to be added soon. Try either option (e.g., ☎ 32(0) 14 95 was 32 14 95 but will become 320 14 95.)

TELEPHONE NUMBERS WITH EXTENSIONS

Direct-dial extension numbers (*Durchwahlen/Klappe*) are placed at the end of the phone number, preceded by a slash (/) or a hyphen (-). You can dial the entire number, including the digits after the slash or hyphen, in order to be connected directly to that extension. Usually a 0 after the hyphen means there are many extensions, so dialing 0 will connect you to the main switchboard or operator, who will direct your call (e.g., Vienna's main hospital, *Allgemeines Krankenhaus*, has a main listing of ☎ 404 00-0).

TELEKOM CUSTOMER SERVICE
☎ 0800 100 100
Mon - Fri, 7 AM - 6 PM

For information about telephone, fax and other telecommunication services, contact *Telekom Austria*. Wait through several messages until an operator answers and then ask for an English speaker.

FREE TELEPHONE SERVICES

Call Waiting

Call waiting—where you can receive another incoming call while already on the line—is only available to those with digital phone lines. To install this function on your phone, first listen for a dial tone, then press the star button (*), 43 and the pound button (#, which looks like a small square) located to the right of 0. A recording will say, *"Ihr Auftrag wird aufgenommen"* ("Your instructions have been received"). Now, when you're on the phone and a second call comes in, you'll hear a short, intermittent beep. If you want to answer the other call, simply press the "R" button located to the left of 1, and the first caller will be placed on hold while you take the incoming call. Pressing "R" again will return you to the original caller. If you'd like to cancel the call-waiting function, press # (pound/square), 43 and # (pound/square).

Automatic Redial

If you have a "W" button, you can use it to redial (*Wiederholen*) the last number called.

Automatic Call Answering

If you don't want to be disturbed by the phone ringing, you can select a prerecorded message that says you can't answer the phone now and asks the caller to please call back. To do this, first listen for the dial tone, then press *, 24, *, 02, # (pound/square). 02 is English; 01 is German; 03 is French; and 04 is for all three languages. The phone will no longer ring and callers will receive the message. To cancel this service, listen for the dial tone, then press #, 24, #. You can also substitute the following for the 02: 06 (message in German that says to call back tomorrow) or 07 (message in German that says to call back the next business day). Canceling these two is the same procedure as above.

CORDLESS PHONES

If you're using a cordless phone and it begins to beep, this means the connection is about to be terminated. Press the star button (*) to maintain the connection.

TELEPHONE DIRECTORIES

The Vienna telephone directory consists of three books. The first two are white pages, the third is the yellow pages (*Gelbe Seiten*). These are delivered to your door once a year (usually in the early winter); a notice is either mailed to your home or posted in your building informing you of the delivery date. This is your only chance to get them, so you may need to ask a neighbor to accept delivery for you. There also may be a minimal fee. You should get the directory when your phone is installed, but if not, call ☎ 712 11 87 (German only). Additional phone books (or books for other parts of Austria) can be ordered from:

2000/2001

Telefonbuch
☞ telekom

BUNDESLAND M - Z

Feuerwehr 122 Polizei 133 Rettung 144

HEROLD

HEROLD BUSINESS DATA AG
2340 Mödling, Guntramsdorfer Strasse 105
☎ 02236 401 169
Fax 02236 401 736
www.otb.at
Mon - Thurs 8 AM - 4:30 PM, Fri 8 AM - noon
An English speaker should be available to arrange mailing the books to you

The *Gelbe Seiten* has an English/German cross-reference section located in the back of the book. At the front of the A-H telephone book are also numbers for prerecorded messages (*Tonbanddienste*) that offer information in German on a variety of topics.

You can also view the directories online for all of Austria. The sites have full search capabilities and are viewable in English and German.
www.etb.at   White Pages
www.gelbe-seiten.at   Yellow Pages

OUT-OF-ORDER TELEPHONE

Reporting an out-of-order telephone can be done in German (but try asking for an English speaker) by dialing ☎ 11120 and telling the Breakdown Office (*Störungsstelle*) what's wrong. You will have to set up an appointment for someone to come repair the line.

TELEGRAMS

Telegrams are sent through the local post office. The necessary forms are found at the *Telegramme* window. The message can be written in English. Telegrams can also be sent by telephone by calling ☎0800 100 190. Don't hang up when you hear the prerecorded message— wait for an operator and you can speak English. A telegram must contain a minimum of seven words, although the address counts toward the number of words.

FAX MACHINES

Fax machines are used more frequently in Austria than in the United States. It's less expensive and faster to send a fax than a letter. If you bought your fax/copier in the United States, you'll also need a large transformer (2,000 amps/watts). Be sure to tell the telephone installer that a U.S. fax machine will be connected. Also mention if a modem will be used on the same line.

CELLULAR PHONES
Handies

Many people now also use mobile phones *(Handies)*. There are several networks to choose from. The three most common are: A1 (operated by Telekom Austria), ONE and max.mobil. You can purchase these from electronic stores (look under *Mobiletelefon* in the phonebook). They take your application and set up your account. A1 can also be purchased at *Telekom*. Handy prices start out at ATS 0.- (under special promotions) and go upwards according to features and namebrands. Depending on the program you choose and the price you are willing to pay, your handy can have a pre-paid amount loaded on your chip (great for teens) or unlimited calling all over the world, including via satellite. Also, a combination of a fixed net telephone (Festnetz) and a handy under the same number and account is now available. You can even have your telephone hooked up via your cable TV together with your computer and handy. (Not all districts in Vienna have the cable installed for this purpose yet.)

ONEderful Mobile Communication

Having launched on October 26, 1998, ONE set new standards as the first nation-wide provider of GSM-1800 technology. Currently ONE's network reaches 96% of the Austrian population. The number of employees (850 at launch in October '98) is continuously growing and will reach 1400 by the end this year. End of May 2000 the number of customers exceeded 700.000, by the end of this year more than one million Austrians are expected to make "rauschfrei" (noise-free) mobile calls. By the end of 2000 18 billion ATS will have been invested, turnover was ATS 2 billion in 1999, and is expected to be ATS 7.1 billion for the year 2000.

ONE is a full-service provider, offering the whole range of telecommunication: mobile telephones with various offers for business as well as for private customers - among those offering High Speed data transfer -, fixed-line telephone and internet access.

In addition, ONE services its customers in its own 21 ONE Worlds in all major Austrian cities and in more than 1500 outlets with the leading retailers of electronic equipment. ONE World Stephansplatz, the flagship store, opened its doors on October 29, 1999. The shop specializes in servicing English-speaking customers.

POST OFFICE *Postamt*

RECEIVING MAIL

Mail is delivered Monday to Friday, excluding holidays.

Mail to you from outside of Austria should be addressed in the following manner:

Name:	Mary Green
Street address (with apartment number):	Ledergasse 12/4
Austrian postal code and city:	A-1010 Vienna
(Province, if outside Vienna)	
Country:	Austria

 Some people find that adding "Europe" to the address helps facilitate delivery, because so much mail is misdirected to Australia.

To pick up a letter or package from the post office, you need a passport or identification card *(Ausweis)* to prove that you're the intended recipient. If a letter is registered *(Eingeschrieben)*, only the addressee can claim it.

For information on available U.S. mail-collection services, call the AWA office at ☎ 320 14 95.

SENDING MAIL

Mailboxes are bright yellow and often mounted on buildings. Those with an orange stripe are also emptied Saturday, Sunday and holidays. Pick-up times are posted on the box.

Mail sent within Austria *(Inland)* should be addressed as follows:

Name:	Barbara Schmidt
Street address (with apartment number):	Stiftgasse 42/3
Austrian postal code and city:	3400 Klosterneuburg
Province, if outside Vienna:	Niederösterreich (or NÖ)

District (*Bezirk*) codes in Vienna are indicated by the second and third numbers of the postal code (e.g., 1010 is the first district and 1190 is the 19th district). The address Ruthgasse 17/4/3/2 indicates the house number (17), building number, if in a complex of buildings (4), stairway or floor (3) and apartment number (2). In most cases, only the house and apartment numbers are used.

POST OFFICE LOCATIONS

The telephone directory's white pages, under *"Post und Telekom Austria"* lists the locations and hours of all post offices by district (*Bezirk*) usually Mon - Fri, 8 AM - noon, 2 PM - 6 PM. The main post office of the district is open Mon - Fri, 7 AM - 7 PM and Sat, 7 AM - 10 AM. The post office at the airport *(Flughafen)* is open Mon - Fri, 7:30 AM - 8 PM. The post symbol is used on all city maps to mark post-office locations. All post offices offer express-mail and faxing services.

POST OFFICES OPEN 24 HOURS

MAIN POST OFFICE *Hauptpostamt*
1010, Fleischmarkt 19

FRANZ-JOSEF-BAHNHOF
1090, Althanstrasse 10

SÜDBAHNHOF
1100, Wiedner Gürtel 1B

WESTBAHNHOF
1150, Europaplatz

INTERNATIONAL COURIERS

DHL, FedEx, TNT and United Parcel Service (UPS) deliver to major cities in Austria, although it's quite expensive and there are restrictions. For locations, look in the white pages under *"Kurierdienste."*

POSTAL RATES

Postal rates (*Postgebühren*) are listed in a booklet, which is revised yearly. Your postal carrier will leave one in your mailbox every December. (See the Tipping section of the Austria chapter.) If you go to you post office, you can also pick one up (along with stamps) at the letter-receiving counter (*Briefannahme*), which only accepts cash.

The postage for letters (up to 2,000 grams) is calculated differently for mail within Austria or worldwide. With worlwide you can send Priority (air mail) or non-priority.

SENDING PACKAGES
Päckchen, Pakete

There are several categories of packages with different rates:

SMALL PACKET OR PARCEL
Päckchen

Whereas in the past the post office differentiated between small and large packages, now there is only the category "package" (up to 31.5 kg) nationally and outside of Austria.

FOUR WAYS TO MAIL PACKAGES

Airmail *Flugpost*
A package to the United States usually takes 10 working days and it is also rather expensive.

Surface Air Lifted (SAL)
This is less expensive than airmail and faster than surface.

Surface *Gewöhnlich*
This is the least expensive of the three, but it also takes the longest (sometimes up to two months), so if you want to know how long, ask, *"Wie lange dauert es?"*

EMS (Express Mail Service)
This is the fastest way to send a package, but also the most expensive. You may want to compare prices and delivery times with the courier services.

POSTAL FORMS

Austria requires a variety of forms to be filled out in order to mail letters and packages. The following section shows you sample forms as well as how to fill them out.

You can sometimes find these forms at a side counter, or you may need to stand in line to get them from a clerk.

Text at the top of the form: The sender is required to fill in the area outlined in bold.

Aufgabeschein Postal form

Empfänger Addressee

Name Name

Bestimmungsort Destination city, state, country

Postleitzahl Postal/ZIP code

Wert Value—in ***Schilling*** (S) and ***Groschen*** (g) (in the shaded areas)

Nachnahme Cash on delivery (COD)

Der Absender wird gebeten, den stark umrandeten Teil auszufüllen
Aufgabeschein

	Name						
Empfänger	Bestimmungs-art	Postleitzahl					
Wert		S	g	Nach-nahme		S	g
eingeschriebene Briefsendung					Wertbrief		Paket

	Aufgabe-nummer		
Postvermerke	Gewicht kg g		
	Entgelt S g		
	Besondere Vermerke		

661 011 500   GZ: 101857 - PE/97

Bitte Rückseite beachten !

Bitte Rückseite beachten! Please note reverse side.

The text on the reverse reminds you to fill in the form in dark (not colored) permanent ink and to keep the form in case you need to trace the package. Should that need arise, you are requested to inquire during nonpeak business hours, preferably late morning or early afternoon.

P.S.K. BANK

Most post offices also serve as branches of the *Postsparkasse* (*P.S.K.*) *Bank*, which are open Mon - Fri, 8 AM - 5 PM. This way, you can take care of your banking and postal needs at the same time. (See the Banking chapter.)

 TIP ## SUBSCRIPTION EXTENSIONS

Subscriptions will be automatically extended in Austria if you don't inform the publisher within a specified period. Your warning is the following: *"Dieser Vertag verlängert sich um ein weiteres Jahr, wenn er nicht drei Monate vor Ablauf der vereinbarten Vertragsdauer gekündigt wird"* ("This contract will be extended for another year if it is not terminated three months before the expiration of the agreed-upon duration of the contract"). You should cancel in writing and send it as registered mail.

✆ **Post & Telekom Austria** post

Aufgabeschein

BITTE FEST AUFDRÜCKEN!

VON | Name und Anschrift des Absenders | Allfällige Bezugszahl des Absenders | Nummer des Paketes

①

AN | Name und Anschrift des Empfängers mit Angabe des Bestimmungslandes | Das Paket kann von Amts wegen geöffnet werden

②

Wertangabe (in Schilling) – in Buchstaben ③ – in Ziffern (ATS)

Nachnahmebetrag (in Schilling) – in Buchstaben ④ – in Ziffern (ATS)

Postscheckkonto Nr. ⑤ P.S.K. A-1018 Wien

Zollerklärung

Inhaltsangabe (und Anzahl der Gegenstände) ⑥a | Ursprungsland der Waren ⑥b | Tarif-Nr. (falls bekannt) ⑥c | Nettogewicht ⑥d | (Zoll-)Wert ⑥e

In den EU-Raum nicht erforderlich ! (Siehe Anleitung auf der Rückseite des letzten Blattes!)

Bemerkungen

☐ Warenmuster ⑦ ☐ Dokumente ⑧ ☐ Geschenk ⑨ | Anzahl der Rechnungen und Bescheinigungen ⑩ | Stempel des Aufgabeamtes

Besondere Vermerke ⑪ | Wertangabe in SZR | Namenszeichen

Vorverfügungen des Absenders für den Fall der Unzustellbarkeit *) | Gesamt-Brutto-gewicht | Gebühr

⑫ ☐ Unzustellbarkeitsmeldung an den Absender | ⑮ ☐ unverzügliche Rücksendung an den Absender

⑬ ☐ Rücksendung an den Absender nach ... Tag(en) | ⑯ ☐ als preisgegeben behandeln bei Rück-/Nachsendung | Die/der Unterfertigte bestätigt, daß diese Sendung keine gefährlichen, nach den Postbestimmungen verbotenen Gegenstände enthält sowie, zutreffendenfalls, die Richtigkeit der im Abschnitt „Zollerklärung" gegebenen Auskünfte und hat auch zur Kenntnis genommen, daß sie/er im Falle der Unzustellbarkeit die aus der Durchführung der nebenstehenden Verfügung(en) erwachsenden Kosten zu tragen hat.

⑭ ☐ Nachsendung an den Empfänger an folgende Anschrift | ☐ auf dem preisgünstigsten Weg ⑰ ☐ auf dem Luftweg ⑱ | Datum und Unterschrift des Absenders ⑲

*) Bitte Zutreffendes ankreuzen

CUSTOMS DECLARATION FORM *Zollerklärung* and INSTRUCTIONS FOR UNDELIVERABLE PACKAGES *Unzustellbarkeit*

(This form is not needed for countries within the EU.)

VON: From:

1. Name und Anschrift des Absenders
Name and address of sender

AN: To:

2. Name und Anschrift des Empfängers mit Angabe des Bestimmungslandes
To: Name and address including country of addressee

3. Wertangabe (in Schilling) - In Buchstaben - in Ziffern
Value in ATS - in words - in number

4. Nachnahmebetrag (in Schilling)
Amount for cash on delivery in ATS

5. Postscheckkonto Nr.
Checking account number with post office

Zollerklärung: Customs Declaration:

6 a. Inhaltsangabe (und Anzahl der Gegenstände)
Contents and number of items in package

b. Unsprungsland der Waren
Country of origin (of the goods)

c. **Tarif-Nr. (falls Bekannt)**
Tariff number (if known)
d. **Nettogewicht**
Net weight
e. **(Zoll-) Wert**
Customs value
7. **Warenmuster**
product sample
8. **Dokumente**
Documents
9. **Geschenk**
Gift
10. **Anzahl der Rechnungen und Bescheingungen**
Number of invoices and certificates
11. **Besondere Vermerke**
Special remarks
Vorverfügungen des Absenders für den Fall der Unzustellbarkeit
In case of inability to deliver
12. **Unzustellbarkeitsmeldung an den Absender**
Inform sender of inability to deliver
13. **Rücksendung an den Absender nach... Tag(en)**
Return to sender after... day(s)
14. **Nachsendung an den Empfänger an folgende:**
Deliver to addressee at this address:
15. **unverzügliche Rücksendung an den Absender**
Return immediately to sender
16. **als preisgegeben behandeln**
Dispose of at free will
bei Rück-/Nachsendung
For return shipment/shipment to new address
17. **auf dem preisgünstigsten Weg**
Most economical way
18. **auf dem Luftweg**
Air mail
19. **Datum und Unterschrift des Absenders**
Sender's signature and date.
By signing, sender certifies he is not sending dangerous goods that
are counter-regulatory to postal codes, that information in the
custom section is correct and that he is responsible for shipping
costs in case of inability to deliver the package.

POSTAL TERMS

Absender Sender

Anschrift Address

Anschriftsänderung Change of address

Aufgabeschein Receipt for registered mail

Briefkasten Mailbox

Briefmarke(n) Postage stamp(s)

Dringend Urgent

Drucksache Printed matter

Eigenhändig To addressee only

Eilbote Express delivery

Eilsendung Express item

Eingeschrieben Registered mail

Einschreiben To register mail

Empfänger Addressee

Flugpost Airmail

Flugzuschlag Air surcharge

Gebühr Rate, charge

Hauptpostamt Main post office

Inhalt Contents

Lagerfrist Period of retention

Nachforschung Inquiry

Nachnahme Cash on Delivery (COD)

Nachsenden To forward or redirect

Nachsendungsantrag Request to redirect

Offen/Geöffnet Open/opened

Paket Parcel

Päckchen Small packet (sent as a heavy letter)

Postamt Post office

Postanweisung Money order

Postausweiskarte Postal identity card

Postleitzahl Postal (ZIP) code

Rückschein Notice of receipt for official mail

Rückscheinbrief (RSB) Registered mail

Schnellpostsendungen Express-mail service

Sich ausweisen To identify yourself

Sonderpostmarke Special-edition stamp

Sperrig Bulky

Wertbrief Insured letter

Zerbrechlich Fragile

Zollamt Customs office

Zustellen To deliver

Zustellgebühr Delivery fee

RADIO & TELEVISION
Radio und Fernsehen

Radio and television are government-owned and regulated in Austria. Each residence owning a radio and television must acquire a radio and television permit (*Rundfunk-und-Fernsehhauptbewilligung*) and pay a bimonthly charge for reception (see Utilities section of Essentials chapter). This is also required for car radios. Go to the post office for radio and television registration (*Radio- und Fernsehanmeldung*) forms. Payment of the bimonthly fees can be arranged with your bank (see Banking chapter). Once a year in January, there is an additional charge for artistic patronage (*Kunstförderung*).

TELEVISION

ORF presents German-language programming on two channels, *ORF* 1 and *ORF* 2. Broadcasting begins at 6 AM. Occasionally, *ORF* does present programs in the original English format with German dubbing or subtitles. Some of the German-dubbed movies can also be heard in English by viewers owning a stereo TV with an A/B function. In newspaper listings, these movies can be indicated in a variety of ways: *OmU* , *OF* or two intersecting circles, one of which is black. Although each daily newspaper has a radio and TV section, most Friday editions carry weekly program guides. There are also television guides, such as *TV Media*, available at newsstands and by subscription *(Abonnement)*.

CABLE TV *Telekabel*

The alternatives to state-broadcast TV are cable and satellite TV. If your apartment or house already has cable installed, then subscription is possible by paying a monthly fee. Otherwise, installation is expensive and depends on your location, both the district and house. For more information, contact:

TELEKABEL WIEN
    1100, Erlachgasse 116
    ☎ 960 60 600
    Fax 960 60 960

This office will put you in touch with your neighborhood subsidiary.

UPC TELEKABEL

The Telekabel TV-Package guarantees unlimited entertainment by offering a lot of multinational, premium-channel programs (CNN, NBC Super Channel, MTV, etc.) for the international community in Vienna.

Additionally, there is a new form of television: Austria's first pay-per-view system, which allows customers to order films at the press of a button via a decoder. Film-Highlights can be seen there long before they're broadcast on free TV. At the top of the list you have common programs like BBC World, BBC Prime, BET, Muzzik, etc.

With the digital set-top-computer as a part of the modern world of television, it can additionally guarantee the highest quality along with different services, like Near-Video-On-Demand and a great variety of TV channels and special-interest programs. Through an "Interactive Entertainment Guide" you will gain access to games, eMail and lots of interactive, multimedia features. You'll be informed about the newest developments by the UPC Telekabel Service Line.

UPC Telekabel also offers internet access via "chello". Connection through a cable modem has brought a new dimension to surfing by paying an attractive flat, monthly rate.

Priority Telecom is a private, fixed-network telephone service from UPC Telekabel which offers highly competitive pricing as well as high quality.

For more information contact:
UPC Telekabel
1100, Erlachgasse 116
Service Line: ☎ 960 60 600
eMail: office@telekabel.co.at
Homepage: www.telekabel.at

SATELLITE TV

With a south-facing building and permission from your landlord, you can install a satellite receiver system. For a reasonable one-time fee, you can get a satellite system with an 60-cm or larger dish. Stores specializing in the necessary equipment are listed under *"Satelliten-empfangsanlagen"* in the yellow pages.

You can align your receiver to one of many satellites offering various language and program options. The Astra satellite provides access to more than 20 channels in English, including British news and movie channels, CNN International, the Cartoon Network, Discovery Channel, Disney Channel and TNT.

TV & VCR OPTIONS

* A standard European television and VCR allow for viewing and taping of the standard European PAL format. Connection to cable or a satellite dish is also possible.

* A multisystem TV and VCR allow you to tape and view programs broadcast here (including via satellite), and will accommodate NTSC (U.S. -made) and PAL tapes. Connection to cable or satellite is also possible

* A North American TV and VCR will work with a transformer, but the TV can't receive broadcasts here, and the VCR will not play PAL tapes.

For a list of video stores renting tapes in English, see the Video Rental section of the Recreation chapter.

TRANSLATORS

Translators are listed by language in the yellow pages under *"Dol-metscher."* You should use a translator for any official documents. The AWA office also has a list of bilingual people who are willing to help with unofficial, general translations.

At the grocery store, bank, school, office or our own home - we have to work with computers. We choose to use them as a tool to make our lives easier, as a source of entertainment, or both. For some of us, the computer has become an intricate part of our lives, either by bringing the office home or just keeping in contact with friends and loved-ones via eMail. In this chapter we provide you with some information on how computers are bought, connected and repaired within Austria along with some suggested internet sites and virtual cafés.

BEFORE YOU MOVE

There are a few things you should check on and consider doing before you move your computer. Perhaps the most important thing is to backup your data. A computer, although expensive, is replacable, whereas your data may not be. Make back up copies of your files either on Zip disks, floppy disks or CD-ROMs and store them together with the original program disks in a sturdy container, preferably a fire-proof lockbox. This may be a bit time-consuming, but you will thank yourself if something should happen.

EQUIPEMENT CHECK

Make sure your equipment is 110/220v compatible. Most of the newer computers enable you to change with the flip of a switch or by changing your power pack. Of course you can use a transformer for 110v equipment, but having the correct voltage can save you aggravation in the future.

You may also want to check your monitor. Generally, monitors from the United States will not work in Europe. The magnetic fields are different here than in North America. It is best to contact your manufacturer for specifications.

MOVING YOUR COMPUTER

Before moving your computer, there are certain procedures to follow which will protect your system from mechanical failure or damage due to normal physical shock, which occurs during transport. If the following steps are taken prior to moving your computer, your system should arrive safely at its destination.

FLOPPY DISK DRIVE PREPARATION

Remove any floppy diskettes from the drives and insert a cardboard disk or an old floppy disk in the drive and close the drive door. This prevents the drive heads from touching each other during movement.

HARD DISK PREPARATION

On newer models the hard disk is atomatically parked whenever the computer shuts down. However, older models may require you to take steps to park the heads via a program. Check the instructions for your computer.

PRINTER PREPARATION

If you plan to move a laser printer, remove the ink cartridge as the ink may spill and contaminate the laser engine. If moving a pin printer, you should insert a piece of paper in the platen to secure the print head.

MISCELLANEOUS HARDWARE

Such computer hardware as a Zip drive, scanner, CD-ROM drive and others generally do not need special care to be moved. However, it is always best to consult your manual or hardware dealer for instructions.

SOFTWARE

Bring it with you! English-language software is available here, but often the price is much higher and it may be difficult to find specific titles.

PACKING AND SHIPPING

The original box your system came in is the best choice. The rigid styrofoam packing material will hold the equipment securely in place. In the event your original box is not available, your carrier can provide a sturdy packing container and materials.

COMPUTERS IN VIENNA

You can purchase computer equipment here, but they usually do not include the software packages available in the United States. Also, the software that is included is normally in German unless your system is special order.

WHICH SYSTEM TO BUY

There are a variety of computer systems and componets those systems are built with. With the computer industry's current growth rate, the options for a system can sometimes be overwhelming. The best thing to do is take a step back and assess your individual needs for your own personal computer. You may want to consider exactly what you plan to use the computer for before making a purchase. If it is for business, you may need special hardware and software programs like network capabilities and office programs. If you want a computer for entertainment purposes perhaps you will need a fast processor and a good graphics card for gaming. Or if you just want a computer for general home use, you may just need the basics with a good eMail program to keep in contact with friends and family back home. In general, the more you plan to use your PC, the more you should invest in one.

COMPUTER DEALERS

Look in the telephone book under *Computer.*

Most of the computer componets and terms are the same in German as in English, so if you have some knowlege about what you want before you go there, you should not have any language problems. There are many computer stores throughout Vienna, so there's probably one in your neighborhood - check your telephone book. A few of the major dealers are:

Actron Computersysteme
www.actron.at

Birg Computer HandelsgesmbH
www.birg.at

Media Markt
(great for software)
www.mediamarkt.at

Niedermeyer
www.niedermeyer.at

You may also want to try:

 B & D Computer Services

☎ & Fax 603 75 75
eMail frifro@teleweb.at
www.bddesign.hypermart.net

Custom computer equipment for the home and small business. He builds custom computer systems and does upgrades. Speaks German and English.

COMPUTER REPAIR

Look in the telephone book under *Computer Reparatur und Service.*

Computer service in Vienna is the same as in most countries. They prefer that you bring your equipment to them. If you wish to have a technician come to your home, you should ask for the rates in advance and have the necessary equipment available when the technician arrives (eg. CD-ROMs, passwords, etc.)

IBM - PC

MY PC-SERVICE
1030, Erdberger Strasse 202
☎ 796 35 88
Fax 796 35 88-47

This service has a hotline to solve computer problems, home repair service or you can take your computer there. English is spoken.

GAMMAG COMPUTERSYSTEME
☎ 278 87 13
Fax 278 87 13-18

This service can send someone to your home or you can take your computer to them. English is spoken.

MACINTOSH

 ### TOOLS AT WORK

1020, Zirkusgasse 40
☎ 216 55 85-15
Fax 216 55 85-19
eMail:
bkuntner@toolsatwork.at
Mon - Fri, 9 AM - 5 PM

The owner, Berenice Kuntner, is very helpful and speaks fluent English. Call first to determine whether you need to bring in your computer. She can come to your home for an additional fee. Eurocheques are accepted.

GETTING CONNECTED

If you want to use the internet for such things like surfing or eMail, you will need an ISP (Internet Service Provider). Your first step is to check with your landlord. If any installation of wiring and equipment is necessary, you must often have written permission from your landlord before companies will preform the work. And depending on your choice for connection, you may need special hardware for your computer such as modems and network cards.

i-ONE – Internet for free for all

The telecommunication provider ONE (Connect Austria) offers customers free Internet access (i-ONE). On the portal, www.one.at, you can find a variety of services such as the latest news (headlines, business news, the story of the day, sports, lifestyle, events, and weather) as well as information about ONE, an SMS gateway, and chatrooms. i-ONE provides up to 6 free e-mail addresses (not only for i-ONE customers) and 10 MB free webspace for one's own homepage.

i-ONE is easily and quickly installed by means of a CD-ROM, which is available for free at all ONE points of sales. When you purchase a ONE mobile phone, the CD-ROM is automatically included, or you may also order it under the toll-free phone number 0800 7777 99. If you already have access to the Internet, you can download the software online from www.one.at.

i-ONE is for everyone – no matter if you are a ONE customer or not. It can be used via the fixed line as well as mobile, and there is no monthly fee or contractual commitment .
The magazine "e-media" awarded i-ONE best Internet service provider in a test of 13 providers in its issue of June 10, 2000.

CONNECTION OPTIONS

There are currently five options available in Vienna:

• **Telephone Connection** - This is a standard internet connection using a dial-up account via your computer modem and your telephone line. The connection speed depends on the modem you have installed (usually 56k). Unlike the United States, you must pay a per-minute fee when using your phone line for this type of connection, regardless of who your internet provider is. This type of service is readily available either by the phone company *Telekom Austria* or a commercial company. Look in the phonebook under *Internet Providers* for a complete list.

• **ISDN** - This service requires an ISDN modem. It runs over dual phone lines which have two seperate phone numbers. The advantage over a regular connection is the speed (128+k) and the fact that you can still use your phone while you are connected. However, you do have to pay for both phone lines and there is still the per-minute charge.

- **Cable Connection (*Chello*)** - This service is provided by your cable television company (*Telekabel*). The benfits of this type of service is a faster (300k), flat rate connection with no per-minute charges. You will however, need a network card for your PC because the connection operates over a LAN (Local Area Network). Once you have your network card, they come to your home, connect their modem to your television and computer, and then install their software. It has no effect on your telephone. For more information contact:

UPC TELEKABEL
    1100, Erlachgasse 116
    ☎ 960 60 600
    eMail office@telekabel.co.at
    www.telekabel.at

- **ADSL** - This service is similar to a cable connection, however it runs over a special phone line installed by your telephone company (*Telekom Austria*). You still need a network card, they provide the modem and software, and it is a flat-rate charge with your base telephone fees included. There are no per-minute fees and your telephone still operates while online. The big advantage is the connection speed (500k). You can find out more by calling:

TELEKOM CUSTOMER SERVICE
    ☎ 0800 100 100
    Mon - Fri, 7 AM - 6 PM

- **Satellite** - This new service is said to be the fastest connection available. However, with it being the newest, the hook-up and monthly prices are high. With special hardware, your computer is connected to your satellite dish and can recieve information at high speeds. Unfortunately, you still need a dial-up connection in order to transmit to the satellite.

Each of these connection options vary in price according to the level of service you choose. Most provide an eMail account and some plans provide you with webspace if you want to claim your own little corner of cyberspace. If you are interested in having your own business or personal webpage designed, look in the phone book under *Internet*.

aZahradnik WebDesign
    ☎ 02252 206 201 or 0676 729 9982
    eMail contact@azahradnik.com   www.azahradnik.com

Custom webpages and graphics in English or German. She is American and also does computer tutoring.

THE INTERNET

Now that you're connected, you may be asking what to do now. The internet is a vast resource for virtually every topic, and it's all at your fingertips. We have collected a few suggestions for informational sites on Vienna and Austria. All of the listed sites have information available in English.

American Women's Association (AWA)
Information on the club and activities.
www.awavienna.com

Austria Academic Portal
Find universities, reasearch centers and libraries throughout Austria.
www.ac-info.at

Austria Cafe
Austrian recipes, history, customs and more with links to a zip code guide, exchange rates and weather updates.
www.austria-cafe.com

Austria National Tourist Office
Everything a tourist needs to know about Austria.
www.anto.com and www.austria-tourism.at

Austrian Press & Information Service
Information on everything from visa regulations to video tours.
www.austria.org

Austrian Trade Commission
Upcoming trade fairs, events and exhibitions in Austria.
www.austriantrade.org

Austrosearch
Austrian news headlines in English.
http://news.austrosearch.at/austrianews

Corporate Information
Austrian business information with a company search available.
www.corporateinformation.com/atcorp.html

Electronic Telefonbuch (ETB)
The site for finding telephone numbers and addresses in Vienna or all of Austria.
www.etb.at

Expat Guide
Great resource for Austrian customs, holidays, phrases, etc.
www.austriaquide.com

Gelbe Seiten (the Yellow Pages)
Search for any company throughout Austria.
www.gelbe-seiten.at

Österreichische National Bibliothek (Austrian National Library)
You can search for books available in English, including complete on-line books ready to read.
www.onb.ac.at

Österreichische Post AG
Find the nearest post office to you, zip code directory, postal rates, tracking, stamp catalog and all about the postal service in Austria,
www.post.at

Virtual Vienna
Everything you need to know about Vienna, complete with message boards and classifieds. Make new friends, look for a job and more!
www.virtualvienna.net

Wien Online
Maps, events calendar, sights, music, etc.
www.wienonline.at/english

Wiener Linien (Vienna Public Transportation Site)
When you need to go somewhere new, this is the place to get directions. Just type in your destination point and they give you many options complete with links to printable maps. (Starts in German, but the search results are in English.)
www.wienerlinien.at

THE VIRTUAL CAFÉ

If you ever need to eMail, fax, scan, copy or print something and either you don't have the equipment or yours is unavaiable - these are the places to visit. You can even sit back, relax, enjoy a coffee and surf the internet. The staff is usually very helpful and, like with most computer-related business, English is not a problem.

BIGnet Internet Café
1010, Hoher Markt 8-9
☎ 533 29 39
Fax 533 29 39-20
eMail office@bignet.at
www.bignet.at

Café Bierbeisl Einstein
1010, Rathausplatz 4
☎ 405 26 26
Fax 405 26 26-24
eMail albert@einstein.at
http://einstein.at

Mediencafe im Amadeus
1010, Kärntner Strasse 19
☎ 513 14 50-17
eMail mwd@artibus.at
www.amadeusbuch.co.at

g-Zone
1010, Universitätsstrasse 11
☎ 407 81 66
Fax 407 81 66-19
eMail office@g-zone.at
www.g-zone.at

Blue Box
1070, Richtergasse 8
☎ 523 26 82
eMail bluebox@ping.at
www.ping.at/bluebox

Café Stein
1090, Währingerstrasse 6-8
☎ 319 72 41-0
Fax 319 72 41-2
eMail c.stein@magnet.at
www.cafe-stein.com

Café-Royal
1100, Absberggasse 25/6
☎ 602 35 00
Fax 602 35 00
eMail cafe-royal@teleweb.at
http://members.teleweb.at/
cafe-royal

VIVA- Snack
1200, Adalbert Stifter Str. 67
☎ 330 32 42
Fax 330 32 42-13
eMail omvfazekas@aon.at
www.omvfazekas.at

Libromania
1220, Donaustadtstrasse 1
☎ 202 52 55
Fax 202 52 55-99
eMail libromania@libromania.at
www.libromania.co.at

M oney is one thing you can't do without, no matter where you are. In Vienna, however, not only are you dealing with a different currency, but also a different system of payment and banking. This chapter explains the different types of bank accounts and services, as well as methods of payment in Austria. Before you know it, you will be filling out payment forms *(Zahlscheine)* like a native!

AUSTRIAN CURRENCY

Austria is among the 11 founding countries in the European Monetary Union. Since January 1, 1999, its official currency is the EURO (€). However, the *Austrian Schlling* remains in circulation as a sub-unit of the EURO until July 1, 2002. Businesses are allowed to complete the transfer to the new currency until January 1, 2002. Therefore, currently, the medium of exchange remains the *Austrian Schilling* (ATS) or the *Österreichische Schilling* (ÖS). One *Schilling* equals 100 *Groschen*. Coins (*Münzen*) come in denominations of 10 *Groschen*, 50 *Groschen*, one *Schilling*, five *Schilling*, 10 *Schilling* and 20 *Schilling* (although this one is rare). Bills *(Scheine)* come in denominations of 20 *Schilling*, 50 *Schilling*, 100 *Schilling*, 500 *Schilling*, 1000 *Schilling* and 5000 *Schilling*. Like most Europeans, Austrians use punctuation differently than in the United States (e.g., ATS 1,000.00 is usually written ATS 1.000,–. Note the "–" for the two empty places after the decimal point).

WRITING NUMBERS

Some numbers look different when written in typical Austrian handwriting. The most obvious are the 1 (written with a sloping line up and then down) and the 7 (which has a horizontal line through the middle to keep it from being confused with a 1—and to keep us foreigners on our toes!).The 4 is often written like a zigzag (with hardly any line on the upper right), and the 9 is often reversed with the loop on the right side instead of the left.

SAYING NUMBERS

To further complicate matters, in German, two-digit numbers above 20 are said in the reverse order (e.g., one-and-twenty is 21). A trick to keep from getting confused about a number being said in German is to write it as you hear it (be sure to leave a place for the tens digit). For example, as someone is saying the number 121 as "one-hundred-one-and-twenty" *(einhunderteinundzwanzig)*, write 1 (for the 100), leave a space and write 1 (as you hear it) and go back to write in the 2 as you hear 20 *(zwanzig)*. This is very helpful with monetary amounts as well as telephone numbers and addresses.

Austrians usually do not say anything to identify the decimal place. The amount ATS 121,50 will be spoken as "one-hundred-one-and-twenty-fifty" (einhunderteinundzwanzigfünfzig). The numbers are all strung together when written and are spoken with only a short pause between zwanzig and fünfzig. If you are confused about an amount or a number, don't feel stupid about asking the person to repeat it slowly ("Langsam, bitte").

BANK ACCOUNTS
U.S. BANKS

You will probably want to check with your bank at home to see if it is able to offer any special services to expatriate customers (e.g., automatic bill paying in your home country while you are out of the country or transferring funds to you abroad). Many banks also have internet banking available. In the United States, Citibank and Chemical Bank offer such programs to both corporations and relocating employees. For more information, call the banks in New York:

CITIBANK'S PERSONAL BANKING FOR OVERSEAS EMPLOYEES
☎ 001 (212) 307-8511
Fax 001 (212) 307-8404
www.citibank.com

CHEMICAL BANK'S INTERNATIONAL EMPLOYEE BANKING
☎ 001 (212) 638-0300
Fax 001 (212) 638-7259

CURRENCY EXCHANGE
Wechselstuben, Geldwechsel

One of the first things you'll need to do after arriving in Austria is to exchange your currency for Austrian Schillings. "Wechselstube/Cambio/Change" signs indicate foreign-currency-exchange services, which are located at the airport, train stations and banks in the city center.

Automatic teller machines that display credit-card logos also accept major credit cards, including those issued overseas, for cash advances, with a daily limit of ATS 5.000 (see Bankomat section of this chapter). Any interest charged on the cash advance will depend on your credit-card company or issuing bank.

AUSTRIAN CURRENT ACCOUNTS

Even if you've made arrangements with your bank back home, you should consider finding a bank here. Keep in mind, however, that banking functions are handled differently in Austria than what you may be accustomed to. A major difference is that, as with the rest of Europe, Austria functions on a cash-and-bank-transfer level, with credit-card and automatic-banking transactions increasing in use. Personal checks (i.e., checks written "PAY TO THE ORDER OF" a specific person) are not used within continental Europe.

As a foreigner living in Austria, you are considered a "foreign-resident customer" *(Deviseninländer)*. To open a current account *(Girokonto)* in Austrian Schillings, you just need your passport and cash *(Barerlag)*, or you can arrange to have funds transferred to your new account. As you will read later in this chapter, a *Girokonto* usually serves as your main source of readily accessible cash.

If funds are being transferred from abroad, be sure to have the money transferred for deposit to your *Girokonto*—and not to a savings account *(Sparbuch)* you also may have opened—because the funds will clear more quickly.

You also can deposit a personal check drawn on a U.S. bank, which can take a few days to a week to clear, depending on the bank. It is unlikely that you'll be able to cash a personal check in Austria and receive the cash immediately. Banks are reluctant to risk having the check returned due to insufficient funds, especially because they're used to the Eurocheque system, which guarantees each Eurocheque for up to ATS 2.500.

BANK TRANSFER *Überweisung*

How long a bank-to-bank transfer *(Überweisung)* will take depends on how direct the relationship is between the two banks (e.g., if they have to route the funds through intermediary banks, it will take longer). Ask both banks how the funds will be sent, though it shouldn't take longer than a week. Having the transfer made by Telex should be faster, but there is usually an extra charge. You can expedite the process by asking your home bank, before leaving for Austria, how best to communicate transfer instructions.

When transferring or depositing funds in a different currency, the rate of exchange *(Devisenkurs)* does not vary among banks, but the foreign-exchange fee *(Devisenspesen)* and a possible service charge *(Spesen)* may depend on how well the bank knows you. Be sure to ask beforehand.

ACCOUNT MAINTENANCE & SERVICE CHARGES

Account maintenance and service charges (*Kontoführungsprovision* and *Spesen*) vary among banks because these fees depend on the level of banking activity and types of services. Ask your bank to explain its services and corresponding fees.

OVERDRAFT

You earn no interest to very little on positive balances in a current account, but in contrast to the United States, you can arrange for an overdraft limit (often twice your monthly income in the account). This allows you to overdraw a current account without filling out an additional application and without having any payment instructions or cash withdrawals being denied. In effect, this is the convenient equivalent of a small loan or cash advance. The bank will, of course, charge you interest on the overdrawn balance. The amount of your overdraft limit and the amount of interest varies, so ask your bank. In general, banks will settle all account charges, including overdraft interest, on a quarterly basis by debiting your account. Details of the charges will appear on your account statements.

BANK-ACCOUNT STATEMENTS

Account statements (*Kontoauszüge*) are usually issued each time there is activity on the account, which may be as often as once a day. Therefore, your statements and any transaction notices (*Belege*) are usually held at the branch where you opened the account for you to pick up. If you wish to have them mailed, there is usually a service charge.

Most banks have machines to print out account statements (*Konto-ausdrucker*). The accounts are centralized within each banking institution by computer, so you can go to any branch of your bank to do this. Simply insert your bank card as pictured on the machine (with some, you withdraw the card again immediately; with others, the machine will hold it and then return it to you), and all your statements since you last requested one will be printed, showing starting and ending balances and all transactions.

Elongated ring binders for statements can be purchased in most stationery stores and the paper-goods section of some large supermarkets.

BANK CARD

Every current account comes with a bank card, which includes the account number and serves as your identification card at the bank when depositing, withdrawing or conducting any other banking transaction. It can also be used to print out account statements and to open the door after hours at a self-service banking center *(Selbstbedienung or SB)*, which usually has machines to print out statements, withdraw cash and check balances with an ATM card *(Bankomatkarte; see Bankomat Card section)*.

OPTIONAL SERVICES FOR CURRENT ACCOUNTS

In addition to the above, you can also add the following two optional services to your bank card for an extra fee: Eurocheque Card *(Eurochequekarte)* and ATM card *(Bankomatkarte)*.

There is one yearly charge for a bank card with both Eurocheque and Bankomat functions, which is standard among banks and supersedes the single Eurocheque Card fee mentioned below.

EUROCHEQUE & EUROCHEQUE CARD

Instead of personal checks, European banks use the Eurocheque system (also valid in bordering Mediterranean countries). The check *(Scheck)* can be used to pay for most goods and services. A few businesses will charge a small handling fee, which is rare and usually confined to small or low-cost stores. Please note that paying with Eurocheques will decrease slowly. It is intended that banks will not provide cheques anymore from 2002 onwards. A Eurocheque, once completely filled out (see example), is like cash (it is not made out to any specific person or firm). Here are some important things to remember about Eurocheques:

- A bank provides only one set of 10 Eurocheques at a time in case of loss or theft.

- In addition to filling in the currency, amount, place, date and your signature (see sample Eurocheque in this section), you must write your Eurocheque Card number on the back and present the card as proof of your signature and the account number. You may be asked for a form of identification (e.g., passport or Austrian ID Card) as well. *Never* write your signature or your card number on a Eurocheque until you have filled in the amount. A check will *not* be accepted without your Eurocheque Card (unless the recipient knows you personally).

- Banks will guarantee only up to ATS 2.500 per check, or its equivalent in other currencies, regardless of your account balance. The standard currency abbreviations are found at the bottom of your check register (*Währungsbezeichnungen*; see example). If you write the check in a foreign currency, your account will be debited in Austrian Schillings at the exchange rate on the day the transaction is posted against your account.

If you need to make a larger payment, you may be asked to write additional checks (up to three at a time) in order to guarantee that they will all clear. However, some businesses may allow you to write one large amount on one check. Once the check has been accepted as payment, you are no longer liable in the event that it's lost by, or stolen from, the recipient.

If your Eurocheques are lost or stolen, immediately report it to the nearest police station and your bank. If an unauthorized person uses the checks, you are responsible for 10 percent of the total amount or a minimum of ATS 1.000. Your bank guarantees the rest of the damages (if the funds cannot be recovered), but only up to 15 checks per year, per account. You are fully liable for all additional checks.

Eurocheques cost about ATS 25 for a package of 10, and you usually will be given a free checkbook (*Scheckheft*) when you open your account or receive your first set of checks. There also is an annual fee for the Eurocheque Card. These fees are standard in Austria and do not vary among banks.

SAMPLE EUROCHEQUE CARD

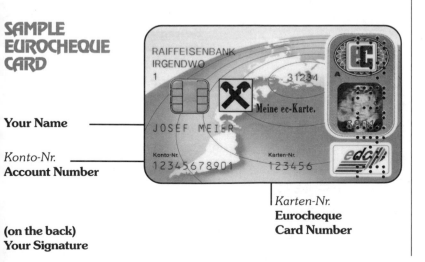

Your Name

Konto-Nr.
Account Number

(on the back)
Your Signature

Karten-Nr.
Eurocheque
Card Number

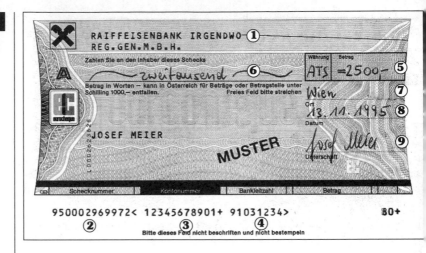

SAMPLE EUROCHEQUE

Printed:

① Name of the bank
② Eurocheque number
③ Account number
④ Bank code

Fill in the following:

⑤ **Währung** Currency abbreviation (ATS = Austrian Schilling. See check register for most other currencies.)

Betrag Amount (in figures) (An elongated = closely precedes first digit of amount.)

⑥ **Betrag in Worten** Amount (in words, which you can write in English)

⑦ **Ort** Place

⑧ **Datum** Date

⑨ **Unterschrift** Your signature

N° (on back)
Eurocheque Card number

DON'T GIVE THIEVES A CHANCE!
Geben Sie Dieben keine Chance!

You'll be asked to sign for each set of Eurocheques you receive and will be given the following security tips as well:

- Do not keep your Eurocheques and your Eurocheque Card in the same place (e.g., both in your wallet).

- Do not carry more than three Eurocheques at a time and keep the rest in a safe place.

- Never leave your Eurocheques and Eurocheque Card unattended in your car, purse, luggage (especially while traveling by train) or a dressing room.

- Do not assume that nothing can go wrong while traveling abroad. Carry some additional form of payment (e.g., cash, traveler's checks or credit cards) when traveling.

We would also add: Never send a check by mail! Use another form of payment. If you must use a check, write *"nur zur Verrechnung"* ("for deposit only") diagonally across the front (which provides a way to trace it, if necessary).

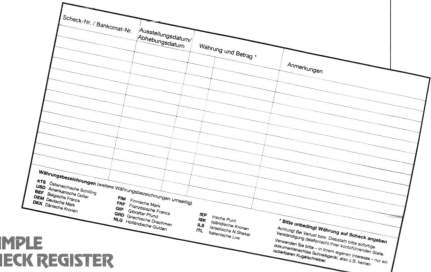

SAMPLE CHECK REGISTER

Note the foreign-currency abbreviations at the bottom.

BANKOMAT CARD

This is the optimal function of your bank card and is the equivalent of an ATM card in the United States. The Bankomat Card, issued with a Personal Identification Number (PIN) code, allows you to withdraw cash 24 hours a day by using a Bankomat machine (identified by a bright blue-and-green B) at any bank in Austria and in much of Europe (look for the Eurocheque emblem, EC, when outside of Austria). Unlike in the United States, you won't be charged for withdrawing money from a bank other than your own. Should you forget your PIN code, notify your bank, which will cancel it immediately and issue you a new one.

Many Austrian banks also have cash *(Bargeld)* withdrawal machines where you can also check your account balance. These, however, can only be used at a branch of your own bank. You can withdraw the maximum amount listed on each machine up to ATS 5.000 total (or its equivalent in other currencies) daily. Should you need to withdraw more than that, you can do so in cash *(Barausziehung)* at the bank's cashier window *(Kassa)* during regular business hours.

Bankomat machines dispense ATS 100 and ATS 1000 bills only (and sometimes run out of 100s, in which case, only 1000s will be available until the machine is refilled). Occasionally you will find a machine with a red sign near where you insert your card, which means the machine is out of order *(ausser Betrieb)*. For your convenience, there is a list of the nearest alternate Bankomat machines. A green sign *(in Betrieb)* means the machine works.

PAYING WITH A BANKOMAT CARD

More and more businesses in Austria and Europe allow you to pay for your purchases with a Bankomat Card. You simply insert your card as shown on the machine at the cashier, type in your PIN code, confirm the amount for payment, and your account will automatically be debited. There is a limit of ATS 10.000 per week and ATS 30.000 per month (this is in addition to the daily limit of ATS 5.000 for cash withdrawals).

"QUICK" SYSTEM

The latest function for the Bankomat Card is the *"Quick"* system of payment. Banks are installing machines (or adding the function to their existing ones) so that you can load up to ATS 1.999 (ATS 1.000 at a time) on your Bankomat Card, which can then be used to pay even the smallest amounts at any business with the corresponding machine. If your bank does not have the machine yet, you can do this at the cashier's window. Banks are encouraging all types of businesses, including bakeries and newsstands, to get these machines, which—thanks to the microchip on the Bankomat Card—can read the amount loaded onto the card, confirm the amount to be paid and then verify the new balance onto the card—all without using your PIN code. This will be quite convenient, but because no PIN code is required, if your card is lost or stolen, the balance of the card cannot be refunded to you. You can, however, replace a damaged card or transfer the balance back to your account at your bank.

HOW TO USE A BANKOMAT MACHINE

You should insert your card as shown, type in your PIN code when prompted, then the amount, confirm with the green button marked *"BESTÄTIGUNG" twice*, correct a mistake with the yellow button marked *"KORREKTUR"* and cancel the transaction with the red button marked *"ABBRUCH."* Your card will be returned to you and your cash will come out through the other longer slot. Should you mistype your PIN code, you will get two more chances. Then, as a security measure, the machine will keep your card. In this event, or if your card is lost or stolen, report it at once to the police and your bank.

TELEPHONE ACCOUNT

This optional service goes by different names at different banks, but the basic idea remains the same. If you are comfortable speaking German on the telephone, or if you're able to deal with someone who speaks English, you may find it convenient. For an annual fee (which varies among banks, so check), you will be given another PIN code to identify yourself over the phone and can then make inquiries, order bank transfers and check your balances and status of payments from anywhere in the world. An added advantage is that the telephone services have longer operating hours than the banks.

SAVINGS ACCOUNTS

ANONYMOUS SAVINGS ACCOUNTS
Anonyme Sparbücher

Although not as famous for its banking secrecy as Switzerland, Austria has a 200-year history of anonymous savings accounts (where the bank doesn't know the account holder's name because a password is used instead) and numbered securities accounts (where usually only two bank employees know the account holder's name), which are both still quite prevalent. Austrians value their banking anonymity as a symbol of personal freedom, but this form of savings account will soon disappear. It is intended that from November 2000 onwards, one will have to show an identity card for opening a new savings account. For credits and withdrawals on these new accounts no identity card will be required, unless the bank has a suspicion of money-laundering. For the exisiting 26 million anonymous savings accounts, there will be a special regulation. Up to June 30, 2002, it will be possible to withdraw money without disclosure requirement. For additional payments into the accounts after November 1, 2000, everybody will need an identity card. The issue of acceptable banking privacy will stay a topic in Austria. Currently, Austrian banks will only release information under an Austrian court order in the case of a criminal offense. With these new regulations, the controversy about the anonymity will soon find an end.

There are next to no restrictions on the movement of funds in and out of Austria, but above a certain amount, the bank processing the transaction is obliged to notify the central bank (Österreichische Nationalbank) as a matter of record.

INTEREST RATES

All savings accounts will earn interest, though the amounts vary among banks. The simple savings book earns the lowest interest rate (but can sometimes be negotiated to a higher percentage) and is accessible at any time. Fixed deposits (ranging in term from six months to six years) will earn higher interest rates the longer the term of the investment. These types of accounts have different names at different banks (e.g., *Vermögenssparbuch*, *Kapitalsparbuch*, *Prämiensparbuch*) but are basically like certificates of deposit (CDs) in the United States. In the event of an emergency, you usually can withdraw money before the term expires, although most of the interest will be lost. Ask about such conditions before committing your money.

SECURITIES ACCOUNT *Wertpapiere*

It is also possible to arrange for a securities (*Wertpapiere*) account. Since 1996, however, these accounts are no longer allowed to be anonymous, although they can still be numbered.

TAXES

Be aware that the local banks will automatically deduct withholding tax on interest earned. Also, Austrian dividends are subject to the withholding tax. At the moment a flat rate of 25% of the capital income will be transferred to the financial authorities. For a resident individual, this tax-deduction is considered as a final income tax. That means you don't have to state this income on your Austrian tax return. No net worth tax is levied in Austria presently.

If an individual has no residency in Austria, he/she has to show proof of this status *(Devisenauslanderschaft)* at the bank and no withholding tax will be deducted from the interest payments. According to the tax treaty between the home country and Austria, withholding tax on dividends may be reduced. Thus, the individual has to declare this income in his/her country of residency for tax purposes. In this case however, being a member of the diplomatic mission of a foreign country or having no residency in Austria, the individual will not qualify for certain government subsidies (e.g. *Bausparkassenprämie*).

SAVINGS & LOAN ACCOUNT
Bausparkassenkonto

Bausparkassenkonto is a popular option in Austria because of its adequate interest rate and government subsidy, which, despite its German name, does not have to be an investment toward future home building or improvements. A predetermined amount is deposited each year (currently ATS 13.760), or automatically withdrawn from your current account in monthly installments, for six years, at the end of which it can be rolled over. For the fixed yearly amount, the government will grant a subsidy. Additional amounts can be deposited on these accounts, but there will be no extra subsidy on these. Your account officer can show you exactly how much money will accumulate over the six-year term based on your investments.

MISCELLANEOUS BANKING SERVICES

FOREIGN-CURRENCY ACCOUNT

Most large Austrian banks also offer current or savings accounts in the major currencies. So if you would like a local account in your home or other currency, ask your account officer for specific terms and conditions.

GOLD COINS

Austria has one of the highest per capita ratios of gold in the world. The Austrian mint *(Münze Österreich AG)* issues the prestigious *Wiener Philharmoniker* and other types of commemorative and bullion gold coins in various sizes, which you can purchase through banks.

SAFE-DEPOSIT BOXES *Safes*

You can rent a safe-deposit box *(Safe)*—which is a good place to store your gold coins, precious jewelry, anonymous account books and other valuables—at any major bank. Here, however, anonymity is not possible because the boxes must be rented under your name. They range in price (per year) depending on the box size. As is true elsewhere, you and the bank will each have a key. You must unlock the box together, but you can deal with the contents privately.

METHODS OF PAYMENT

CREDIT CARDS *Kreditkarten*

Although you may be quite comfortable with using credit cards *(Kreditkarten)*, there are some differences here of which you should be aware. Your bank will issue you one Visa or Eurocard/MasterCard. But, unlike in the United States, if you want another card, you must go to another bank or apply with the credit-card company directly.

There are two levels of annual credit-card fees: one without travel insurance and one with travel insurance (but with either option, the first year you only pay half the fee). Ask your bank or credit-card company for more details. Otherwise, the cards basically function the same way, with one major exception. If you wish, you can arrange to have your monthly balance automatically withdrawn from your current account. You will receive a credit-card statement in the mail indicating the total amount to be deducted from your account, which gives you time to deposit the necessary funds or contact your bank to arrange for a partial payment and carry the balance over at the set interest rate.

Your credit limit will depend on your relationship with the bank issuing the card and your income level. Be sure to clarify this when applying for the card.

If your credit card is lost or stolen and you report it to the credit-card company within 24 hours (the telephone number is issued with the card, or see Emergency ☎ appendix), then you won't be held liable for any misuse of the card. If you report it after 24 hours, your liability is limited to ATS 1.000.

BANK TRANSFER

By far the most prevalent method of payment in Austria, bank transfers are quite efficient. They can be used to pay a bill *(Rechnung)* from a current account for almost any large purchase as well as for many services (including doctors' visits, plumbing, electrical work and local charity donations). However, this is only an option with a current account. If you wish to have access to funds in a savings account, you must transfer them first to a current account and then make the bank transfer.

There are three basic types of bank transfers, but the principle remains the same. Banking information—which includes name, address, bank account number, bank routing code *(Bankleitzahl or BLZ)* and name of the bank—is entered for both the person ordering the payment and the recipient on the appropriate form. The payer signs the form and submits it to his or her own bank, which will stamp all copies of the form, return one as a receipt *(Quittung)* and then process the payment. The amount will appear as a debit on the payer's account by the next day and will reach its destination in a day or so. At this point, it is no longer the payer's responsibility, and the stamped receipt is your confirmation of your order to the bank to make payment *(Bestätigung)*.

SAMPLE ZAHLSCHEIN

There are two parts, so you have to write the same information in two places.

Fill in the following information:

① *Betrag S g* Amount *(Schilling and Groschen)*

② *Eingezahlt von* Your name and address

③ *Hinweise* or *Verwendungszweck* Reference information or purpose

④ *Auftraggeber Konto-Nr.* Your account number

⑤ *Unterschrift des Auftraggebers* Your authorized signature

⑥ *Empfänger* Person or organization to receive payment (may be preprinted)

⑦ *Auftragsbestätigung* Portion as your receipt

PAYMENT ORDER
Zahlschein, Erlagschein

The two different terms reflect their historical origin. The *Erlagschein* was originally a product of the Postal Bank; the *Zahlschein* of the regular banks. The two are, for all intents and purposes, interchangeable. Any organization or business can obtain these preprinted forms, which already contain all the necessary banking information. They will fill in the amount due to them and the reference number (and sometimes even your name and address, but *never* the rest of your banking information), and give it to you or send it with their bill. You fill in the rest of the information, sign it and submit it to your bank for payment from your account. If you prefer, you can also take it with cash to a bank for payment. If you don't have an account at that bank, there is a small charge for this.

If the amount due is still in question (e.g., a mail-order catalog lets you return items you don't want, so you only need to pay for what you keep), then the amount will be left blank and you will have to fill this in as well. Many popular local charities (e.g., *Licht ins Dunkel*, *Nachbar in Not*, *Rettet den Stephansdom*) have their preprinted forms (*Zahlschein* or *Erlagschein*) available at various banks for those who want to contribute.

SAMPLE ERLAGSCHEIN

There are two parts, so you have to write in some information twice.

Fill in the following information:

① **Betrag S g** Amount **(Schilling and Groschen)**

② **Kontonummer des Auftraggebers** Your account number

③ **Auftraggeber/Einzahler** Your name and address

④ **Verwendungszweck** Purpose of payment

⑤ **Unterschrift des Auftraggebers** Your authorized signature

ACCOUNT-TO-ACCOUNT TRANSFER
Überweisung

Überweisung are blank forms available at your bank (which may have the bank's name and routing code preprinted, but nothing else). You use them when you need to make a payment but have not been given a *Zahlschein* (e.g., a doctor has given you his bill for services, or *Honorarnote*, providing his bank information without a form). Many European businesses include their banking information on their letterhead and submit their bills this way.

SAMPLE ÜBERWEISUNG

There are still two sections, but one may be a carbon copy.

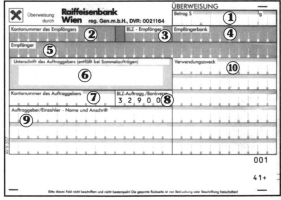

Fill in the following information:

① **Betrag S g**
Amount
(Schilling and
Groschen)

② **Kontonummer des Empfängers** Recipient's account number

③ **BLZ–Empfänger** Recipient's bank-routing code

④ **Empfängerbank** Recipient's bank name

⑤ **Empfänger** Recipient's name

⑥ **Unterschrift des Auftraggebers** Your authorized signature

⑦ **Kontonummer des Auftraggebers** Your account number

⑧ **BLZ–Auftraggeber** Your bank's routing code (may be preprinted)

⑨ **Auftraggeber/Einzahler** Your name and address

⑩ **Verwendungszweck** Purpose (or reference information)

You must fill in all the banking information for both yourself and the recipient, sign the form and take it to the bank, where you'll receive a stamped copy. In the case of a private doctor, this copy would be your proof of payment to submit to the Austrian Health Authority for any reimbursement. Ask your bank to give you extra forms so you can prepare them in advance and save time at the bank.

For both types of transfers, make sure your name and the reference number (e.g., invoice number) of the payment is clear. Otherwise, the recipient may not be able to identify the source and will continue to consider your bill outstanding. While the forms vary slightly from bank to bank, and sometimes from branch to branch, the information and where it goes is the same. Also, some forms are carbon copies so you only have to enter the information once (and your address and banking information will be blackened out on the recipient's copy). With other forms, you have to enter the same information in two or three places.

STANDING PAYMENT ORDER

Any sort of regularly recurring bill can be paid this way. If the amount and monthly date of payment are fixed, the order is called a *Dauerauftrag*. If the amount and date of payment vary from month to month, the order is called an *Einziehungsauftrag* or *Abbuchungsauftrag*. Your account officer will prepare the necessary forms if the payment recipient does not have prepared forms. Either the exact date and amount of payment are determined by you, or you authorize your bank to pay bills received from a specific source. In the latter case, you will usually receive advance notification of the amount and date of the upcoming payment so that you can deposit enough money or question the bill. These standing orders can be changed or canceled at any time by contacting your bank.

Bills often paid by standing orders are for rent, gas, electricity, telephone service, radio/television reception, insurance premiums, tuition and credit-card balances. The monthly installments of a yearly public-transportation pass (*Jahreskarte*) can only be paid this way (the Vienna Public Transit Authority will ask for your banking information on the application, which you sign. It will then be routed to your bank; see Transportation chapter). Your bank is responsible for making the accurate payments on time. Should it make a mistake, which is rare, and the payment is delayed or incorrectly routed, the recipient will still receive it eventually. If your bank makes a payment in error (e.g., pays an order that you just canceled) and you catch it the same day (e.g., by checking your statements) and notify the bank immediately, the payment can usually be reversed the next day without any further complications.

You can also issue a standing order (*Dauerauftrag*) to have a specific amount from your current account automatically transferred to a savings account. This type of order is sometimes called an *Abschöpfungsauftrag*. Any fees charged by your bank for this type of transfer will depend on the account-maintenance plan chosen for your current account. Generally, even the most basic account will include a number of standing orders free of charge, with a nominal fee for changes or cancellations. If you have a higher level account, your standing orders will most likely be free. As usual, check with your account officer.

BANKS IN VIENNA

BRANCH STAFF & SETUP

As you can see from the preceding sections, it is extremely important to find an account officer who is helpful and easy to communicate with. As in most countries, account officers sit at desks away from the main banking area. These personal bank officers (*Betreuer*) not only open accounts but also arrange for credit cards and standing orders, and offer advice on the bank's own investment options and services. They tend to speak better English and are usually more helpful and have more time to discuss your questions and concerns (this is, after all, their job!) than the bank tellers.

Most larger Austrian banks also have a separate department to deal with foreign private customers as well as customers who do not reside in Austria (*Devisenausländer*). Should you wish to maintain a relationship with your Austrian bank after you return to your home country, you will be transferred to this department and your current account will be changed into a "free Schilling" account (*freies Schillingkonto*) or a free account in whatever currency you prefer. You will receive a new account number, Eurocheques, bank card and PIN code. This is required by Austrian banking regulations as different conditions apply to nonresidents, regardless of nationality. But as long as you live in Austria, your banking business will be conducted through the local branch offices.

Other aspects of the overall branch setup (regardless of size) are somewhat different than what foreigners may be used to. Behind a long counter (*Schalter*), various bank employees sit at desks. One of them should approach the counter to see what you need (there is rarely any organized line here). This is where you go to pick up your statements and any transaction notices, order and pick up additional sets of Eurocheques, new bank cards and PIN codes. This is also where you submit any bank transfers for payment or checks for deposit. In fact, just about any business not involving cash or a savings book is conducted at the counter.

CASHIER *Kassa* & CURRENCY EXCHANGE *Change*

The *Kassa* and *Change* are located at separate windows, where there are distinct lines, sometimes quite long. The *Kassa* takes care of all cash transactions (e.g., making change, accepting cash deposits, paying out cash withdrawals) and makes all entries into savings accounts using a machine to verify passwords and enter transactions into savings books. The *Change* window will exchange all major currencies (in smaller branches, this is often the same window as the *Kassa*, if they have this service at all). If you need a large amount or a minor currency, you should contact your bank in advance so it can arrange to have it ready for you to pick up.

BANKING HOURS
Mon - Wed, Fri 8 AM - 12:30 PM, 1:30 PM - 3 PM
Thurs 8 AM - 12:30 PM, 1:30 PM - 5:30 PM
Sat - Sun & Holidays Closed

The main branches (*Zentralen*) of major banks, located in the first district, are usually open through the lunch hour, Monday to Friday (see list on next page).

MAIN BANK LOCATIONS

Major banks offering a full range of banking services and facilities include those listed below. The addresses given here are their main offices in or near the first district, so they should have English-speaking staff. These banks also have branches throughout Vienna and Austria. International-customer or general-customer information numbers (where you can find an English-speaking operator) are also provided.

BANK AUSTRIA AG
  1010, Am Hof 2
  1030, Vordere Zollamtsstr. 13
  ☎ 711 91-0
  ☎ 711 91-6501 (international private banking)

BANK FÜR ARBEIT UND WIRTSCHAFT (BAWAG)
  1010, Seitzergasse 2-4
  ☎ 534 53-0

CREDITANSTALT BANKVEREIN
  1010, Schottengasse 6-8
  ☎ 531 31-0
  ☎ 531 31-4740
  (private customers)

DIE ERSTE ÖSTERREICHISCHE SPARKASSE-BANK AG
  1010, Graben 21 (main office)
  1010, Neutorgasse 2-8
  ☎ 531 00-0 (central operator)

ÖSTERREICHISCHE POSTPARKASSE AG (P.S.K.)
  1018, Georg-Coch-Platz 2
  ☎ 514 00-2986
  (international customers)

RAIFFEISENBANK WIEN
  1010, Michaelerplatz 3
  (Looshaus)
  ☎ 531 73-0
  1030, Am Stadtpark 9
  (next to Vienna Hilton)
  ☎ 717 07-1308
  ☎ 717 07-2614 (customer information)

Creditanstalt offers a very special account package called Club Suxess:

In addition to the complete range of account-related services – e.g. standing orders, cheque card with Bankomat features, CA-Master Card and Diners Club Card – you will benefit from Club Suxess membership.

If you want to get a 25% reduction on restaurant bills, pay half the regular rate at over 1,100 quality hotels worldwide, save 5% on travel arrangements with the "travel bonus service" (also when paying with credit card) and have instant access to cash in an emergency, the Club Suxess account is precisely what you need. Come to Creditanstalt and ask for our "Club Suxess – all benefits at a glance" brochure.

Modern times make it possible – 24-hour banking by computer.

If you have Internet access, you can use the services of CA-b@nking. Visit our Website at "www.creditanstalt.co.at".

Also, feel free to make appointments after our opening hours if you need special advice, e.g. about loans or bigger investments.

e-mail:
christine.wunderbaldinger@creditanstalt.co.at
www.creditanstalt.co.at
Tel.: 320 66 01, Fax: 320 13 25

 CREDITANSTALT

1190 Wien
Sieveringer Straße 3

AUSTRIAN POSTAL BANK
Österreichische Postsparkasse

Österreichische Postsparkasse (P.S.K.) is a unique institution and therefore deserves further explanation. About 2,300 Austrian branches are independent institutions or are located inside post offices. This means you can do your banking while buying stamps and mailing letters or packages. The only real drawbacks are that the staff may be less likely to speak English than at other banks and their services and banking expertise can be somewhat limited.

In addition to all regular banking services, the P.S.K. has some unique features:

- Most post offices open Mon - Fri 8 AM - noon, 2 PM - 6 PM. Banking windows *(Kassenschalter)*, however, close at 5 PM.

- Cash is available in any post office or can be delivered to you by your postal carrier.

- There is no charge for mailing monthly statements.

- There is no charge for envelopes and postage for payment orders.

Even if you don't have an account with P.S.K., you can buy a postal money order *(Postanweisung)*, which is sent to an address, not to a bank account.

The main office of the P.S.K., on Georg-Coch-Platz in the first district, is not only the most likely location for English-speaking staff, but it's also an architectural landmark. Designed by Otto Wagner and built during 1904 - 1906, this building is world famous as an embodiment of the Art Nouveau *(Jugendstil)* style.

VIENNA'S STOCK EXCHANGE *Börse*

The *Börse* is located in the first district on the Schottenring and is the only stock exchange in the country. Founded by imperial decree in 1771 as the main capital market of Central and Eastern Europe, it reopened after World War II in 1948 as a domestic financial market. The exchange has had a volatile recent history, experiencing a boom through the 1980s and peaking in March 1990 at a level that the ATX (*Börsenindex*) has not been able to reach since. The initial boom was largely due to investor overenthusiasm at the collapse of communism in Eastern Europe.

Trading in the stock market must be done through a bank or independent brokerage house. Most of the large banks have securities departments that offer stocks (*Aktien*) and bonds (*Anleihen*) in over-the-counter (OTC) trading, for which they charge a commission. Some of them may also offer discount brokerage services, charging lower commissions. If you're interested, talk to your bank or a financial-services company.

In addition to the banks, Merrill Lynch, a major U.S. brokerage firm, offers full brokerage services in Vienna. Call first to make an appointment.

MERRILL LYNCH
1010, Bauernmarkt 2   Mon - Fri, 8:30 AM - 6 PM
☎ 531 40-0   Mon - Fri, 8:30 AM - 10 PM (telephone)

FINANCIAL SERVICES

Allgemeiner Wirtschaftsdienst (AWD), which is based in Germany with representatives in Austria, Switzerland and Italy, is the largest independent financial-services company in Europe with more than 600,000 clients. Instead of representing one financial institution or product, AWD works with more than 300 international companies, including banks and investment and insurance companies. Financial consultants provide clients with free financial advice and transaction services (they collect fees from the financial institutions themselves). For more information, call the following two AWA members who work with AWD in Austria. Both are fluent in English, German, Spanish and Swedish and would be able to help with general financial planning as well as discuss international investment opportunities.

VIVECA HAMEDER   **EMIRA SOCORRO-REICHENBACH**
☎ 589 19-0   ☎ 589 19-0 or
Mobile ☎ (0664) 231 94 64   ☎ 505 33 03 (home)

BANKING TERMS

Abbuchungsauftrag Standing order

Aktien Stocks

Auftraggeber Party authorizing a payment

Bankleitzahl (BLZ) Bank sorting code

Bankomat Automatic Teller Machine (ATM)

Bankomatkarte ATM card

Barabhebung Cash withdrawal

Barerlag Cash deposit

Bargeld Cash

Beleg Transaction advice

Bestätigung Confirmation slip

Betrag Amount

Börse Stock exchange

Buchung Booked entry

Change Foreign-currency exchange

Dauerauftrag Standing payment order (fixed date and amount)

Devisenausländer Foreign nonresident customer

Deviseninländer Foreign-resident customer

Devisenkurs Foreign-exchange rate

Einziehungsauftrag Standing payment order (variable date and amount)

Empfänger Party to receive a payment

Eurochequekarte Eurocheque Card

Girokonto Current account

Hinweise Reference information

Kassa Cashier

Kontoausdrucker Machine to print account statements

Kontoauszüge Account statements

Kontoführungsprovision Account maintenance fee

Kontonummer Account number

Kreditkarten Credit cards

Münzen Coins

Passwort, Losungswort Password

Postanweisung Postal money order

Quittung Receipt

Rechnung, Honorarnote Bill for payment

Safe Safe-deposit box

Schalter Counter

Scheckheft Checkbook

Scheine Paper money

Selbstbedienung (SB) Self-service center

Sparbuch Savings account (also savings book itself)

Spesen Fees

Überbringer Bearer

Überweisung Transfer

Verwendungszweck Purpose of payment

Währung Currency

Währungsbezeichnungen Currency abbreviations

Wertpapiere Securities

Zahlschein, Erlagschein Preprinted transfer forms

Zentrale Main office

Establishing your own business, starting professional activities or taking residence in Austria will have the effect that individuals and companies will become subject to Austrian taxes. Choosing a good set up, finding the optimal form of organization for the individual needs, etc. requires lots of information concerning the local tax situation, social security systems and international treaties. Without these treaties, income could become taxable in two or more countries. There is quite a lot of bureaucracy and a real jungle of laws to go through. Professional help from a local tax advisor or an accounting company can be a great advantage in different matters, not only in keeping the tax burden as low as possible. You can request a list of registered professionals and companies from the Austrian Chamber of Accountants and Advisors "Kammer der Wirtschaftstreuhänder" 1120, Schönbrunnerstrasse 222-228/1/6/2, ☎ 811 73 0.

TAXATION OF INDIVIDUALS

Resident individuals are liable for Income Tax *(Eink*ommensteuer) on their world-wide income and on some types of capital gains. Austrian-source dividends and bank deposit interest received by a resident individual are usually subject to final withholding taxes. Individuals are considered residents if they have a dwelling in Austria that they apparently intend to retain and occupy, or if they spend more than six consecutive months in Austria. Nationals of countries that are part of the European Economic Union are also treated as residents for tax purposes on request if at least 90% of their income is Austrian source or if their other income does not exceed certain limits.

 Spouses are taxed separately, and children are taxed separately from their parents.

Taxable income of individuals comprises income arising from agriculture and forestry, business or trade, independent professional services, employment, capital investments, rentals and royalties, and miscellaneous income (including some capital gains). Taxable income is ascertained by aggregating the net income of these catagories (after deducting expenses incurred in earning the income of each catagory) and deducting from the net total special personal expenses and extraordinary charges. Income tax is not deductible.

•   Compulsory Social Security Premiums are 100% deductible, whether domestic or foreign. Employers and employees must both make social security contributions, which are calculated as a percentage of employees' monthly gross earnings up to a maximum in the year 2000 of ATS 43.200 per month. Employee contribution rates for the year 2000 are 17.65% for salaried employees and 18.2% for workers. Employer contribution rates are 21.65% for salaried employees and 24.05% for workers. Exemption from or a refund of contributions may be available in the case of foreign employees under the terms of a relevant social security treaty.

• Special Personal Expenses include, as a rule, life insurance premiums, home construction and improvement expenses, subscriptions to new issues of qualifing shares, certain recurring charges and annuities, and tax advisor fees.

• Extraordinary Charges are unusually burdensome expenses, such as those arising from an accident or illness.

• Income tax payable by a resident taxpayer is reduced by various lump-sum credits. There is a general credit, a credit for a married taxpayer whose spouse's income does not exceed ATS 30.000, or for a single person with children. Credits for dependent children are also available. A credit is given as relief for travel expenses to work, and a credit is given for a taxpayer with employment income subject to wage tax.

• Income Tax Rates range from 21% up to 50% with a base income of ATS 50.000 at 0%.

Employers must withhold wage tax (*Lohnsteuer*), a form of income tax, paid to resident and non-resident employees. The tax is usually the final tax on employment income, unless for some reason an income tax assessment is required. Residents need not file tax returns if their income is below stated limits or subject to Wage or Withholding Tax.

EXPATRIATE RELIEF

Up to 35% of an expatriate employee's taxable income may be paid to the employee tax free if the employer reimburses certain expenses. To qualify for the relief, the employee may not have been resident in Austria in the preceding ten years, must have been sent to Austria on behalf of his or her foreign employer and must now be on the payroll of an Austrian group company, must be seconded for no more than five years, and must maintain his or her foreign residence for the term of the Austrian employment. The following expenses are covered, provided that they are reimbursed by the employer: moving expenses, double household costs, schooling costs for children, and travel expenses to the foreign headquarters and residence. Limits are imposed on the amount of individual expenses that may be deducted.

DIPLOMATIC STATUS

Members of the diplomatic mission in Austria, their family and their house-employees are not liable to Austrian income tax on compensations for their functions, if they are not Austrian citizens and are not permanent residents in Austria. Other income from Austrian sources will be treated as income received by a non-resident person.

FORMS OF BUSINESS ORGANIZATIONS

The main forms of business organizations in Austria are the stock corporation *(Aktiengesellschaft - AG)*, limited liability company *(Gesellschaft mit beschränkter Haftung - Ges.mbH)*, general commercial partnership *(Offene Handelsgesellschaft - OHG)*, and limited partnership *(Kommanditgesellschaft - KG)*. Other forms include cooperatives, branches of domestic and foreign companies, and partnerships formed under civil law. Of these forms, foreign investors usually choose the Ges.mbH. With the exception of civil law partnerships, OHGs and KGs, all of the entities mentioned above are subject to corporate income tax. Partnerships, OHGs and KGs are not chargeable entities for corporate or personal income tax purposes; the partners themselves are taxed on their shares of the partnership's profits.

•   Foreigners may own 100% of an Austrian enterprise. Austrian participation in the management of the enterprise is not required.

•   A resident company is liable for corporate income tax *(Körperschaftsteuer)* of 34% on its world-wide profits, including capital gains. A minimum tax regulation exists. A company is resident in Austria if its legal seat or place of management is located there.

•   Most Austrian tax treaties exempt foreign-source income from corporate income tax, but the foreign tax credit is the usual method for relieving double taxation in the case of dividends, interest and royalties.

•   The remuneration of management board members is usually fully deductible; that of supervisory board members is only 50% deductible.

OTHER TAXES

VALUE ADDED TAX
(Umsatzsteuer - USt)

Umsatzsteuer - USt). VAT, is levied on the delivery of goods and performance of services in Austria by an entrepreneur, for consideration, in the course of business and on the importation of goods from non-EU countries, unless the transaction is specifically exempted. Entrepreneurs can generally credit the VAT they have been charged by suppliers against the liability for the VAT that they charged to customers within the same period. The standard rate is 20%. A 10% rate applies e.g. to the rent paid for apartments and other homes, to sales of food and farm products and other essentials. Members of a diplomatic mission in Austria have the right to buy goods and services free of Austrian VAT as long as they do not have Austrian citizenship or permanent residency in Austria. Please note that there are special rulings for the procedure.

INHERITANCE AND GIFT TAX
(Erbschafts und Schenkungssteuer)

(Erbschafts und Schenkungssteuer).Individuals are liable for inheritance and gift tax on property acquired by reason of death or by way of gift. The tax applies to property located in Austria and abroad, unless the beneficiary and the deceased person or donor are both non-resident; in that case, the tax applies only to specified types of Austrian property set out in the law. Rates vary from 2% to 60%, depending on the recipient's degree of relationship to the deceased or donor and the value of the property transferred. Bonds subject to Austrian final taxation and Austrian savings books are exempted from inheritance tax.

 Add valorem and fixed-sum duties are levied on a variety of documents and legal transactions.

CAPITAL TRANSFER TAX
(Kapitalverkehrssteuer)

Contributions to the capital of a domestic corporate entity or to the assests of a branch of a foreign company are subject to a 1% Capital Transfer Tax. Transfers of securities are subject to a 0.02% to a 2.5% transfer tax,

A FEE IS LEVIED IN ADDITION TO VAT ON AUTOMOBILES

(*Normverbrauchsabgabe* - NOVA). This fee is calculated by applying a percentage based on fuel consumption to the net value of the automobile, excluding VAT. VAT at the standard rate is levied on the net value plus the fee.

REAL ESTATE TAXES

A municipal **Real Estate Tax** (*Grundsteuer*) is levied annually on owners of Austrian real estate at rates ranging from 0.8% to 1% of the tax value which is considerably below market value.

Transfers of Real Estate are generally subject to a 3.5% tax (*Grunderwerbsteuer*) on the sales price or market value. In addition, a 1% registration fee will be triggered.

This chapter has been provided by Deloitte & Touche, Austria

Food—we can't live without it. But when you first arrive—and don't know a word of German—you may think you'll go hungry before you can understand a label or even ask the grocer for some apples. Moreover, you miss your favorite foods from home and soon realize that finding the necessary ingredients here is not so easy. Don't be discouraged, however. Many have found what they needed or have adapted recipes. Better yet, try some of Austria's specialities and add new creations to your repertoire. And what better place to initiate your taste buds than at Vienna's markets?

The Austrian Seal of Quality (*goldenes AUSTRIA-Gütesiegel*) indicates Austrian products that have been tested in state-run or state-authorized testing facilities. A product bearing this symbol is of proven quality.

KINDS OF STORES

Apotheke	Pharmacy (carries some baking ingredients)
Bäckerei	Bakery
Drogerie	Drugstore (carries some health food)
Feinkost, Delikatessen	Delicatessen
Fischhandlung	Fish shop
Fleischerei	Butcher
Konditorei	Pastry shop
Lebensmittelladen	Grocery store
Obst & Gemüse-Geschäft	Fruits and vegetables (produce) store
Papiergeschäft	Stationery store (for paper napkins, candles, place cards)
Reformhaus	Health-food store
Weinhandel	Wine shop

SPECIALTY STORES

While all markets carry the basic items, the following stores also sell international goods and gourmet specialties. They are listed in order by district, and business hours are only indicated for those that don't have standard schedules.

BILLA CORSO
1010, Kärntner Ring 9-13
(in the *Ringstrassen Galerien*)
☎ 512 66 25

This upscale supermarket has a bakery, delicatessen, Italian-food counter, seafood counter and imported products (*Fauchon*).

DA CONTE ALIMENTARI
1010, Judenplatz 1
☎ 533 64 46-0

In addition to Italian packaged and fresh specialties to take out, this Italian deli has a small area, inside to sit and eat, as well as outdoor seating in warm weather (Mon-Sat noon-3 PM, 6:30 PM-midnight).

GEBRÜDER WILD
1010, Neuer Markt 10-11
☎ 512 53 03

This is an old Viennese store that sells meat, wine, imported canned goods and salads and sandwiches. They also offer party services.

WALTER REIMER
1010, Wollzeile 26
☎ 512 14 33

It carries cake-decorating supplies.

JOH. SCHÖNBICHLER & CO.
1010, Wollzeile 4
☎ 512 18 68 or ☎ 512 18 16

This tea importer also stocks spices, essences and a limited selection of condiments and Asian food items.

AINHORN
1020, Grosse Stadtgutgasse 7
☎ 214 56 21
Mon-Thurs 9 AM - 5:30 PM,
Fri 8 AM - noon

This store sells kosher meat, poultry and cold cuts, as well as some canned, frozen and packaged foods.

NELLY MALKOW
1020, Tempelgasse 86
☎ 214 83 94
Mon-Thurs 9 AM - 7 PM
Fri 10 AM - NOON

This shop carries 100-percent kosher wine, canned and frozen foods, and cheese.

REBENWURZEL & CO.
1020, Grosse Mohrengasse 19
☎ 216 66 40
Mon - Thurs 11 AM - 6 PM,
Fri 9 AM - noon

This shop sells kosher food, including frozen (and occasionally fresh) meat, and has a deli section.

ASIA SHOP
1040, Rechte Wienzeile 9A
☎ 586 62 33 or ☎ 587 64 99

This shop, located in the *Naschmarkt*, sells Chinese, Japanese and Korean items.

NIPPON YA
1040, Faulmanngasse 5
☎ 586 10 84

This shop carries Japanese specialties.

JULIUS MEINL AM GRABEN
1010, Graben 19
(corner of Naglergasse)
☎ 532 33 34
Fax 532 33 34-20

The Julius Meinl flagship store was recently completely rebuilt and now offers on two levels the finest gourmet foods from all over the world. The shopping experience here is world class. An attractive stairway and elevators lead to the upper floor food departments. There is an excellent restaurant with a beautiful view of the Vienna city centre. Regular culinary events take place. You can follow what's happening at www.meinl.com on the Internet.

For the coming Holiday Season they will offer an internet-based ordering system for gifts and holiday products.

You can phone or fax orders for pick-up or delivery.

BOBBY'S

1040, Schleifmühlgasse 8
☎ 586 75 34
Fax 587 26 63

This store carries British products, including sausages and pastries. They also carry light-and dark-brown sugar, British icing sugar (very close to American confectioner's sugar), Karo light and dark corn syrup, Cheerios, Dr. Pepper, root beer, canned pumpkin, and brownie and muffin mix. They can also order specific items for you. Free delivery is available for minimum orders of ATS 2.000, otherwise fees depend on where you live.

ASIA FOOD CENTER

1050, Wiedner Hauptstrasse 114
☎ 544 23 46

This store sells Chinese, Japanese, Korean and Thai products, including fresh Chinese vegetables and kitchenware/cooking utensils.

PICCINI

1060, Linke Wienzeile 4
☎ 587 52 54

Across from the *Naschmarkt*, this shop specializes in imported pasta, cheese, wine, olive oil and other Italian items.

VIENNA DEKOR SÜSSWAREN

1080, Josefstädter Strasse 30
☎ 405 67 53
Fax 403 74 98

This stores carries everything you need to decorate a cake, including a wide selection of novelty decorations.

CASA MEXICO

1090, Fuchsthallergasse 4
☎ 315 45 39

This store carries imported Mexican favorites. They make fresh corn and flour tortillas and carry a variety of frozen prepared foods.

METRO

1110, Landwehrstrasse 6
2331, Vosendorf, Ortsstrasse 23-27 (this location is bigger)

At this membership warehouse/bulk goods store, you'll find everything from fax machines to frozen shrimp. If you have a *Legitimationskarte* (blue or red), you'll receive a temporary membership card to use at the checkout counter, and they will not charge you VAT if you spend over ATS 1.000.

L'ORA GUISTA

1190, Billrothstrasse 14
☎ 369 52 20

This shop carries imported Italian foods including prosciutto and cheeses. Fresh pasta made daily and antipastos are available for take out or eating inside. They also cater.

FRUITS & VEGETABLES *Obst und Gemüse*

There are produce stands and stores in every neighborhood. They carry fresher items than most supermarkets—though not quite as fresh as open-air markets like the *Naschmarkt*. Usually, the salesperson selects produce for you, so avoid touching, picking and squeezing, unless you're told it's okay.

FRUIT *Obst*

Apples *Äpfel*
Apricots *Marillen, Aprikosen*
Avocado *Avocado*
Bananas *Bananen*
Blueberries *Heidelbeeren*
Cantaloupe *Zuckermelone,*
Melone
Cherries *Kirschen*
Coconut *Kokosnuss*
Cranberries *Preiselbeeren*
Currants
Ribisel, Johannisbeeren
  Black *schwarz*
  Red *rot*
  White *weiss*
  Dried *Korinthen*
Dates *Datteln*
Elderberry *Hollunder, Holler*
Figs *Feigen*
Gooseberries *Stachelbeeren*
Grapefruit *Grapefruit*
Grapes *Weintrauben*
Honeydew *Galiamelone,*
Honigmelone
Kiwi *Kiwi*
Lemons *Zitronen*
Lime *Limone, Limonette*
Mango *Mango*
Nectarines *Nektarinen*
Oranges *Orangen*
Peaches *Pfirsiche*
Pears *Birnen*
Persimmon *Persimone*
Pineapple *Ananas*

Plums *Zwetschken, Pflaumen*
  Greengage plums
  Ringlotten
  Prunes *Dörrpflaumen*
Pomegranate *Granatapfel*
Pumpkin *Kürbis*
(but this also means "squash")
Raspberries *Himbeeren*
Strawberries *Erdbeeren*
Tangerines *Mandarinen,*
Satsumas, Clementinen
Tomatoes *Tomaten, Paradeiser*
  Cherry tomatoes *Kirsch-*
  tomaten, Partytomaten
  Plum tomatoes *italienische*
  Tomaten, längliche Tomaten
  Sun-dried tomatoes
  getrocknete Tomaten
Watermelon *Wassermelone*

Asparagus & Mushroom Seasons

In early spring, the appearance of fresh asparagus is reason for celebration. It's available in abundance so restaurants use it to create special dishes. This period is known as *Spargelzeit* (asparagus time). In the fall comes another tasty treat. *Pilzwochen* (which means "mushroom weeks") signals the time when a variety of fresh edible mushrooms appear in markets and are featured in restaurant specials.

VEGETABLES Gemüse

Artichoke *Artischocke*

Asparagus *Spargel*

Aubergine/eggplant *Melanzani*

Beans *Bohnen*
  Dried white beans *Weisse Bohnen*
  Green beans *Fisolen*
  Kidney beans *Kidney Bohnen*
  Lentils *Linsen*
  Lima beans *Dicke Bohnen*
  Yellow beans *Spargelbohnen*

Belgian endive/chicory *Endivie*

Broccoli *Broccoli*

Brussel sprouts *Kohlsprossen*

Cabbage *Kohl*
  Napa/Chinese cabbage *Chinakohl* (sometimes *Japankohl*)
  Red cabbage *Rotkraut*
  White (regular) cabbage *Weisskraut*

Carrots *Karotten, Möhre*

Cauliflower *Karfiol*

Celery greens *Zellergrün*

Celery root *Zeller*

Celery stalks *Stangensellerie*

Chicory/Belgian endive *Endivie*

Corn *Mais, Kukuruz*

Cucumber *Gurken*

Eggplant/aubergine *Melanzani*

Fennel *Fenchel*

Kale (curly) *(Grün) Kohl*

Kohlrabi *Kohlrabi, Kohlrüben*

Leeks *Porree, Lauch*

Lettuce *Salat*
  Endive lettuce *Frissee, Endiviensalat*
  Iceberg lettuce *Eisberg salat, Bummerlsalat*
  Leaf lettuce *Grüner Salat, Blattsalat*
  Romaine lettuce *Romaine*

Mushrooms *Pilze, Schwammerln*
  White button mushrooms *Champignons*
  Boletus mushrooms *Herrenpilze, Steinpilze*
  Chanterelle mushrooms *Eierschwammerl, Pfifferlinge*
  Shitake *Shiitake*

Okra *Okra*

Onions *Zwiebeln*
  Green onions *Jungzwiebeln*
  Red onions *rote Zwiebeln*
  Yellow onions *Zwiebeln*

Parsley root *Petersilwurzel* (good in soups)

Parsnips *gelbe Rüben*

Peas *Erbsen*
Snow peas/mangetout *Zuckererbsen* (but these can also be regular sweet peas)

Pepper *Paprika*
Green pepper *grüner Paprika*
Red pepper *roter Paprika*
Yellow pepper *gelber Paprika*

Potatoes *Erdäpfel, Kartoffeln*
Red potatoes *rote Erdäpfel, rote Kartoffeln*
Kipfler
Good for potato salad
Sieglinde
Available year-round;

good for boiling and making salads
Runde Good for baking, mashing and making dumplings

Radishes (red) *Radieschen*
White/daikon radishes *Rettich*

Shallots *Schalotten*

Spinach *Spinat*

Squash *Kürbis* (also pumpkin)

Sweet potatoes *Süsskartoffeln*

Turnips *weisse Rüben*

Water chestnuts *Wasserkastanien* (available at Asian markets and the *Naschmarkt*)

Yams *Yamswurzel*

Zucchini/courgette/marrow *Zucchini*

STAPLE FOODS

Anchovies *Sardellen*

Baking powder *Backpulver* (in small envelopes)

Baking soda *Natron, Speisesoda* (in small envelopes)

Bouillon *Bouillon*
Beef *Rindsuppe*
Chicken *Hühnersuppe*
Vegetable *Gemüsesuppe*

Bread crumbs *Paniermehl, Semmelbrösel*

Chocolate, baking *Kochschokolade, Haushaltsschokolade*
Chocolate chips *Schokoladetropfen* (in small box in baking section)
Chocolate, semisweet *Zartbitter*

Couscous *Couscous*

Condensed milk, (sweetened) *Gezuckerte Kondensmilch* (in tubes or jars)

Cornmeal *Maismehl*
Coarse *Maisgriess*
Fine *Fein*
Polenta *Polenta*

Corn starch *Maisstärke* (*Maizena* is a brand name)

Corn syrup Not available

Cream of tartar *Doppelweinstein, Weinsteinsäure* (available at drugstores and pharmacies)

Farina *Griess*

Flour *Mehl* (available in various grades and textures)

All-purpose flour *700 glatt, Universal (480 glatt)*
Buckwheat flour
Buchweizenmehl (found in health-food stores)
Double-sifted *doppelgriffig*
Extra-fine flour
Mehl extra fein
Potato flour *Kartoffelmehl*
Sifted *griffig* (for breads)
Whole-grain flour
Vollkornmehl
Whole-wheat flour
Vollweizenmehl

> **TIP** *Universal* flour is not for cakes and cookies.

Food coloring
Lebensmittelfarbe

Frozen food *Tiefkühlkost*

Gelatin *Gelatine* (packaged in sheets in baking section)

Graham crackers Not available, but an adequate substitute in recipes is Digestive Biscuits, from British-import stores (see Specialty Stores section of this chapter)

Honey *Honig*

Horseradish *Kren, Meerrettich*

Jam *Marmelade*

Ketchup *Ketchup*

Lard *Schweineschmalz*

Maple syrup *Ahornsirup*

Mayonnaise *Mayonnaise*

Mincemeat pie filling
Available at British shops (see Specialty Stores section)

Miso paste Available at Asian markets (see Specialty Stores)

Molasses *Melasse*

Mustard *Senf* (in many varieties)
Noodles *Nudeln*
Nuts *Nüsse*
  Almonds *Mandeln*
  Chestnuts *Maroni*
  Hazelnuts *Haselnüsse*
  Peanuts *Erdnüsse*
  Pine nuts *Pinienkerne*
  Walnuts *Walnüsse*

Oatmeal *Haferflocken*

Oil *Öl*
  Corn oil *Maiskeimöl*
  Olive oil *Olivenöl*
  Sunflower oil
  Sonnenblumenöl
  Vegetable oil *Pflanzenöl*

Olives *Oliven*

Peanut butter *Erdnussbutter*

Pickles
  Sweet pickles *Essiggurken*
  Tart (not really dill) pickles *Salzgurken*

Powdered milk *Fix Milch* brand of *Milchpulver* (not readily available)

Raisins *Rosinen*

Rice *Reis*
  Brown rice *Naturreis*

Salsa *Salsa*

Shortening *Ceres, Frivissa* (coconut-oil shortening)

Soy sauce *Soyasoß*

Stuffing (dried bread cubes)
Semmelwürfel

Sugar *Zucker*
  American brown sugar
  Rohr-Zucker Feinkristall)
  Cane *Rohrzucker*

Confectioners'/icing
Available at Bobby's (see
Specialty Stores section)
Cube *Würfelzucker*
Glazing *Staubzucker*
(tends to have gritty texture)
Powdered *Streuzucker* (so
fine that it's used only for
dusting baked goods)
Rock *Kandiszucker*
White crystal *Normal-
kristall-* and *Feinkristallzucker*

Tofu Available at Asian markets
and the *Naschmarkt*

Tomatoes (crushed) *Tomaten-
fruchtfleisch in Stücken*

Tomatoes (whole) *ganze
Tomaten*

Tomato paste *Tomatenmark*

Tomato sauce *passierte
Tomaten*

Tuna *Thunfisch*
Vinegar *Essig*
  Balsamic vinegar
  Aceto Balsamico
  Cider vinegar *Apfelessig*
  Red-wine vinegar
  Rotwein Essig
  White vinegar *Säureessig*
Wasabi Available at Japanese
stores (see Specialty Stores section)
Wheat germ *Weizenkeim* (in
health-food sections and stores)
White-bread crumbs
Semmelbrösel
Yeast *Hefe*
  Dry *getrocknet*
  (in small envelopes)
  Moist cubes *Frischhefe*
  (in dairy case)

SPICES & HERBS *Gewürze und Kräuter*

Allspice *Piment*
Almond extract
Bittermandelöl
Arrowroot *Pfeilwurzelmehl*
Basil *Basilikum*
Bay leaves *Lorbeerblätter*
Caraway seed *Kümmel*
Cayenne pepper
Cayennepfeffer
Celery salt *Selleriesalz*
Celery seed *Selleriesamen*
Chervil *Kerbel*
Chili pepper *Chili-Pfeffer*
Chili powder *Chili gemahlen*
Chives *Schnittlauch* (fresh in the
produce section)
Cilantro/coriander *Koriander*
(found at the *Naschmarkt*, Meinl
am Graben & Billa Corso)
Cinnamon *Zimt*

Cloves *Nelken*
Cumin (ground) *Kreuzkümmel*
Cumin gemahlen
Curry powder *Curry*
Dill (weed) *Dille, Dillspitzen*
Fennel seeds *Fenchelsamen*
Garlic *Knoblauch*
  Granulated *granuliert*
  Powder *Pulver*
  (It also comes as a paste in a
  tube and as cloves in a jar.)
Ginger *Ingwer* (also found fresh
in the produce section)
Juniper berries
Wacholderbeeren
Lemon peel *Zitronenschale*
Lovage *Liebstöckel*
Mace *Muskatblüte*
Marjoram *Majoran*
Mint *Minze*

Mustard seed *Senfkörner*
Nutmeg *Muskatnuss*
Onion powder *Zwiebelpulver*
Orange peel *Orangenschale*
Oregano *Oregano*
Paprika *Edelsüss*
  Mild *mild*
  Hot *scharf*
Parsley *Petersilie*
  Curled *Krauspetersilie*
  Flat/Italian *italienische
Petersilie*
Pepper *Pfeffer*
  Black pepper *Pfeffer
schwarz*
  White pepper *Pfeffer weiss*
Peppercorns *Pfefferkörner*
Peppermint *Pfefferminze*
Poppy seed *Mohnsamen*
Poultry seasoning *Geflügel-
gewürz, Brathendlgewürz*
Rosemary *Rosmarin*

Sage *Salbei*
Savory *Bohnenkraut*
Sesame seeds Available at
Asian markets
Tarragon leaves *Estragon*
Thyme *Thymian*
Turmeric *Gelbwurz, Kurkuma*
Sorrel *Sauerampfer*
Salt *Salz*
  Iodized *mit Jod, jodiert*
  (all salt is iodized)
  Sea salt *Meersalz*
  Table salt *Tafelsalz*
Vanilla *Vanille*
  Liquid extract *Extrakt*
  Vanilla beans
  Vanilleschoten (in glass tubes
  in the spice section)
  (*Vanillezucker* in small enve-
  lopes is what Austrians use.)

TIP Vanilla essence can be made by slicing two vanilla bean pods, adding 100ml alcohol (Weingeist, available from an Apotheke) and letting the solution sit for three weeks.

BAKING SUPPLIES

Baking-pan liner *Backpapier*
(baking-pan and cookie-sheet
liner)
Cheesecloth *Seihtuch*
Cupcake papers *Papier-
Backförmchen*
Pastry bag *Tortenspritztüte*

Plastic bags *Plastiksäcke*
  Sandwich (snack) bag
  Jausen-Beutel, Jausensäcke
  Trash/rubbish bag
  Müllbeutel, Müllsäcke
Toothpicks *Zahnstocher*
Waxed paper *Butterbrot-
Papier*

BAKING-INGREDIENT CONVERSIONS

7-gram envelope of *Germ* =
(sold in packets of 3 envelopes)

2 TBSP + $^1/_4$ tsp yeast
(= $^1/_2$ cube fresh yeast)
(enough for $^1/_2$ kg flour)

14-gram envelope of *Natron* =
(sold in packets of 3 envelopes)

2 tsp baking soda

16-gram envelope of *Backpulver* =
(sold in packets of 5 envelopes)

1 TBSP baking powder

KITCHEN SUBSTITUTIONS

- *Kalle 2000 Extra-Grösse Brat-Folie* is a long sheet of heatproof plastic that is the same circumference as American cooking bags for meat up to 12 pounds. Whereas American brands are constructed as bags with tie closures, the Austrian brand can be cut to any length and the cook ties both ends off. A six-kilogram turkey can be forced inside.

- Austrian recipes call for *Vanillezucker* **(vanilla sugar),** which comes in eight-gram envelopes (usually sold in packets of three). For liquid vanilla extract, try Julius Meinl am Graben or one of the British-import stores (see Specialty Stores).

- For 1 $^1/_2$ cups **corn syrup,** dissolve one cup sugar in one-half cup water.

- *Preiselbeerenkompott* (found in jars in the jam section of the supermarket) is equivalent to **cranberry sauce** with whole berries.

CONVERTED AMERICAN MEASUREMENTS

Ounces to Grams

KEY

grams	g	**tablespoon**	TBSP
ounces	oz	**teaspoon**	tsp
pounds	lb		

All measurements are approximately equal to.
Sources vary, so it's always best to weigh your own ingredients.

Almonds	1 cup		150 g
Bread crumbs	1 cup fresh crumbs	2 $^3/_4$ oz	83 g
	1 cup dry crumbs	3 oz	90 g
Butter & other fat	1 cup	8 oz	227 g
	1 stick $^1/_4$ lb	4 oz	115 g
	1 TBSP	$^1/_2$ oz	15 g
Cheese	1 cup grated	4 oz	115 g
	1 TBSP grated	$^1/_2$ oz	7 $^1/_2$ g
Chutney	$^1/_4$ cup		75 g
Cocoa	1 cup	4 oz	115 g
	1 TBSP	$^1/_2$ oz	15 g
Cottage cheese	1 cup	8 oz	227 g
Cream cheese	1 cup		230 g
Currants/sultanas	1 cup	8 oz	227 g
Eggs	1 medium egg		55 g
	1 large egg	2 oz	60 g
	6–8 egg whites	1 cup	
Flour	1 cup	4 oz	115 g
	4 TBSP	1 oz	30 g
Honey	1 cup		330 g
Meat	1 cup cubed/diced	8 oz	227 g
Mushrooms	2 cups fresh		250 g
Nuts	1 cup ground		90 g
Nuts	1 cup chopped		155 g
Oats (rolled)	1 cup		100 g
Onions	1 cup chopped	5 oz	145 g
Raisins	1 cup	5 $^1/_2$ oz	160 g
Rice	1 cup uncooked		200 g
	4 cups cooked		200 g
Salt	1 TBSP		15 g
Shallots	1 TBSP minced		15 g
Sugar	$^1/_2$ cup granulated		100 g
	1 cup granulated	6 $^1/_2$ oz	220 g
	1 cup powdered	4 $^1/_2$ oz	130 g
	$^1/_2$ cup American brown		70 g
Yogurt	$^1/_2$ cup	4 $^1/_4$ oz	125 g

CONVERTED METRIC MEASUREMENTS

Grams to Ounces

100 grams

Butter or other fat	3 ¹/₂ oz	¹/₂ cup less 1 TBSP
Cheese (grated)	3 ¹/₂ oz	1 cup less 2 TBSP
Bread crumbs (fresh)	3 ¹/₂ oz	1 ¹/₄ cups
Cocoa	3 ¹/₂ oz	1 cup less 2 TBSP
Cottage cheese	3 ¹/₂ oz	¹/₂ cup less 1 TBSP
Currants/sultanas	3 ¹/₂ oz	¹/₂ cup less 1 TBSP
Flour	3 ¹/₂ oz	1 cup less 2 TBSP
Meat (cubed)	3 ¹/₂ oz	¹/₂ cup less 1 TBSP
Onions (chopped)	3 ¹/₂ oz	³/₄ cup less 2 TBSP
Raisins	3 ¹/₂ oz	³/₄ cup less 1 TBSP
Rice	3 ¹/₂ oz	¹/₂ cup less 1 TBSP

DAIRY PRODUCTS *Milchprodukte*

Dairy products are packaged in smaller quantities, and the refrigerator shelf life seems to be much shorter than for North American products. Fat content is listed as *"Fettgehalt."*

MILK MILCH

Buttermilk *Buttermilch*
Evaporated milk *Alpenmilch*
(available in bottles near coffee
section)
Fortified milk *Kindermilch*
Fresh milk *Frischmilch*
(has a shorter shelf life and lower
bacterial count)

Low-fat milk *Magermilch,
Fettarm Milch, Leicht Milch*
Sour milk *Sauermilch*
**Whole (homogenized)
milk** *Vollmilch*
Yogurt *Joghurt*

> **TIP** *Haltbarmilch* is milk with an extended shelf life, which
> is found on regular store shelves (and available in different fat
> contents). It doesn't require refrigeration until opened, after
> which it keeps for two to three days. The expiration date is
> stamped on top of the container.

BUTTER & CREAM *Butter & Rahm, Obers*

Butter *Butter*
  Lightly salted butter
  Teebutter mild gesalzen
  Sweet butter *Teebutter*

Cottage cheese *Cottage cheese,
Löffelkäse*

Cream *Rahm, Obers*
  Coffee cream *Kaffeeobers*
  Sour cream *Sauerrahm*
  **Whipping/heavy/
  double cream** *Schlagobers*

Cream cheese *Doppelrahm-
stufe, Rahmkäse* (available as
Philadelphia cream cheese)

Curd *Topfen*

Margarine *Margarine*
(*Rama, Vita* and *Thea* are
some common brands)

> **TIP** Some glass and clear-plastic yogurt containers can be
> returned for deposit (*Pfand*). See the Bottle Deposits section
> of this chapter and the Recycling chapter for more information.

CHEESE *Käse*

The variety of cheese is so astounding, you may leave Vienna without having sampled every one(though you can certainly try). To start, taste the typical Austrian cheese spread *Liptauer*, which is seasoned with paprika and found at most deli counters and new-wine taverns (*Heurigen*) throughout Vienna. Although whole-milk and cream cheeses are more common, low-fat (*Magerkäse*) and reduced-fact (*fettarm*) cheeses are available.

BAKED GOODS

BREAD *Brot*

Breads are plentiful and delicious in Vienna. Be aware, however, that bakery breads don't contain preservatives, so buy only what you can eat in a day (or two for dark breads). You can buy a half loaf (*halbes*) of most breads or a quarter (*ein Viertel*) of the large round ones. The standard favorites are *Roggenbrot* (rye bread) and *Semmeln* (Kaiser rolls). Let the clerks and your taste buds help you decipher all the names. Heavy white bread is either *Sandwich* or *Zeppelin*.

 BAKERY CHAINS

The breads from small bakeries are wonderful, but chain bakeries such as **Anker** and **Der Mann** are also good—as well as convenient—sources of freshly baked breads and pastries. Some locations have small tables where you can stand to have a typical Austrian breakfast of coffee and a *Semmel* with butter and jam.

SPECIALTY BAKERIES Bäckereien

If you're looking for special baked goods, try one of the following Bäckereien:

STRÖCK

1020, Praterstern (U1 station)
1030, Drorygasse 20
1090, Friedensbrücke (U4 station)
1110, Simmeringer Hauptstrasse
1200, Klosterneuburger Strasse 37
1220, Süssenbrunner Strasse 62

In addition to a variety of baked goods, this chain carries **American-style donuts,** both glazed and unglazed. Look for other locations in the telephone directory's white pages.

ARTHUR GRIMM

1010, Kurrentgasse 10
☎ 533 13 84-0

This bakery carries **bread for diabetics and those with celiac disease (bei Zöliakie).** These products are available Monday (order by Saturday 10 a.m.) and Thursday (order by Wednesday 6 p.m.). If you'd like a comprehensive list faxed to you, call them or visit their website at www.grimm.at.

SMÖREBRÖDS FEINBÄCKEREI

1150, Haidmannsgasse 2
(behind church near Westbahnhof)
☎ 893 42 14
Fax 893 05 50
Mon - Sat 5 AM - 12:30 PM,
Fri 2:30 PM - 6 PM

This bakery makes **bagels** and will deliver orders of more than ATS 150 (about 12 bagels). Be sure to order one day in advance. English is spoken.

At the **Naschmarkt** (see Markets section), you can find a variety of foreign and domestic breads in larger sizes and sometimes lower prices than in bakeries. Here you will find **pita bread** and an unleavened thin bread that can be used in place of **flour tortillas.**

Challah, called *Barches* in Vienna, can be ordered by calling the following bakeries a day in advance:

KARL HAAG

1010, Neuer Markt 9
☎ 512 99 65
1050, Pilgramgasse 20
☎ 587 81 54

LEOPOLD JANELE

1010, Laurenzerberg 3
☎ 533 29 68
1040, Wiedner Hauptstrasse 48
☎ 581 46 77

ENGLÄNDER EDIT

1020, Hollandstrasse 7
☎ 214 56 17

Fresh *challah* (*Barches*) is available every Friday.

CAKES, PASTRIES & CANDY
Kuchen, Backwaren und Süsswaren

Most of the previously mentioned bakeries also sell pastries and cakes, but the following pastry shops (*Konditoreien*) are justifiably famous for theirs and will prepare special orders to take out (*zum Mitnehmen*). For others, look in the telephone directory's white pages under *"Kaffeehäuser"* ("Coffeehouses").

AIDA is a chain with numerous locations throughout the city, some of which have nonsmoking areas.

KURKONDITOREI OBERLAA-STADTHAUS
1010, Neuer Markt 16
☎ 513 29 36
Daily 8 AM - 8 PM

This pastry shop sells exclusive pastries, specialty truffles and chocolates. It also serves warm meals until 3 PM.

L. HEINER
1010, Kärntner Strasse 21
Mon - Sat 8:30 AM - 7:30 PM
Sun 10 AM - 7:30 PM
1010, Wollzeile 9
Mon - Sat 8:30 AM - 7 PM
Sun 10 AM - 7 PM

COMMON VIENNESE PASTRIES

Apfelstrudel	Apples, raisins, nuts and sugar baked in a flaky crust
Krapfen	Donut, either plain or filled with apricot (*Marillen*) or prune (*Powidl*) preserves, or vanilla creme
Obsttorte	Sponge cake topped with glazed fruit
Sachertorte	Rich chocolate cake with apricot (*Marillen*) glaze and hard chocolate shell

(Also see the Coffeehouses section of the Dining chapter.)

MEAT *Fleisch*

Those coming from overseas may be in for a shock when trying to buy meat for the first time. Except for stores and markets where meat is prepackaged, like American supermarkets, butchers are available to cut meat as requested. Try to be patient and learn the system. When dealing with a butcher (*Fleischer*), know what and how much you want ahead of time (e.g., for one and a half kilograms of roast beef, say, *"eineinhalb Kilo Rostbraten, bitte"*). If language is a problem, write it down (*1.5 kg Rostbraten*). Meat is normally requested by weight, but you can ask for pieces (*Stücke*) or slices (*Schnitte*) when applicable (e.g., three thin pork or veal cutlets would be *"drei dünne Schweinsschnitzel"* or *"drei Kalbsschnitzel, bitte"*).

When you buy *Schnitzel*, your butcher might ask if he should pound it for you. The word to listen for is *"klopfen."* Your answer of *"Ja, bitte"* will save you time and effort and make him think you know what you're doing.

Beef	*Rindfleisch*	**Pork**	*Schweinefleisch*
Lamb	*Lammfleisch*	**Veal**	*Kalbfleisch*

Pork, beef, veal and lamb are cut differently in every country. Comparisons are nearly impossible. Some terms that might prove helpful follow.

CUTS OF MEAT

Loin/filet *Lungenbraten*
Ribs *Rippen*
Sirloin *Beiried*
Bones *Knochen*
  With marrow *mit Mark*
Brains *Hirn*
Heart *Herz*
Kidney *Niere*
Liver *Leber*

Ground, minced *faschiert*
Tender *zart*
Tough *zäh*
Thin *dünn*
Thick *dick*
Whole *im Ganzen*
Pieces *in Stücken*
Sliced *geschnitten*

BEEF *Rindfleisch*

Beiried Sirloin

Faschiertes vom Rind
Ground round (very lean)

Gulaschfleisch Stew beef

Lungenbraten Filet

Ochsenschlepp Ox tail

Rindsschnitzel im Ganzen
For roasting

Rostbraten Roast beef

Schnitzel Cutlet

Tafelspitz Flank steak

 Rump steak and *Entrecôte* are *Schnitzel*s from the porterhouse; roast beef is a big piece of *Beiried*. Beef steak and filet steak, as well as *Tournedos* and *Chateaubriand*, are cut from the *Lungenbraten* (tenderloin).

PORK *Schweinefleisch*

Schnitzel Cutlet
(*Schweinsschlögel* is sirloin and therefore the best for *Schnitzel*, though it is expensive.)

Schulter Shoulder

Schweinskotelett Pork chop

Schweinslungenbraten Pork loin

Schweinsbraten Pork roast

  Langes Karree With long bone (can be cut into chops)

  Kurzes Karree With short bone (can be cut into chops)

Selchfleisch/Geselchtes
Smoked meat (must be cooked unless it says "*essfertig*"—"ready-to-eat")

Schweinshaxe Pig's feet

Speck Bacon (American-style bacon is sometimes available in packages in the dairy case of Julius Meinl am Graben; see Specialty Stores section.)

Surfleisch Pork cured in brine

Beinschinken im ganzen
Whole smoked ham

Faschiertes gemischt Mixed ground pork and beef

LAMB *Lamm*

Lammkotelett Lamb chop

Lammschlögel Leg of lamb

Lammgulasch Cubed lamb

Lammschulter ausgelöst Lamb for stew

At the *Landstrasser Markt* (U3 station Landstrasse), you can find lamb in the Islamic butcher shops.

VEAL *Kalb*

Kalbsbraten Veal roast
Kalbsschnitzel Veal cutlet

Kalbskotelett Veal chop

POULTRY & GAME FOWL
Geflügel und Wildgeflügel

Huhn, Hendl Chicken
   Hühnerbrust Chicken breast
    ohne Haut Without skin
   Flügel Wings
   Hühnerkeulen Legs (thighs
   & drumsticks)

Ente Duck
Fasan Pheasant
Gans Goose
Pute, Truthahn Turkey
Puter Tom turkey

Most poultry shops also sell take-out chicken that's grilled, fried or roasted.

GAME *Wild*

Austrians (and hunters in particular) have an entire vocabulary to describe meats in this category. Here is some general terminology:

Gemse Mountain goat
Hase Wild hare
Hirsch, Wildbret Venison

Kaninchen Rabbit
Reh Roebuck (deer)
Wildschwein Wild boar

Many stands at the *Naschmarkt* sell poultry and wild game.

DELI COUNTER

All butcher shops and most supermarkets carry sausages and cold cuts. Some even make their own (*hausgemacht*). Here are some common varieties:

Debreziner Sharp, paprika-spiced sausage (should be boiled)

Extrawurst Bologna

Frankfurter Similar to a North American hot dog (should be boiled)

Kalbsbratwurst Mild veal sausage (should be fried)

Knackwurst, Knacker Large *Frankfurter* (should be boiled, fried or used cold in salad)

Krakauer Like *Extrawurst* with pieces of ham

Pariser Veal bologna

Salami Salami (many varieties)

Saunaschinken Boiled ham

Schinken Ham

Schweinsbratwurst Seasoned pork sausage (should be fried)

Würstl Sausage (should be fried or grilled)

FISH *Fisch*

You can buy prepared seafood at Nordsee restaurants throughout the city and fresh fish at the *Naschmarkt* location, near Karlsplatz. If you need larger quantities of fish (and want to save some money), try one of the following wholesale markets (*Abholmärkte*):

CERNY-FISCHHANDELS
1220, Hermann-Gebauer-Strasse 18
☎ 288 13
Mon - Fri 6 AM - 2 PM

Seafood *Meeresfrüchte*
  Freshwater *Süsswasser*
  Saltwater *Meerwasser*
  Ocean fish *Seefische*
Carp *Karpfen*
Cod *Kabeljau*
Cuttlefish/squid *Tintenfisch*
Flounder *Flunder*
Halibut *Heilbutt*
Herring *Hering*
Octopus *Oktopus*
Pike/perch *Zander*
Plaice/Dover sole *Scholle*

NORDSEE
1110, Döblerhofstrasse 14/3
☎ 740 16
Mon - Fri 6 AM - noon

Salmon *Lachs, Salm*
Sardine *Sardine*
Shellfish *Schalentier* (unlike *Meeresfrüchte*, which includes octopus and squid, not just shellfish)
  Crab *Krabbe*
  Lobster *Hummer*
  Scallops *Jakobsmuscheln*
  Shrimp *Garnele*
Stockfish *Stockfisch*
Swordfish *Schwertfisch*
Trout *Forelle*
Tuna *Thunfisch*

HEALTH FOOD *Bio-Kost*

Food labeled *"bio—aus biologischer Landwirtschaft"* ("from biological agriculture"), or with similar designations, have been produced without synthetic chemical fertilizers or synthetic pesticides. Animals are not mass-produced. Austria, as a member of the European Union, adheres to EU regulations and directives, but in some areas, Austrian purity standards are even more stringent.

There are many health-food stores (*Reformhäuser*) throughout Vienna that carry a wide range of foods, juices, some organically grown produce, diet packages and natural cosmetics. Look in the yellow pages under *"Reformhäuser"* for specific stores. Also, most supermarkets have an organic corner (*Bioecke*), where health food, though more expensive, can be found.

Food intended for special dietary use must undergo an official approval procedure before being sold. They must be labeled as follows:

- **Baby food and infant formula** labeled *"ab sechs Monate zu verwenden"* means "can be used by babies six months and older."

- **Diabetic products** are labeled *"zur Ernährung bei Diabetes mellitus."*

- **Products for those with celiac disease** (a sensitivity to wheat or rye grains, which disrupts digestion) are labeled *"bei Zöliakie"*

CATERERS *Caterers*

For smaller social affairs, try the deli counter of your local supermarket for platters of meats, *Wurst* and cheeses. For larger functions, especially if you also need a banquet room, check with Vienna's hotels.

 = Member recommendation

BON APPÉTIT CATERING
1100, Knöllgasse 66/7
☎ 667 84 20

From dinner for six to cocktails for 200—and even frozen meals for working women—this catering service can do it all in international style. It can even take care of details such as flower arrangements and serving staff. The owner, Teresa Pialek-Ely, is British. She doesn't accept credit cards.

DA CONTE RESTAURANT
1010, Kurrentgasse 12
☎ 533 64 64
Mon - Sun noon - 3 PM,
6 PM - midnight

This authentic Italian restaurant also does catering and can provide Italian wines and serving staff. English is spoken and Eurocard/MasterCard and Visa are accepted.

DO & CO PARTY SERVICE AND CATERING
1100, Dampfmühlgasse 5
☎ 740 00
Fax 740 000 131

This fine restaurant can cater an elegant party with everything from hors d'oeuvres to desserts to full-course dinners. It can also take care of every detail, including serving staff, place settings, tables and chairs. English is spoken, but they don't accept credit cards.

LE BISTRO
1090, Währinger Strasse 32
☎ 319 76 89 (after 10 AM)
Fax 317 57 14

Owner Thomas Seiler teaches French cooking, runs the restaurant and teaches at Vienna's specialty school for hotel and tourism management. He speaks French, German and English. He has no fixed list, but he does prepare food according to your preferences. Tables, table settings and serving staff can be provided. You can use the restaurant Saturday and Sunday for private parties. Visa & Eurocard are accepted.

GEBRÜDER WILD

1010, Neuer Markt 10-11
☎ 512 53 03
Fax: 513 95 19
Mon - Fri 8:30 AM - 6:30 PM,
Sat 8:30 AM - 1 PM
This market offers a party service that can prepare everything from cocktails to dinners. It can also provide serving staff and tableware.

EXQUISIT PARTY SERVICE, ROSWITHA KAMP

1130, Fasangartengasse 103
☎ 804 87 77
Fax 804 17 47
Dinners for 10 people, buffets for 500, receptions for 1,000—Frau Kamp can handle them all, including table settings and serving staff. She speaks English but doesn't take credit cards.

Serving Staff
MODUL HOSPITALITY CENTER

1190, Dänenstrasse 1
☎ 47 67 00
Fax 47 67 02-17

Modul is the Viennese school for hotel and tourism management. Herr Joseph Schuster can arrange for trained students (who all speak English) to serve at a party.

BERNHOLZ CATERING

1020, Czerningasse 8/4
☎/Fax 214 91 40
This business does kosher catering (also for airlines), has meat prepared under the supervision of a rabbi and has a deli counter. You can order pre-made meals for religious holidays. They speak English but don't take credit cards.

ORBIE AUSTRIA A. WITZ DONUT & PANCAKE

Brunnerstrasse 33/3/7
2700 Wiener Neustadt
☎ 02622 66 77 0
Fax 0664 423 45 46
This company can bring a machine to your large party to make fresh donuts and pancakes/crepes as your guests watch. Ask for Frau Witz, who speaks English.

CHINA, GLASS & SILVERWARE RENTAL

If you need to rent party furniture or table settings, look in the yellow pages under *"Partyservice."* If you only need table settings, contact the following:

UNITED NATIONS CAFETERIA

1400, Vienna International Centre
☎ 26060 48 76

Those with UNO-City identification cards can rent glasses, plates, silverware and even napkins and tablecloths. You can also buy paper napkins and ice cubes. Order forms, with prices, are available at the cafeteria service desk.

SUPERMARKETS

Supermarkets (*Supermärkte*) and grocery stores (*Lebensmittelgeschäfte*) in Vienna do not take your purchases to your car, bag your purchases (with rare exceptions) or provide free bags. Therefore, you will have to learn to do things on your own. (See the Bridging the Cultural Gap section of the Austria chapter for additional shopping information.)

 Billa, Interspar/Spar, and **Merkur** are the largest supermarket chains with locations throughout Vienna.

HOW TO SHOP

Hours: After countless years of limited business hours, stores are now allowed to stay open until 7:30 PM on weeknights and 5 PM on Saturdays (closed Sundays). You should still check each store's posted hours. Some smaller stores close for an hour or more during lunchtime.

Grocery bags: Bring bags (preferably cloth), a basket (like a true Austrian) or a mini shopping cart to carry your groceries. If you forget, there are always paper or plastic bags for a nominal fee at the checkout counter.

Shopping carts: At larger stores or those with parking lots, you may have to insert an ATS 5 or ATS 10 coin as a deposit in order to unlock one cart from another. The coin is released when you reconnect the cart to another in a collection area.

Produce: You usually have to weigh your own fruits and vegetables. Above or below a produce item is the name of it and either a price per piece (*per Stück*), in which case you don't weigh it, or a corresponding number (to use when weighing it). You then place your bag or individual item on a nearby scale (*Waage*) and press the corresponding number (sometimes it's a picture). Put the printed-out sticker on your bag or item before heading to the checkout area.

GROCERY TERMS

abgepackt Packaged
Aktion Special offer
Bioprodukte Organic product
Bitte auf Waage Nr. 30
Please press button number 30
(on the scale).

Bund Bunch, bundle
per kg Per kilogram
per Stk, per Stück
Per piece
Taste 72 Press button 72
(on the scale).

SERVICE COUNTERS

At some counters, customers may stand in line or take a number from a nearby dispenser (so learn your German numbers quickly). If you're waiting in line, carefully watch for your turn so you can place your order before someone else does (it will happen if you hesitate too long). It's okay to say, *"Ich bin die* (or *der* for men) *Nächste"* ("I'm next").

ORDERING BREAD, MEAT & DELI ITEMS

With rolls or pastries, you can order per piece (e.g., if you want two Kaiser rolls, say, *"zwei Stück Semmeln, bitte"*). You can ask for a quarter (*ein Viertel*) or half (*ein halbes*) loaf of large breads. Ask for meat, cold cuts and cheese by weight (e.g., kilograms, grams or dekagrams). Keep in mind that although deli items are often priced per 100 grams, you should order in dekagrams per units of 10 (e.g., if you want 100 grams of bologna, which is 10 dag, say, *"zehn Deka Extrawurst, bitte"*). You can request certain items by quantity, too (e.g., if you want four pork chops, say, *"vier Schweinskoteletten, bitte"*).

BOTTLE DEPOSITS

Glass beverage (and plastic milk and yogurt) bottles have deposits. Look for the word *"Pfand"* ("deposit") on bottle labels. Even though you won't see it on those for beer, there is a deposit. There are usually conveyor belts at larger supermarkets, where you place your bottles and either wait for a credit receipt (*Flaschenzettel*) from a clerk or press a button for the machine to print out your receipt. You then present the *Flaschenzettel* to the cashier, who deducts the amount from your grocery bill. In small stores, you may give the bottles directly to the checkout clerk. (See the Recycling chapter for more details.)

CASHIER *Kassa*

There are no express checkout lines (patience is a virtue). It is, however, customary to let people with a few items (usually what can be carried in their bare hands) go ahead, or they may ask for your permission. The cashier may ask for your *Flaschenzettel*. Be prepared to pack fast (most Austrians load items back into the cart, then take them over to a side counter to pack into bags). Julius Meinl am Graben (see Specialty Stores section), however, packs your groceries into free bags.

PAYMENT

You're expected to pay in cash (*Bargeld*), by Eurocheque with a Eurocheque Card or, in larger supermarkets, with your Bankomat Card (see Bankomat Card section of Banking chapter).

 STORES OPEN LATE & ON SUNDAY

Although business hours are constantly changing, at the time of publication, the following stores stay open later and on traditionally closed days:

BILLA
1020, Bahnhof Wien Nord
Daily 7 AM - 7 PM

BILLA
Vienna International Airport,
Lower level (follow shopping-cart signs)
Daily 7:30 AM - 10 PM

BILLA
Franz-Josefs-Bahnhof
(Tram D, 5, or 33)
Daily (including holidays:
7 AM - 7:30 PM

OKAY
1070, Westbahnhof
Daily 6 AM - 10:50 PM

Gas stations often carry a variety of packaged foods and drinks (including milk) and have extended hours.

MARKETS *Märkte*

You will find the widest selection of fresh foods in Vienna's open-air markets. Located throughout the city, they are usually made up of stalls operated by independent vendors. Customers line up in front of stands when necessary, usually with several clerks helping them. You generally order produce by weight (e.g., *zwei Kilo Äpfel* is two kilograms, or about four pounds, of apples), though you can order by quantity, too (e.g., *vier Äpfel* is four apples). One *dag*, or *deka*, (short for decagram) equals 10 grams, a measure often used for smaller, lighter items, such as cheese or sandwich meat.

The vendor selects the items for the customer, followed by the question *"Alles?"* or *"Noch etwas?"* meaning "Anything else?" When you're done, say, *"Alles"* or *"Das ist alles."* Then the vendor will tell you your total, so pay attention. Although items are usually bagged in paper or plastic bags, it helps to have your own reusable shopping bag or small cart to make carrying it all easier.

Opening hours are always changing. A general rule of thumb is that open-air markets open early and close in the late afternoon or at dusk. Late shoppers risk buying picked-over products. The best resource for detailed information, including the history of the markets, is *Die Wiener Märkte* (see Books appendix). Although it's in German, you can find all the necessary addresses, and with a little German knowledge, you can even decipher the accompanying comments.

FAMOUS NASCHMARKT

The **Naschmarkt** is located in the fourth district, between the Linke and Rechte Wienzeile and between Getreidemarkt and Kettenbrücken-gasse (take the U4 to Kettenbrückengasse because parking is difficult to find). This is the most well-known outdoor market in Vienna with stalls selling everything from the freshest produce (often at the best prices) to delicious Austrian and Turkish specialties. You'll also find tropical fruits, baked goods, fresh meat and seafood, unusual spices, nuts, olives, cheeses, teas, flowers and much more. There are four Asian markets selling Chinese, Japanese and Korean products, Islamic butchers with pork-free stalls, a Saturday flea market and the **best bargain in all of Vienna—huge lamb-and-fresh-vegetable-filled pita-bread sandwiches (*Döner Kebabs*).** The only problem with the *Naschmarkt* is the overwhelming temptation to buy too much.

The Origin of "Naschmarkt"

There are two stories regarding the origin of the name *"Naschmarkt."* The first claims that it originates from the shouts in the marketplace of *"An aschen"* or *"Eine Asche,"* meaning "ashes," which were originally sold as washing powder and later as a soap ingredient. The second story says the name comes from the German word *"naschen,"* which means "to eat sweets and dainties on the sly" or "to nibble, pick or pilfer." Today, the second explanation seems more appropriate when you see all the people nibbling—or inhaling—all the *Naschmarkt* treats.

YEAR-ROUND MARKETS

INDOOR MARKETS

Don't let bad weather keep you from buying fresh meat and produce. Try one of the following indoor markets instead:

LANDSTRASSER MARKT
    1030, Invalidenstrasse 2 (*Wien Mitte*)

Housed on two floors in a building across from the Vienna Hilton, you can reach this market by taking an elevator from the *U-Bahn* station. This is a good place to buy game (*Wild*), such as rabbit (*Hase*), venison (*Hirsch, Wildbret*), wild boar (*Wildschwein*) and pheasant (*Fasan*).

NUSSDORFER HALLE
    1090, Nussdorfer Strasse & Alserbachstrasse

Built in 1882 and reopened in 1995, this is the only unchanged market hall still in existence in Vienna. In addition to its architectural charm, it's a good food market. It also has places to sit and drink coffee or wine.

OUTDOOR MARKETS

In addition to the large markets, some districts have their own markets full of fresh fruits and vegetables. You may discover one in your own neighborhood. Two that might be of special interest are listed below:

OLD VIENNA FARMERS MARKET (*Altwiener Bauernmarkt*)
    1010, Freyung
    1st & 3rd Fridays and Saturdays in the month

Farmers come here to sell their homemade products, including wines, honey, breads, sausages and cheeses.

GROSSMARKT WIEN-INZERSDORF
1230, Laxenburger Strasse 365

This is the wholesale market where shop and restaurant owners buy in bulk, so it opens and closes early (Mon - Sat 4:30 AM - 8:30 AM). There's also the Flower Hall (*Blumenhalle*), open Mon - Sat 5 AM - 8 AM, which sells flowers in bulk (good for special events or occasions). In addition to cut flowers, you can buy plants.

SEASONAL MARKETS

LENT & EASTER MARKETS
Fasten- und Ostermärkte

OSTERMARKT FREYUNG
1010, Freyung

This well-established *Ostermarkt* opens two Mondays before Easter Sunday. Some stalls sell charming and authentic handmade goods. The sight of the small mountain of hand-painted eggs in the market center alone makes a visit worthwhile.

ADVENT MARKETS
Christkindlmärkte

Christkindlmärkte usually open in late November and run until Christmas Eve. The Vienna Tourist Information Office (see Info Offices appendix) has a brochure in English on the market in front of City Hall (*Rathaus*).

OLD VIENNESE ADVENT MARKET
(Altwiener Christkindlmarkt)
1010, Freyung

This is one of the most traditional and authentic *Christkindlmärkte*, selling handmade gifts as well as food and hot mulled wine (*Glühwein*).

ART AT HEILIGENKREUZER-HOF
(Kunst im Heiligenkreuzer-Hof)
1010, Heiligenkreuzer-Hof
Saturdays and Sundays only

This market sells crafts such as leather goods, quilted items, paintings and ceramics made by local artisans.

CITY HALL ADVENT MARKET
(Christkindlmarkt Rathaus)
1010, Rathausplatz

Vienna's largest *Christkindlmarkt* turns *Rathauspark* into a winter wonderland for the children in all of us, but it, however, lacks authenticity and genuine old-world charm. (Also see the Recommended Activities section of the Children chapter.)

TOSTMANN TRACHTEN'S
OLD VIENNA CHRISTMAS MARKET
1010, Schottengasse 3A

This is a shop for traditional Austrian clothing, but at Christmastime, its ancient multiple-level cellar *(Keller)* is filled with thousands of Christmas decorations.

CHRISTMAS AT SPITTELBERG
(Weihnachten am Spittelberg)
1070, Spittelberggasse

The setting of Baroque houses complements the beautiful handicrafts sold at this favorite market of the Viennese.

CULTURE AND CHRISTMAS MARKET SCHÖNBRUNN
PALACE
(Kultur- und Weihnachtsmarkt Schloss Schönbrunn)
1130, Schloss Schönbrunn (in front of palace)

Although the palace is an unbeatable backdrop, this relative newcomer to the *Christkindlmarkt* scene sells a few authentic and many less-traditional Christmas items.

EMERGENCY RATIONS

In today's world you never know what to expect. In case of an event such as the Chernobyl nuclear accident, officials in Austria recommend that you keep on hand a 14-day supply of staples such as rice, pasta, sugar, honey, canned/tinned fish and meats, condensed milk, dried peas and beans, and oils. To this list we would add bottled water, canned soup, cereal and nuts.

H ome, sweet home—and with it all the goods and services to make and keep it that way. When you first arrive in Vienna, you may be overwhelmed by the number of household needs you have simultaneously: lights to see in the dark, an electrician to install them, closets to hold clothes, detergent to wash them in, rugs for bare floors, curtains for bare windows and even a piano tuner so children can resume lessons. This chapter provides all the basic household information you'll need—or at least points you in the right direction.

Household goods and services are grouped by category and listed in alphabetical order in this chapter.

CATEGORIES

General Information

Major Malls & Shopping Areas
All-Purpose Stores
Consumer Tips

Household Goods & Services

Antiques, Antique Dealers & Furniture Repair

Carpets/Rugs, Carpet Cleaning & Repair

Ceramics, China, Crystal, Glass & Porcelain, Glass Repair & Engraving

Cleaning Products

Clock & Watch Repair

Computer Service

Department Stores

Do-It-Yourself

Domestic Help

Donations

Dry Cleaning & Laundry

Electricians & Repair Shops, Electrical Appliances

Flowers (Real & Artificial), Plants, Gardening, Plant Doctor, Garden Furniture

Furniture

Gas for Grills

Gifts

Glass, Glaziers & Mirrors

Interior-Design Fabric, Curtains, Drapery & Upholstery

Keys & Locksmiths

Kitchen Equipment & Hardware

Lights, Lamps & Lampshades

Linens for Bed & Table

Metalwork, Gold & Silver

Pianos & Piano Tuners

Picture Framing & Restoration

Secondhand Shops & Flea Markets

Television

Transformers for Electrical Current

Within these categories, businesses are listed alphabetically by district. Where applicable, the main/home/anchor store (*Mutterhaus*) is listed. Check the telephone directory's white pages for one in your area. If there is a special distinction, it is noted in the comments following the phone or fax number. You will find English translations corresponding to the German listings in the yellow pages, as well as some useful terminology.

MAJOR MALLS & SHOPPING AREAS

Although each district has its own group of shops, the following are considered Vienna's major shopping areas:

1010, Kärntner Strasse & the Graben

These two streets make up Vienna's exclusive shopping area, which is filled with clothing, shoe, china, silver and souvenir stores. **Steffl, Benetton** and **J. & L. Lobmeyr** are just a few of the well-known names here.

1060 & 1070, Mariahilfer Strasse

For fashion, Viennese women say they look on Kärntner Strasse, then go buy on Mariahilfer Strasse. This extremely long street of stores stretches from behind the *Kunsthistorisches Museum* to *Westbahnhof*, with everything imaginable on sale, including furniture and household-goods stores such as **Interio, Leiner** and department stores such as **Gerngross** and **Peek & Cloppenburg.**

1110, Simmeringer Haide

This shopping complex off the southbound A-4 going toward the airport has an **Interspar** supermarket, **Media Markt** (electronics store) and **Metro** (bulk-goods warehouse where membership or diplomatic card is required), along with many smaller stores.

1210, Shopping Center Nord

This smaller mall houses clothing, shoe, book, stationery, sporting-goods, pet and pet supplies, and appliance stores. There is also a famous gourmet-sandwich shop and other small stores.

1220, Donauzentrum

This two-story mall across the street from the U1 terminal (Kagran) has a little bit of everything: **Kika** (furniture and housewares), **Niedermeyer, Interspar** (groceries), clothing, sporting goods and a food court.

2334 Vösendorf-Süd, Shopping City Süd

The largest mall in Europe has two levels that house **IKEA, Leiner** (furniture and housewares), **Bauhaus** (hardware), clothing, shoe, sporting-goods and food stores, as well as a variety of restaurants, including **Nordsee.** The sprawling complex surrounding it includes a minimall (with eclectic stores, a food court and a multiplex movie theater) and a number of freestanding businesses like **Bellaflora** (fresh, silk and dried plants), **Betten-Reiter** (curtains, sheets and towels), **Media Markt** (electronics and appliances), **Baumax** (hardware), **Kaindl** (housewares and appliances), **Interio** (furniture and housewares), **Toys 'R' Us** and many more.

ALL-PURPOSE STORES

When you first arrive, you'll probably need many things at once. The following stores supersede categorization and therefore serve as all-purpose sources of household goods and furnishings at relatively reasonable prices. Closets (*Schränke*) will most likely be your first priority because most apartments have none or very few. The following stores sell quick do-it-yourself solutions that should complement your existing furniture. Also note that the following stores do not accept credit cards. They do, however, usually accept Bankomat (ATM) Cards and Eurocheques with a valid Eurocheque Card (see Bankomat and Eurocheque & Eurocheque Card sections of Banking chapter).

IKEA

2334, Vösendorf
Shopping City Süd

This large Swedish store meets almost every household need—from furniture and lights to dishes and towels— all at reasonable prices. Goods can be returned or exchanged. You can pay by Bankomat Card or Eurocheque. Delivery costs extra. For a small fee, you can receive a Family Club card that gives you a 15-percent discount at the cafeteria (which serves Scandinavian dishes and has a nonsmoking section) and other specific discounts (check for details). The furniture is predominantly build-it-yourself, and it comes in various styles and colors. The large fabric department's selection varies by season. You measure and cut the fabric yourself, then take it to a clerk, who weighs, prices and seals it in a bag for you. An IKEA bus (see IKEA Bus section of Transportation chapter) regularly departs from opposite the Opera House (*Oper*) in the first district.

INTERIO

1220, Wagramerstrasse,
Donauzentrum
1060, Mariahilferstrasse 19-21
1210, Brünner Strasse 73A
2334, Vösendorf Süd,
Shopping City Süd (just before
IKEA and Multiplex)

This store features modern and Scandinavian-style build-it-yourself furniture. It has a selection of housewares, frames, lights and decorator and seasonal items. It also has a selection of window blinds and cotton decorator fabrics at reasonable prices. Credit cards and Bankomat Cards are accepted.

KIKA

1190, Kreilplatz 1
(above Pam Pam)
1220, Donauzentrum
1220, Wagramer Strasse 246
2334, Vösendorf,
Dr.-Robert-Firneis-Strasse
(north of Shopping City Süd)

This store is popular for its variety of furniture. It also carries curtains, some fabric, linens and housewares. The Bankomat Card is accepted.

LEINER

1070, Mariahilfer Strasse 18

2334, Vösendorf Süd,
Shopping City Süd

This large household-goods store sells reasonably priced furniture, kitchen and bathroom units, as well as baby items. It also carries drapery fabrics, linens and decorator accessories. The huge multilevel store on Mariahilfer Strasse has a nearby parking garage. Credit cards and Bankomat Cards are accepted.

LUTZ/MÖBELIX

1210, Brünner Strasse 57A

1030, Kelsenstrasse 9 (Möbelix)

1150, Hütteldorfer Strasse 23
(Lutz)

2345, Brumman Gebirge
Hubatschstrasse 4
(Across from Shpping
City Süd)

This is another large furniture, home and garden store. You can find discount prices at Möbelix, but you must be careful of the quality.

MICHELFEIT

1100, Favoritenstrasse 130

1100, Laxenburger Strasse 145/
Raxstrasse

1160, Sandleitengasse 26-30

This store carries household items and furniture (at the second location) at reasonable prices. It also has stores outside Vienna and will deliver. The Bankomat Card, Eurocard/ Master- Card and Visa are accepted.

MÖMA

2334, Vösendorf Süd,
Shopping City Süd area

This large warehouse-style furniture store features build-it-yourself furniture. You can find mirrors and odd lamps here at reasonable prices, too.

CONSUMER TIPS

Sales in Austria are concentrated in January and July–August, usually to empty stores of merchandise in order to prepare for the following season. Terms you need to know are:

Aktion Special

Saldi Sale

Winterschlussverkauf
Winter closeout sale

Sommerschlussverkauf
Summer closeout sale

Totalabverkauf Total sellout

 In Austria, exchanging goods is not customary. You're only entitled to do this if you reserve that right in writing before making the purchase. Even so, this would include only items that show no sign of wear. Your reservation of the right to exchange never entitles you to receive your money back. All sales are final.

TIP The following are tips from the Austrian Consumer Information Association (*Verein für Konsumenteninformation*):

- **If you buy something from an uninvited door-to-door salesperson, you can cancel the contract within a week.** If you initiated the contract or purchase, it is valid from the time of sale or signing.

- **When purchasing an item you can't take with you, be sure to stipulate a delivery date in writing, though this doesn't mean you'll get it on that date.** If delays will be a problem, write *"Fixgeschäft,"* which means that if delivery is late by even one day, you can cancel the contract.

- **Once you've accepted delivery of defective goods, they are yours. There is no warranty on goods with apparent defects that you may have overlooked.** If you're unable to inspect the items upon delivery (e.g., if they're still packed), write *"mit Vorbehalt"* ("with reservation") next to your signature on the delivery slip.

- **The following are other rights that must be stipulated in writing:**
  - The right to exchange an item (*Umtauschrecht*)
  - Discounts for cash payments

- **For any business transaction, keep all the paperwork.**

Verein für Konsumenteninformation also publishes a monthly consumer magazine, *Konsument*, in German. Although it does report on consumer issues, it is not the same as *Consumer Reports* in the United States. If you'd like to receive a 12-month subscription (for ATS 468), call the association at the following number, or go in person to pick up an individual issue:

VEREIN FÜR KONSUMENTENINFORMATION (VKI)
  1060, Mariahilfer Strasse 81
  ☎ 587 86 86-0

- For repairs and services, labor is charged by the hour, so it's a good idea to note the time when the service person arrives as well as any interruptions.
- Keep in mind that it often costs more to repair than to replace a unit.
- You should also obtain a written estimate before actual work begins.
- A *Wegzeit* is a travel charge (about ATS 300–ATS 500) in addition to labor costs.

ANTIQUES *Antiquitäten*

Look in the yellow pages under:

Antiques *Antiquitäten*

Antique Dealers *Antiquitätenhandlungen*

Restoration *Antiquitätenrestauratoren, Restauratoren*

Carpenter *Tischlereien*

Craftsmen *Antiquitätentischlerei, Kunsttischlereien*

Secondhand Shops *Altwaren*

For quality merchandise (with the associated prices), start in the first district between the Graben and the *Hofburg*. The book *Antiquitäten in Wien* (see Books Appendix) lists 300 addresses for antique stores and flea markets. Although in German, you can pick out the addresses.

Dorotheum

In the heart of this area of antique shops in the first district is the Dorotheum, which is well worth a visit, even if you have no interest in buying antiques. The Dorotheum is an auction house/pawnshop run by the state. The main location is at:

DOROTHEUM

1010, Dorotheergasse 17   Mon - Fri, 10 AM - 6 PM, Sat 9 AM - 5 PM

☎ 515 60-0   Mon - Fri, 8 AM - 3 PM (office)

There are branches throughout Vienna as well as in other cities in Austria. It accepts all major credit cards for direct purchases.

Articles are both bought and sold here. A charge of 10 percent (12 percent in the art section, or *Kunstabteilung*) is added to the price you pay for an article. In addition, there is either a 12-percent (plus VAT) or 18-percent (includes VAT) buyer's fee. Public auctions are held at 2 PM daily in different rooms on different days. For instance, the *Franz-Josef-Saal* has auctions on Wednesday, and the *Ludwigsdorff-Saal* is used on Friday (except on holidays, in which case, special notices are posted). There are usually three preview days to look at displayed articles. Each item has a tag with a call number (*Ausrufnummer*), description and starting price for bids (*Ausrufpreis*).

SELLING

There is a commission fee of 9.6 to 18 percent. If you want to pawn something, the interest charge is two percent per month, or 24 percent annually.

BUYING

In order to buy, you either can go to the auction yourself or employ a proxy (*Sensal*) to bid for you (ask in advance about charges). There are also rooms where items are priced for cash and carry (*Freiverkauf*).

ANTIQUE DEALERS & FURNITURE REPAIR

 STEFAN HEILDBORGH

1030, Neulinggasse 48/23
☎ 714 78 58
This carpenter/cabinet maker makes and repairs furniture. He speaks four languages, including English, and enjoys dealing with foreigners. Call to set up an appointment.

 PATRICK KOVACS KUNSTHANDEL

1040, Rechte Wienzeile 31
☎ 587 94 74
Fax 586 08 40-85
www.kunstnet.at/kovacs
Here you will find true *Jugendstil* and typically Viennese furniture.

 DREIMÄDERL-HAUS

1040, Wiedner Hauptstrasse 69
☎ 505 41 67
Here you can find a variety of things, including furniture and paintings.

GERHARD HIRSCHLER
1120, Korbergasse 10
☎ 813 14 19
Mobile ☎ (0663) 88 23 14
Herr Hirschler speaks a little English. For ATS 800, he will come to give a cost estimate for repairs. Call to set up an appointment.

 = Member recommendation

CARPETS/RUGS *Teppiche*

Look in the yellow pages under:

Carpets/Rugs *Teppiche*
Carpeting *Teppichböden*
Carpet Cleaning *Teppichreinigungen*
Carpet Dealer *Teppichhändler*

Carpet Invisible Mending *Teppichkunststopfereien, Kunststopfereien*
Carpet Repair *Teppichreparatur*

 ADIL BESIM KG

1010, Graben 30
☎ 533 09 10
Fax 533 09 10 30
eMail:
adil-besim@adil-besim.co.at
www.adil-besim.co.at

This a family business established in 1946 with seven stores in Austria. They sell old, antique and new carpets, rugs, Kilims and tapestries. Parternership with many producers in Turkey, Iran, Pakistan and Nepal. They also have a service workshop. Very friendly and English is spoken. Visit their great online site with lots of helpful tips on carpets.

CARPET CLEANING & REPAIR

ADIL BESIM KG

1010, Graben 30
☎ 533 09 10
Fax 533 09 10 30
Mon - Fri, 9:30 AM - 6 PM,
Sat, 9:30 AM - 5 PM

This carpet dealer also does cleaning and repairing. English is spoken.

VARTIAN

1010, Rotenturmstrasse 15
☎ 533 63 96
Mon - Fri, 9 AM - 6 PM,
Sat, 9 AM - 5 PM

This carpet store also does cleaning and repairing. A little English is spoken.

GEORGE & AZNIF

1050, Zentagasse 9
☎ 545 35 92

1090, Kinderspitalgasse 1
☎ 405 83 34
Mon - Fri, 9 AM - 6 PM,
Sat, 9 AM - 1 PM

This couple cleans and repairs carpets at both locations. Pickup and delivery are also available. Old carpets can be treated with lanolin. They both speak English.

SERVICE MASTER

1130, Dostojewskigasse 12
☎ 876 42 40

Both locations clean carpets and upholstery.

TEPPICHKLINIK POLLISCHANSKY

1190, Sieveringer Strasse 33
☎ 320 32 67
Mon - Fri, 7:30 AM - 5 PM

This place specializes in cleaning and repairing carpet and upholstery. English is spoken.

Do-It-Yourself Carpet Cleaning

You can rent a large professional rug-cleaning machine, complete with shampoo, at some large drugstores (*Drogerien*) and hardware stores.

CERAMICS, CHINA, CRYSTAL, GLASS & PORCELAIN

Look in the yellow pages under:

Ceramics *Keramik*
China Stores *Porzellan und Porzellanwaren*
China/Glass Repairs *Porzellanreparaturen, Kunstkittereien, Restaurierer*

Glass Engraving *Glasgraveure*
Glassware *Glaswaren*

CERAMICS

KERAMIK AUS GMUNDEN
1010, Kärntner Durchgang
☎ 512 58 24

This store sells the swirled, dotted and flowered ceramics Austria is known for. It accepts all major credit cards.

PAWLATA KERAMIK
1010 Kärntner Strasse 14
☎ 512 17 64

This store has a huge selection of ceramics in its lower-level show-rooms. It accepts all major credit cards.

WIENER KERAMIK MANUFAKTUR E.J. KERNSTOCK
1150, Mariahilfer Strasse 164
☎ 892 23 17
Mon - Fri, 10 AM - 12:30 PM, 2 PM - 6 PM, Sat 10 AM - noon

A little English is spoken. No credit cards are accepted.

CHINA & CRYSTAL

Vienna has numerous china shops, but the following are three of the most famous, and one even has a bargain basement:

WIENER PORZELLAN-MANUFAKTUR AUGARTEN
1010, Stock am Eisenplatz 3-4
☎ 512 14 94
1020, Schloss Augarten
Obere Augartenstrasse 1
☎ 211 24 18
1060, Mariahilfer Strasse 31
☎ 587 92 18

Augarten is famous for its high-quality porcelain produced in Austria. Each piece is signed and numbered in accordance with the long-standing belief that each piece is a work of art. It accepts all major credit cards. There is a small factory and group tours can be arranged by calling ☎ 211 24 10. Individual tours are conducted Mon - Fri at 9:30 AM.

J & L LOBMEYR
1010, Kärntner Strasse 26
☎ 512 05 08

This exclusive store carries china, *Herend Porzellan* from Hungary and crystal. This is by far Vienna's most famous crystal and chandelier shop. It accepts all major credit cards.

SLAMA
1060, Mariahilfer Strasse 71
☎ 587 36 21

Although the shop carries china, crystal and ceramics, the attraction is its bargain basement. It accepts all major credit cards except American Express.

GLASS REPAIR & ENGRAVING

Glass engraving is an Austrian tradition, where friends often present specially engraved pieces to commemorate significant events or just to immortalize the friendship. The following locations engrave and repair glasses:

J & L LOBMEYR
1010, Kärntner Strasse 26
☎ 512 05 08
Mon - Fri ,9 AM - 6 PM,
Sat, 9 AM - 5 PM

This crystal store also does engraving; friendship glasses are a specialty. English is spoken. All major credit cards are accepted.

PAUL DENK
1010, Gluckgasse 5
☎ 512 59 25
Mon - Thurs, 9 AM - noon,
1 PM - 5 PM, Fri, 9 AM - 2 PM

Herr Denk, who speaks English, can grind off chipped rims of glasses.

ERIKA BAKIC-ROSENBERGER
1040, Opernpassage 23
☎ 586 10 00
Mon - Fri, 8 AM - noon,
2 PM - 5 PM

This shop does engraving and will monogram or copy a favorite scene onto a vase or bowl. Very little English is spoken.

CLEANING PRODUCTS

Most cleaning products are sold at supermarkets, though many are only available at drugstores (*Drogerien*) or hardware stores (*Eisenwaren*). **Drogeriemarkt (DM)** and **Bipa** are well-known chains that carry beauty, health, baby, cleaning and household products, as well as some pet supplies. Hardware-store chains such as **Bauhaus, Baumax, Obi** and **Hornbach** all carry cleaning and household products. The best prices and largest selection are at supermarkets such as **Hofer, Merkur** and **Interspar.** Department stores often have a selection in their basements or household-goods (*Haushaltswaren*) departments.

Warning Symbols

 Extremely flammable, highly flammable

 Very toxic, contains carcinogens

 Harmful (detrimental to health, irritant, contains carcinogens)

 Corrosive chemicals

Below is a list of products, their German translations and some brand names, which are provided as examples and not intended as recommendations. Trial and error will help you determine your own preferred brands. A complete line of cleaning products can be found under the brand name *Frosch*. Products marked *"Umweltfreundlich"* are considered "environmentally friendly."

Cleaning Product *German Translation*	**Where Found** *Brands*
Ammonia *Salmiakgeist*	Drugstore (*Drogerie*)
Bleach *Bleichmittel*	Supermarket *Danclor*
Chrome cleaner *Chromreiniger*	Supermarket, auto-supply store
Dishwasher detergent *Maschinenspülmittel*	Supermarket *Calgonit, Somat, Sun*
Dishwasher rinse aid *Klarspüler*	Supermarket *Calgonit, Somat, Sun*
Dishwasher salt *Regeneriersalz*	Supermarket *Calgonit, Somat, Sun* (needed in European dishwashers)
Dishwashing soap (liquid) *Geschirrspülmittel (flüssig)*	Supermarket *Calgonit, Palmolive*
Disinfectant *Desinfektionsmittel*	*Drogerie* *Danclor, Lysoform*
Drain cleaner *Abflussreiniger*	Supermarket *Airjet, Rohrfix*
Fabric softener *Weichspüler*	Supermarket *Kuschelweich, Lenor*

Fine wash/hand wash	Supermarket
Feinwaschmittel	*Coral, Fewa, Woolite*
Floor wax	Supermarket, hardware store
Bodenwachs	
Floor-wax remover	Supermarket, hardware store
Bodenwachsentferner	*Rax*
Furniture polish	Supermarket
Möbelpflege, Möbelpolitur	*Pronto, Opti, Estalin*
Laundry detergent	Supermarket
Waschmittel	*Ariel, Omo, Persil*
Liquid cleaner	Supermarket
Flüssiger Haushaltsreiniger	*Cif, Ajax*
Nonchlorine bleach	Supermarket
Fleckensalz	*Dr. Beckmann*
Nonscratch cleaner	Supermarket, hardware store
Kratzfreireiniger	*Gerafix, Sidol, Cif* (for ceramic surfaces and chrome is *ohne zu kratzen*)
Oven cleaner	Supermarket
Ofenreiniger	*K2R, Back & Grill*
Powder cleanser	Supermarket
Pulverreiniger	*Vim, ATA*
Prewash treatment	Supermarket
Vorwaschmittel	*Shout, Tru, Sil*
Spot remover	*Drogerie*
Fleckentferner,	*Dr. Beckmann*
Fleckenroller aus Gallseife	(by type of stain; see following box)
Spray starch	Supermarket
Sprühstärke	(refillable spritz bottle)
Starch	Supermarket
Stärke	*Ideal, Jubilee*
Steel wool	Supermarket, hardware store
Stahlwolle	*Brillo*
Stovetop cleaner	Supermarket
Stahlfix	*Potzblitz Fluessig*
Toilet cleaner	Supermarket, hardware store
WC Reiniger	*Blue Star, Tofix*
Tub & tile cleaner	Supermarket
Badezimmerreiniger	*Cif, Mr. Proper*
Window cleaner	Supermarket
Fensterputzmittel	*Ajax, Cif, Clin*

Stain Terms

Ballpoint pen, beer, liquor, stamp-pad ink
Kuli, Bier, Likör, Stempelfarbe
Blood, milk, protein *Blut, Milch, Eiweiss*
Coffee, tea, yellowed stains *Kaffee, Tee, Gilb*
Fat, oil *Fett, Öl*
Felt-tip pens *Filzschreiber*
Fruit, red wine, jam *Obst, Rotwein, Marmelade*
Glue, chewing gum, White-Out, nail polish
Kleber, Kaugummi, Tipp-Ex, Nagellack
Tar, resin, candle wax *Teer, Harz, Kerzenwachs*

SPECIAL-RISK SYMBOLS ON LABELS

R 20   Harmful by inhalation
R 35   Causes chemical burns
R 45   May cause cancer
S 2   Keep out of reach of children.
S 24/25   Avoid contact with skin and eyes.
S 45   In case of an accident, or if you feel sick, seek
              medical attention   immediately (show the
              label when possible).

CLOCK & WATCH REPAIR

Look in the yellow pages under:

Clock-, watchmaker *Uhrmacher*
Watches *Uhren*

The following businesses have English speakers, accept credit cards
and can repair all types of watches. You may find less expensive repair
services in your own neighborhood, but they may not speak English
and probably won't accept credit cards.

KARL HOFER (HAUS DES UHRENMUSEUMS)
  1010, Schulhof 2
  ☎ 533 45 77

RUDOLF HÜBNER
  1010, Graben 28
  ☎ 533 80 65

COMPUTER SERVICE

IBMs/ PERSONAL COMPUTERS

MACINTOSH

MY PC-SERVICE
1030, Erdberger Strasse 202
☎ 796 35 88
Fax 796 35 88-47

This service has a hotline to solve computer problems, home repair service or you can take your computer there. English is spoken.

GAMMAG COMPUTERSYSTEME
☎ 278 87 13
Fax 278 87 13-18

This service can send someone to your home or you can take your computer to them. English is spoken.

 TOOLS AT WORK

1020, Zirkusgasse 40
☎ 216 55 85-15
Fax 216 55 85-19
eMail bkuntner@toolsatwork.at
Mon - Fri, 9 AM - 5 PM

The owner, Berenice Kuntner, is very helpful and speaks fluent English. Call first to determine whether you need to bring in your computer. She can come to your home for an additional fee. Eurocheques are accepted.

DEPARTMENT STORES

Austrian department stores include **Steffl** on Kärntner Strasse in the first district and **Gerngross** and **Herzmansky** on Mariahilfer Strasse in the seventh district. There are no major department stores in any of the malls.

DO-IT-YOURSELF
Bastlerbedarf, Selbstbaumöbel

Hardware Terms	
Builders Baumeister	**Paint** Farbe
Building materials Baustoffe	**Turpentine** Terpentin
Do-it-yourself Bastlerbedarf, Selbstbaumöbel	**Stripper** Abbeizer
	Wood Holz

The following stores carry building supplies, paints and some hardware items. For other locations and stores, check the yellow pages under "Baustoffe."

BAUHAUS
1030, Arsenalstrasse 5
1220, Wagramer Strasse 196
2334 Vösendorf,
Shopping City Süd

BAUMAX
1140, Albert-Schweitzer-Gasse2A
1220, Gwerbepark Stadlau
2310, Schwechat
1120, Wienergerbstrasse 31-39
2334 Vösendorf-Süd,
(Shopping City Süd area)
3400 Klosterneuburg,
Aufeldstrasse 42

OBI
2334, Vosendorf
Triesterstrasse 14

HORNBACH
1220, Stadlauerstrasse 37
2345 Brann am Gebirge, Johann
Steinbock Strasse 7A

DOMESTIC HELP

A housekeeper (*Bedienerin* or *Putzfrau*) can be employed hourly or monthly on a regular salary basis in Austria. Other than by word of mouth, the best way to find household help is to advertise in the local newspapers *Kurier* or *Bazar*. The current minimum hourly rate is ATS 120 plus transportation costs. It's customary to provide a meal (lunch) for a full day's work. Be sure to request references from the applicant and check for official papers (e.g., *Meldezettel*). Those who employ a domestic are required to pay contributions to the state's health insurance and retirement funds if the person earns more than ATS 3.600 per month (this amount is adjusted every calendar year). For information on where and how to register, call the Chamber for Workers and Employees (*Kammer für Arbeiter und Angestellte* or *Arbeiterkammer*) at ☎ 501 65-0.

DONATIONS

If you'd like to donate old furniture, clothing or other household goods, contact the AWA office at ☎ 320 14 95, the United Nations Women's Guild at ☎ 206 024 276 or the following organization:

DER WÜRFEL
1070, Myrthengasse 17
☎ 523 98 807

This unique organization, which employs the unemployed, provides such services as interior painting, wallpaper hanging, and laying, sanding and lacquering wood floors. It can pick up your donations of old clothes, dishes, books and other small items.

DRY CLEANING & LAUNDRY

Look in the yellow pages under:

Dry Cleaning *Textilreinigung*   **Laundry** *Wäscherei*

Laundry Terms

Bleach *Bleichen*

Boxed (shirts) *Zusammen-gelegt, gefaltet*

Coin-operated machine *Münzwäscherei*

Detergent (powder) *Pulver, Waschpulver*

Dry cleaning *Chemische Putzerei, Putzerei*

Drying *Trocknen*

Express (costs more) *Express*

Fabric softener *Weichspüler*

Ironing/pressing *Bügeln*

Laundromat *Wäscherei*

Laundry by the kilogram *Kilo-Reinigung*

Needs spotting (costs more) *Spezial*

Normal (cleaning) *Einfach*

On the hanger *am Kleiderbügel*

Starch *Stärken, gestärkt*

Wash *Wäsche*

LAUNDRY FACILITIES

Laundry facilities with coin-operated washers and dryers are not widely available, but the following are a few conveniently located ones. Bring lots of ATS 5 and ATS 10 coins and detergent. Wash-load size is determined by weight. Don't be afraid to cram a washer full of clothes in order to get your money's worth.

RICHARD KARLBERGER
   1030, Schlachthausgasse 19
   ☎ 798 81 91

   1030, Fiakerplatz 8
   ☎ 713 24 24
   Mon - Fri, 7:30 AM - 6 PM,
   Sat, 7:30 AM - 1 PM

This facility's machines hold up to six kilograms.

Clothing Labels

⊔ Washable

△ Bleachable

▣ Can be machine-dried

⊿ Can be ironed

○ Dry clean only

DRY CLEANERS

The following businesses have several locations throughout the city, so check the yellow pages under *"Textilreinigung"* ("Textile Dry Cleaners") for the location nearest you. Also look around your own neighborhood. Most dry cleaners require payment in advance.

SALESIANER
  1030, Gärtnergasse 1
  1113, Hietzinger Hauptstrasse 82
  1114, Linzer Strasse 104-110

These locations also have laundry services.

STROSS
  1010, Hoher Markt 2
  1030, Landstrasser
  Hauptstrasse 41

These locations also offer one-hour dry cleaning.

ELECTRICIANS & REPAIR SHOPS, ELECTRICAL APPLIANCES

Look in the yellow pages under:

Electrical Appliances
Elektrogeräte
Electrical Heating
Elektroheizungen
Electricians *Elektroinstallation*

Transformers (see Transformers section)
Transformatorenbau
Electrician *Elektriker*

When you purchase an appliance, try to arrange installation with the seller because it will be cheaper than having someone else do the job. Many firms, such as Philips, Miele and Siemens, have their own repair departments. Check the telephone directory's white pages for addresses. Some electrical-appliance stores also do repairs and servicing. Look under *"Kundendienst"* ("Customer Service") in individual listings.

ELECTRICAL-APPLIANCE REPAIR SHOPS
Elektroreparatur

Having a small appliance repaired is often not worth it because the cost of repair usually exceeds the cost of buying a new one. There may, however, be times when you need to deal with an *Elektroreparatur*. You should get any agreement in writing. Cost estimates are free of charge unless you're told in advance otherwise. There are two types of estimates:

* Binding (guaranteed) cost estimate (*verbindlicher Kostenvoranschlag*).

* Nonbinding cost estimate (*unverbindlicher Kostenvoranschlag*), where the indicated amount cannot exceed 15 percent. If the costs will be higher than that, the repairer is obligated to inform the customer immediately. At this point, you can legally terminate the agreement, but you're still obligated to pay for services rendered up to that point.

Your signature implies that you agree to the full text of the contract.

If you want to know if an appliance can be repaired, take it to a repair shop or service location specified by the manufacturer. You can also look in the yellow pages under the product name, followed by *"Kundendienst/Servicestelle"* ("Customer Service/Service Location"). Ask someone *"Können Sie (das) reparieren?"* ("Can you repair this?").

If a service call is necessary, you will have to pay a travel fee of about ATS 800 just to have someone come to your home. Even if your appliance is not repaired, you must still pay this fee.

ELECTRICAL-APPLIANCE STORES

The following stores all have several locations throughout Vienna. Check the telephone directory's white pages for stores near you.

Cosmos
This store carries small and large appliances at competitive prices, but it doesn't take credit cards.

Interspar
This is an enormous supermarket (at Donauzentrum, Shopping City Süd and Simmeringer Haide) where you also can buy a variety of appliances. Although it doesn't take credit cards, it does accept the Bankomat Card.

Media Markt
This huge store sells competitively priced home appliances, TVs, stereos, VCRs, computers, photo equipment and videos and CDs. It doesn't take credit cards but accepts the Bankomat Card.

Niedermeyer
This electronics store sells smaller items such as cameras, camcorders, phones and answering machines. Not all locations have a full selection, with stores being product-specific. All major credit cards are accepted.

 You also can visit showrooms (*Ausstellungsräume*) of large companies such as Miele, Philips and Siemens. Prices may be the same, but the selection and product information should be more comprehensive. Check the telephone directory's white pages for locations. Product instructions often come (or are available) in multiple languages, including English, so be sure to ask.

New appliances are usually guaranteed for six months from the date of purchase. Upon request, firms will send someone to your home during this period to service the machine. If the person finds nothing wrong, however, you must pay the service charge. You're better off taking an appliance to a designated service center instead of the store where you bought it. Although the store may handle the repair, it's generally not free, and replacement or service can take a long time. When buying a new machine, ask if the store will be responsible for the installation and warranty because it's generally not included in the purchase price.

FLOWERS *Blumen,* PLANTS *Pflanzen* & GARDENING

Gardening Terms

Advice service *Beratungsdienst*

Bouquet *Blumenstrauss*

Bulbs *Blumenzwiebel*

Florists *Blumenhandlungen*

Flowerpot, large *grosser Blumentopf*

Flowerpot, small *kleiner Blumentopf*

Flowers *Blumen*

Flowers, fresh-cut *frische Schnittblumen*

Garden *Garten*

Garden center *Gartencenter, Gartenbedarf*

Garden furniture *Gartenmöbel*

Garden tools *Gartengeräte*

Landscaping/design *Gartenanlagen, Gartenarchitekten*

Nursery *Gärtnerei*

Plant protection *Pflanzenschutzmittel*

Planters *Blumenbehälter*

Seeds *Samen*

Sets *Setzlinge*

Soil *Erde*

FLOWER SHOPS

Flower shops are everywhere in Vienna—from established stores to little stalls. The city's many markets (e.g., **Naschmarkt** on Saturday and **Viktor Adler Markt**) are also good sources of fresh-cut flowers. In addition, **Holland Blumenmark,** a chain with branches throughout the city, offers a variety of plants and flowers at reasonable prices. Large stores like **IKEA, Bauhaus** and **Metro** also carry a selection of indoor plants and pots.

GARDEN CENTERS

The following are two large specialty garden centers:

BELLAFLORA
1220, Pergostrasse 33
☎ 259 76 72

2334 Vösendorf,
Shopping City Süd area
☎ 699 87 47

GARTENCENTER STARKL
2331 Vösendorf,
Konsumstrasse 6-8
☎ 69 27 61 or ☎ 69 62 25

3430 Tulln, Frauenhofer 1
☎ 02272 642 42

The Tulln location is also open
Sun, 9 AM - 5 PM.

PLANT DOCTOR

If your plant needs professional attention, contact the following organization (bring a German speaker with you if possible):

AUSTRIAN GARDEN ASSOCIATION
Österreichische Gartenbaugesellschaft Verein
   1010, Parkring 12
   ☎ 512 84 16
   Wed, 4 PM - 6 PM

This group is affiliated with the English Garden Association. It gives advice on hydroculture and offers free diagnosis of plant diseases. Its membership fee includes a subscription to the monthly magazine *Garten* (in German). It also carries books and magazines in English.

M. EIFLER & CO
   1010, Petersplatz 11
   ☎ 533 61 03

This store specializes in seeds, but will also provide advice on plant problems.

DRIED FLOWERS & SILK FLOWERS
Trockenblumen und Kunstblumen, Seidenpflanzen

Many florists carry dried flowers as well, and **Bellaflora** also carries silk flowers. The following store specializes in artificial flowers and plants:

PLANTAS
   2334 Vösendorf, Shopping
   City Süd, Europaring 18
   ☎ 69 91 20 0

This store carries individual stems and arrangements of silk flowers.

GARDEN FURNITURE *Gartenmöbel*

Look under *"Gartenmöbel"* in the yellow pages. All big household stores (e.g., **IKEA, Bauhaus, Kika** and **Leiner**) carry garden, patio and terrace furniture seasonally. In addition is the following store:

BLAHA GARTENMÖBEL
   2100 Korneuburg, Kleinengersdorfer Strasse 110
   ☎ (02262) 750 66
   Mon - Fri , 8 AM - 6 PM, Sat, 8 AM - 5 PM (March - Sept),
   Mon - Fri, 8 AM - noon (Oct - Feb)

Located outside Vienna, this store has 7,000 m² of garden furniture. English is spoken. Only cash and Eurocheques are accepted.

FURNITURE Möbel

Look in the yellow pages under:

Furniture Möbel
Furniture Dealers Möbelhandel

Furniture Stores
Einrichtungshäuser

Although all districts have some furniture shops, you can also find a variety of smaller ones in the seventh district, which is known as the furniture quarter (*Möbelviertel*). Try Spittelberggasse, Siebensterngasse and Breitegasse. Nearly all shops deliver for a fee. All the all-purpose stores listed at the beginning of this chapter sell furniture.

Very few apartments and houses have built-in closets (*Einbauschränke*) or wardrobes (*Schränke*). Secondhand shops, the Dorotheum (see Antiques section of this chapter) and moving sales are also options.

SPECIALTY FURNITURE

The following stores carry specific styles of furniture. Also look in the yellow pages under:

Period Furniture Stilmöbel

TRANSANTIK
1050, Rechte Wienzeile 45
☎ 587 92 97

1060, Esterhazygasse 23
☎ 587 44 28

These stores carry natural-pine country furniture, new and antique. No credit cards are accepted, and English is not spoken.

KARNER & KARNER LEBENSRÄUME
1070, Siebensterngasse 4
☎ 524 40 28
Fax 524 40 29

This store carries teak and coconut furniture from Southeast Asia, as well as ceramics from Morocco, international textiles and primitive art. English is spoken, and Eurocard/ MasterCard and Visa are accepted.

KRAUS: SKANDINAVISK MØBELHUS
1230, Altmannsdorferstr. 153
☎ 665 95 95

This store stocks Scandinavian solid-wood furniture. English is spoken, but credit cards are not accepted.

> **TIP** There is a large amount of designer furniture stores in Udine, Italy, on the border to southern Austria. Many deliver free to Vienna and have reasonable prices.

COUNTRY HOUSE
ENGLISCHES WOHNEN

1080, Auerspergstrasse 11
☎ 403 24 93-0
Fax 403 24 93-14
1090, Liechtensteinstrasse 6
☎ 310 74 74
Fax 310 74 74-14

English Antiques and
Eccentricities
1010, Freyung 3
Courtyard Palais Harrach
☎ 532 43 44

These specialist stores feature classical English- and French-made reproduction furniture, furnishings and accessories. They offer free interior-design advice, work to given budgets, speak English and accept Credit Cards. Country House is a real haven for friends of the traditional Classic Look in Austria. (see inside back cover).

Furniture Terms
Armoire/wardrobe *Schrank*
Chair (arms) *Sessel*
Chair (no arms) *Stuhl*
Couch/sofa *Couch/Sofa*
Desk *Schreibtisch*
Dresser *Kommode*
Shelves *Regale*

GAS FOR GRILLS

ING.
H. GRUBER

1170, Wattgasse 66
☎ 486 33 68
Fax 486 33 68-9
Mon - Fri, 8 AM - noon, 1 PM - 6 PM

This store can fill tanks with U.S.-type fittings. Herr Gruber speaks a little English.

GIFTS *Geschenke*

Gift and souvenir shops abound, but if you need an authentic Austrian gift, try one of the following shops:

NIEDERÖSTERREICHISCHES HEIMATWERK

1010, Herrengasse 6-8
☎ 533 34 95

This shop specializes in cottage-industry gifts produced traditionally in Lower Austria. Goods include *Trachten* fabrics, ceramics, ornaments and Austrian cookbooks printed in English. English is spoken, and all major credit cards are accepted.

ÖSTERREICHISCHE WERKSTÄTTEN

1010, Kärntner Strasse 6
☎ 512 24 18

This multilevel store stocks goods produced by Austrian artisans. Works of glass and metal, jewelry, decorative items and ornaments are supplemented by seasonal items. English is spoken, and all major credit cards are accepted.

GLASS, GLAZIERS & MIRRORS
Glas, Glasereien & Spiegel

In Austria, all services for windows, furniture glass, picture frames and mirrors are performed by *Glasereien*. Look in the yellow pages under:

Glass Studios (glass ceilings and doors, glass furniture, custom-designed mirrors, Tiffany-style work and art glass) *Glasatelier, Kunstglasereien*

Glazier (windows, furniture glass, picture frames and glass and mirrors) *Glasereien* (listed alphabetically by district)

In the case of window (*Fensterglas*) replacement, some shops may require you to bring the broken window in for repair.

INTERIOR-DESIGN FABRIC, CURTAINS, DRAPERY & UPHOLSTERY

Decorating Terms

Blinds *Jalousien*

Carpets *Teppiche*

Cornices/pelmets *Karniesen*

Curtains/drapes *Vorhänge*

Curtain rods *Vorhangstangen*

Decorator *Dekorateur*

Drapery cleaning *Vorhang-reinigung*

Fabric *Stoff*

Home-furnishing stores *Einrichtungshäuser*

Upholstered furniture *Polstermöbel*

Upholsterer *Tapezierer*

Upholstery cleaning *Polstermöbelreinigung*

Upholstery material *Möbel-stoffe*

Wallpaper *Tapeten*

Wallpaper hangers *Tapeten-arbeiter*

DECORATOR FABRICS *Dekorstoffe*

The all-purpose stores (e.g., **IKEA, Interio, Kika** and **Leiner**) listed earlier also carry decorator fabrics at reasonable prices. The stores listed on the following page stock a different selection and often offer decorating services.

BACKHAUSEN
1010, Kärntner Strasse 33
☎ 514 04-0

This famous store carries furnishing materials, carpets, accessories and souvenirs. It has one-of-a-kind fabrics from its own studios and *Jugendstil* reproduction designs. It accepts all major credit cards, and English is spoken.

INDIA TRADING LTD.
1010, Strobelgasse 2
☎ 512 51 96
Fax 512 93 08
eMail pravin@india.co.at

This store carries a wide selection of pure silks in a rainbow of colors. All major credit cards are accepted, and English is spoken.

KA INTERNATIONAL
1010, Wildpretmarkt 2-4
☎ 533 17 12

This shop carries a colorful array of decorator fabrics and offers a decorator service. It has some furniture in stock, but you can also custom-order. Decorative borders and tassels, wallpaper and borders, and sisal carpets are available to order. It also custom-makes curtains and drapes. All major credit cards are accepted, and English is spoken.

LAURA ASHLEY
1010, Weihburggasse 5
☎ 512 93 40

This well-known store carries fabric, women's clothing and wallpaper. It accepts all major credit cards, and English is spoken.

LES TISSUS COLBERT
1010, Vorlaufstrasse 4
☎ 535 80 87

This shop stocks French fabrics in regular and extra-wide widths (1.40 m-2.80 m), as well as some accessories. It accepts all major credit cards, and English may be spoken.

COUNTRY HOUSE VORHANG DESIGN
1090, Liechtensteinstrasse 6
☎ 310 74 74

This store specializes in drapery fabrics in English patterns. It accepts all major credit cards, and English is spoken.

KEYS & LOCKSMITHS
Schlüssel und Schlossereien

Look in the yellow pages under:
Lockouts *Aufsperrdienste, Schlüsseldienste*
Locksmith (to install locks) *Schlosserei*

Many security keys (for apartments and houses) cannot be duplicated. You have to ask the landlord or house manager, who will often provide the extra keys for a fee (be aware that security keys can cost ATS 500 each). For those that can be duplicated, spare keys can be made quickly at department stores, supermarkets, shoe-repair services, hardware stores or at one of the many **Mister Minit** outlets (in all major shopping malls and areas). Check the telephone directory's white pages for the location nearest you. If you're locked out or need to replace a lost suitcase key, try the following locksmith:

JOSEF SAIBEL
1020, Karmelitergasse 3
☎ 216 33 00-0

This locksmith is on duty 24 hours a day, seven days a week (including holidays). He can copy keys as well as install security locks and doors. If you've lost a suitcase key, you can bring your suitcase to see if he can make a duplicate. He speaks English.

 LOST KEYS

If you've lost your keys, go to the nearest police station (*Polizei*) to check whether they have been turned in (a one-week wait is suggested). The police will also call a locksmith for you if you're locked out. For added protection, you can register your keys with the following office:

KEY-RETURN CENTER *Schlüsselfundzentrale*
1080, Lerchenfelderstrasse 44/Stiege 2 (2nd staircase)
☎ 406 13 25

There is a small fee per calendar year for a bundle of keys. You receive a metal tag with a registration number and instructions to take found keys to the police. The police will call the service if they receive your keys, and then the service calls you. It also pays a reward to the finder. English is spoken.

DROP YOUR KEYS IN THE SEWER?! Call MA 30 at ☎ 795 14 93-00 anytime, and someone will come to retrieve them within 30 minutes (ATS 800 weekdays, ATS 1.600 evenings and holidays).

EQUIPKITCHEN EQUIPMENT & HARDWARE
Küchengeräte und Eisenwaren
Look in the yellow pages under:
Hardware Stores *Eisenwarenhandlungen* (mostly tools, nuts, bolts)

HOUSE & KITCHEN EQUIPMENT
Haus- und Küchengerätehandlungen
Many of the larger household and department stores listed earlier sell kitchen equipment and a limited supply of hardware items. If you're looking for Tupperware plastic containers, call the following numbers:

TUPPERWARE
1190, Formanekgasse 23
☎ 369 28 59
Tues, 8 AM - 12:30 PM,
1:30 PM - 5 PM
(call ahead for other times)

Two other locations are listed in the telephone directory's white pages, but keep in mind that Austrian Tupperware differs significantly from U.S. styles.

**SANDRA
SCHWEIGHOFER-COOPER
(U.S.-style Tupperware)**
1190, Sandgasse 37-39/1/1
☎ 320 72 69
Mobile ☎ 0664 337 08 03

This AWA member takes orders in the summer and winter and goes back to the United States to pick up the requested items.

LIGHTS, LAMPS & LAMPSHADES
Leuchten, Lampen und Lampenschirme
There are many lighting shops throughout Vienna, but all major household and department stores also sell lights. Most apartments come without lighting fixtures, so you'll have to purchase a few right away. Depending on how many rooms you have, this could add up—you may want to try more affordable stores like **IKEA.** You'll find a limited selection of mainly modern fixtures in stores such as **Leiner, Kika, Michelfeit** and **Cosmos.** Hardware stores such as **Bauhaus** and **Bauwelt** also sell indoor and outdoor lighting.

**LEUCHTENZENTRUM
MOLECZ & SOHN**
1070, Neubaugasse 23
☎ 523 17 06
1230, Oberluaerstrasse 271-283
☎ 616 40 65

This store produces and sells a wide selection of light fixtures. It carries many replacement glass shades.

**WIENER MESSING
MANUFAKTUR**
1070, Kellermanngasse 8
☎ 526 43 70

If you're looking for *Jugendstil* lamps, try this store. It also takes special orders and restores old fixtures.

Returning Old Fluorescent Tubes

You pay deposits on fluorescent tubes, so when you buy replacements at a lighting store, bring the old ones back to avoid paying another deposit.

LINENS FOR BED & TABLE

Linen Terms

Bedding/linens *Bettwaren*
Comforters/duvets *Tuchent*
Comforter cleaners
Bettfedernreinigung
Mattresses *Matratzen*

Pillowcases *Polsterüberzüge*
Pillows *Polster*
Sheets *Leintücher*
Table linens *Tischwäsche*

All major household and department stores have linen departments, but you should be aware that sizes may differ from your home country (e.g., bed linens are not the same size as U.S. ones). In Austria, you'll find down comforters with a cover (*Überzug*) used in place of a top sheet and blankets. Pillows (*Polster*) are square, so be aware when buying pillowcases (*Polsterüberzüge*). Various latex and hypoallergenic products are also available. The following stores specialize in linens and also carry American sizes and styles:

GANS
  1010, Brandstätte 1
  ☎ 533 35 60

This specialty store has several locations throughout the city so refer to the telephone directory's white pages for the location nearest you. All major credit cards are accepted, and English is spoken.

GUNKEL
  1010, Tuchlauben 11
  ☎ 533 63 01

All major credit cards are accepted, and some English is spoken.

ZUR SCHWÄBISCHEN JUNGFRAU
  1010, Graben 26
  ☎ 535 53 56 or ☎ 535 53 57

Founded in 1720, this shop stocks American sizes and brands such as Fieldcrest. It will custom-make and embroider bedding. It accepts all major credit cards, and English is spoken.

METALWORK, GOLD & SILVER *Metallwaren-erzeugung, Gold und Silber*

Look in the yellow pages under:

Coppersmith *Kupferschmied*
Goldsmith *Goldschmied*
Metalwork *Metallwarener-zeugung*
Silver Plating/Replating *Versilberungen*

Silversmith *Silberschmied*
Wrought Iron *Kunstschmiede-waren, Schmiedeeisen*

BERNDORF
1010, Wollzeile 12
☎ 512 29 44

Berndorf is an Austrian manufacturer of cutlery. In addition to selling its own products, this store offers silver replating (which takes two to three months) and repair. It accepts all major credit cards, and English is spoken.

PIANOS & PIANO TUNERS *Klaviere und Klavierstimmer*

Look in the yellow pages under:
Piano Dealers *Klavierhandlungen*
Piano Rentals *Klavierleihanstalten*

While there are many piano dealers in the city of music, the following is considered one of the best worldwide:

BÖSENDORFER KLAVIERFABRIK
1010, Bösendorferstrasse 12
☎ 503 31 18

This world-renowned piano maker, in business since the late 18th century, handles tuning, sales and rentals. Ask for Herr Blum, who speaks English.

PIANO TUNERS

The Austrian Blind Industry (*Österreichische Blindenindustrie*) has recommended the following two piano tuners who speak English and whom you can call directly:

MR. GERHARD HYDEN
☎ 480 03 15

MR. KURT TOMISCHEK
☎ 985 07 50

PICTURE FRAMING & RESTORATION
Restaurierung

Look in the yellow pages under:

Picture Frames *Bilderrahmen*

Restorers *Restauratoren*

If you want a mat around your picture, ask for a *Passepartout*. The following location does picture framing and restoration:

KUNSTVERLAG WOLFRUM
1010, Augustinerstrasse 10
☎ 512 53 98

This shop also carries old etchings, art calendars, note cards and books. Many languages are spoken.

SECONDHAND SHOPS & FLEA MARKETS
Altwaren und Flohmärkte

Secondhand Shops are listed in the yellow pages under *"Altwaren."* You can also find used goods at flea markets (*Flohmärkte*). Check the Antiques section of this chapter for a book listing flea markets.

NASCHMARKT
1060, Wienzeile

In the sixth district, at the end of the *Naschmarkt* near the U4 Kettenbrückengasse exit is a flea market every Sat, 6 AM - noon. Get there early for the best buys.

VISPTA SKI SALE
1220, Strasse der
Menschenrechte 1
☎ 203 55 95

Held in late October or early November every year, this is a huge secondhand winter-sports-equipment sale and flea market sponsored by the PTA of the Vienna International School. Call for details.

FRANZ-JOSEFS-KAI
1010, Franz-Josefs-Kai
(below Schwedenplatz)

This market is spread out along the Danube Canal (*Donaukanal*) below Schwedenplatz. It operates during the summer.

Sat, 3 PM - 6 PM,
Sun, 10 AM - 8 PM
(times may vary).

The parent-teacher organizations of both the American International School and the Vienna International School sponsor spring and autumn flea market/bazaars. See the Education chapter for addresses and phone numbers.

You can also find many secondhand shops on the following streets:

1040 & 1050, Schönbrunner Strasse

1040, Favoritenstrasse, Margaretenstrasse and Wiedner Hauptstrasse

1180, Währinger Strasse

SECONDHAND FURNITURE WAREHOUSES

CARITAS-LAGER
(Storehouse)
    1050, Mittersteig 10
    ☎ 505 96 37
    Mon, 9 AM - 8 PM,
    Tues, Fri 9 AM - 6 PM, Sat, 9 AM - noon

This large warehouse has four halls containing furniture ranging from kitchen units to bedroom suites. Parking is plentiful and delivery is available. Major credit cards are accepted.

SECONDHAND ELECTRONICS

A good source is people leaving Austria. Check bulletin boards and newsletters of the United Nations, embassies, international schools and the AWA. Also look in the *Bazar* newspaper (see Publications appendix) and online at www. virtualvienna.net.

TELEVISION

Look in the yellow pages under:

Television *Fernsehapparate*
Television Repair *Fernsehservice*

If you want someone to come to your home, look for the word *"Heimservice"* in advertisements and yellow-page listings. For information on cable and satellite reception or VCRs, see the TV & Radio section of the Communications chapter. For purchase options, see the Electrical Appliances and Secondhand Shops sections of this chapter.

TRANSFORMERS FOR ELECTRICAL CURRENT

If you've brought electrical equipment from the United States, you must use a transformer. The American current is 110 V, 50 cycle, while the Austrian current is 220 V, 60 cycle, so without a transformer, your appliances will burn out within seconds. Transformers are less expensive in the United States, so try to buy them there. They come in various sizes and capacities; the power-handling capability should be as large as, or slightly larger than, the appliance's power requirements. Never connect an appliance to a transformer with a smaller power rating because you risk blowing fuses, damaging appliances and possibly causing a fire. Transformers only adapt voltage and do not convert cycles, which affect the speed of some appliance functions (e.g., tape recorders may play faster and clock radios won't keep time properly).

Transformers may develop some heat while in use, which is not detrimental. However, if one becomes hot to the touch, the appliance you're using may be defective. If you've come without transformers, try buying used ones from people from the United Nations, international schools, embassies or the AWA, who often sell theirs before leaving Austria. Check the bulletin boards or publications of these organizations for sale notices. If you would like one made to order, contact one of the following companies:

JOSEPH BARTH
    1100, Neilreichgasse 45
    ☎ 604 22 98
    Mon - Thurs, 7 AM - 4 PM,
    Fri, 7 AM - 11:30 AM

Herr Barth, who speaks English, builds transformers to specifications and also repairs them.

ARNOLD RUSA
    1180, Schumanngasse 36
    ☎ 405 33 85
    Mon - Thurs, 8 AM - 4 PM,
    Fri, 8 AM - noon

This company makes transformers to order, and some English is spoken.

 To determine the size of the transformer needed for any given appliance, multiply the number of amperes by the voltage: **Amps x Volts = Watts.**

Transformer Care

- Turn transformer off or unplug it when not in use.
- Never handle one with wet hands or feet.
- Do not handle or move transformer while equipment is plugged.
- Keep transformer well-ventilated.

Recycling

Vienna produces 800,000 tons of waste annually. Everyone, however, can help reduce this amount by practicing the three R's: reduce, reuse and recycle. When shopping, avoid excess packaging, throwaway containers and products that will become hazardous waste. Also, buy products that can be reused, such as cloth napkins instead of paper, returnable bottles rather than throwaways and cloth sacks rather than plastic. Regardless of how we shop, there will still be waste. An important contribution to reducing waste is to separate domestic waste, which can be classified into three categories: recyclable, hazardous waste and bulk waste.

This symbol refers to anything that can be recycled.

This symbol refers to a product that has been deemed environmentally friendly by the Association for Consumer Information (*Verein für Konsumenteninformation*), which means it has met certain standards for production, usage, disposal, air pollution, packaging and overall environmental impact.

This symbol signifies that a fee has been paid for recycling the packaging of the product.

RECYCLABLES

Recyclables are reusable waste materials. By collecting them separately, incinerated or dumped waste can be reduced by up to 25 percent. Recyclables include waste paper, clear and colored glass, beverage cans, waste metal, plastic wrap, aluminum foil, textiles and organic garden and kitchen waste.

HAZARDOUS WASTE

Hazardous waste includes substances that, when carelessly thrown away, can endanger human, plant and animal life. Batteries, oils and pharmaceutical drugs are some such items. If you fail to take hazardous waste to a collection center, you are creating a direct threat to the environment.

BULK WASTE

Bulk waste is anything too large for a regular container due to its size and/or weight. This includes building debris, used tires, furniture and wood. These items are collected separately in special bulk containers at waste dumps.

SEPARATING YOUR RECYCLABLES

You will often find recycling containers located in your apartment complex or in a central location outside for communal use. Remember to rinse out all containers. Also, when your hands are full, use the foot bars at the bottom of the bins to automatically open the lids. If you carry your recyclables in a plastic bag, remember to empty the contents into the appropriate container and dispose of the bag in the plastics bin. The following are the names of the containers and acceptable recyclable materials for them.

WASTE PAPER *Altpapier*
goes in the container with the **RED LID**

You CAN recycle:

+ newspapers, magazines, catalogs, brochures
+ letters, writing paper, envelopes (plastic windows removed)
+ books, notebooks, telephone directories
+ paper bags
+ cardboard boxes, corrugated boxes (unfolded and/or cut into pieces)

You CAN'T recycle:

– wax-coated containers or boxes (e.g., milk, juice, frozen-food or cigarette packages)
– carbon paper, copying paper, fax paper
– dark-colored gift-wrapping paper
– soiled or greasy paper
– plastic bags

PLASTIC WRAP/PACKAGING
Kunststoffverpackungen
goes in the container with the **YELLOW LID**

You CAN recycle:

+ shopping and other plastic bags (one m² or more)
+ packaging wrap/film (one m² or more)
+ household plastic wrap/film (one m² or more)
+ plastic beverage bottles (1/2 liter or more)

You CAN'T recycle:

– rigid plastics
– dairy-product containers
– plastic containers for fruit and meat
– formed/molded plastics
– plastic bottles and containers used for household, do-it-yourself and industrial purposes

CLEAR GLASS *Weissglas*
goes in the container with the GRAY LID

You CAN recycle:

+ clear disposable bottles
+ clear preserves/jam jars
+ clear wine and liquor bottles
+ condensed-milk and soft-drink bottles
+ drinking glasses

You CAN'T recycle:

− slightly colored glass (e.g., light green or light brown)
− screw caps, tops, lids, corks
− metal neck rings and tops (e.g., from screw-top closures)
− earthenware bottles, porcelain, china
− mirrors, window glass
− plastic bags or bottles

COLORED GLASS *Buntglas*
goes in the container with the GREEN LID

You CAN recycle:

+ colored or slightly colored disposable bottles
+ colored or slightly colored wine and liquor bottles

You CAN'T recycle:

− clear glass
− screw caps, tops, lids, corks
− metal neck rings and tops (e.g., from screw-top closures)
− porcelain, stoneware, china
− plastic bags or bottles

BOTTLES FOR DEPOSIT *Pfand*

Before you drop your glass bottles and jars into the recycling bins, look for the word *"Pfand"* (which means "deposit") on them. To get your deposit back, take these to a supermarket with a bottle-return machine or conveyor belt, both of which are usually located in the bottled-beverage section or near the store entrance. While you can use the machine on your own, you must ring the bell if the conveyor belt is unattended. A clerk should then turn on the belt to take your returnables and give you a receipt (*Flaschenzettel*) to present to the cashier, who will deduct the amount from your grocery bill.

BEVERAGE CANS *Metall-Dosen*
go in the container with the BLUE LID

You CAN recycle:

+ aluminum or tin beverage cans (e.g., beer or soft-drink cans)
+ aluminum foil

You CAN'T recycle:

– aerosol cans (e.g., hair spray, household cleaners)
– bicycles

BIODEGRADABLE FOOD WASTE *Biotonne*
goes in the container with the BROWN LID

You CAN recycle:

+ grass, weeds, leaves, tree branches, hedge and bush clippings, crop waste, shrubs, windfall
+ fruit, dairy products, tea leaves and coffee grounds

You CAN'T recycle:

– meat, bones, greasy or salted food, glass, metal, plastic, batteries, composite materials (e.g., baby diapers, milk containers), all chemicals, furniture varnish, paint, oil, newspapers, colored prints, paper, drugs, dust and dirt removed from vacuum cleaners, textiles, wood, cat litter, dog droppings
– plastic bags used to carry organic waste to bins (The basic rule regarding compost materials is to bring only the kind of waste you would dump in your own compost pile.)

RECYCLING WAX-COATED DRINK CARTONS

Wax-coated milk and juice cartons can be recycled from your home. Once a year, individual collection boxes (*Der Bag*) are left on your doorstep so you can fill them up with cleaned, flattened cartons and leave them outside your house or apartment building. These will then be replaced with new boxes. Pick-up dates are listed on the *Bag* lid. For more information (in German), call ☎ 406 60 00.

TEXTILES

Textiles can be taken to:

- **Waste dumps year-round**
- **Mobile collection centers in April and October**
- ***Humana* boxes throughout the city (often near other recycling bins)**
- **Biannual clothing drives, which collect used clothing directly from your home.** Acceptable textiles include: all clean clothing, underwear, linens, wool and cotton blankets, feathers in fabric sacks, fabric remnants measuring at least 30x30 cm (to be turned into cleaning rags). Unacceptable items include: soiled textiles, leather goods, shoes, hats, bags, nylon stockings, carpet, mattresses, fabric pieces smaller than 30x30 cm.

STYROFOAM

Styrofoam items can be returned to any waste dump and some grocery stores, including Billa, Merkur and Spar. The in-store collection site is usually in the bottle-return area.

WASTE-DISPOSAL SYMBOLS

 Anything with this symbol can be thrown into the appropriate household-waste container.

 Anything with this symbol cannot be removed with household waste. You must take it to a special-waste collector or to a nearby problem-material collection point (*Problemstoffsammelstelle*). Return toxic substances (e.g., paint, paint thinner, car oil) to the store where purchased.

 Anything with this symbol is forbidden from being dumped into the sewer system, so don't empty it into sink drains or toilets. Feminine-hygiene products, nylon stockings, leftover pet food and cigarette butts should all go into the household-waste (*Hausmüll*) container. Take other products to the store where purchased, a special-waste collector or problem-material collection point.

HAZARDOUS WASTE

Batteries

Used batteries can be returned to any waste dump, some Post Offices, some grocery stores (near the check-out or in the bottle-return area) and stores where they were purchased. Car batteries can be taken to gas stations.

Lightbulbs

Burnt-out lightbulbs should be returned to the stores where they were purchased.

Medicine

Return all unused medicine to any pharmacy (*Apotheke*) or problem-material collection point.

Motor Oil

Used motor oil can be returned to a gas station or taken to a problem-material collection point.

Bulk Waste

The following items can be taken to a waste dump:

- Building debris
- Tires
- Furniture
- Wood
- Mattresses

Waste dumps also provide containers to separately dispose of bulky recyclables such as cardboard, metals and organic waste.

WASTE DUMPS *Mistplätze*

All types of waste—recyclables, hazardous waste and bulk waste—are accepted at the locations listed below. You are allowed to take a maximum of one car-trunkful of bulk waste to any dump site free of charge, or you can have it all taken from your house—for a fee. For pick-up information, call ☎ 546 48 (Mon - Fri, 6 AM - 10 AM).

Waste dumps are open Mon - Tues, Thurs - Fri 7 AM - 6 PM, Wed 7 AM - 8 PM, Sat 10 AM - 6 PM.

- 1020, Dresdner Strasse 119
- 1100, Sonnleithnergasse 30
- 1110, Döblerhofstrasse 18
- 1120, Wundtgasse/ Jägerhausgasse
- 1140, Zehetnergasse 7-9
- 1160, Kendlerstrasse 47
- 1170, Richthausenstrasse 2-4
- 1190, Grinzinger Strasse 151

- 1190, Leidesdorfgasse 1
- 1210, Fultonstrasse 10
- 1210, Stammersdorfer Strasse (next to 224)
- 1220, Vienna Waste Treatment Plant (*Abfallbehandlungsanlage der Stadt Wien*), Percostrasse 2
- 1230, Südrandstrasse 2

RECYCLING INFORMATION

The list of products accepted for recycling (especially plastics) is constantly changing. For the most recent list, or for answers to other questions regarding recycling and/or waste disposal, call:

The Waste Line (*Mist-Telefon*) ☎ 546 48
(Mon - Fri 8 AM -3 PM)

This service can provide information in English on the separate collection of recyclable and hazardous domestic and industrial waste.

It can also give you the location of the nearest problem-material collection point (*Problemstoffsammelstelle*).

SPECIAL SERVICES

CAR DISPOSAL

For a sizable fee, you can have a wrecked or old car towed away by mailing the model identification information and a release form (available from any police station) to: MA 48, 1050, Einsiedlergasse 2 (call ☎ 760 43 87-0 to request towing). For more information, call ☎ 588 17-0 (English is spoken).

MOBILE WASTE-COLLECTION CENTERS

These centers operate in April and October, so look for advertisements in the local papers.

FLEA MARKET OF WASTE
Mistflohmarkt

To buy or sell junk, go to:

MISTFLOHMARKT
1220, Stadlauer Strasse 41A
(Tues - Sat 9 AM - 3 PM)

Vienna is a food lover's dream, offering a variety of hearty entrées and decadent desserts. When you're in a hurry or short on cash, a sausage stand (*Würstelstand*) or snack shop (*Imbiss*) lets you fill up and go (though you'll probably have to stand). A pub (*Beisel*) or inn (*Gasthaus*) offers a cozier setting and moderately priced local cuisine. If you have a caffeine craving or a sweet tooth, a coffeehouse (*Kaffeehaus*) or pastry shop (*Konditorei*) is just the place. Weekends, especially during the summer, are perfect for visiting the nearby wine taverns (*Heurigen*) serving this year's local vintage and offering a buffet to accompany their homegrown wines. Vienna also supplies international flavor with everything from Chinese *dim sum* to Mexican *fajitas*. So explore the city and discover your own favorite neighborhood restaurant (*Lokal*).

Guten Appetit!

HOW TO EAT OUT IN VIENNA

- **BRING CASH.** Many restaurants in Vienna do not accept credit cards, so if you plan to use one, call or ask ahead (*"Nehmen Sie Kreditkarten?"*). Also, you may want to ask which days, if any, the restaurant is closed (*"Haben Sie Ruhetag?"*).

- **SEAT YOURSELF, UNLESS YOU HAVE A RESERVATION.** If you want to make a reservation, say, *"Ich möchte einen Tisch reservieren."*

- **DON'T EXPECT TO FIND A NONSMOKING (*Nichtraucher*) SECTION.** With very few exceptions, there is no such thing, so try to find a corner table or sit outside.

- **ASK FOR A MENU (*"Die Speisekarte, bitte"*).** Then the waiter (*Herr Ober*) or waitress (*Fräulein*) will ask what you want to drink (*"Zu trinken?"*). Keep in mind that all menu prices include tax and a service charge.

- **IF YOU WANT TAP WATER, ASK FOR IT (*"Leitungswasser, bitte"*) OR ORDER MINERAL WATER (*"Mineralwasser, bitte"*).** Water isn't a regular service here. And you'll have to ask for refills, too. Also, there are no free refills of coffee.

- **KEEP YOUR VOICE DOWN.** Like many people, Austrians appreciate quiet conversation inside restaurants (and outside those located in residential neighborhoods). Also, if you're speaking a language other than German, you're likely to call more attention to yourself.

- **IF YOU NEED A DOGGIE BAG, SAY, *"Können Sie mir das einpacken, bitte?"*** Austrians don't normally take home leftovers, but if you ask in German, the server should oblige.

- **ASK FOR THE CHECK (*"Zahlen, bitte"*).** Your server may ask if the check will be paid together (*"Zusammen?"*) or separately (*"Getrennt?"*), then will calculate the bill. (You will also be charged for each piece of bread eaten.) You give a sum that usually includes a 5 to 7 percent tip (e.g., he or she says, "100." You give the exact amount plus tip and say, *"Das stimmt schon"* or *"Danke."* Or say, "105" and wait for your change. It's impolite to leave the tip on the table, unless you've paid a cashier or you are leaving something for the busboy.

- **TO EAT IN OR TO GO?** If you're at a fast-food place, tell the cashier whether you want your order to go (*"Zum Mitnehmen"*) or to eat in (*"Zum Hier-Essen"*).

RESTAURANT KEY

$	**Inexpensive** Less than ATS 100*
$$	**Moderate** ATS 100 - ATS 180*
$$$	**Expensive** ATS 180 and above*

* This reflects the average cost of an entrée.

AE	American Express	**JCB**	Japanese Credit Bureau
DC	Diners Club	**V**	Visa
EC/MC	Eurocard/MasterCard	**RR**	Reservation required

RESTAURANTS

Here's a short list of restaurants in Vienna (in district order) to get you started. You can buy *Wien, wie es ißt ...* , a yearly guide to 4,000 of Vienna's restaurants, cafés and bars, published by Falter Verlag (www.falter.at.) Also available is *Österreich A La Carte* and *Gault Millau Österreich*, yearly restaurant and wine guides for all of Austria. These are all available at Freytag & Berndt (1010, Kohlmarkt 9) and at many bookstores. Also look in the yellow pages under *"Gastronomieseiten."*

Austrian/Viennese

GRAND CAFÉ $$$
(Ana Grand Hotel)
   1010, Kärntner Ring 9
   ☎ 515 80 91-20
   Daily 6:30 AM - midnight
   AE, DC, EC/MC, JCB, V

MELKER STIFTSKELLER $$
   1010, Schottengasse 3
   ☎ 533 55 30
   Tues-Sat 5 PM - midnight
   DC, EC/MC, V

LUSTIG ESSEN
(Eclectic Sampler Plates) $
   1010, Salvatorgasse 6
   ☎ 533 30 37
   Daily 11:30 AM - midnight
   EC/MC

OFENLOCH $$
   1010, Kurrentgasse 8
   ☎ 533 88 44
   Daily 11:30 AM - midnight
   AE, DC, EC/MC, V

PÜRSTNER $$
   1010, Riemergasse 10
   ☎ 512 63 57
   Daily 10 AM - midnight
   AE, DC, EC/MC, V

ZU DEN DREI HACKEN $$
   1010, Singerstrasse 28
   ☎ 512 58 95
   Mon - Sat 9 AM - midnight
   AE, DC, EC/MC, V

ZUM KUCKUCK $$$/RR
1010, Himmelpfortgasse 15
☎ 512 84 70
Mon - Sat noon - 2:30 and
6 PM - midnight
AE, DC, EC/MC, JCB, V

AMON $$
1030, Schlachthausgasse 13
☎ 798 81 66
Wed - Sat 10 AM - 11:30 PM,
Sun 10 AM - 10 PM
AE, EC, V

FREIHAUS $$
1040, Schleifmuehlgasse 7
☎ 587 16 65
Daily 5:30 PM - 2 AM
EC/MC, V

BOHÈME $$$/RR
1070, Spittelberggasse 19
☎ 523 31 73
Mon - Sat 6 PM - midnight
AE, DC, EC/MC, V

**SPITTELBERGER
PLUTZER BRÄU** $$
1070, Schrankgasse 2
☎ 526 12 15
Daily 11 AM - 2 AM
EC/MC, V

RESTAURANT GLACISBEISL $$
1070, Messeplatz 1
☎ 526 67 95
Daily 10 AM - midnight
AE, DC, EC/MC, V

STOMACH $$/RR
1090, Seegasse 26
☎ 310 20 99
Wed - Sat 6 PM - 11:30 PM,
Sun noon - 9:30 PM

HIETZINGER BRÄU
(*Tafelspitz*) $$$/RR
1130, Auhofstrasse 1
☎ 877 70 87
Daily 11:30 AM - 3 PM,
6 PM - 10:30 PM
(mid-July - mid-Aug closed)
DC, EC/MC, V

ECKEL $$$
1190, Sieveringer Strasse 46
☎ 320 32 18
Tues - Sat noon - 2:30 PM,
6 PM - 10:30 PM
AE, DC, V

HÄUSERL AM STOAN $
1190, Zierleitengasse 42A
☎ 440 13 77
Wed - Sun 11 AM - 11 PM

STRANDCAFÉ (Spare Ribs) $$
1220, Florian-Berndl-Gasse 20
☎ 203 67 47
Daily 11 AM - 10 PM

American

LIVINGSTONE $$$/RR
(California Cuisine)   (for dinner)
1010, Zelinkagasse 4
☎ 533 33 93
Daily 5 PM - 4 AM
AE, DC

PIZZA HUT $
1010, Rotenturmstrasse 29
☎ 535 85 80
Mon - Thur 11:30 AM - 11 PM,
Fri - Sat 11:30 AM - 1 AM,
Sun noon - 10 PM
AE, DC, EC/MC, V

PIZZA HUT
1010, Schottengasse 2
☎ 533 18 10
Mon -Sat 11 AM - 10 PM,
Sun noon - 10 PM
AE, DC, EC/MC, V

1070, Mariahilfer Strasse 120
☎ 524 06 45
Daily 11 AM - 9 PM,
AE, DC, EC/MC, V

1210, Franz Jonas Platz
☎ 271 66 40
Mon - Thu 11:30 AM - 8 PM,
Fri - Sat 11:30 AM - 9 PM
Sun noon - 9 PM
AE, DC, EC/MC, V

T.G.I. FRIDAYS $$
1010, Neuer Markt 8
☎ 513 77 89
Daily 11:30 AM - midnight
(Bar stays open longer)
AE, DC, EC/MC, V

TEXAS STEAK HOUSE
(Barbecue) $$
1150, Hütteldorfer Strasse 33
☎ 985 81 22
Mon - Sat 11 AM - midnight,
Sun 11 AM - 8 PM
(June -Sept Sat - Sun closed,
July closed)

Asian

ASIA (Chinese/Dim Sum) $$
1010, Himmelpfortgasse 27
☎ 512 72 77
Daily 11 AM - 3 PM,
5:30 PM - 11:30 PM
EC/MC, V

WOK (Asian Cuisine) $$
1040, Operngasse 20B
☎ 585 21 02
Daily 11:30 AM - 2:30 PM,
5:30 PM–11 PM
EC/MC, V

GREEN COTTAGE $$$/RR
(Chinese/Sichuan)
1050, Kettenbrückengasse 3
☎ 586 65 81
Mon - Sat 6 PM - 11:30 PM

THAI KITCHEN (Thai) $$
1050, Schönbrunner Strasse 23
☎ 586 78 85
Tues - Fri 6 PM - midnight,
Sat - Sun noon - 2:30 PM,
6 PM - midnight

NEU OST WIND (Chinese) $$
1060, Hofmühlgasse 7
☎ 597 12 57
Daily 11:30 AM - 2:30 PM,
6 PM - 11:30 PM
AE, DC, EC/MC, V

OSTWIND (Chinese) $$
1070, Lindengasse 24
☎ 523 41 82
Daily 11:30 AM - 2:30 PM,
5:30 PM - 11:30 PM
EC/MC, V

TSING TAO $$
(Chinese/Dim Sum)
1070, Burggasse 123
☎ 522 04 57
Daily 11:30 AM - 3 PM,
6 PM - 12:30 AM

1150, Gerstnerstrasse 5
☎ 892 32 27
Daily 11:30 AM - 3 PM,
6 PM - midnight
AE, DC, EC/MC, JCB, V

HAPPY BUDDHA $$
(Chinese/Dim Sum)
1150, Mariahilfer Gürtel 9
☎ 893 42 17
Daily 11:30 AM - 2:30 PM,
5:30 PM - midnight
AE, DC, EC/MC, V

JADE (Chinese) $$
1190, Grinzinger Strasse 71-73
☎ 320 68 96
Daily 11:30 AM - 3 PM,
5:30 PM - midnight
AE, DC, EC/MC, V

1190, Heiligenstädter Strasse 34
☎ 602 62 95
Daily 11:30 AM - 2:30 PM,
5:30 PM - 11:30 PM
EC/MC, V

SHUSI WONG $$
(Chinese/Dim Sum)
1190, Krottenbachstrasse 183
☎ 479 51 97
Daily 11:30 AM - 2:30 PM,
5:30 PM - 11 PM

French

LE CIEL $$$/RR
1010, Kärntner Ring 9
(ANA Grand Hotel)
☎ 515 80 91-00
Mon - Sat noon - 2:30 PM,
7 PM - 10:45 PM
AE, DC, EC/MC, JCB, V

EL FONTROUSSI $$
1030, Reisnerstrasse 39
☎ 712 54 30
Mon - Fri 11:30 AM - 2:30 PM,
6 PM - 11 PM, Sat 6 PM - 11 PM

Greek

ACHILLEUS $$
1010, Köllnerhofgasse 3
☎ 513 83 28
Mon - Fri 5:30 PM - midnight
Sat - Sun 11:30 AM - 3 PM,
5:30 PM - midnight
AE, DC, EC/MC, V

ORPHEUS $$
1010, Spiegelgasse 10
☎ 512 38 88
Sun - Thurs noon - midnight,
Fri - Sat noon - 1 AM
EC/MC, V

DER GRIECHE $$
1060, Barnabitengasse 5
☎ 587 74 66
Daily 11:30 AM - 2:30 PM,
6 PM - 11:30 PM
EC/MC, V

Indian

KOH-I-NOOR $$
1010, Marc-Aurel-Strasse 8
☎ 533 00 80
Daily 11:30 AM - 2:30 PM,
6 PM - midnight
AE, DC, EC/MC, V

RAAGINI $$
1010, Franz-Josefs-Kai 49
☎ 533 03 32
Daily 11:30 AM - 2:30 PM,
6 PM - 11 PM
DC, MC, V

DEMI TASS $$
1040, Prinz-Eugen-Strasse 28
☎ 504 31 19
Mon - Sat 11:30 AM - 2:30 PM,
6 PM - 11:30 PM
AE, DC, EC/MC, V

BOMBAY $$
1070, Neubaugasse 75
☎ 523 44 50
Daily 11 AM - 3 PM,
6 PM - midnight
AE, DC, EC/MC, V

TANDOOR $$
1180, Antonigasse 9
☎ 406 41 16
Tues - Sun 11:30 AM - 2:30 PM,
6 PM - 11 PM

International

SHEBEEN - THE INTERNATIONAL PUB $$
1070, Lerchenfelderstrasse 45
☎ 513 83 28
Mon 5 PM - 2 AM,
Tues - Fri 5 PM - 4 AM,
Sat 1 PM - 4 AM,
Sun 10 AM - 2 AM

RESTAURANT HANSEN $$/RR
1010, Wipplingerstrasse 34
☎ 532 05 42
Mon - Fri 9 AM - 8 PM,
Sat 9 PM - 5 PM

Irish

FLANAGAN'S IRISH PUB $$
1010, Schwarzenbergstrasse 1-3
☎ 513 73 78
Sun - Thurs 11 AM - 2 AM,
Fri - Sat 11 AM - 4 AM
AE, DC, EC/MC, V

BILLY BONES $$
1090, Schlickplatz 4
☎ 310 97 80
Sun - Thurs 5 PM - 1 AM,
Fri - Sat 5 PM - 2 AM

CHARLIE P's $
1090, Währinger Strasse 3
☎ 409 79 23
Mon - Thurs 10 AM - 2 AM,
Fri - Sat 10 AM - 3 AM,
Sun noon - 1 AM
AE, DC, EC/MC, V

Italian

AL CAVALLINO $$
1010, Dorotheergasse 19
☎ 512 39 36
Mon - Fri 11:30 AM - 2:30 PM,
6 PM - 11 PM
Sat 11:30 AM - 2:30 PM

CANTINETTA ANTINORI $$$/RR
1010, Jasomirgottstrasse 3-5
☎ 533 77 22
Daily 11:30 AM - midnight
AE, DC, EC/MC, V

DA CAPO $$/RR
1010, Schulerstrasse 18
☎ 512 44 91
Daily 11:30 AM - 11:30 PM
DC, V

DA CONTE $$$/RR
1010, Kurrentgasse 12
☎ 533 64 64
Mon - Sat noon - 3 PM,
6 PM - midnight
AE, DC, EC/MC, JCB, V

DANIELI $$$/RR
1010, Himmelpfortgasse 3
☎ 513 79 13
Daily 9 AM - 2 AM
AE, DC, JCB, V

NOODLES & CO. $$
1010, Karlsplatz 5
☎ 505 38 39
Sun - Fri 11 AM - 3 PM,
6 PM - 2 AM,
Sat 6 PM - 2 AM
AE, DC, EC/MC, V

NOVELLI $$$
1010, Bräunerstrasse 11
☎ 513 42 00
Mon - Sat noon - 2:30 PM,
6 PM - 11 PM
Bar: Mon - Sat 11 AM - 1 AM
DC, EC/MC, V

PROSCUITTO & COMPANY $$
1010, Führichgasse 3
Mon - Fri noon - 3 PM,
5 PM - 11 PM
Sat noon - 11 PM

A TAVOLA $$
1010, Weihburggasse 3-5
☎ 512 79 55
Mon - Sat noon - 3 PM,
6 PM - midnight
AE, EC/MC, V

TRATTORIA $$
AL CAMINETTO
1010, Neuer Markt 8a
☎ 512 34 42
Mon - Sat 10 AM - midnight
AE, DC, EC/MC, V

LA TAVOLOZZA $$
1080, Florianigasse 37
☎ 406 37 57
Tues - Sun 6 PM - 12:30 AM,
Sat - Sun noon - 3 PM

SARDEGNA $$
1090, Grünentorgasse 21
(corner of Servitengasse 14)
☎ 319 77 63
Daily 11:30 AM - 2:30 PM,
6 PM - midnight
AE, DC, EC/MC, V

Japanese

AKAKIKO (Sushi) $$
1010, Heidenschuss 3
☎ 533 85 14

1070, Mariahilferstrasse 40-48
(Gerngross, 5th floor)
☎ 524 06 16

1130, Am Platz 3
☎ 877 02 43
Daily 10:30 AM - midnight

SUSHI BAR K2 $$$
1010, Fleischmarkt 6
☎ 535 68 28
Mon - Sat noon - 2 PM,
6 PM - 11 PM
AE, DC, EC/MC, V

UNKAI (Japanese/
Weekend Sushi Buffet) $$$/RR
1010, Kärntner Ring 9
(ANA Grand Hotel)
☎ 515 80 91-10
Daily Noon - 2:30 PM,
7 PM - 10:45 PM
DC, EC/MC, JCB

YUGETSU
(Sushi & Teppan-Yaki) $$$
1010, Führichgasse 10
☎ 512 27 20
Daily noon - 2:30 PM,
6 PM - 11 PM
(Jan-March Closed Sun)
AE, DC, EC/MC, JCB, V

TOKO RI (Sushi) $$
1020, Franz-Hochedlinger-
Gasse 2
☎ 214 89 40
Mon - Sat noon - 2:30 PM,
6 PM - 11 PM
DC, EC/MC, V

RIKYU (Japanese) $$
1030, Marxergasse 15
☎ 713 37 34
Daily 11:30 AM - 2:30 PM,
6 PM - 11:30 PM
AE, DC, EC/MC, JCB, V

HANIL SUSHI (Japanese) $$
1180, Gymnasiumstrasse 26
☎ 478 54 29
Mon - Sat Noon - 2:30 PM
5:30 PM - 10:30 PM

Kosher/Jewish

ARCHE NOAH $$
1010, Seitenstettengasse 2
☎ 533 13 74
Sun - Fri 11:30 AM - 3:30 PM,
6:30 PM - 11 PM
Sat 11:30 AM - 2:30 PM
(winter 11:30 AM - 2:30 PM,
6:30 PM - 11 PM)

Latin American & Mexican

MARGARITAVILLE (Mexican) $$
1010, Bartensteingasse 3
☎ 405 47 86
Mon - Sat 6 PM - 2 AM,
Sun 6 PM - midnight
AE, EC/MC, V

MICHL'S $$$
CHURRASCARIA
(All-You-Can-Eat Brazilian Grill)
1010, Schellinggasse 12
☎ 512 04 45
Daily 11 AM - 1 AM

1150, Sechshauser Strasse 76
☎ 893 61 07
Daily 6 PM - midnight

1190, Nussdorfer Platz 8
☎ 370 62 37
Mon - Sat 6 PM - midnight,
Sun noon - 2:30 PM
EC/MC, V

TASCARIA MAREDO $$
(Argentinian Steaks)
1010, Opernring 3-5
☎ 586 77 22
Daily 11:30 AM - midnight
AE, DC, EC/MC, JCB, V
Non-smoking section

MÁS! (Mexican) $$/RR
1080, Laudongasse 36
☎ 403 83 24
Daily 6 PM - 2 AM
AE, DC, EC/MC, V

MARIA'S CANTINA $$
(Mexican)
1090, Schubertgasse 13
☎ 310 65 73
Sun - Thurs 6 PM - 2 AM,
Fri - Sat 6 PM - 4 AM

Middle Eastern

LEVANTINER SPEZIALITÄT
RESTAURANT $$
1010, Wallnerstrasse 2
☎ 533 18 95
Daily 11 AM - 11:30 PM

LEVANTE $$
1010, Wollzeile 19
☎ 512 47 21
Daily 11 AM - 11:30 PM

1070, Mariahilfer Strasse 88A
☎ 523 63 01
Daily 11 AM - 11:30 PM

1080, Josefstädter Strasse 14
☎ 408 53 06
Daily 11:30 AM - 11:30 PM
AE, EC/MC, V

Russian

FEUERVOGEL $$/RR
1090, Alserbachstrasse 21
☎ 317 53 91
Mon - Sat 5:30 PM - midnight
AE, DC, EC/MC, V

Spanish

BODEGA ESPAÑOLA $$/RR
1040, Belverderegasse 10
☎ 504 55 00
Mon - Sat 6 PM - 1 AM

BODEGA MANCHEGA $$/RR
1090, Nordbergstrasse 12
☎ 319 65 75
Daily 6:30 PM - 1 AM
AE, DC, EC/MC, V

Turkish

KEBABHAUS $
1040, Operngasse 26
☎ 587 53 08
Sun - Thurs 11:30 AM - 11:30
Fri - Sat 11:30 AM - 4 AM

LOKANTA SARIKOÇ $$
1090, Währinger Strasse 18
☎ 319 99 87
Daily 11 AM - midnight
EC/MC, V

Vegetarian

LEBENBAUER $$
1010, Teinfaltstrasse 3
☎ 533 55 56-0
Mon - Fri 11 AM - 3 PM,
5:30 PM - 10:30 PM
Sat 11 AM - 2 pm
AE, DC, EC/MC, V

SIDDHARTHA $$
1010, Fleischmarkt 16
☎ 513 11 97
Mon 11:30 AM - 3 PM,
Tues - Sat 11 AM - 3 PM,
6 PM - 11 PM

WRENKH $$
1010, Bauernmarkt 10
☎ 533 15 26
Daily 11 AM - midnight

1150, Hollergasse 9
☎ 892 33 56
Mon - Sat 11:30 AM - 2:30 PM,
6 PM - midnight PM
AE, DC, EC/MC, JCB, V

VEG $$
(Coffeehouse/Restaurant)
1070, Neubaugasse 81
☎ 522 59 07
Daily 11 AM - 3 PM,
6 PM - 11 PM
AE, DC, EC/MC, V

DREIKLANG $$
1090, Wasagasse 28
☎ 310 17 03
Mon - Fri 9 AM - 10 PM

MENU TERMS

Biere Beers

Krügel 1/2 liter of beer
Seidl 1/3 liter of beer
Pfiff 1/8 liter of beer

Suppen Soups

Bouillon mit Ei ~ Consommé with egg
Bohnensuppe ~ Bean soup
Erdäpfelsuppe/Kartoffelsuppe ~ Potato soup
Frittatensuppe ~ Beef broth with pancake strips
Gulaschsuppe ~ Goulash soup
Knoblauchcremesuppe ~ Cream of garlic soup
Leberknödelsuppe ~ Liver dumpling soup
Linsensuppe ~ Lentil soup
Zwiebelsuppe ~ Onion soup

Salate Salads

Gemischter Salat ~ Mixed salad (usually includes marinated cucumbers, potato salad and sauerkraut salad)
Grüner Salat ~ Green salad

Hauptspeisen Main Courses

Hendl/Pute ~ Chicken/Turkey
Backhendl ~ Deep-fried breaded chicken
Brathendl ~ Oven-baked chicken
Eierspeise ~ Scrambled eggs
Hühnerschnitzel ~ Deep-fried breaded chicken cutlet
Putenschnitzel ~ Deep-fried breaded turkey cutlet

Rindfleisch/Schwein ~ Beef/Pork
Bauernschmaus ~ Smoked ham, roast pork, sausage, sauerkraut and dumplings
Beuschl ~ Lungs stew
Blunzen ~ Black pudding
Fleischlaberl ~ Fried meatballs
Geröstete Leber ~ Roasted liver strips with onions
Schweinsschnitzel ~ Pan-fried pork cutlet
Stelze ~ Pork shanks/hocks
Tafelspitz mit Kren ~ Boiled beef with horseradish
Vanillerostbraten ~ Rump roast with garlic and vanilla bean
Wiener Schnitzel ~ Deep-fried breaded pork or veal cutlet
Zwiebelrostbraten ~ Rump roast with fried onions

Fische ~ Fish

Kabeljau ~ Cod	***Flunder*** ~ Flounder	***Forelle*** ~ Trout
Heilbutt ~ Halibut	***Karpfen*** ~ Carp	***Lachs/Salm*** ~ Salmon
Seezunge ~ Sole	***Thunfisch*** ~ Tuna	***Zander*** ~ Pike-Perch

Gegrillt ~ Grilled   ***Gebacken*** ~ Breaded and deep-fried
Gebraten ~ Pan-fried

Beilagen ~ Side Dishes

G'röstl/Röstkartoffeln ~ Fried potato slices with onions
Knödel ~ Dumplings
Reis ~ Rice
Petersilkartoffeln ~ Parslied potatoes
Pommes Frites ~ French fries

Nachspeisen Desserts

Kaiserschmarren mit Kompott ~ Pancake pieces with compote
Palatschinken ~ Crepes/pancakes

HEURIGEN

Heuriger (which literally means "this year's") is young wine from the current year and a *Heurigen* is a wine tavern that serves it. The *Heuriger* becomes "old" (*alt*) after St. Martin's Day, November 11. *Heurigen* are strictly regulated by law: They are only allowed to be open certain hours on certain days and cannot stay open more than 300 days a year. You can tell when one is open by looking for a pine branch (*Buschen*) hanging outside the door. A few open for lunch and most from 4 PM until midnight. Reservations are advised for large parties. If you see a sign saying *"Strassenverkauf,"* you can buy bottles "sold from the street" to take home. Just ring the doorbell.

Wiener Heurigen/Wine Taverns of Vienna is an English brochure listing various Heurigens, including their locations, business hours, and details. Available at the Vienna Tourist Information Office on Kärtner Strasse.

HOW TO ENJOY A HEURIGEN

- **Seat yourself, unless you have a reservation.** Large parties should make reservations, especially during the summer.

- **Order only your drinks from the server.** White (*weiss*) or red (*rot*) wines can be ordered by the liter (*Liter*), half liter (*Halber Liter*), quarter liter (*Viertel*) and eighth liter (*Achtel*).

- **Unless the *Heurigen* has a food menu, order meals at the buffet counter.** In a *Heurigen*, a buffet doesn't mean all-you-can-eat, but rather self-serve. You'll also have to pay for your food there. The buffet usually consists of cooked meats, sandwich meats, cheeses, salads and breads. Meat is charged by weight. You may also be able to order dishes like *Wiener Schnitzel* or whatever else the kitchen offers. If you need your bread sliced, simply say, *"Aufschneiden, bitte."*

- **Tip the strolling musicians.** Don't be surprised if they stop at your table to play a few songs. A tip of about ATS 20 is appreciated.

- **Ask for the check (*"Zahlen, bitte"*) and pay and tip the server for your drinks.** If you've paid the owner directly, you can leave a tip on the table for the server.

HEURIGEN DRINKS

Most* — Unfiltered nonalcoholic grape juice (cloudy-looking but sweet)

Sturm* — Fermented grape juice, not yet wine (sweet and packs quite a punch, so be careful!)

Staubiger* — Unfiltered young wine (literally means "dusty")

* These are seasonal (available only in the autumn).

Eiswein — Wine pressed from frozen grapes (very sweet)

Gespritzer — Mixture of wine and soda water (wine and water can be ordered separately)

Almdudler — Nonalcoholic herbal soda (tastes a bit like ginger ale)

Kracherl — Lemonade

HEURIGEN FOOD

Auflauf ~ Soufflé

Brot ~ Bread

Fisolensalat ~ Green-bean salad

Geselchtes ~ Salted and smoked ham

Kartoffelsalat ~ Potato salad

Krautsalat ~ Warm shredded cabbage lightly marinated in vinegar

Liptauer ~ Cream-cheese-and-paprika bread spread

Sauerkraut ~ Pickled shredded cabbage

Saumaisen ~ Pork dumpling

Schinken ~ Ham

Schmalz ~ Lard bread spread

Schwarzwurzelsalat ~ Root (like asparagus) salad with cream

Schweinsbraten ~ Roast pork

Semmel ~ Kaiser roll

Surschnitzel ~ Fried brine-marinated pork cutlet

Wiener Schnitzel ~ Deep-fried breaded pork or veal cutlet

Roter Rübensalat ~ Pickled red-beet salad

HEURIGEN AREAS

We'll just point you in the direction of some areas in and outside of Vienna known for their *Heurigen*. If you'd like a complete guide, buy *Wiener Heurigenführer* at any bookstore. Remember that most public transportation stops at about 12:30 AM. *"Prost!"*

Grinzing & Sievering
In the 19th district, this is the area most frequented by tourists. Beware of crowds on the weekends (though you'll find plenty of English speakers). For Grinzing, take tram (*Strassenbahn*) 38 to the end of the line and head for Cobenzlgasse. For Sievering, take bus (*Autobus*) 39A to Daringergasse.

Heiligenstadt/Nussdorf
Also in the 19th district and a bit touristy, take the U4 to Heiligenstadt, and you'll find *Heurigen* on Grinzingerstrasse and Kahlenberger Strasse. Take *Strassenbahn* D to Nussdorf.

Hietzing
In the 13th district, *Heurigen* here are a little more spread out. Take the U4 to Ober St. Veit, *Autobus* 55B two stops, then walk to Firmiangasse.

Klosterneuburg/Weidling
These two areas—which are situated on a hillside near the famous *Klosterneuburg* abbey—are beautiful settings for *Heurigen* along the Weidlingbach and the Hauptstrasse. Take the U4 to Heiligenstadt and *Autobus* 341 or 439 (to Klosterneuburg), or Autobus 239, 241 (to Weidling), .

Neustift am Walde
This area is also in the 19th district and visited by many tourists. Take *Autobus* 35A to Neustift am Walde.

Perchtoldsdorf
A wine-farming village on the edge of Vienna, its Hochstrasse and Sonnbergstrasse offer a variety of less expensive *Heurigen*. Take a map and *Strassenbahn* 60 or *Autobus* 257 or 259 to Rodaun.

Stadtheurige
The first district also has *Heurigen*. Often located under what were the vintners' houses or under former abbeys, you will find these on the side streets.

AUSTRIAN WINES

You can also order older wines at *Heurigen* and, of course, at restaurants. Below are some common ones, which can be ordered in the same sizes mentioned earlier. Keep in mind that only wines deemed high in quality receive the official Austrian Seal of Quality for Wine (*Österreichisches Weingütesiegel*).

Weissweine   White Wines

Grüner Veltliner ~ Fruity, crisp
Neuburger ~ Nutty
Rheinriesling, Welschriesling ~ Delicately aromatic
Traminer ~ Fruity, sweet
Weissburgunder ~ Semidry
Zierfandler ~ Full-bodied with a fine bouquet

Rotweine   Red Wines

Blauer Portugieser, St. Laurent ~ Full-bodied
Blaufränkisch, Blauer Burgunder ~ Fruity
Zweigelt ~ Velvety, fruity

Roséweine   Rosé Wines

Schilcher ~ Crisp

COFFEEHOUSES

In Vienna, coffee isn't just a beverage, but rather a cultural icon with the old coffeehouse (*Kaffeehaus*) as its sanctuary. A coffeehouse not only offers endless caffeinated choices but also provides a relaxed atmosphere to read newspapers (which it often provides), meet friends and, of course, indulge in decadent cakes and pastries. There's no need to rush—take your time and enjoy. Desserts are usually displayed in a glass case. You can order from the case or tell your waiter what you want. Most coffeehouses also serve alcohol and other beverages, as well as sandwiches, soups and main courses.

Here are some of the best-known coffeehouses. They can be a bit pricey for a cup of coffee (about ATS 30 - ATS 60), but they're an integral part of Vienna's culture and are worth an indulgence.

DEMEL (*Konditorei*)
1010, Kohlmarkt 14
Daily 10 AM - 7 PM
Non-smoking section
AE, DC, EC/MC, V

CAFÉ CENTRAL
1010, Herrengasse 14
Mon - Sat 8 AM - 8 PM
AE, DC, EC/MC, V

DIGLAS KAFFEEHAUS
1010, Wollzeile 10
Daily 7 AM - midnight
AE, DC, EC/MC, V

CAFÉ GRIENSTEIDL
1010, Michaelerplatz 2
Daily 8 AM - 11:30 PM
Non-smoking section
AE, DC, EC/MC, V

CAFÉ LANDTMANN
1010, Dr.-Karl-Lueger-Ring 4
Daily 8 AM - midnight
AE, DC, EC/MC, V

CAFÉ HAWELKA
1010, Dorotheergasse 6
Wed - Sat, Mon 8 AM - 2 AM,
Sun 4 PM - 2 AM

This coffeehouse serves hot jam-filled buns (*Buchteln*) after 10 PM.

CAFÉ MUSEUM
1010, Friedrichstrasse 6
Daily 8 AM - midnight
Non-smoking section

CAFÉ SACHER
(*Sachertorte*)
1010, Philharmonikerstrasse 4
(Hotel Sacher)
Daily 8:30 AM - 11:30 PM
Non-smoking section
AE, DC, EC/MC, JCB, V

CAFÉ SCHWARZENBERG
1010, Kärntner Ring 17
Sun - Fri 7 AM - midnight,
Sat 9 AM - midnight
Non-smoking section
AE, DC, EC/MC, JCB, V

CAFÉ TIROLERHOF
1010, Führichgasse 8
Mon - Sat 7 AM - 9 PM,
Sun 9:30 AM - 8 PM

CAFÉ GLORIETTE
1130, Schloss Schönbrunn
(on palace grounds overlooking
Vienna)
Daily 9 AM - 5 PM (May - mid-Sept)

COFFEEHOUSE DRINKS
Kaffeehaus Getränke

Einspänner ~ Black coffee with whipped cream in a glass
Eiskaffee ~ Coffee with vanilla ice cream and whipped cream
Heisse Schokolade ~ Hot chocolate with whipped cream
Kaffee mit Schlag ~ Coffee with cream
Kapuziner ~ Black coffee with a dash of frothed milk
Kleiner/Grosser Brauner ~ Small/large coffee
with a shot of milk or cream
Kleiner/Grosser Mokka ~ Small/large strong black coffee
Koffeinfreier Kaffee ~ Decaffeinated coffee
Kurzer ~ Small shot of espresso
Mazagran ~ Cold coffee with ice and rum
Melange ~ Half coffee and half steamed milk
Mokka Gespritzt ~ Black coffee with rum
Obers ~ Cream
Piccolo ~ Shot of black coffee with whipped cream
Portion Kaffee ~ Pot of coffee and pot of hot milk
Süssstoff/Saccharine ~ Artificial sweetener/Saccharin
Schale licht ~ Café au lait
Schlagobers ~ Whipped cream
(In Vienna, whipped cream is not sweetened.)
Schwarztee/Früchtetee (mit Zitrone oder Milch) ~
Black tea/herbal tea (with lemon or milk)
Türkischer Kaffee ~ Turkish coffee (very strong)
Verlängerter ~ Watered-down strong coffee
Zucker ~ Sugar

CAKES *Torten*

Apfelstrudel ~ Sliced apples and raisins in a flaky pastry

Dobostorte/Dobosschnitten ~ Sponge cake
with chocolate-butter-cream filling and caramel topping

Linzertorte ~ Almond pastry
filled with raspberry, apricot or red-currant jam

Malakofftorte ~ Layers of ladyfingers
with whipped-cream filling

Milchrahmstrudel (Millirahmstrudel) ~
Hot cream-cheese pastry with vanilla sauce

Mohnstrudel/Mohntorte ~ Poppy-seed strudel/cake

Mohr im Hemd ~ Warm nut cake with melted chocolate sauce
and whipped-cream topping

Sachertorte ~ Rich chocolate cake with apricot-jam glaze
under hard chocolate shell

Schwarzwälderkirschtorte ~ Black Forest cherry cake

Topfenstrudel ~ Cream-cheese-filled pastry

* *Torte* is a round cake;
Schnitte is a piece from a sheet cake.

The Party Palace
Jagdschloss Magdalenenhof

Built in 1905, the villa "Jadgschloss Magdelenenhof" is situated in a beautiful park with old trees and a lovely English garden. Coffee and cake are served Wednesday through Sunday, from 11 AM - 6 PM, in a smoke-free atmosphere. For special occasions, you may rent the Coffee House for the day, with or without service, or have them fully cater your cocktail party, buffet or wedding reception for 10 to 70 guests. Smoking is permitted during private parties. Amenities include rooms for sleeping babies or playing children, as well as a garden and a playground 50 meters from the front gate.

Elizabeth Dobie-Sarsam, a Canadian, and Hassan Sarsam have run the restaurant since 1987. Both speak fluent English and German. The kitchen offers a pleasing choice of traditional Viennese and international cuisines, and the kitchen garden guarantees the food is generously seasoned and garnished with fresh herbs and flowers. Fees are middle range.

Jagdschloss Magdalenenhof, located in the 21st district on the Bisamberg at the end of Senderstrasse, bordering Langenzersdorf. Tel. & Fax: 292 41 09; Mail: Magdalenenhof@aon.at.

O ut of necessity, this chapter covers a lot of territory—from pregnancy past puberty. The emphasis, however, is on pregnancy and babies, because during this time, you will probably need the most information and advice. The line dividing babies and children is not clear; many topics relevant to both are covered in the earlier babies section. There are some suggestions, tips and ideas for shopping for and coping with children in Vienna, from clothing-size conversions to car-seat laws to fun outings. Because teens can appear to be practically another species, and because they would never believe anything a strange adult told them, we recruited a teen to write their section.

PREGNANCY

If you are pregnant or plan to have a baby in Vienna, you should contact the American Women's Association (AWA) Stork Club and the AWA Vienna Childbirth Trust (see Organizations chapter). In both of these groups, mothers with their babies meet regularly to share experiences and information. Furthermore, they serve as a welcome support group of new and expectant mothers. Many of the members have given birth here recently so their recommendations of doctors and hospitals, and advice on pregnancy, delivery and breastfeeding can be very helpful and timesaving.

FINDING A GYNECOLOGIST/ OBSTETRICIAN

The German word for gynecologist/obstetrician is *Facharzt für Frauenheilkunde und Geburtshilfe*. These are a few resources for finding one:

AWA STORK CLUB & AWA VIENNA CHILDBIRTH TRUST
☎ 320 14 95

VIENNA MEDICAL ASSOCIATION
SERVICE DEPARTMENT FOR FOREIGN PATIENTS
1010, Weihburggasse 10-12
☎ 515 01-213   This service can recommend
Daily 8 AM - 4 PM   English-speaking doctors.

U. S. CONSULATE
☎ 313 39-7538
Mon - Fri 8:30 AM - noon, 1 PM - 4 PM

CHOOSING A DOCTOR

When choosing a doctor, ask if he or she has an ultrasound machine in the office and what his or her childbirth philosophy is. You should expect to have an ultrasound and internal exam at each visit, so in-office facilities would save you a lot of running around. But don't fret—most doctors do have their own machines because it allows for more comprehensive care.

As Austrian doctors' practices vary, it is extremely important to discuss beforehand your wishes regarding your delivery and postpartum care. To get an idea of how your doctor works, consider asking the following questions:

- Does the doctor intervene as little as possible with the natural birth process?
- Does the doctor perform many caesarean sections?
- How long will the doctor wait past your due date before he or she will induce labor?
- Does the doctor support Lamaze techniques?
- At which hospitals does the doctor deliver?

Some doctors do not encourage the use of Lamaze and those who perform epidural caesarean sections are rare. You might also consider writing a birth plan, having it translated and discussing it thoroughly with your doctor. Give the doctor a copy and include another one with your chart at the hospital.

WHAT TO EXPECT FROM YOUR DOCTOR

Once you've chosen a doctor, he or she will issue you a *Mutter Kind Pass* (Mother and Child Passport), in which all examinations during your pregnancy, including birth information, as well as regular exams and vaccinations for the child up to age five will be recorded. Take your *Mutter Kind Pass* to all office visits during your pregnancy and to the hospital when you deliver.

TOXOPLASMOSIS

Before the 16th pregnancy week, you should be sent to a lab for a blood test, which will be checked for various things, including whether you are *toxoplasma* positive or negative. If you are *toxoplasma* positive, it means your body has had the undetectable parasite and therefore has built up the antibodies to fight *toxoplasmosis*. If, however, you are *toxoplasma* negative, you do not have these antibodies. If you're not immediately treated, the parasite can cause birth defects.

In Austria and Central Europe, *toxoplasma* is not only in animal fecies (as in the United States) but can also be in certain foods. *Toxoplasma* can sometimes be found in raw animal proteins, so if you are *toxoplasma* negative, you must avoid all foods containing raw eggs and raw meat while you are pregnant. This includes: ice cream from local shops, chocolate mousse, tiramisu, homemade mayonnaise, smoked meats (e.g., prosciutto, salmon, salami), sushi, caviar and beef tartar. If you eat any meat—including steaks, be sure it's well-done and not pink or bloody inside. Another source of *toxoplasma* is cats and some other animals, so if you have pets, ask your doctor what precautionary measures you need to take.

CHOOSING A HOSPITAL

Most hospitals welcome expectant mothers and will gladly show you around their maternity wards. Hospital policies can also vary, so be sure to confirm the following information.

PUBLIC HOSPITALS

If you have Austrian Health Insurance (*Krankenkasse*), then you can deliver at a public hospital at no charge, though the delivery will be made by whichever doctor is on duty and you will share a room and bathroom with other patients. Another alternative is to receive private care in a public hospital, which allows you to choose from one of the hospital's staff doctors to deliver your baby and to have a private room. If you have supplementary private insurance (*Zusatzversicherung*), then it will cover the additional costs. If not, you must pay them.

PRIVATE HOSPITALS

The third option is to go to a private hospital. In this case, you must bring your own doctor, who will be solely responsible for your care. Unless an emergency arises, a midwife will attend to you during labor and your doctor will deliver the baby. If you prefer a different arrangement, tell your doctor. You will get a private room with a bathroom that you share with another person. At a private hospital, a single room usually is not completely covered by insurance, so you would be responsible for the additional cost. If you are a private patient without *Krankenkasse*, then both the public and private hospital would require a large deposit. Before you commit to any hospital, ask how much that would be.

HOSPITAL FACILITIES

You may want to ask the following questions regarding the hospital's medical facilities: Does the hospital have facilities to do a caesarean section? Can the father be present during a C-section? (Almost all hospitals permit fathers to stay during normal deliveries.) Does the hospital have a birthing chair or underwater-birthing facilities? Will the newborn receive vitamin K injections, and eye drops?

PRENATAL EXERCISE &
BIRTH PREPARATION CLASSES

Most hospitals offer both prenatal-exercise and birth-preparation classes in German. The exercise classes usually cover breathing and relaxing techniques along with birthing positions. You can often participate even if your German is limited. Call the Midwife Center (*Hebammen-Zentrum*) at ☎ 408 80 22 (Mon - Thurs 9 AM - 1 PM, Wed 2 PM - 5 PM) or the Counseling Center for Natural Childbirth (*Beratungsstelle für natürliche Geburt*) at ☎ 523 17 11 (Mon - Wed 10 AM - 12:30 PM, Mon, Thurs 3 PM - 5:30 PM) to find out if an English course is available. Also, there are usually experienced English-speaking midwives or nurse-practioners in Vienna who teach such classes. AWA members can call the office at ☎ 320 14 95 to see if someone is currently available.

EPIDURALS

If you want to have an epidural, discuss this with your doctor ahead of time because it is not a common practice in Austria. To ensure that you receive an epidural during labor, you must be adamant with your doctor and make the necessary arrangements well in advance. Vaginal shaving and the use of enemas are also rare, so talk to your doctor.

NEONATAL CARE

Many hospitals do not have neonatal-care units to treat ill or prematurely born babies. Check to see if your hospital has neonatal care or where the baby would be transferred and how far away that hospital is. Also ask if the mother can be transferred with the infant.

ROOMING-IN

Find out if your baby will be allowed to stay with you the whole time. Ask how many mothers will be in a room with you. Check into the hospital's visitor policy, as some have strict rules regarding who is allowed to visit, when and for how long. There may also be restrictions on bringing flowers to the room.

BREASTFEEDING & BABY CARE

If you ask, most hospitals will demonstrate feeding, bathing and dressing the baby. If you plan to breastfeed, make sure the hospital supports your decision and will respond to your requests. In some cases, you must insist on the baby always being breastfed. Do not rely solely on the hospital for breastfeeding advice because sometimes the information can be incomplete or inaccurate. Also, rest assured that nursing discreetly in public is acceptable in Austria.

Contact the La Leche League (LLL) before the birth for the best breast-feeding counseling. The LLL is a self-help group that meets regularly to discuss breastfeeding. It sells a handbook in English and provides many other information sheets in English because everything comes from the United States and is then translated into German. For more information, contact one of its English-speaking counselors:

LILLI OLIVARES-DIAZ
☎ 876 58 27 (evenings only)

ANNA MARIE HOFSTADLER
☎ 440 23 62

LENGTH OF HOSPITAL STAYS

In general, hospital stays in Austria are much longer than those in the United States. A stay of five to six days is typical for a normal delivery, while a caesarean delivery often requires a 10-day stay. If you have arranged to leave six to eight hours after your baby is born (*Ambulante Geburt*), you may sign yourself out of the hospital at your own risk, as long as you have arranged to have a midwife regularly visit you at home.

HOSPITALS

You will deliver your baby at the hospital with which your doctor is affiliated. If, however, you would like to find a hospital on your own, look in the yellow pages under *"Krankenhäuser und Kliniken"* or ask other new mothers. The following list is just to get you started in your search.

Private Hospitals

GOLDENES KREUZ
1090, Lazarettgasse 16-18
☎ 401 11-540
Fax 401 11-505

This is a popular private hospital with a friendly, patient-oriented, English-speaking staff. Rooms have TVs, telephones and bathrooms. Rooming-in is allowed 24 hours a day. Many choose this hospital because it's close to the *Allgemeines Krankenhaus (AKH)* and University Children's Hospital, in case neonatal care is needed.

PRIVATKLINIK DÖBLING
1190, Heiligenstädter Strasse 57-63
☎ 36 06 60

This is a newer hospital with very pleasant surroundings. The staff is friendly and very accommodating, and some speak English. The delivery room has a bathtub, and husbands can be present during C-sections with the doctor's consent. The rooms are large with changing tables, sofa beds, bathrooms and balconies. Telephones and TVs are also available. The baby and father can stay in the room. Visitors are welcome anytime and can be received in an enclosed winter room. The hospital respects your wishes regarding nursing.

RUDOLFINERHAUS
1190, Billrothstrasse 78
☎ 360 36

This is a popular, quiet hospital with spacious rooms and friendly staff who speak some English. An English- and French-speaking gynecologist is on call 24 hours a day. Full rooming-in is permitted with diaper-changing facilities provided upon request. Telephones and TVs are available. The hospital has a lounge and coffee shop, a pleasant garden for patients, and parking is available.

Public Hospitals

ST. JOSEF WIEN-HACKING
1130, Auhofstrasse 189
☎ 878 44

Formerly private, this Roman Catholic hospital is run by nuns, who provide a friendly, pleasant atmosphere. Rooming-in rooms have four to five beds, but private rooms are available for an extra fee. Each private room has one bed with a telephone. Most of the doctors speak English, but the nuns do not.

IGNAZ SEMMELWEIS FRAUENKLINIK
1180, Bastiengasse 36-38
☎ 476 15

This hospital is very patient-oriented and offers baby-care classes to couples. Full rooming-in is allowed. Experienced midwives often deliver, though a physician is always on duty. You are not allowed to bring your own doctor.

SOZIALMEDIZINISCHES ZENTRUM OST KRANKENHAUS DONAUSPITAL (SMZ OST)
1220, Langobardenstrasse 122
☎ 288 02

This is a brand-new hospital with modern facilities and a neonatal-care unit. You should register as soon as you find out you're pregnant because it's often booked up. The hospital strongly encourages breastfeeding.

KRANKENHAUS KORNEUBURG
2100 Korneuburg (Niederösterreich), Wiener Ring 3
☎ (02262) 725 81-0

This is a popular hospital—even though it's outside the city—so you need to sign up six to seven months before the birth. Full rooming-in is available and breastfeeding is encouraged.

HOME BIRTHS & BIRTHING HOMES

Although many doctors tend to advise against home births, it is still a viable option. There are several independently practicing midwives in the Vienna area, some of whom speak English. Your midwife will help you prepare for the birth through regular prenatal visits and will be on call for your delivery. She will deliver the baby, register it and visit daily for seven to 10 days after the birth to check on both you and the baby. If a hospital visit is necessary, she can accompany you.

Midwives

Information on practicing midwives can be obtained from the following:

COUNSELING CENTER FOR NATURAL CHILDBIRTH AND LIFE WITH CHILDREN
Beratungsstelle für natürliche Geburt und Leben mit Kindern
1070, Zollergasse 37   Mon - Wed 10 AM - 12:30 PM,
☎ 523 17 11   and 3 PM - 5:30 PM

MIDWIFE CENTER *Hebammen-Zentrum*
1090, Lazarettgasse 6/2/1
☎ 408 80 22
Mon - Thurs 9 AM - 1 PM, Wed 2 PM - 5 PM

Birthing Homes

GEBURTSHAUS NUSSDORF
1190, Heiligenstädter Strasse 217
☎ 370 49 37

This clinic offers natural childbirth only and is run by two Viennese obstetrician/gynecologists. An experienced midwife—whom you meet during your prenatal classes and checkups—delivers the baby. In case of complications, you will be transferred to a hospital because the clinic doesn't have the facilities to do a C-section. An obstetrician and a pediatrician are always either on call or on duty. You can usually take your baby home eight hours after the delivery, and the midwife will make follow-up visits for about a week. The care is very mother-oriented and personal. Some of the midwives speak English. If you have private insurance, all expenses will be covered. If you only have *Krankenkasse*, the fee will be ATS 30.000 to ATS 40.000, depending on which package you choose. There is an informational meeting the first Friday of each month at 5:30 PM.

PREPARING FOR THE BABY

Maternity Clothes

To find maternity shops, check the yellow pages under *"Umstandsmode."* Here are a few shops:

BOUTIQUE MIMI
1070, Mariahilfer Strasse 22
☎ 523 53 98

MAMI SHOP
1070, Westbahnstrasse 1B
☎ 522 35 84

BEBE
1090, Viriotgasse 6
☎ 319 25 83

Baby Furniture & Accessories

Look in the yellow pages under *"Kindermöbel"* and *"Kinderwagen."* Also check the AWA Stork Club and the spring and fall flea markets at the American International School and Vienna International School (see Education chapter for addresses), which are valuable sources of good-quality used children's and baby clothing, furniture and accessories. Here are a few stores:

BAUMGARTEN
1170, Hernalser
Hauptstrasse 110
☎ 486 53 53

This is a store carrying everything from cribs to clothes. There are additional locations.

IKEA
2334 Vösendorf,
Shopping City Süd
☎ 690 00

This is a moderately priced Swedish do-it-yourself furniture/housewares store. You'll find baby and children's furniture, bedding, fabrics, lamps, toys, rugs, etc. They also have a free catalog. (See the All-Purpose Stores section of the Home chapter.)

INSTITUT BSTÄNDIG
1010, Freyung 5
☎ 533 73 04

1060, Mariahilfer Strasse 95
☎ 596 12 85

This store sells a wide range of accessories and also rents medical equipment, such as electric nursing pumps, lamps and scales. A free catalog is available.

KIKA
2334 Vösendorf, Dr.-R.-Firneis-Strasse
☎ 69 26 11

This is a furniture/housewares store selling all your baby needs.

LEINER
1070, Mariahilfer Strasse 18
☎ 521 53

This is a furniture store stocked with all your baby needs, including strollers, car seats, cribs, changing tables and high chairs.

Baby Shopping Terms

Backpack *Rucksack*	**High chair** *Hochstuhl*
Bassinet *Stubenkorb*	**Infant seat** *Kindersitz*
Bathtub *Badewanne*	**Johnny-jump-up** *Wippe*
Carry cot *Tragtasche*	**Pacifier** *Schnuller*
Car seat *Autokindersitz*	**Playpen** *Gehschule*
Changing table *Wickeltisch*	**Rubber crib mat** *Gummiunterlage*
Cradle *Wiege*	**Sling carrier** *Tragtuch*
Crib *Gitterbett*	**Stroller/pram** *Kinderwagen*
Fitted sheets *Spannleintücher*	**Travel bed** *Reisebett*

**Public Bathrooms
with Diaper-Changing Facilities**

1010, Graben	1010, Stephansplatz *U-Bahn* station
1010, Operngasse	1010, Schwedenplatz *U-Bahn* station
1010, Rathauspark	1020, Volksprater, Knusperhäuschen
1020, Messeparkplatz	1120, Philadelphiabrücke *U-Bahn* station

FINDING A PEDIATRICIAN

A pediatrician is not normally present at the delivery, although the doctor examines the baby shortly afterward. A complete pediatric examination is done within the next few days. Start looking for a pediatrician before the baby is born. Contact the AWA Stork Club or the AWA Health Care Professionals group, or ask your obstetrician for a referral. If you want to have your pediatrician examine the baby while you are still in the hospital, you must notify the hospital in advance. If you want to have a pediatrician present at the delivery, discuss this with your obstetrician.

CIRCUMCISIONS

Circumcisions are seldom performed here and are considered a more serious procedure than in the United States. If you would like to have your baby boy circumcised, tell your doctor before the birth so that arrangements can be made.

HIP CHECKS

Doctors examine newborn babies for a congenital hip deformity, which is not unusual in Central and Eastern European countries. Many pediatricians can do the ultrasound in their offices. If not, they will send you elsewhere for one. If your baby has a hip deformity, you will be told either to use an extra-wide fabric diaper on top of the disposable one or to use a hip brace. This should prevent discomfort and the need for surgery.

IMMUNIZATIONS

The hepatitis B immunization is not routinely given here in Austria (as it is in the United States). If you want your child to be immunized, tell your pediatrician because the vaccine is available in pharmacies with a prescription. You can have your child immunized by your pediatrician or through a public immunization program offered by the city of Vienna, which is less expensive. Your local Parents Information Center (*Elternberatungsstelle*) in your district office (*Bezirksamt*) has more information.

DIAPERS

While there is no cloth-diaper service in Vienna, there are several disposable diapers on the market, available at stores like DM, Bipa and Toys 'R' Us. When buying diapers, be sure to look for *Höschenwindeln* (not *Vlieswindeln* or just *Windeln*, as both of these are rectangular absorbent pads to be inserted in cloth diapers or snap pants). Regular cloth diapers are available at some children's clothing stores like *Dohnal* and *Kindermode Mary*. *Windelhaus Popolino* specializes in selling cloth diapers, offering different types of highly absorbent cloth diapers, which are used in combination with disposable liners. For more information, contact:

WINDELHAUS POPOLINO
2334 Vösendorf, Shopping City Süd
☎ 609 13 09

BABY FOOD & FORMULA

Baby formulas only come in powdered form, to which you must add water. It is safe to use Viennese tap water. There are special formulas available, such as Soya, if your baby is lactose-intolerant or has diarrhea, so ask your doctor for details. Electric bottle warmers are available, but they don't plug into car cigarette lighters. Styrofoam bottle containers are commonly used to keep bottles warm.

The "Milton Method" is the quickest and easiest way to sterilize bottles, nipples, pacifiers and small toys. A plastic container is filled with water and a small amount of Milton solution. Usually after soaking for two hours, the contents are sterilized. Milton containers are available throughout Vienna at all pharmacies (*Apotheken*) and drugstores (*Drogerien*).

There is a variety of jarred baby food and instant cereals, which can be found at supermarkets, pharmacies and drugstores. If you want organic food, look for the word *Bio*. If you want to avoid certain ingredients, look for the following words:

No artificial colors *ohne Farbstoffzusatz*
No artificial flavors *ohne Aromazusatz*
No preservatives *ohne Konservierungsstoffe*
No sugar *ohne Zuckerzusatz*

INFANT FIRST-AID KIT

You should make a baby's first-aid kit before or shortly after the birth. Include things like fever suppositories (commonly used here), teething gel, ear drops, nose drops, etc. Consult your doctor for recommended brands and dosages.

FINDING HELP
AFTER THE BABY IS BORN

The city of Vienna MA 47 (Magistrate Office Dept. 47) and Caritas (a Catholic charity organization) jointly offer an in-house-help program (*Familienhilfe*), which is available to any family where the mother is seriously ill, injured or recovering from delivery. After a birth, you can receive help for up to four weeks. Costs to participate are based on your income and rent. Help arrives within one to two days of a request, though overnight care is not available. In case of an emergency, help will arrive the next day. With planned operations or expected due dates, however, you should try to sign up in advance. To register for *Familienhilfe*, contact one of the following:

MA 47	FAMILIENZENTRUM DER CARITAS
1010, Schottenring 25	1020, Lassallestrasse 2/4
☎ 531 14-857 92	☎ 728 68 62
Mon - Fri 7:30 AM - 3:30 PM	Mon - Thurs 8 AM - 4 PM,
	Fri 8 AM - 2 PM

BABYSITTERS

If you're looking for a babysitter, contact one of the following organizations for a referral. The AWA office also has a list of babysitters for its members.

WIENER FAMILIENBUND
1070, Neubaugasse 66/2
☎ 526 82 19   Mon - Fri 8:30 AM - 1:30 PM

This service will give you the names and phone numbers of three babysitters, all of whom speak English, have liability insurance and have taken a course in babysitting. Most are students at least 16 years old. Some are available mornings, but most work afternoons, evenings and weekends. You also can use this service to find a long-term babysitter. The referral itself is free, though they recommend you pay the sitter ATS 70 an hour, making all arrangements yourself. This service also sells a brochure with a list of all public and private *Kindergartens*, as well as one for all schools.

INSTITUTE OF EUROPEAN STUDIES
1010, Johannesgasse 7   Mon - Fri 9 AM - 5 PM
☎ 512 26 01

The Institute refers students who are interested in babysitting.

KINDERDREHSCHEIBE
1050, Wehrgasse 26/1   Mon - Wed 10 AM - 4 PM,
☎ 581 38 81   Thurs 8 AM - 4 PM

This service will help you find a babysitter and/or a private *Kindergarten*.

WIENER KINDERFREUNDE
1080, Albertgasse 23   Mon - Thurs 8 AM - 4:30 PM,
☎ 401 25-0   Fri 8 AM - 3 PM

This organization offers child guidance and organized children's activities.

WILFRIEDE KARUTZ
1180, Schulgasse 2/11
☎ 405 28 05   Mon - Fri 8 AM - 4 PM (Aug. closed)

Wilfriede and Grete offer a babysitting service for one- to three-year-olds in a nursery-school environment. Both of these women are qualified nursery-school teachers, and Wilfriede speaks fluent English. You pay ATS 50 an hour, though the rate decreases the more hours you use per week. If you live near the 18th district, this is a great service for daytime babysitting. You need to call to reserve a space and can use this service on a regular or occasional basis.

AMERICAN INTERNATIONAL SCHOOL
1190, Salmannsdorfer Strasse 47   Mon - Thurs 8 AM - 4:30 PM,
☎ 401 32-0   Fri 8 AM - 3 PM

Each fall the school prepares a list of high-school students interested in babysitting, but they are only available evenings and weekends.

DAY CARE

Along with one-on-one babysitting, there are companies that employ stay-at-home mothers to care for a small group of children (no more than five). This is also a great way for your child to learn German. If you're interested, contact one of the following:

SOZIALES HILFSWERK DER ÖVP   WIENER KINDERFREUNDE
1010, Falkestrasse 3   1080, Albertstrasse 23
☎ 515 43 91   ☎ 401 25-0

VEREIN FÜR TAGESMÜTTER TAGESZENTRUM
1080, Pfeilgasse 8/4
☎ 408 60 06 or ☎ 403 78 22

AU PAIRS

If you're looking for an au pair, call one of the following agencies:

KATHOLISCHES JUGENDWERK
1010, Johannesgasse 16   Mon, Wed 2 PM - 4 PM,
☎ 512 16 21   Tues, Thurs 9 AM - noon

All these au pairs come from EU countries to avoid work-permit problems.
There is usually a waiting list to get an au pair, so call to check.

ÖKISTA (AUSTRIAN STUDENT TRAVEL AGENCY)
1090, Garnisongasse 7   Mon - Fri 9 AM - 5:30 PM
☎ 401 48

CITY-SPONSORED SERVICES FOR NEW MOTHERS

In every district, there's an Office for Youth and Family (*Amt für Jugend und Familie*) that offers a book in German called *Rund ums Baby*, which tells you what you need to know when having a baby, especially what you are entitled to by Austrian law. This is important because you have more rights and privileges here than in the United States. To get a free copy of the book, check the telephone directory's white pages under *"Bezirksämter"* for the office in your district. Go to the *Jugendamt* department and simply show your *Mutter Kind Pass*.

Women who have been employed for at least one year receive 18 months of paid maternity leave (*Wochengeld* und *Karenzurlaubsgeld*). Call the *Krankenkasse* or Labor Office Insurance Service (*Arbeitsmarktservice Versicherungsdienste*) for more information.

Women who have resided in Vienna for at least six months before the birth receive a children's package. They can choose from either a newborn package (*Säuglingsausstattung*), which includes diapers, clothing, a receiving blanket, packaged food and other supplies; or the toddler package (*Ausstattung für Kleinkinder*), which includes a towel, jogging suit, pajamas and other items for one- to two-year-olds. If you had your baby at a public hospital, you will receive your package directly from the hospital. If you had your baby at a private hospital, you need to pick up your package at your local district *Jugendamt*, where you must show the mother's *Meldezettel*, the *Mutter Kind Pass* and the baby's Austrian birth certificate.

Check to see if you qualify for family financial aid (*Familienbeihilfe*). This is a monthly monetary grant allocated per child to families paying taxes here.

Available at your local *Bezirksamt* is *Mutterberatung* (counseling for mothers). This service is provided at a free walk-in clinic, usually open once a week. Here, you can have your baby weighed, measured and examined by a pediatrician, or you can simply ask questions about feeding, immunizations, childhood diseases, etc. All *Mutter Kind Pass* examinations can be done here. They also offer a series of baby-care classes for new parents (*Elternschule*), where fathers are also welcome. Of course, these are only offered in German, but they're still worth checking into.

REGISTERING THE BABY'S BIRTH

Birth Certificate *Geburtsurkunde*

After the baby is born, the first thing to do is to register its birth in Austria. The hospital will have filled out a preregistration form and sent this to the registrar (*Standesamt*) serving the district (*Bezirk*) where the birth occurred and not the one where you live. The hospital will give you a card to take to the *Standesamt*. To find the address, look in the telephone directory's white pages. You might want to call in advance to find out the exact amount of tax stamps (*Stempelmarken*) you will need for each document. Some *Standesämter* sell *Stempelmarken*, but you can also buy them from a tobacconist/newsstand (*Tabak-Trafik*). Either the mother or father can register the birth. You will need the following documents:

- Certified copy of marriage certificate with a certified translation
- Mother's birth certificate
- Both parents' passports
- Parents' police registration (*Meldezettel*)
- *Stempelmarken*
- Card from the hospital

Make sure to check the spelling of all names on the birth certificate very carefully, as all future documents will be based on this one. You can request additional copies of the birth certificate. You should also request an international birth certificate (*Auszug aus dem Geburtseintrag*), which is certified and comes in seven languages. *Stempelmarken* are required for each copy.

U.S. PASSPORT & REGISTRATION

Most children born abroad to a U.S. citizen acquire U.S. citizenship at birth. After receiving the Austrian birth certificate, contact the U.S. Consulate. When it has been determined that the child has acquired U.S. citizenship, you can register for a "Consular Report of Birth Abroad of a Citizen of the United States of America" (Form FS 240). This important document is recognized by the U.S. government as proof of acquisition of U.S. citizenship and is an acceptable proof of citizenship for such purposes as obtaining a passport or enrolling in school.

When applying for the Consular Report of Birth Abroad, you can also apply for your child's passport and Social Security card at the same time. You need to make an appointment to apply for all these documents, so call the U.S. Consulate at ☎ 313 39-7546. Also, ask what the fee is, where U.S.-size passport photos can be taken and what documents are required. Citizens of other countries should call their own consulates (see Embassies appendix).

AUSTRIAN RESIDENCE PERMIT
Aufenthaltsbewilligung

For a child to obtain an Austrian residence permit, you will need the following:

- Parents' *Meldezettel*
- Child and both parents' passports
- Child's Austrian birth certificate

POLICE REGISTRATION *Meldezettel*

Apply at your district police station (*Bezirkspolizeikommissariat*) within one week of your baby's birth. You will need to purchase a *Meldezettel* form with five pages at a *Tabak-Trafik*. Take the following with you to the police:

- Child's Austrian birth certificate
- Child and both parents' passports
- Child's Austrian residence permit
- Parents' *Meldezettels*
- *Meldezettel* form filled out for child

(See the Documents section of the Essentials chapter.)

BIRTH ANNOUNCEMENTS

Most stationery stores (*Papierwaren*) sell birth announcements (*Geburtsanzeigen*). Custom-made ones can be ordered at some stores or, more commonly, at a print shop (*Druckerei*).

BABY & CHILDREN'S CLOTHING

New Clothing

For baby and children's clothing stores, look up *"Kinderbekleidung"* in the yellow pages. Two large chains are Mary Kindermoden and Dohnal Kindermoden, both with several locations. Department stores like H&M, C&A, Gerngross and Herzmansky also carry children's clothing. Along the Danube Canal (*Donaukanal*) in the first district (particularly on Salzgries, a street parallel to the Kai) is the garment district. There, you can purchase retail from wholesale stores, as long as you see the sign *"Einzelhandel"* or *"Detailverkauf."*

Used Clothing

Here are a couple of secondhand stores that carry children's clothing:

TAUSCHZENTRALE FÜR KINDERARTIKEL
1070, Westbahnstrasse 27
☎ 523 93 94

This store has a lot to choose from, but you must be selective.

AMERICAN INTERNATIONAL SCHOOL NEARLY NEW SHOP
1190, Salmannsdorfer Strasse 47
☎ 401 32   Tues, Thurs 8:30 AM - 3 PM

Located on campus, this shop also allows you to sell your old clothes on consignment. Also check out the semiannual flea markets at AIS and VIS (see the Secondhand Shops & Flea Markets section of the Home chapter).

SIZE CONVERSION CHART

SHOE SIZES

2	18
3	19
4	20
5	21

CLOTHING SIZES

U.S.	Europe
Premie	50
0–3 months	56
3–6 months	62
6–9 months	68
9–12 months	74
18 months	80
2T	92
3T	98
4 years	104
6 years	116
8 years	128
10 years	134
12 years	140

TOYS

There are excellent toy stores throughout Vienna. For locations near you, check the yellow pages under *"Spielwaren."* Some stores specialize in wooden and/or educational toys, games and books. Toys 'R' Us and Minimundus are two chains that usually have lower prices.

Here are a few other toy stores:

SPIELZEUGSCHACHTEL
1010, Rauhensteingasse 5
☎ 512 44 94

Located directly behind the Steffl department store, this is a nice place to browse because everything is displayed so you can look and touch. Friendly and informative salespeople can help you with a large selection of wooden toys, puzzles and board games.

ED WITTE
1010, Domgasse 2   1060, Linke Wienzeile 16 (across the *Naschmarkt*)
☎ 512 61 67   ☎ 586 43 05

Try this store for party favors and decorations, Carnival (*Fasching*) or Halloween costumes, helium-tank rentals or fireworks.

SPIELWAREN HEINZ
1130, Hietzinger Hauptstrasse 22   1190, Obkirchergasse 37-39
☎ 877 61 00   ☎ 32 33 43-10
There are many locations throughout Vienna.

A. BANNERT
1220, Wagramer Strasse 56
☎ 203 55 89

CHILDREN

 ## PARENTS' LEGAL RESPONSIBILITY

In Austria, parents are legally liable if their child suffers from a serious injury or illness—such as from a bicycle accident or poisoning—while under their supervision. In such an event, the examining doctor is required to report the incident and it will be investigated.

BICYCLE & CAR-SEAT LAWS

Children younger than 10 years old are not allowed to ride their bikes alone in the street. (See the Transportation chapter for additional information.)

Car-seat laws concern children up to the age of 12 and up to the height of 1.5 meters. Newborns to nine-month-olds need to be in an infant car seat. If you don't want to buy one, you can rent one from the ÖAMTC (ATS 350 for members and ATS 450 for nonmembers). There's a required returnable deposit of ATS 1.390 or ATS 1.490, depending on the model you choose. (See the Automobile Clubs section of the Driving chapter.) Nine-month-olds to about three-and-a-half-year-olds (up to 18 kg–20 kg) must be in a regular car seat. You should stop using the car seat when the child's head sits higher than the back of the car seat. Three-and-a-half-year-olds (18 kg–20 kg) to 12-year-olds (up to 1.5 m tall) need to sit in a booster chair in the car. Once they reach age 12 and are at least 1.5 m tall, they can sit in the car's regular seat with a seat belt. Austrian law requires children younger than 12 to sit in the back seat of the car, which is safer, especially if there's an air bag on the front-passenger side.

EDUCATION FOR CHILDREN

Schools, including preschools, are listed in the Education chapter.

ACTIVITIES FOR CHILDREN

Vienna offers many great cultural and outdoor activities for you and your children. Brochures in German and English with programs and events are available from City Hall (*Stadtinformation Rathaus*; see Info Offices appendix). Also available is the following brochure:

FAMILIENTAGE (FAMILY DAYS)
1082, Friedrich-Schmidt-Platz 5
☎ 4000 84-368

Call to receive this booklet filled with current activities for children. You will also receive a discount card *(Aktionskarte)* entitling children 15 and under to a variety of discounts.

RECOMMENDED PLAYGROUNDS

AUGARTEN - 2ND District
PRATER - 2ND District
TÜRKENSCHANZ - 19TH District
DONAU PARK - 22ND District

RECOMMENDED ACTIVITIES

The following are just a few places you can take your children. Also, see the Entertainment and Recreation chapters for more ideas.

BUTTERFLY HAUS
1010, Burggarten
☎ 533 85 70
Apr - Oct: Mon - Fri 10 AM - 5 PM, Sat - Sun 10 AM - 6:30 PM
Nov - Mar: Daily 10 AM - 4 PM
all ages

Just 300 meters from the Opera is a tropical rainforest encased in a beautiful *Jugendstil* glasshouse with hundreds of live, free-flying tropical butterflies. Watch your feet for the pigmy quail running around.

NATURHISTORISCHES MUSEUM
(MUSEUM OF NATURAL HISTORY)
1010, Maria-Theresien Platz
☎ 521 77 0
Mon, Thurs 9 AM - 6:30 PM, Wed 9 AM - 9 PM, Tues - closed
ages 3 and up

Room after room filled with different stuffed (taxidermy) animals. Kids will simply love it here.

WIENER TEDDYBÄREN MUSEUM

1010, Drahtgasse 3
☎ 533 47 55
Mon - Sat 10 AM - 6 PM, Sun 2 PM - 6 PM
ages 2 and up

This boutique/museum features new
and antique teddy bears, some of
which are handmade and painted by
local and international artists. Teddy-
bear accessories are also available.

HAUS DES MEERES (AQUARIUM)

1060, Esterhazypark
☎ 587 14 17
Daily 9 AM - 6 PM
all ages

Residing inside one of Vienna's concrete air defense towers are over 1,000
living sea animals.

ZOOM KINDERMUSEUM

1070, Museumplatz 1
☎ 522 67 48
Open Daily - call for exact times and programs
ages 4 and up

This children's museum features special exhibits from local and international
artists, as well as interactive exhibits.

SCHÖNBRUNNER SCHLOSS-MARIONETTENTHEATER

1130, Schloss Schönbrunn
☎ 817 32 47
Open Daily (except Tues.) Showtimes - 4 PM and 7 PM

In this intimate theater, beautifully dressed puppets perform full-length musicals. Be aware that shows often last 2 - 3 hours and adults often attend, so
children should be old enough to sit quietly for long periods.

SCHÖNBRUNNER TIERGARTEN (ZOO)

1130, Schönbrunn Park
all ages

The world's oldest zoo is being completely renovated into an animal-friend-
lier environment. Besides the thrill of lions, tigers and bears, young children
will love sliding down into the petting zoo and trying out the playground.
Don't forget to take the short hike up the hill in the back through some
woods to the authentic Haidachhof Tyrolean farmhouse, which was moved
from Tyrol to Vienna. An annual pass can be purchased for about ATS 550.

IMAX FILMTHEATER

1140, Mariahilfer Strasse 212
☎ 894 01 01

This theater presents science and nature IMAX films on a five-story-tall screen with a state-of-the-art sound system.

ALTE DONAU

The perfect place to rent a boat for an hour. Try the places around Wagramer Strasse 48 or on An der oberen Alten Donau 20, 29 or 184-186.

DONAUINSEL (DANUBE ISLAND)

Stroll, skate or ride your bike along the paths of the Donau. here you can also rent roller-blades, water slide or try out the BMX track.

PRATER

Visit what has been called as "the lungs of Vienna". Here you have it all -

Wurstl (Amusement Park) *Prater* - roller-coasters, merry-go-rounds, pony rides, burlap slides, bumper cars, bungee chairs, etc. Definately something for everyone.

Grün (Green) *Prater* - 4.5 km of paved, car-free road that is perfect for roller-blading, biking, walking, jogging, etc. In addition, you will find a skate boarding area, lots of playgrounds, duck ponds, and wooded paths. Bikes and blades can also be rented.

RECOMMENDED OUTDOOR POOLS

ANGELIBAD
1210, An der oberen Alten Donau
☎ 263 22 69

DÖBLING
1190, Geweystr. 6
☎ 318 01 40

GÄNSEHÄUFEL
1220, Moissigasse 21
☎ 269 90 16

SCHAFBERG
1180, Josef-Redl-Gasse 2
☎ 479 15 93

SEASONAL ACTIVITES

JANUARY - MARCH
Ice-skating at City Hall (Rathaus)

BEGINNING OF APRIL:
Children's Flea Market - Donau Canal
(between Schwedenplatz and Schottenring) From April - Sept., every third Saturday of the month starting at 10 AM

END OF APRIL:
Prater Spring Festival
"Wurstl" (Carnival) Prater officially re-opens

MAY 1:
May festival for children
Afternoons on the Kaiserwiese in Prater

END OF JUNE:
Donauinsel Festival
Something for everyone - Bands for older kids and a children's island near the Brigittenauer Bridge (Brücke)

OCTOBER:
Vienna Autumn Kite Festival
On the Donauinsel near the Florisdorfer Bridge (Brücke)

DECEMBER:
Advent Activities at City Hall (Rathaus)
Activities for children 3 and up, such as baking, painting, woodwork and crafts are available in the Volkshalle. A large tent has also been recently added allowing children the chance to play and warm up from the cold while their parents get a break as well. Babysitting is also available.

BIRTHDAY PARTY IDEAS

Birthday Party in Zoo
Birthday kids can celebrate with friends at the Zoo in Schönbrunn. The Birthday package includes: entrance into park, special tour (according to interests), sculpturing of zoo animals and birthday snack - approx. 1 1/2 hours. English tours are also available.
For reservations call Mon - Fri, 8 AM - 10 AM
☎ 877 92 94 228

Birthday Party at McDonald's

They provide the room and food and you provide the kids and money. Check local restaurants for details.

Karaoke Birthday

Parties, talent contests, complete service with all the technical necessities. Programs in English available.

Verena Kleindienst and Manfred Schauer
1160., Wilhelminenstraße 184/6
☎ 489 18 71

Kosilo's Children's Island

A portable playground with Indian teepees, trampoline, baby playground, painting, crafts, make-up and lots of toys. Can be booked for several days. Clown Kosilo can also come to private parties. Programs in English available.

KosArt Productions
Walter Kosar
1080, Neudeggergasse 14
☎ 408 46 62

Birthday at Schloß Wilhelminenberg

Birthday parties are given under a certain theme and three hours of entertainment to this theme are offered. The parties also include gifts for the kids and snacks.

Schloß Wilhelminenberg
1160 Wien, Savoyenstr. 2
☎ 485 85 03

FAMILY FRIENDLY RESTAURANTS

BRUNCH:

Hilton
Family Brunch Buffet
1030, Am Stadtpark
☎ 717 00-357
Sat & Sun, noon - 3 PM

The Vienna Hilton offers a complete buffet for adults and a special buffet table for children. Children ages one to six eat free, age seven to 14 eat for ATS 20 for each year (e.g., a 9-year old would be charged ATS 180)

Marriot Hotel
Family Brunch Buffet
1010, Parkring 12A
☎ 515 18 0
Sunday, 12 PM - 3 PM

Kids 6 and under eat for free while ages 6 - 12 pay half the full price. There is a playroom with child care and toys.

DAILY:

Bamkraxler
1190, Kahlenberger Straße 17
☎ 318 88 00
Tue - Sat 4 PM - midnight, Sun 11 AM - midnight

Beautiful garden with chestnut trees and its own large playground. During the colder months there is also a stage with a puppet show every second Saturday.

Luftberg
1020, Prater 128, Waldsteingartenstr.
☎ 729 49 99
Daily 11 AM - midnight (closed in Oct.)

A large playground, elephant slide and *Luftburg* (air mattress for jumping). Large indoor playroom as well.

Schweizerhaus
1020 Prater, Straße-des-Ersten-Mai 116
☎ 728 01 52
Daily (during Prater season) 10 AM - midnight

Playground next to outside tables

TEENS

Laws in Austria set minimum requirements on a
number of specific child and parent behaviors.
Your child's school will have the latest information. In general, though, at age 16, teens can
legally drink beer and wine. At 18, they can
drink any alcohol legally.

TIPS FOR TEENS NEW TO VIENNA

Like anywhere else, Vienna can seem pretty dull if you don't know
people and don't have a clue where to meet them. Of course the city
looks better if you have someone to show you around, but you can get
around and have fun even if you don't know anyone. Vienna has
something for everyone – whether you like sightseeing, checking out
art exhibits, hanging out at malls, going out on the town, or moving
mass and muscle.

WATERING HOLES

There are hundreds of pleasant cafes scattered around Vienna where
you can get a caffeine kick – or a hot chocolate with lots of whipped
cream (schlagobers), a light snack, sweet or ice-cream. In summer,
sidewalk cafes are a great place to watch the world go by, or relax in
an inner garden – and there's no pressure to move on in a hurry.
However, young foreign teens are not such café fans and tend to
congregate in some of the following places:

Mc Donald's
  1010, Schwedenplatz 3-4
  Mon - Thurs 7 AM - 11 PM
  Fri - Sat 7 AM - 2 AM
  Sun 8 AM - 11 PM
  ☎ 533 4494

Mc Donald's
  1190, Grinzinger Allee 3
  Mon - Sat 7 AM - 11:30 PM
  Sun 8 AM - 11:30 PM
  ☎ 328 28 07

TGI Friday
  1010, Neuer Markt 8
  Mon - Thurs 11:30 AM - 11 PM
  Fri - Sat 11:30 AM - 12 PM
  ☎ 513 7789

Mac Café
  1060, Mariahilferstrasse 85-87
  Mon - Sat 8 AM - 12 PM
  Sun 9 AM - 12 PM
  ☎ 585 49 490

Burger King
  1220, DonauPlex
  Daily 11 AM - 1 AM

PARTYING VIENNESE STYLE

Vienna always has some kind of festival going on. For young people, at the end of June, the Danube Island Festival (*Donauinselfest*) is a weekend of partying with dozens of stages set up for music and cabarets, stalls selling food and skateboarders showing off their stunts. At the end of June the Free Party sends musicians around the Ring on trucks. New Year's Eve (*Silvester*) in Vienna turns the first district into one big outdoor party. There are bands playing and stands selling champagne all over the first district, especially around Stephansplatz and the Rathaus, but watch out for the fireworks and popping corks. At Christmas, the Advent Markets (*Christkindlmaerkte*) all over town are a good place to browse for gifts or drink a mug of hot mulled wine (*Gluehwein*).

CHEERS

Many Viennese teens like to go out drinking. Austrian law says you must be at least 16 to drink wine and beer and 18 to drink hard alcohol. But even this isn't strictly enforced because Vienna doesn't have major problems with rowdy drunks. To most places it is more fun to go out in a group, or with at least one other person, because it isn't easy to meet people right off the bat.

If you are looking to meet people, try the local bars. The Bermuda
Triangle (Bermuda-Dreieck) is an area of about 15 bars near
Schwedenplatz. The area got its name because it is so easy to move
from one bar to the next - and if you have a drink at every bar, you're
likely to end up lost – just like boats and planes in the place of the
same name in the Atlantic! Each bar has a slightly different feel (e.g.
different music and drink specialities). Most bars are open until about
2 AM Sunday to Thursday and 3 or 4 AM Friday and Saturday. The
following list gives some of the Viennese bars frequented by expatriate
teenagers:

Paddy O'Briens
1010, Passauer Platz 2
☎ 535 96 82
An Irish pub with live music and
regular events.

Kix Bar
1010, Bäckerstrasse 4
☎ 513 79 34
Bright and modern decor. Jazz
music.

Aera
1010, Gonzagagasse 11
☎ 533 53 14
Cabaret music

Steinzeit
1010, Fischerstiege 9
Plays all sorts of music (60's,
Rock, Pop and *Neu Deutschen
Welle*).

Miles Smiles
1080, Lange Gasse 51
Live modern Jazz

Benjamin's
1010, Salzgries 11-13
For sports fans. There is a large
screen showing sports ranging
from football to the Superbowl.

Crossfield's Australian Pub
1010, Maysederg 5
☎ 513 0881

Z'eng
1010 Goldorfstrasse 2
☎ 535 97 37
As the name says, kind of
small.

DISCO FEVER

If you'd rather do more than sit on a bar stool, then why not try a disco? Vienna is the city of dance and it doesn't have to be at the Opera Ball. Most discos have cover charges (from about ATS 80 -120) and drinks are more expensive than elsewhere. The appropriate dress for any place changes from time to time. In general Austrian teens like dressing up but the disco crowd prefers fashionable to classical. Some recommended discos are:

Volksgarten
1010, Burgring 1
Daily 10 PM - 8 AM

Sofiensäle
1030, Marxergasse 17
☎ 710 77 66

Havana
Copa Cagrana,
Danube Island Sunken City
Summer 6 PM - 3 AM

Club Vienna U4
1120,
Schönbrunnerstrasse 222

RACK 'EM UP

Playing pool (billards) is another option. You can rent tables by the hour, quench your thirst and in some places even go online. In cafés you have to consume to play. Here are a few places to try.

KÖÖ
1010, Salzgriesstrasse 1
Mon - Thurs 9 AM - 2 AM
Fri, Sat 9 AM - 4 AM
☎ 535 8775
16 pool tables as well as darts and table football.

1050, Siebenbrunnengasse 21
Daily 10 AM - 2 AM
☎ 545 72 71
This is a café/bar has 26 pool tables.

1220, Donauplex
Sun - Thurs 9 AM - 1 AM
Fri - Sat 9 AM - 3 AM
☎ 204 3139
This is also a café/bar and has 37 tables, darts and table football.

Café Roter Engel
1010, Seitenstettengasse 5
Sun - Thurs 3 PM - 8 PM
Fri, Sat 5 PM - 3 AM
☎ 535 5368

Wiedner Billard Center
1040, Rechte Wienzeile 35
Mon - Fri 8 AM - 2 AM
Sat, Sun 11 AM - 2 AM
☎ 587 1251
This place has 40 tables.

For those who like to have a choice of entertainment, Fun Planet in the Donauplex is a large arcade with video games, pool tables, table football and darts.

CATCH A FLICK, A PLAY OR A CONCERT

For the movie buffs there are a few theaters that play English language movies in the original (see the cinemas/movies theaters section of the Entertainment chapter) for ATS 90 to ATS 110, and Monday is discount-ticket day. Renting videos or DVD's is also an option. (See the Video Rental section of the Recreation chapter). For those who like it live, Vienna's English theater produces experimental theater as well as the classical. (See the Entertainment Chapter.)

Vienna is not only a city of classical music and the jazz capital of Europe, but there is something for fans of almost every kind of music and well-known performers do come to Vienna from time to time. Check what is coming and where you have to get tickets through the club ö3 web page (www.oe3.orf.at) or call the free number 0800 600 603 - English is usually no problem. For those who are crazy about concerts it may be worth becoming a member of club ö3 because you get reductions on some events (membership forms available at the tickets office outside Virgin. See SHOP TILL YOU DROP below). Members also receive a magazine (in German) that has the concert program as a center pull out. You can order tickets at the number above and tickets are sold at the office outside the entrance to Virgin. Tickets can usually be purchased for concerts about two months in advance and tickets for the well known performers sell out quickly, so get in quick.

SHOP TILL YOU DROP

There are several malls around Vienna. The Donauplex (take the U1 to Kagran), the Millenium tower and Shopping City Süd, which is outside Vienna (Take the *Badner Bahn* to Vösendorf-SCS or the IKEA bus from the Opera; see the Transportation chapter), and is the largest shopping mall in Europe. For those addicted to brand name clothing, the shopping village *Parndorf* near *Neusiedlersee* offers brands such as Nike, 30 - 40 % cheaper than elsewhere. A favorite place for young people to go shopping is Mariahilferstrasse, a long street in the 6th and 7th district where you will find a large variety of shops. Clothes are a matter of taste and budget and trendy clothes shops tend to come and go, so it's a matter of looking around and finding what you like. Check the following stores:

H & M
1060, Mariahilferstrasse 41-43
1060, Mariahilferstrasse 53
1070, Mariahilferstrasse 106-108

Clothes for young people in style, size and price.

Sports Experts
1070, Mariahilferstrasse 38-40

Sports clothes and equipment.

Kleider Bauer
1060, Mariahilferstrasse 67
1070, Mariahilferstrasse 74B
1060, Mariahilferstrasse 111
(plus 13 other outlets)

A bit conservative, but some surprises.

C & A
1060, Mariahilferstrasse 96
(plus 5 other outlets)

Not only for young people, but good value for the money. Easy to exchange whatever you don't like.

Peek and Kloppenburg
1070, Mariahilferstrasse 26-30

More expensive and a tedious system of payment, but some good buys.

Mango
1070, Mariahilferstrasse 56

Medium price range and limited selection, but changes regularly.

MEDIA

You can find just about everything in Vienna. Belonging to the EU has created a lot of competition so prices are not too bad. For computer buffs almost everything is available, so don't worry about the cable you lost in the move, and you can usually find someone who speaks English to help. However, other than the odd game, you will not find much English language software. Try Saturn or order over the internet. There are also very good deals around for mobile telephones. It is a highly competitive market and constantly changing, so shop around. If you tend to run up high bills, you can use a prepaid card. In a foreign city, having a mobile phone can be a real asset. If you get lost on the way to meet someone, you just let them know - and parents can keep their stress in check by calling to be sure you're still out there!

Saturn
1060, Mariahilferstrasse 37-39
On the top floor of Gerngross

Niedermeyer
(locations all around Vienna)
There's bound to be one near you

Media Markt
Shopping City Süd

This is an enormous shop with electronic equipment as well as a selection of videos.

MUSIC, VIDEOS, DVD'S

There is no shortage of music in Vienna. It is also not difficult to find English language videos, however, they are not cheap.

Amadeus

A large bookstore with a small collection of English books, but also English videos and DVD's

Libro

Upstairs you can find videos and DVD's.

Virgin Megastore

This is a huge CD store. They also have a small collection of English books for the young generation, a reasonable collection of English language videos and a growing collection of DVDs. If you are looking for sheet music other than classical this is a good place to go.

MAGAZINES

For those missing their favorite magazines, the bookshop in West Bahnhof has a good selection from *Seventeen* and *Popular Science* to sport and movie magazines. Check also the American magazine store in the Donauplex. Virgin (see above) also has a few magazines including *Seventeen* as well as music and movie magazines.

OUT AND ABOUT

Vienna is full of parks and recreation areas. The occasional stroll around the *Volksgarten, Rathauspark, Burggarten, Stadtpark,* even the grounds of Schönbrunn Palace is pleasant, but if you want to lounge on the grass or need more action, head for the *Kurpark* at Laerberg, the *Donaupark,* Old Danube (*Alte Donau)* or the Danube Island (*Donauinsel).* At the latter two you can also go swimming if you don't mind the odd topless or naked body - not only among the young. You can also walk, bike or rollerblade 17 km from one end of Danube Island to the other. If you don't have your own, there are rollerblades and bikes for hire near the U1 station *Donauinsel* (on the UN city side). A short walk from here, you will also find a water-ski lift and the wind in Vienna means you can speed around on a windsurfer, if that is your idea of fun. If you don't fancy swimming in the Danube, there are plenty of swimming pools around. Of course, they charge an entrance fee, but you can spend all day there.

Although there are skateboarders all over the city, the U-Bahn station on Danube Island is a meeting place. A new *Skaterparadies* is being established in Kurpark for skaters and boarders, and Friday Night Skating is beginning in Vienna. For information, check the skaters webpage (www.oersv.or.at). It is only in German, but the dates and events don't take much deciphering. Don't miss the Ring skating event in July. The Austrian-Inline-Skating Academy offers courses for private groups, and you could organize your own group. For the bikers, there are bike lanes in many parts of the city center and around Vienna, and there are plans to connect all of Vienna in the next few years. Buy yourself a bike map of Vienna (see the section on Bicycling in the Recreation chapter). There are also suggestions for bike tours online at www.wien.at/radfahren. Again, the information is only in German, but maps are provided. You can take bikes on public transport (see the Transportation chapter). Danube Island is not the only place you can hire a bike - check the internet address above for other places.

If this is not enough exercise, there are gyms and health clubs where you can burn calories or pump weights. Most of these clubs have all sorts of exercise classes from aerobics to spinning. If there's a sport you love but haven't found yet, check www.askoe.or.at, under types of sport (*Sportarten*). There is somebody who plays almost everything in Vienna from American football to cricket. And if you're a couch potato, there's always MTV - it's different from the United States, but it's still MTV.

For those who really want to make the most of what's happening in Vienna, and can manage just a little German, try the following publications:

Falter

City

Treffpunkt (meeting point) in the newspaper *Kurier* every Thursday.

Freizeit (free time) in the *Kurier* every Saturday.

W e are as young as we feel. One look around Vienna will show you that many seniors here are as active and fit as younger folks. Whether you like to exercise, travel or just meet with friends, there are numerous opportunities you can enjoy in Vienna. This chapter introduces some of them and offers advice on other topics that may be of interest.

In Austria, senior citizens are women 60 years and older and men 65 and older. In order to qualify for senior-citizen discounts, you'll need to show photo identification with your date of birth on it.

 Please be aware that the following information applies to seniors only and times listed are usually designated specifically for senior use.

TRANSPORTATION TICKETS

There are two categories of public-transportation tickets for seniors in Vienna. Anything labeled *"Pensionisten"* is for retirees/pensioners officially registered with the Austrian government. Those qualifying will know who they are. Tickets and opportunities designated for *"Senioren"* are available to anyone fulfilling the age requirements (see beginning of chapter). The city has begun issuing a new pass that will replace all previous senior (*Senioren*) and retiree (*Pensionisten*) passes.

Seniors can buy yearly passes (*Jahreskarten*) for half the regular price at any presale ticket window (*Vorverkaufsstelle*). You will need to bring a passport or driver's license as proof of age and a passport-sized photo to be attached to the *Jahreskarte*. There is also a form to fill out; because it is in German, you may want to take it with you and bring it back with your bank-account information for automatic monthly withdrawal. You can also purchase a senior ticket for two rides (*Seniorenfahrschein für 2 Fahrten*) at a price significantly lower than the usual adult fare. With the Austrian Railway Senior ID Card (*Seniorenausweis der Österreichischen Bundesbahn*), which can be purchased at any train station (*Bahnhof*), you get half off all train tickets for trips within Austria. Again, you need proof of age and a passport-sized photo.

Pensionisten (but not *Senioren*) can also get half-price individual tickets (*Halbpreisfahrscheine*) or a half-price four-day strip ticket (*Streifen-karte für 4 Fahrten zum Halbpreis*).

For more information on getting around in Vienna, see the Transportation chapter.

RECREATION

SWIMMING

The following are city pools (*Städtische Schwimmbäder*) that have special times and prices for retirees. Seniors can usually swim for two hours for ATS 25. If a longer swim time is available, it usually costs ATS 35.

AMALIENBAD
1100, Reumannplatz 24
☎ 607 47 47
Tues - Sun, noon - 3 PM

BRIGITTENAUER SPORTCLUB
1100 Troststrasse 51
☎ 603 99 67
Mon - Tues, noon - 4:30 PM

HALLENBAD SIMMERING
1110, Florian-Hedorfer-Strasse 5
☎ 767 25 68
Mon 3 PM - 5:30 PM (winter only)

HALLENBAD HIETZING
1130, Atzgersdorfer Strasse 14
☎ 804 53 10 or ☎ 804 53 19
Daily 12:30 PM - 3 PM

OTTAKRINGER BAD
1160, Johann-Staud-Strasse 11
☎ 914 81 06
Mon, noon - 5 PM

HALLENBAD DÖBLING
1190, Geweygasse 6
☎ 318 01 40
Mon, 3 PM - 5:30 PM

HALLENBAD GROSSFELDSIEDLUNG
1210, Oswald-Redlich-Strasse 44
☎ 258 25 64
Mon, 9 AM - 3 PM

This pool has water gymnastics (*Acqua Turnen*) on Monday at 10:30 AM (at the same price).

HALLENBAD DONAUSTADT
1220, Portnergasse 38
☎ 203 43 21
Wed, noon - 6 PM

This time is for adults only; no children are allowed.

All of the above pools have saunas, which charge about ATS 100 per session, but they're often for *both* genders together. If you're uncomfortable with public nudity, you should inquire before going. Under *"Bäder"* in the telephone directory's white pages, there is a listing of all indoor (*"Hallen"*) and outdoor (*"Frei-, Sommer- und Strandbad"*) swimming pools, which charge various fees, so you should call first.

BOWLING

These alleys offer special prices for seniors during the times given:

BRUNSWICK BOWLING HALLE

1020, PraterHauptallee 124
☎ 728 07 09-0
Daily 10 AM - 4:30 PM

1170, Schumanngasse 107
☎ 486 43 61
Daily 10 AM - 4:30 PM

BOWLING CENTER FLORIDSDORF

1210, Pitkagasse 4
☎ 271 40 51
Daily 10 AM - 6 PM

ICE SKATING

Only one ice rink in Vienna has a special discount for seniors:

WIENER EISLAUF VEREIN

1030, Lothringerstrasse 22
☎ 713 63 53 or ☎ 712 14 46

Mon - Fri, 9 AM - 1 PM
Price does not include skate rental.

BILLIARDS, BRIDGE & CHESS

The following are cafés where people meet to enjoy different games. Naturally, German is the language spoken. If you speak only English, you and your friends can still meet at one of them to play. One advantage is that this eliminates the need to "entertain" (i.e., at a café, everyone buys her or his own drink).

CAFÉ MUSEUM

1010, Friedrichstrasse 6
☎ 586 52 02

Chess players meet here.

CAFÉ PRÜCKEL

1010, Stubenring 24
☎ 512 61 15

Bridge games start after 1 PM.

CAFÉ HEINE

1020, Heinestrasse 39
☎ 214 51 58

You can find chess and cards played here.

CAFÉ AM HEUMARKT

1030, Am Heumarkt 15
☎ 712 65 81

People play billiards or chess Mon - Fri. Stamp collectors also gather here.

CAFÉ SPERL

1060, Gumpendorfer Strasse 11
☎ 586 41 58

Billiards, chess and cards are activities here.

CAFÉ-RESTAURANT WUNDERER

1140, Hadikgasse 62
☎ 894 62 25 or ☎ 894 61 94

Chess and cards are the games of choice.

AGE HAS ITS ADVANTAGES— SPECIAL DEALS

CULTURE AT LUNCHTIME (*Kultur-Mittag*)
1010, Mahlerstrasse 5/48
☎ 512 55 81

Concerts are held at 12:30 PM once a month at the Old City Hall (*Altes Rathaus*), 1010, Wipplingerstrasse 8. Admittance to hear beautiful music from first-class musicians costs ATS 80 for seniors. Call for the specific dates.

HAIR CARE

COIFFEUR KARL
1030, Landstrasser
Hauptstrasse 13
☎ 712 91 96

A wash, cut and style is half price for seniors.

COIFFEUR BEA
1220, Schüttaustrasse 4
☎ 263 62 22

This salon with English-speaking staff, located near the Vienna International Centre, offers a 10-percent discount for seniors on Wednesday.

MEAL DEALS

CAFÉ GRIENSTEIDL
1010, Michaelerplatz 2
☎ 535 26 92

This café-restaurant offers a senior plate (*Seniorenteller*), which is a smaller portion for half price. It also has a nonsmoking section.

**SENIOR SNACKS
(*Senioren-Jausen*)**

The Viennese newspaper *Kurier* organizes afternoon coffees with light entertainment. Look in Monday's *Kurier* "Senior Section" ("*Senioren-Seite*") for more details.

**ROSENBERGER
STADT-RESTAURANT**
1010, Maysedergasse 2
☎ 512 34 58

There is a *Senioren-Club* every day from 3 PM - 5 PM in the *Biedermeier-Stüberl*. For ATS 38, you get a piece of cake and a *Melange* in a cup you can take with you.

HEALTH & LIFESTYLE

A booklet in English, "Vienna for Guests with Handicaps," is available at Vienna Tourist Information Offices (see Info Offices appendix). It contains information on everything from transportation to public toilets with wheelchair accessibility in Vienna, but you should confirm the information before depending on it.

U.S. MEDICARE

The U.S. Medicare system only covers its citizens traveling to Canada and Mexico. Therefore, it's important to check your Medicare supplement for overseas coverage. Also, remember to alert all senior citizens planning to visit Europe to check their coverage.

FOR THOSE WITH ELDERLY PARENTS IN THE UNITED STATES

A U.S.-based government agency can help locate medical and legal assistance, home care, meal deliverers and nurses for elderly people living in the United States. It has the telephone numbers of agencies nationwide, and you can request a brochure. For more information, call one of the following numbers:

**NATIONAL ASSOCIATION
OF AREA AGENCIES ON AGING**
☏ 001 (800) 677-1116 (toll-free in the United States)
☏ 001 (202) 296-8130
Mon - Fri, 9 AM - 9 PM (E.S.T.)

SOCIAL

Contact groups (see Organizations chapter), cross-generational English- and German-speaking people gathering monthly for coffee and conversation, meet in many districts. They welcome seniors.

IF YOU CAN SPEAK SOME GERMAN

There are many opportunities for those speaking some German (and those wanting to improve their fluency). If you can call these places for information and understand their replies, you have enough German knowledge to participate in their activities.

CENTER HIETZING
1130, Trauttmannsdorfgasse 5
☎ 876 44 84
Mon - Fri, 8 AM - noon

All the center's proceeds go to charity. The center has professional English-speaking staff to help with psychological or legal problems. It also offers activities such as bridge lessons, gymnastics with music, creative dancing, health gymnastics and *Ismakogie* ("awareness of one's muscles").

SENIOR PASS *Kurier Senioren-Pass*

You can pick up this pass at the daily newspaper *Kurier* Customer Center (*Kurier Kundenzentrum*) in the *Opernpassage* (the underground passage between Kärntner Strasse and Ringstrasse), but you'll need to bring a photo ID and a passport-sized photo. The pass entitles you to discounts with *WAT*, which, among other things, organizes canoe trips through the *Donau-Auen* (a national park passing Hainburg and Orth) and to the *Kamptal-Stauseen*. For more trip information, contact:

COLUMBUS-REISESERVICE
(*Der Reiseservice des Wiener Seniorenbundes*)
1010, Biberstrasse 7
☎ 513 27 70 or ☎ 513 82 77
Mon - Fri, 9 AM - 5 PM

Although only Austrian retirees can become members, with this travel service, nonmembers can book any tour at the same price as Austrian retirees, with a few exceptions.

SENIOREN REISEN
1090, Alserbachstrasse 23
☎ 31 37 20
Mon - Fri, 8 AM - 5 PM

This travel service arranges trips for Austrian retirees. Nonmembers must pay an additional fee for tours in Austria lasting more than three days.

WAT (*Wiener Arbeiter Turn und Sportverein*)
1120, Sagedergasse 10-12
☎ 804 85 32
Mon - Thurs, 9 AM - 1 PM,
Fri, 1 PM - 5 PM

VIENNESE SENIOR CENTER IN WUK (*Wiener Senioren Zentrum im Wuk–Werkstätte und Kultur*)
1090, Währinger Strasse 59
☎ 408 56 92
Mon - Fri, 10 AM - 3 PM

This senior center is run by a self-help group not affiliated with any political party or religion. There are no membership fees. Activities are published in the *Kurier "Senioren-Seite."*

Kurier's *"Senioren Seite"* often has very attractive travel offers (e.g., stay three weeks, pay for two). Several times a year, it offers a three-week all-inclusive trip to spas in Slovakia for half the price of a stay at an Austrian spa.

If you plan to retire in Vienna, be aware that Viennese retirement homes (*Wiener Pensionistenheime*) are only for Austrian citizens.

There is an adult education program (*Volkshochschule*) in almost every district offering classes in everything from art to computer training (see Recreation chapter). The following adult-education information service can tell you about classes for seniors:

EBIS
(*Erwachsenenbildungs-Informations Service*)
1040, Mayerhofgasse 6/3
☎ 504 58 88
Mon - Fri, 8 AM - 6 PM

W hen in need of medical care, we are the most vulnerable, both physically and psychologically. The added complications of differing cultural expectations, language barriers and emotional stress make the situation even more difficult for both doctor and patient. The information in this chapter is intended to alleviate some of these apprehensions. Although only an introduction, it should provide a basic understanding to help you cope with the many medical situations you may encounter in Vienna.

EMERGENCIES

AMBULANCE *Rettung*

| In a **MEDICAL EMERGENCY**, call | ☎ **112** |
| or an **AMBULANCE** *Rettung* | ☎ **144** |

- **Be very specific with your address (including apartment number, floor and staircase, if necessary).**

- **Give your telephone number.**

Because you can panic and forget things in an emergency, or because someone else may have to call for you, fill in the following information ahead of time:

Your address: (District, city)

_____

(Street, numbers)

_____

Your ☎:

_____

The ambulance will usually bring a doctor who may speak English. Unless your doctor has been notified and has specified a hospital, the ambulance driver will select the destination based on his or her communications with medical facilities. In the case of a suspected heart attack *(Herzanfall)*, tell the dispatcher when you call, and the ambulance will most likely bring a physician and staff trained in cardiac emergency care.

The German word *"Ambulanz"* means emergency room, or more specifically, the outpatient clinic, and *"Rettung"* means "ambulance." So don't panic if a hospital calls to tell you that someone is at its *Ambulanz*, and don't confuse the two in an emergency. If you say "ambulance," they may assume you're going to the outpatient clinic on your own.

ACCIDENTAL POISONING

In case of suspected poisoning, call the

Poison Antidote Service
Vergiftungsinformationszentrale (VIZ)
☎ **406 43 43**

- Say: "I only speak English" (so the person can transfer your call or speak English to you).
- State clearly what was ingested, if you know, and how much.
- This is a 24-hour service, available seven days a week, staffed by English-speaking physicians.

EMERGENCY TERMS

Accident *Unfall*	**Severe bleeding** *starke Blutung*
Appendicitis *Blinddarmentzündung*	**Severe breathing difficulties** *schwere Atemnot*
Choking *Ersticken*	**Severe hemorrhage** *schwerer Blutsturz*
Emergency *Notfall*	
Heart attack *Herzanfall*	**Severe pain** *heftige Schmerzen*
Loss of consciousness *Bewusstlosigkeit*	**Chest** *die Brust*
Serious accident *schwerer Unfall*	**Heart** *das Herz*

MINOR INJURIES

Should you need immediate attention for minor injuries when your doctor is not available, you can go directly to an accident hospital *(Unfallspital)*. Should your injury not require an ambulance, try taking a taxi because taxi drivers know the fastest routes and will drop you off at the correct entrance. This way you won't have to deal with traffic and parking. There are many *Unfallspitäler* listed under *"Krankenhäuser"* in the white pages of the telephone directory. The following public hospitals are just a few that accept emergencies 24 hours a day, seven days a week.

ALLGEMEINES
KRANKENHAUS (AKH)
  1090, Währinger Gürtel 18-20
  ☎ 404 00-1964

This hospital is affiliated with the University of Vienna.

UNFALL KRANKENHAUS
MEIDLING (UKH MEIDLING)
  1120, Kundratstrasse 37
  ☎ 601 50

LORENZ BÖHLER
UNFALL KRANKENHAUS
  1200,
  Donaueschingenstrasse 13
  ☎ 331 10

Trauma Care
Unfallstation, Unfallaufnahme
Emergency room *Notfallstation, Notfallaufnahme*

MEDICAL CARE AT NIGHT, ON WEEKENDS & HOLIDAYS

For medical attention at these times, **when your own doctor is unavailable,** call one of the following services. Also look in the weekend newspapers under *"Notdienst"* ("Emergency Service").

DOCTORS-ON-CALL SERVICE
(Ärztefunkdienst)
  ☎ 1771
  Mon - Fri, 7 AM - 7 PM

  ☎ 141
  Mon - Fri, 7 PM - 7 AM,
  Sat - Sun & Holidays, 24 hours

This non-emergency medical service, which may have an English speaker, will send a doctor to your home to examine the patient and prescribe the necessary medication.

SPECIALISTS LUGECK
(Fachärzte Lugeck)
  ☎ 512 18 18

This medical group has an English-speaking nurse on duty 24 hours a day, seven days a week. She will contact a doctor, who will then call you. This service is not for children.

MEDICINE DELIVERY SERVICE
(Medikamentenzustelldienst)
☎ 891 44

If you're unable to go to the pharmacy, this service of the Workers' Samaritan Union (Arbeiter Samariter Bund) will pick up your prescription and money, go to the nearest open pharmacy and bring back your medicine for a fee.

ON-DUTY PHARMACY SERVICE
(Apotheken-Bereitschaftsdienst)
☎ 1550

This number provides a recording in German of those pharmacies on duty after hours, on weekends and public holidays, by district. If you want to have this information handy, pick up a calendar listing Vienna's off-hours pharmacies ("Tag-, Nacht- und Sonntagsdienst der Wiener Apotheken") at any pharmacy.

PHARMACIES
Apotheken

Pharmacies (Apotheken) are located in every district of Vienna. Most drugs aren't available over-the-counter and require a doctor's prescription. Nonprescription drugs (e.g., aspirin, cough syrup) are only available at Apotheken, not drugstores (Drogerien). To find a pharmacy, look for the Apotheke sign (above) or look in the white pages of the telephone directory under "Apotheken." They are open regularly:

> **Mon - Fri, 8 AM - noon, 2 PM - 6 PM, Sat, 8 AM - noon**

Pharmacies take turns staying open at lunchtime, overnight and on weekends. A list of the nearest open pharmacies will be posted outside each closed pharmacy, as well as at the local police station and in the weekend papers. You will have to ring or knock on the Apotheke door for a pharmacist to serve you through a small window in the door. There is an extra charge for medicine purchased after hours.

MEDICAL INSURANCE

AUSTRIAN HEALTH INSURANCE
Krankenkasse

Austria has a national health-insurance system known as the *Krankenkasse (KK)*, which is part of a comprehensive Social Security system (*Sozialversicherung*) that also includes accident insurance, workmen's compensation and a pension plan. There is a national umbrella organization, with several smaller funds based on geography or occupation. Those insured by the *KK* should know the name of their fund (*Kasse*). Most people in Vienna are insured by the Vienna Health Insurance Agency *(Wiener Gebietskrankenkasse or WGKK)*.

Participation in the *KK* is compulsory for everyone working in Austria with a "regular" employment contract, those working in certain professions and those with a trade license (*Gewerbeschein*). The premium for coverage is a set percentage of a person's salary (with half to be paid by the employee and half by the employer). Employees of the United Nations and other international organizations can choose between the *KK* and private health insurance.

Anyone, regardless of citizenship, who is a permanent resident of Austria and is not insured under a program of the Austrian Social Security system (i.e., through employment) can still join the Austrian health-insurance plan. If you're interested, you should apply at the Health Insurance Agency (*Gebietskrankenkasse*) in the province *(Bundesland)* where you live (in Vienna, contact the *WGKK*). If you're self-employed, unemployed or in school, this is called self-insurance (*Selbstversicherung*). The premium may be increased if and when Austrian Social Security contributions are increased, though it may also be reduced in cases of individual hardship, upon application. For more information, ask your employer or the *WGKK*.

TREATMENT VOUCHERS
Krankenscheine

Once you have joined the *KK*, you'll receive a treatment voucher called a *Krankenschein*, which is given to the doctor in lieu of payment.

There are three separate *Krankenscheine* (each issued quarterly): one for a general practitioner, one for a specialist and one for a dentist. These are available from the personnel department for the employee and any qualified dependents (or from the *KK* if you're self-insured).

You present your *Krankenschein* at your initial visit to the doctor. This voucher entitles you to three months' treatment from that doctor, with unlimited visits during that period. You're then required to visit this doctor until the end of the quarter, at which time you can present a new voucher to a different doctor. If your doctor goes on vacation during the three-month period, he or she will arrange for a colleague (usually one with an office nearby) to see his or her patients during that time. This information is posted well in advance at your doctor's office on a large pink sign and is usually on the telephone recording as well. You don't need an additional *Krankenschein* for the substitute. If you plan to go on vacation within Austria during the three-month period, you can request a vacation voucher (*Urlaubsüberweisung*) from your doctor so that you can see another Austrian physician during your trip (especially important if you're going skiing).

If your doctor feels it's necessary to refer you to a specialist (or you need to see more than one specialist within a three-month period) or to send you for further tests, he or she will issue a referral voucher (*Überweisungsschein*), which must be presented for treatment within two weeks of its issuance by your doctor. All laboratory tests and prescriptions have to go through a physician.

If you don't bring a voucher with you, the doctor will either ask you to pay a deposit, or *Einlage* (about ATS 300 - ATS 500), or ask you to sign a form promising to submit one within a set time. A doctor who is contracted to the *KK* can still see patients who are not insured with the *KK*, but they are considered private patients and therefore must pay a fee. Vouchers aren't required for emergency treatment by an ambulance (*Rettung*) or by the Doctors-on-Call Service (*Ärztefunkdienst*).

When you visit a doctor during regular consultation hours (*Ordination*), you may have to wait a long time, even for a short visit. To make the most of your appointment, get to the point quickly and have all your questions written down. The *KK* pays doctors very little per patient, so their income is based on the number of patients whose vouchers they have per quarter, and they must see any patient whose voucher they have as many times as that patient comes to see them during that quarter.

KRANKENKASSE BENEFITS

In addition to doctor's visits, the *KK* offers extensive benefits—the most important of which are the following:

- **Annual physical examination**
- **Hospital treatment**
- **Maternity leave**
- **Medical or therapeutic devices**
- **Medication**
- **Payment during sick leave**
- **Treatment in other countries**

Many European countries have reciprocal agreements with Austria. You must have a certificate for foreign care (*Auslandsbetreuenungs-schein*) for the duration of your stay in one of these countries in order to be treated under the national health-insurance system of that country (request one from your employer, or the *KK* if self-insured, before leaving on an extended trip to such countries).

PRIVATE MEDICAL INSURANCE
Nebenversicherung, Zusatzversicherung

Many Austrians have private insurance (*Nebenversicherung, Zusatz-versicherung*) along with the *KK* to cover additional benefits or costs, such as special care (*Sonderklasse*) in a hospital (see Hospitals section), or to see a private doctor who doesn't have a contract with the *KK*. There are numerous Austrian insurance firms that provide such coverage at various levels, either as part of a group insurance plan organized by your employer (as with the *KK*, half the premium is paid by the employer, half by the employee) or as a self-insurance plan. Some foreign insurance companies, such as the one listed below, also are able to provide additional insurance at competitive rates.

GOODHEALTH WORLDWIDE LIMITED

Mill Bay Lane
Horsham, W. Sussex,
England RH12 1TQ
☎ (44) 1403 230 000
Fax (44) 1403 268 429
Insurance is for expatriates only, up to the age of 74.

INSURANCETOGO.COM WORLDWIDE INSURANCE AGENCY

500 Professional Center Dr.
Novato, CA 94947   USA
☎ 01 (415) 898-0584
Fax 01 (415) 898-0877
eMail info@insurancetogo.com
www.InsuranceToGo.com

HOW TO FIND A DOCTOR

Your country's consulate or embassy may be able to provide a list of doctors (*Ärzte*) who speak English or another language. Also, look in the A–H telephone book under *"Ärzte,"* where general practitioners (*Ärzte und Ärztinnen Praktische*) are listed first by district (*Bezirk*). Specialists (*Fachärzte und Fachärztinnen*) follow and are listed by their specialties and by district. Your private-insurance company can recommend doctors who accept your insurance. The following are some other resources:

VIENNA MEDICAL ASSOCIA-TION: SERVICE DEPARTMENT FOR FOREIGN PATIENTS
(Ärztekammer für Wien: Servicestelle für ausländische Patienten)
  1010, Weihburggasse 10-12
  ☎ 515 01 21-3
  Mon - Fri, 8 AM - 4 PM
  ☎ 401 44
  (24-hour emergency calls)
  Fax 401 55 99

This English-speaking organization helps international (both visitor and resident) patients by providing free information about types and length of treatment and prospective costs. It can also make arrangements between doctors, patients and hospitals, and help you find a doctor or specialist who speaks your language.

MEDICAL ASSOCIATION PATIENT SERVICE
(Patientenservice der Ärztekammer)
  ☎ 1771
  Mon - Fri, 7 AM - 7 PM

This organization can help you find a doctor (who may even make house calls) in your neighborhood.

Body Temperatures in Degrees *(Grad)* Fahrenheit & Celsius	°F	°C
	98.6°	37.0°
	99.5°	37.5°
	100.4°	38.0°
	101.3°	38.5°
	102.2°	39.0°
	103.1°	39.5°
	104.0°	40.0°
	104.9°	40.5°

MEDICAL SPECIALTIES

The following specialties are listed in the white pages of the telephone directory under *"Ärzte."*

Augenheilkunde Ophthalmology

Chirurgie Surgery (with many subspecialties)

Frauenheilkunde und Geburts-hilfe Gynecology and Obstetrics

Gefässchirurgie Vascular Surgery

Hals-, Nasen-, Ohren-krankheiten Throat, Nose and Ear

Haut- ung Geschlechtskrank-heiten Dermatology and Venereal Disease

Innere Medizin Internal Medicine

Kinder- und Jugendheilkunde Pediatrics

Lungenkrankheiten Pulmonary Diseases

Medizinisches Labora-torium Medical Laboratory

Neurologie und Psychia-trie Neurology and Psychiatry

Orthopädie und orth. Chirurgie Orthopedics and Orthopedic Surgery

Physikalische Medizin Physical Therapy

Radiologie (Röntgen) Radiology (X-rays)

Urologie Urology

Zahn-, Mund- und Kiefer-heilkunde Dental, Oral and Orthodontic Care

"Dentisten" are not the same as "dentists" in English. The word for "dentist" in German is *"Zahnarzt."*

MAKING A DOCTOR'S APPOINTMENT

If you need to make an appointment, look for the word *"Voranm,"* an abbreviation of *Voranmeldung,* in the doctor's telephone-book listing. Most doctors also list their regular consultation hours *(Ordination or Ord)* when they see patients on a first-come-first-served basis. Many now have telephone recordings switched on after office hours that state consultation times.

The words *"alle Kassen"* indicate that they accept all Austrian *KK* (the alternative being that they may accept patients of a particular *KK* only), and *"keine Kassen"* means they only consult on a private-patient basis. Doctors who are under contract to the *KK* may still see patients privately, which usually means shorter waits and longer consultations for the patient. When you call for an appointment, you should specify that you want to be seen as a private patient.

If you're covered by the *KK* but wish to consult a doctor who is not under contract to the *KK*, it's still possible to have your lab work, X-rays, etc. done through the *KK* by having your general practitioner *(praktischer Arzt)* with a *KK* affiliation rewrite the prescriptions. Also, you may want to apply to the *KK* with proof of payment to a private doctor for the *KK* to partially reimburse you. Consult your private doctor for details.

Be prepared to wait much longer to see the doctor if you go during the consultation hours. When you enter the waiting room, ask, *"Wer war der Letzte, bitte?"* ("Who was the last?"), so you'll know whom to follow (the person who comes in after you will ask, too, so be prepared to raise your hand), and wait to be called.

Many Austrian doctors are still willing to make house calls outside their regular hours. Even if the examination at home is covered by the *KK*, the doctor is allowed to charge a fee for attending to you in your home (but not all do).

 In the Examining Room

Unlike in some other parts of the world, Austrian doctors do not offer examination gowns to their patients and a nurse usually isn't present during an exam. Some who feel uncomfortable doing this bring their own gowns. The phrase *"Bitte, machen Sie sich frei"* is the doctor's request for you to disrobe.

HEALTH-CARE PROFESSIONALS

There are a number of English-speaking health-care professionals (psychologists, dietitians, nurses, speech therapists, physiotherapists) working in Vienna, who can be identified via the AWA Vienna Health Care Professionals Group (call ☎ 320 14 95 for a contact number).

IMMUNIZATIONS
Impfungen

If you have questions about required vaccinations for your child, ask your general practitioner, pediatrician or the school's nurse. Immunizations are not usually covered by the *KK*. Children, however, can be immunized for free or for a minimal charge (depending on the type of immunization) at a Vienna Parental Advisory Office *(Elternberatungsstelle der Stadt Wien)* found in each district (check the white pages of the telephone directory for the location nearest you).

TICK IMMUNIZATION
Zeckenschutzimpfung

The Central European Tick—which is found in many of Austria's wooded areas, such as the Vienna Woods, the Wachau, Styria, Carinthia and Burgenland—transmits an illness called Early Summer Meningoencephalitis, which is an inflammation of the brain and meninges. If you'll be living here for more than a year, you should get the tick immunizations, which are a series of three intramuscular injections, usually given in the late winter/early spring according to the following schedule:

FIRST INJECTION	Late winter/early spring
SECOND INJECTION	An interval of 2-8 weeks
THIRD INJECTION	9-12 months later
BOOSTER INJECTION	Every 3-4 years thereafter
(one single dose)	

Protection starts after the SECOND injection and is COMPLETE after the THIRD one.

Keep in mind that due to greater tick threats in the spring and September, the second injection is given two weeks after the first. These injections can be given by your general practitioner or pediatrician. Call first to make sure your doctor has the serum on hand. If not, you may have to pick it up (at any pharmacy) and keep it refrigerated until it can be administered. Some international-school nurses may administer the immunizations to students for a fee. Adults can receive these shots—as well as others, such as flu shots *(Grippeimpfungen)*—from their District Health Office *(Bezirksgesundheitsamt)*. Check the telephone directory for the one in your district (office hours are posted on the door). If you have any questions, call:

INSTITUTE OF VIROLOGY *(Institut für Virologie)*
1090, Kinderspitalgasse 15
☎ 404 90-601
Mon - Fri, 2 PM - 3 PM, Thurs, 5 PM - 6 PM

The Institute will also administer the tick immunizations during the above hours (no appointment necessary) and point out regions where ticks are found, as well as what to do if you're bitten by a tick. English is spoken.

 If you've been bitten by a tick and have not been immunized, contact a doctor immediately. If left untreated, you could contract *meningoencephalitis*, which can be deadly.

IMMUNIZATIONS FOR INTERNATIONAL TRAVEL
Impfstellen für Auslandsreisende

You can get information on mandatory and recommended immunizations for travelers to foreign countries, as well as the actual shots, from the following:

INSTITUTE OF TROPICAL MEDICINE
(Institut für Tropenmedizin)
1090, Kinderspitalgasse 15
☎ 403 43 92 or ☎ 403 83 43-0
Mon - Fri, 9 AM - 4:30 PM
Mon - Fri, 1 PM - 4 PM (vaccinations)

If you contract an unidentified illness following travel to a tropical or subtropical country, you can contact the following clinic:

OUTPATIENT CLINIC FOR TROPICAL AND TRAVEL DISEASES
(Ambulanz für Tropen- und Reisekrankheiten)
Kaiser-Franz-Josef-Spital
1100, Kundratstrasse 3
☎ 601 91-2476
Mon - Fri, 8 AM - noon

LOCAL HEALTH AUTHORITIES
Gesundheitsämter

The telephone directory's white pages list the addresses and telephone numbers of *"Gesundheitsämter"* under *"Bezirksgesundheitsämter"* and local *KK* administrative offices under *"Krankenkassebezirksstellen."*

HOSPITALS
Krankenhäuser

Hospital care is classified as either general (*allgemeine Klasse*) or special (*Sonderklasse*). The *allgemeine Klasse* can only admit people who have Austrian *KK* or are from a country with a special treaty with the Austrian *KK* (which includes most European countries). Wards vary in size, visiting hours are restricted and there is no choice of doctor (you'll be attended to by the doctor on duty). The quality of medical care should be comparable, but a hospital stay at a *Sonderklasse* is considered more comfortable.

Sonderklasse provides you with a private or semiprivate room, more flexible visiting hours, more personal care and your choice of doctors. Your own specialist can attend to you as long as he or she has privileges at that particular hospital, which might be important for expectant mothers. This also means that in nonemergency admissions, your hospital will be determined by where your doctor has privileges. Most private insurance plans cover the cost for *Sonderklasse*, but unless you also have the Austrian *KK*, you'll be required to make a substantial down payment upon hospital admittance (about ATS 40.000 or more). This deposit may be waived if your foreign insurance company contacts the hospital prior to your admission. There is no direct billing with non-Austrian insurance companies.

Upon admittance, be sure to have your *Sozialversicherungskarte* if you're insured under the *KK* and/or your private-insurance card. Most hospitals in Vienna are fully equipped with modern technology, but you may find that you need to take along your own toiletries (e.g., washcloth, towel, soap, facial tissues, etc.), even in the *Sonderklasse*.

PEDIATRIC FACILITIES

You may want to take your child to a pediatric hospital (*Kinderkliniken*) because regular hospitals often don't have separate pediatric facilities. The main difference among *Kinderkliniken* is that some have surgery facilities and some don't, which could be a consideration if your child has a broken bone or appendicitis. Be aware that you may or may not find an English speaker at the following locations:

Hospitals With Pediatric Operating Facilities

ALLGEMEINES KRANKENHAUS NOTFALLAUFNAHME/ EBENE 6D
1090, Währinger Gürtel 18-20
☎ 404 00-3232

GOTTFRIED VON PREYER'SCHES KINDERSPITAL
1100, Schrankenberggasse 31
☎ 601 13

DONAUSPITAL IM SMZ OST JOURNALDIENST FÜR NOTFÄLLE
1220, Langobardenstrasse 122
☎ 288 02

Hospitals Without Pediatric Operating Facilities

MAUTNER-MARKHOFSCHES KINDERSPITAL
1030, Juchgasse 25
☎ 711 65

ST. ANNA KINDERSPITAL
1090, Kinderspitalgasse 6
☎ 401 70-0

KINDERKLINIK GLANZING
1190, Glanzinggasse 35-39
☎ 476 02-0

You may also want to try this Pediatrician:

 DR. BARBARA GRÖHS

1140, Linzerstraße 434/2/2
☎ 577 27 66
This English-speaking pediatrician takes her time with your children's big and small problems in a warm and friendly atmosphere. She also provides ultrasound, allergy tests, homeopathy and acupuncture.

DENTAL, ORAL & ORTHODONTIC CARE *Zahn-, Mund- und Kieferheilkunde*

EMERGENCY DENTAL TREATMENT

> **For emergency dental treatment, call**
>
> **On-Duty Dentists** ☎ **512 20 78**
> *Zahnarztbereitschaft*
>
> Mon - Fri, 8 PM - 1 AM, Sat - Sun & Holidays, 9 AM - 6 PM
>
> This recording in German gives the names and telephone numbers of dentists on emergency duty in Vienna. This information is also available in the weekend newspapers under *"Notdienst"* ("Emergency Services").

The following emergency dental clinic is open Mon - Fri during limited hours:

UNIVERSITÄTSZAHNKLINIK
   1090, Währinger Strasse 25A
   ☎ 401 81-0 (outpatient)
   ☎ 401 81-2001 (dental prosthesis)

You may get a tape recording (in German) giving office hours.

Emergency Dental Prosthesis Repair

The *"Notdienst"* section of the weekend newspapers also lists an emergency service for the repair of dental prostheses.

DENTISTS *Zahnärzte*

Medically qualified dentists are known as *Zahnärzte* in Austria and are listed in the A–H telephone book in the *"Ärzte"* section, by district. An appointment (*Voranmeldung*) is usually required, but consulting hours (*Ordination*) are also listed. The *KK* system covers only some dental-treatment costs. This is one reason why Austria emphasizes curative measures rather than preventive care. For example, a thorough teeth and gum cleaning isn't covered by the *KK*, so it must be paid for privately (ask your dentist). The following two are an English-speaking dentist and dental hygienist. You also can call the AWA office at ☎ 320 14 95 for a list of English-speaking dentists and approximate costs for services.

 DR. NENAD MIRKOVIC

1090, Garnisong. 3/5
☎ 402 3087

This private dentist and dental surgeon speaks fluent English and is excellent with children.

 DR. CHRISTIAN ZINN-ZINNENBURG

1130, Altgasse 25A/3/1/4
☎ 877 55 42
Mon - Tues, Thurs, 8 AM - 1 PM,
2 PM - 5 PM, Fri, 8 AM - 1 PM

This dentist uses American dental techniques and explains treatment procedures in English. Call for an appointment Mon - Tues, Thurs 10 AM - 1 PM (appointments must be made in German).

 HY LOGAN

1190, Billrothstrasse 78
☎ 369 29 76
Mon - Fri, 8 AM - 1 PM
(to make an appointment)

This American-trained dental hygienist works at the dental clinic in the *Rudolfinerhaus*.

 DR. HERMAN GERM

1200, Allerheilgeneplatz 11
☎ 332 3010 or 332 3011
Mon - Fri afternoons

This Kassa or private dentist speaks fluent English and is also excellent with children.

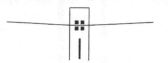
ORTHODONTISTS *Kieferheilkunde*

Some dentists only practice orthodontics, while others practice both orthodontics and dentistry. Your dentist may refer you to the following orthodontic clinic, which provides excellent care, though you may not see the same orthodontist at each visit:

INSTITUTE OF THE VIENNA MEDICAL ASSOCIATION (*Institut der Ärztekammer für Wien*)
> 1060, Gumpendorfer Strasse 83
> ☎ 597 23 85-0
> Mon, Wed, Fri, 8 AM - 4 PM,
> Tues, Thurs, 8 AM - 6 PM

Or you can try one of the following orthodontist:

DR. CLAUDIA AICHINGER-PFANDL
> 1190, Billrothstrasse 58
> ☎ 367 72 22
> Fax 367 72 22-11
> (see advertisement above)

 DR. FRANZ RONAY
> 1010, Rudolfplatz 14
> ☎ 533 51 92
> Mon - Thurs, 9 AM - noon,
> 1 PM - 6 PM

This American-trained, English-speaking orthodontist holds U.S. patents on some procedures and also has an American assistant.

 = Member recommendation

MISCELLANEOUS MEDICAL SERVICES

AIDS HELP *(AIDS Hilfe)*
1080, Wickenburggasse 14
☎ 408 61 86
Mon, Wed, 4 PM - 7 PM,
Thurs, 9 AM - noon,
Fri, 2 PM - 5 PM (HIV testing)

This organization, which has English speakers, provides information and care to HIV-positive people.

ALCOHOLICS ANONYMOUS
(Anonyme Alkoholiker)
1030, Barthgasse 5
☎ 317 88 76 (English)
☎ 799 55 99 (German)

This organization has English-speaking groups that meet in different districts, so call for locations and times.

ALANON *(Anonyme Alkoholiker Angehörigengruppe)*
1170, Geblergasse 45
☎ 408 53 77
Tues, 7:30 PM - 8:30 PM

This group is for people with alcoholic family members. The English speakers usually meet at the time above. Call to confirm the meeting schedule.

AUSTRIAN RED CROSS BLOOD DONOR CENTER
(Blutspendezentrale des Österreichischen Roten Kreuzes)
1040, Wiedner Hauptstrasse 30-34
Mon - Thurs, 8 AM - 5 PM,
Fri , 8 AM - 5:30 PM (blood donation)
☎ 589 00-251

Blood donation is organized by the Austrian Red Cross. English is spoken.

AUSTRIAN SOCIETY OF HOMEOPATHIC MEDICINE
(Österreichische Gesellschaft für homöopathische Medizin)
1070, Mariahilfer Strasse 110
☎ 526 75 75

This English-speaking group can provide a list of homeopathic doctors.

POLLEN ALERT SERVICE
(Pollenwarndienst)
☎ 1529

Call for information (in German) about pollen levels in Vienna.

OUTPATIENT CLINIC FOR PREGNANCY HELP
(Ambulatorium für Schwangerenhilfe)
1010, Fleischmarkt 26
☎ 512 96 31
Mon - Fri, 8 AM - 5 PM,
Sat, 8 AM - noon

This clinic, where English is spoken, offers pregnancy tests, birth control and abortion counseling.

E very culture has its own recreational activities. Vienna, with its plentiful holidays, parks and nearby woods and mountains, is the perfect place to enjoy the outdoors. If you prefer staying indoors, however, there are plenty of specialty stores and clubs to facilitate your interests. The following information should help you find the right people or places to indulge in whatever sport or leisure activity you enjoy. It is in alphabetical order with leisure activities first, then sports.

LEISURE

ART INSTRUCTION

ARTISTIC COMMUNITY SCHOOL
Künstlerische Volkshochschule
1090, Lazarettgasse 27
☎ 405 78 77

This institute, which has a solid reputation and reasonable tuition, offers a variety of courses that focus primarily on art for both children and adults. Drawing, painting, graphics, crafts, gold and silver work, photography, drama and yoga are just a few areas. Many instructors speak English; those who don't ask students to help translate. The school also offers other leisure activities.

ART SUPPLIES

ALOIS EBESEDER
1010, Babenbergerstrasse 3
☎ 587 03 53

This store, which is located directly behind the Museum of Fine Arts (*Kunsthistorisches Museum*), also carries many art and craft supplies. Only German is spoken.

BECK, KOLLER & CO.
1010, Walfischgasse 15
☎ 512 16 95

Although primarily a paint store, it also stocks art supplies and specialty chemicals. English is spoken.

OTTO KUMMER
1070, Schottenfeldgasse 3
☎ 523 84 88

This store has a wide selection of art supplies. English is spoken.

HOBBY & KUNST KRONSTEINER
1030, Landstrasser Hauptstrasse 120
☎ 713 43 09

This store has everything for the do-it-yourself person, including stencils, découpage and ceramics. It also sells dollhouses and dollhouse furniture. Employees can offer advice in English.

Art-Supply Terms

Brush *Pinsel*

Charcoal sticks *Kohlestifte*

Easel *Staffelei*

Oil colors *Ölfarben*

Palette knife *Spatel*

Pastels *Pastellstifte*

Turpentine *Terpentin*

Watercolors *Wasserfarben*

COMMUNITY SCHOOLS *Volkshochschulen*

Volkshochschulen are public institutions with a long tradition and good reputation. They offer a variety of courses in German for adults and children at different levels. A basic German knowledge is necessary, but the instructors and other students are very helpful. There is a *Volkshochschule* in almost every district in Vienna. Free program schedules are available from the schools. Course fees are reasonable and vary with the type and length of a course. Classes are available in aerobics, ceramics, computers, drawing, painting, languages, needlework and music. The winter semester begins in September, the summer one in February. Locations are listed in the telephone directory's white pages under *"Volkshochschulen."* For other educational opportunities in English, see the Education chapter.

DANCING *Tanz*

Dancing plays a very important role in the Vienna social scene, with the Viennese Waltz (*Wiener Walzer*) and other ballroom dancing remaining very popular. (Also see Holidays section of Austria chapter.) If you'd like to learn how to waltz, or simply want to brush up on your moves, contact one of the many dance schools listed in the yellow pages under *"Tanzschule."* These schools not only teach dance steps but also dance etiquette. If you want a complete listing of schools, ask for the brochure *"Küss mich, ich bin ein Tänzer"* ("Kiss Me, I'm a Dancer") at any Vienna Tourist Information Office (see Info Offices appendix). The following is a list of some of the most popular classical-dance schools (*Tanzschule für Gesellschaftstanz*) in Vienna:

ELLMAYER
1010, Bräunerstrasse 13
☎ 512 71 97
Mon - Sat, 3 PM - 10 PM,
Sun, 5 PM - 10 PM
Instructors can teach classes in English.

STANEK
1010, Grashofgasse 1A
☎ 513 42 92
Daily, 5 PM - 10 PM
This school only offers ballroom-dancing classes.

SCHÖNBRUNN
1130, Altgasse 6
☎ 877 32 02
Mon, Tues, Thurs, Fri,
7 PM - 10 PM

IMMERVOLL
1130, Hietzinger Hauptstrasse 6
☎ 877 66 96
Daily, 5 PM - 8 PM

Private lessons in English are available.

WIATER
1180, Martinstrasse 96
☎ 406 57 09
Daily, 5 PM - 10 PM

If you leave your address on the answering machine, this school will send you a class schedule. Classes can be taught in English.

In the summer (May 9 - Sept 22), the First Danube Steamship Company (DDSG) offers Friday- and Saturday-evening dancing excursions (7 PM - 10:30 PM). For reservations, call ☎ 727 50-0 (two weeks in advance) or, for groups, fax 727 50-440. The brochure *"Musik, Tanz, Unterhaltung"* ("Music, Dance, Entertainment") lists restaurants, discos and nightclubs where music and dancing are available. You can pick it up at the City Information (*Stadtinformation*) office (see Info Offices appendix).

HORSE RACING
Pferderennen

Horse racing has been popular in Vienna since the 14th century, when horses used to race down the Landstrasser Hauptstrasse with crowds cheering them on to the finish line.

Today, the *Prater*'s Freudenau Track serves as the official setting for horse races, with an elegant spectator stand dating back to 1836. Races usually start at 12:30 PM and continue until dusk on predetermined days.

For information, contact the following association:

VIENNESE GALLOPING RACE ASSOCIATION
Wiener Galopp-Rennverein
    1020, Freudenau
    ☎ 728 95 35-0
    Mon - Thurs, 8 AM - 4:30 PM, Fri, 8 AM - 12:30 PM

Also at the *Prater*, the *Krieau Trabrennbahn* features trotting races on selected days during the season from Sept - June, with racing commencing at 2 PM and continuing until dusk. For more information, contact the following association:

VIENNESE TROTTING ASSOCIATION
Wiener Trabrenn-Verein
    1020, Krieau
    ☎ 728 00 46
    Mon - Fri, 7 AM - noon

KNITTING
Stricken

Vienna has many yarn shops. Look in the yellow pages under *"Wollgarne."* You can get a list of translated knitting terms and converted needle and hook sizes from the AWA office (see Organizations chapter).

MOVIES
Kinos

There are several English-language and original-format movie theaters (*Kinos*) in Vienna, so you can still watch current American films, albeit a few months or weeks later. For theaters and addresses, see the Cinemas/Movie Theaters section of the Entertainment chapter.

On evenings in July and August, you can see films of famous classical-music and opera performances outdoors on a large screen at *Rathausplatz*, the square in front of City Hall (*Rathaus*). Weather permitting, these free movies start at dusk (around 9:30 PM). Schedules are available at the City Information (*Stadtinformation*) office (see Info Offices appendix). Also see the Cinemas/Movie Theaters section of the Entertainment chapter.

PICNICKING
& PUBLIC BARBECUES

During the summer, Vienna has 14 barbecue and picnic areas open for public use: along the Danube (*Donau*), on Danube Island *(Donauinsel)* and in the 11th, 19th, 22nd and 23rd districts. Many sites have toilet facilities and drinking water. For reservations, call the Grill Telephone (*Grilltelefon*) at ☎ 488 29 96-496 (in German). *"Wien Online"* (www.wienonline.at) lists each site and its layout plan (click on the *Freizeit* button for grill locations).

READING
Lesen

LIBRARIES & BOOKSTORES
Bibliotheken und Buchhandlungen

Your can find a complete list of libraries under *"Bibliotheken"* in the *"Bildungsseiten"* of the yellow pages.

AMERICAN REFERENCE CENTER (ARC)

1080, Schmidgasse 14
☎ 405 30 33
Fax 406 52 60
eMail usis@usia.co.at
www.usembassy-vienna.at
Mon - Thurs 2 PM - 5 PM
(by appointment only)

The center provides current information resources about the United States government and public policy, as well as economic and social issues. The resources are available to Austrian government agencies, the media and people with serious research interests in the United States.

BRITISH COUNCIL AUSTRIA LIBRARY

1010, Schenkenstrasse 4
☎ 533 26 16-82
Fax 533 26 16-85

This library has a 21,000-volume literature collection from all the English-speaking Commonwealth countries in both its circulating and noncirculating sections. There is also an extensive library of fine films, which you can rent for a fee. The library is open to the public, with membership required in order to borrow materials. The annual membership fee is ATS 450. Proof of identity (e.g., passport) is required for registration. Call for hours.

AMERICAN INTERNATIONAL SCHOOL SECONDARY LIBRARY

1190, Salmannsdorfer Strasse 47
☎ 401 32-220
Mon - Fri, 8 AM - 3:30 PM
eMail info@ais.at
www.ais.at

The library subscribes to 200 American magazines, newspapers and journals. Books can be borrowed for up to two weeks, with an overdue fee of ATS 1 per day charged on late returns. The library is closed during school holidays. Parents of AIS students can use the library at no charge. All others must pay a one-time, non-refundable fee of ATS 1.000.

WEBSTER UNIVERSITY LIBRARY

1220, Berchtoldgasse 1
☎ 269 92 93 0
Fax 269 92 93 13

This university library focuses on areas in which the school has programs, such as management, international relations, computer science and psychology. It's open to the international community as a reference-only library (i.e., you can't borrow books). Call for hours.

CITY PUBLIC LIBRARIES
Städtische Büchereien

1080, Skodagasse 20
☎ 40 00-845 50
Fax 40 00-998 45-10
Mon, Thurs, 10 AM - 7:30 PM,
Tues, Fri, 2 PM - 7:30 PM

Vienna's public libraries have extensive collections of books, tapes, CDs and records. Although they primarily stock German-language books, the libraries do have about 20,000 non-German works. To find the nearest branch, look in the telephone directory's white pages under *"Büchereien, Städt."*

UNIVERSITY OF VIENNA LIBRARIES
Universitätsbibliotheken

Main University Library
Hauptbibliothek
1010, Dr.-Karl-Lueger-Ring 1
Mon - Fri, 9 AM - 7:45 PM,
Sat, 9 AM - 12:45 PM

The university has an extensive network of specialized libraries (e.g., business and economics, art history, English literature, music and technology) throughout Vienna. Collections are predominantly in German. If you know what you want—or you have the time to look through the card catalogs—you'll find an adequate amount of material in English. The university's loan policy depends on your residence status. A refundable deposit may be required.

AUSTRIAN NATIONAL LIBRARY *Österreichische Nationalbibliothek*

1010, Josefsplatz 1
☎ 534 10
Fax 534 10-280
eMail onb@onb.ac.at
www.onb.ac.at
Mon - Fri, 9 AM - 7 PM,
Sat, 9 AM - 12:45 PM

For the true library enthusiast, a visit to the *Österreichische Nationalbibliothek* is an absolute must. Take the time to browse through its card catalog, make a few selections, fill out the forms, then pick up your requests the following day and peruse them in the reading room. It's free. There's also a separate periodicals room with many English-language magazines.

BOOKSTORES *Buchhandlungen*

There are a number of bookstores in Vienna that specialize in English-language books, and most of the larger Austrian shops also carry selections in English.

English-Language Bookstores

SHAKESPEARE & COMPANY
1010, Sterngasse 2
☎ 535 50 53
Fax 535 50 53-16

This shop sponsors occasional poetry readings and literary events. It has an extensive collection of fiction and books on art, politics, Viennese history, travel, reference, poetry and theater.

BIG BEN BOOKSHOP
1090, Servitengasse 4A
☎ 319 64 12
Fax 319 64 12 3
eMail:
bookshop@bigben.vienna.at

This store, which is a 10-minute walk from the United States Embassy, carries fiction and history, politics, crime, travel, art and children's books. It also sells audiocassettes and videos.

THE BRITISH BOOKSHOP
1010, Weihburggasse 24-26
☎ 512 19 45 or ☎ 512 26 82
Fax 512 10 26

This store has an extensive selection of best-selling hardcover and paperback fiction and nonfiction, including books on crime, professions, reference (including dictionaries), travel and children's literature. It's also a center for books on teaching English as a second language. It can special-order books for you. (See advertisement on previous page.)

> You can also order books and other media online from www.amazon.co.uk or www.amazon.co.at (in German).

Austrian Bookstores With Some English-Language Books

BUCHHANDLUNG FRICK
1010, Graben 27
☎ 533 99 14 or ☎ 533 99 15

This bookstore has an upstairs section with some books in English; downstairs, it has books on Vienna and Austria in English. It can special-order books.

GEROLD & CO.
1010, Graben 31
☎ 533 50 14-0
Fax 533 50 14-12

This is a specialty shop for international literature. It has a number of fiction and nonfiction books in English. The staff speaks English.

BUCHHANDLUNG MORAWA
1010, Wollzeile 11 (main store)
☎ 515 62-0
Fax 515 62-138

This store has an excellent selection of American magazines, international newspapers and some books in English. It will order and take subscriptions. Morawa has a number of branches throughout the city including a very large one at Westbahnhof.

FREYTAG & BERNDT
1010, Kohlmarkt 9
☎ 533 20 94-0

This shop specializes in maps and travel guides, including books on Vienna and Austria in English. The staff can assist you in English.

ÖBV BUCHHANDLUNG
Österreichischer Bundesverlag
1015, Schwarzenbergstrasse 5
☎ 514 05-227 or ☎ 515 05-228
Fax 514 05-223

This store carries a selection of books printed in Austria and Germany, including textbooks for foreign-language courses.

Book Terms
Book(s) *Buch (Bücher)*
Magazine *Zeitschrift*
Map *Landkarte*
Paperback book *Taschenbuch*

SEWING *Nähen*

Sewing-machine dealers are listed in the yellow pages under *"Nähmaschinen,"* and for sewing-machine repair look under *"Nähmaschinen Reparatur."* The following are some fabric stores:

INDIA SEIDEN
1010, Schulerstrasse 9
☎ 512 54 22 or ☎ 512 51 96
Fax 512 93 08
eMail pravin@india.co.at
www.india.co.at

This store carries only silks, but in a rainbow of colors and textures (see Interior Fabrics section of Home chapter).

SILESIA
1010, Vorlaufstrasse 3
☎ 533 76 46

This store has a wide selection of fabrics, as well as patterns and notions. A customer card (*Kundenkarte*) entitles you to discounts.

Sewing Terms
Cotton *Baumwolle*
Button(s) *Knopf (Knöpfe)*
Fabric *Stoff*
Lining material *Futterstoff*
Needles *Nähnadeln*
Pins *Stecknadeln*
Silk *Seide*
Strong thread *Zwirn*
Thread *Nähseide*
Wool *Wolle*
Zipper *Reissverschluss*

KOMOLKA
1070, Mariahilfer Strasse 58
☎ 523 71 84-0 or
☎ 523 95 91-0

This store carries day and evening fabrics and imports. Fabrics at discounted prices are in the basement.

SEIDEN SEMLER
1120, Meidlinger
Hauptstrasse 75
☎ 813 22 42

This store has some discounted fabrics.

TEXTIL MÜLLER
3420 Kritzendorf,
Durchstichstrasse 2
☎ (02243) 2178
Mon - Fri, 9 AM - 6 PM,
Sat, 9 AM - 1 PM
(first Sat of month 9 AM - 5 PM)

Northwest of Vienna (take the *Schnellbahn* 40 from Heiligenstadt), this store is worth the trip. It is a large discount house with an overwhelming and eclectic selection. There are walls full of buttons. English is spoken. It also carries thin and lacy fabrics for curtains.

For decorator fabrics, see the Decorator Fabrics section of the Home chapter.

EMBROIDERY, NEEDLEPOINT & TAPESTRY
Stickerei

Stores that sell embroidery, needlepoint, tapestry and patchwork supplies (*Zubehör*) are listed in the yellow pages under *"Handarbeiten."*

DAS HANDARBEITGESCHÄFT
1010, Stephansplatz 6
☎ 512 44 43

Employees only speak German so you must know the terminology for what you want.

LUDWIG NOWOTNY
1010, Freisingergasse 4
(Petersplatz)
☎ 533 93 35

Established in 1818, this store can ship fine-art needle works, embroideries and souvenirs worldwide. English is spoken.

EXQUISITY PATCHWORK
1030, Ungargasse 35
☎ 718 96 96

This store has 1,800 bolts of fabric, as well as books and templates. English is spoken.

PFEIFFER
1180, Währinger Strasse 120
☎ 479 68 81

This store carries embroidery and needlepoint supplies. English is spoken.

AWA members can call the AWA office for information about sewing and quilting groups or can check the organization's *Highlights* magazine.

STARGAZING/ASTRONOMY *Astronomie*

URANIA OBSERVATORY
Sternwarte
1010, Uraniastrasse 1
☎ 712 61 91

The Urania Telescope is open to the public for viewing the skies (on clear nights) on Wednesday, Friday and Saturday at 8 PM and, in the summer, at 9 PM. It is closed in August. You can see the moon, Jupiter and its moons, gas clouds and galaxies. Photographs can be taken. There's an admission charge. (Also see the Other Places of Interest section of the Entertainment chapter.) Only German is spoken.

KUFFNER-STERNWARTE
1180, Johann-Staud-Strasse 10
☎ 914 81 30

The telescope is available for viewing Tuesday, Friday and Saturday at 8 PM. There are separate admission fees for adults and children.

PLANETARIUM
1020, Prater
(Oswald-Thomas-Platz 1)
☎ 729 54 94

It is open to the public on Sunday at 5 PM (closed Aug - mid-Sept). Programs (in German) vary, so call for details.

VIDEO RENTAL *Videoverleih*

Many local video-rental shops in Vienna carry some movies in English. The following are stores that specialize in English-language movies:

BLOCKBUSTER VIDEO
1010, Salztorgasse 6
☎ 533 23 21
Mon - Fri, 10 AM - 10 PM,
Sat, 10 AM - midnight

This store, which is affiliated with the huge U.S. video-store chain, has more than 1,200 English-language movies and seven other locations in Vienna (look in the telephone directory's white pages). There is no membership fee, but you need identification (e.g., passport, driver's license or *Meldezettel*). VCRs and games are also available for rental.

PICKWICKS
1010, Marc-Aurel-Strasse 10-12
☎ 533 01 82
Mon - Sat, 10 AM - 10 PM

There is a membership fee (bring a passport or driver's license to sign up); members receive a list of the 7,000 available videos in PAL and NTSC formats (some foreign-language films). There's a discount for same-day return before 8 PM. It also rents VCRs.

ALPHAVILLE
1040, Scheifmühlgasse 5
☎ 585 19 66
Mon - Sat, 10 AM - 10 PM,
Sun, 2 PM - 7 PM

Other video outlets are listed in the yellow pages under *"Videotheken."*

WALKING *Wandern* & JOGGING *Joggen*

Most newcomers find that a good street directory (*Grossraum Buchplan*) is necessary for both business and leisure. Freytag & Berndt at 1010, Kohlmarkt 9, and ÖAMTC (an Austrian automobile club) at 1010, Schubertring 1-3, plus some bookstores, carry a variety of directories. A free city map (*Stadtplan*) is available at hotels and Vienna Tourist Information Offices (see Info Offices appendix).

Walking tours of Vienna are scheduled monthly and listed in the "*Wiener Spaziergänge/*Walks in Vienna" brochure, available from any Vienna Tourist Information Office (see Info Offices appendix). Some of these tours are conducted in English. The fee is payable at the designated meeting point.

For exploring Vienna's surroundings, consider buying *Wanderatlas Wienerwald* (*Vienna Woods Walking Atlas*), which is published and sold by Freytag & Berndt (see address above). Another good resource is the brochure "*Die Wiener Stadtwanderwege*" ("The Viennese City Footpaths"), which describes nine different round-trip walks around the perimeter of the city and is available at the City Information (*Stadtinformation*) office (see Info Offices appendix). The AWA also has two regular walking groups, so call the AWA office for information or consult the AWA *Highlights* magazine (see Organizations chapter).

Vienna has more than 80 public parks—many with statues, an array of interesting animal life and beautiful landscaping—with well-marked paths for walking, running or biking. Each season they display a whole new look, which gives you an excuse to visit each park regularly.

Suggested Walks in Vienna

Vienna Woods *Wienerwald*

The *Wienerwald*, surrounding the city to the north and west, is a wonderful place to go walking. Well-marked trails lead through woods and vineyards and offer some spectacular views. You can also stop at an inn (*Gasthaus*) or new-wine tavern (*Heurigen*) along the way. To get to the *Wienerwald*, take tram (*Strassenbahn*) 38 to Grinzing and then bus (*Autobus*) 38A to Kahlenberg. From there, you can see the whole city. You can walk or take another bus to Leopoldsberg, or follow a path back down to Grinzing or Nussdorf.

Danube *Donau*

The Danube (*Donau*) River is another great place to spend a summer afternoon. As it passes through Vienna, the river splits into two channels, with the Danube Island *(Donauinsel)* separating the shipping channel of the *Donau* from the New Danube *(Neue Donau)*. Along *Donauinsel* and *Neue Donau* is a recreational area where you can walk, bike, rollerblade, picnic, sunbathe, play soccer or fly kites. There are well-maintained paths for walking and biking, and large grassy areas for picnics. Restaurants and businesses are mainly located near the *Reichsbrücke* (a bridge), where you can rent rollerblades and bikes. During the summer, a pedestrian bridge at *Reichsbrücke* links the second-district bank to the *Insel*. This area is easily accessible via the U1. The U6 and the *Schnell-bahn* 45 also provide easy access to the *Donau* for walkers and bikers. For more information, look for the *"Freizeitparadies Donauinsel"* ("Danube Island Leisure Paradise") brochure at the City Information *(Stadtinformation)* office (see Info Offices appendix).

Prater

The *Prater* is an amusement park in the second district with one of Vienna's landmarks, the Giant Ferris Wheel *(Riesenrad)*. It also has a bowling alley, swimming pool, horseback riding and racing, and a large area for walking, biking and rollerblading. Large grassy areas are perfect for playing sports or Frisbee and lounging in the sun. There are a number of playgrounds for children. The five-kilometer pedestrian *Hauptallee* is a great place for a Sunday-afternoon stroll. The view from the *Riesenrad* is spectacular.

Lainzer Animal Park *Lainzer Tiergarten*

You can also walk around the Lainzer Animal Park *(Lainzer Tiergarten)* in the 13th district, where, if you're lucky, you may spot a wild boar. This was originally the private hunting grounds of Empress Elisabeth, wife of Emperor Franz Josef. It has many walking paths and restaurants. There are a number of entrances to the *Tiergarten*. The entrance at the *Nikolaitor*, on Himmelhofgasse, takes you into a quiet, heavily wooded area. Take the U4 or *Schnellbahn* 45 to Hütteldorf, cross the bridge over the freeway and follow the signs to the *Tiergarten*. Inside the gate is a map showing the main paths and locations of restaurants and lookout towers. There are periodic signs on the paths to keep you going in the right direction. The *Lainzer Tor*, on Hermesstrasse, is near the *Hermes Villa* (☎ 804 13 24), which was Empress Elisabeth's country home. There you can find exhibits and a restaurant, as well as more walking paths. Take *Strassenbahn* 60 from Hietzing to Hermesstrasse, then *Autobus* 60B to *Lainzer Tor*. The area around the *Hermes Villa* is open all year and the rest of the *Tiergarten* is open from early March - Nov.

SPORTS *Sport*

Many Austrians are sports enthusiasts year-round and, for obvious reasons, are particularly devoted to skiing. There are, however, many other options available for the sports lover. More detailed information on sports in Vienna and sport clubs can be obtained at the City Information (*Stadtinformation*) office (*see* Info Offices appendix).

AMERICAN FOOTBALL *Amerikanischer Fussball*

For information about American football, contact:

VIENNA VIKINGS
   1180, Gustav-Tschermak-Gasse 4
   ☎ 470 17 86

This is for 10- to 14-year-old children and 14- to 25-year-olds; cheerleaders are 17- to 22-year-olds. Tryouts are held in early October.

BASEBALL *Baseball*

The great American pastime hasn't quite caught on in Austria, so other than getting an informal group together to play, adults may have trouble finding a regular team. The American International Baseball Club, affiliated with Little League International, does organize games for six- to 15-year-olds from April - June. Registration and tryouts are held during the winter, with registration information posted at the international schools, UNO-City and the U.S. Embassy. Games are played at the *Prater* baseball fields.

> **TIP** There is an Austrian league with several Vienna teams. Their schedule can be found online at www.baseballaustria.com. Or for more information contact Österreichischer Baseball-Softball Verband, 1030, Baumgasse 28/1, ☎ 774 41 13, eMail office@baseballaustria.com.

BASKETBALL *Basketball*

School teams (e.g., Vienna International School, American International School and some Austrian schools) compete in several different leagues and in international and Eastern European tournaments. For information on school and other adult Vienna league tournaments, contact:

VIENNESE BASKETBALL FEDERATION
Wiener Basketball-Verband/WBV
1010, Dominikanerbastei 22
☎ 512 74 18
English is spoken.

The Vienna International Centre organizes basketball competitions between the UN Club, UNIDO, IAEA staff and dependents of staff. Games for men (and a few women) are played twice a week. The Inter-Agency Games for staff members are played annually. For more information, call one of the following contacts:

FERENC DEMJEN
☎ 21345 3579 (work)

AHMAD DIK
☎ 21345 4109 (work)

BICYCLING *Radfahren*

Biking is a popular Viennese pastime. You can ride on more than 500 kilometers of special bicycle paths, bike lanes and bike routes in areas with little traffic. For safety reasons, children, and adults, should wear bicycle helmets. If you plan to ride around city streets, you should buy a map of Vienna for cyclists called *"Stadtplan Wien für Radfahrer"* ("Vienna City Map for Bicycle Riders"), which shows recommended routes (mostly side streets) with arrows indicating the direction of traffic, dangerous stretches and areas where bicycling is not allowed. It's available in German at bookstores, though you can read the map easily. For more maps and information (in German), look for *"Logbuch Radwege Wien"* ("Logbook of Vienna Bike Paths") and *"Radwanderführer rund um Wien"* ("Bike Riding Guide Around Vienna") in bookstores as well.

On *Donauinsel*, there are 40 kilometers of paths. The routes along *Donaukanal*, through the *Prater* and throughout the city await the keen biker. For off-road bikers, there are many steep and unpaved paths through the *Wienerwald* accessible from various districts.

The Danube bike trail (*Donau Radweg*), which runs along the entire length of Austria's *Donau* from Passau on the German border to Hainburg, near the border of Hungary and Slovakia, is a route suitable for cyclists of all levels. The bike path is 305 kilometers long, so it's possible to travel for a day or a week. Actual travel will also depend on how many times you stop to have ice cream or visit a *Heurigen*. Don't forget, you can always buy a train ticket for yourself and your bike if you get too tired to ride home (see the following and Bicycles on the *U-Bahn* & *Schnellbahn* section of Transportation chapter).

Taking Bicycles on Public Transportation

Bikes are permitted on the subway/underground (*U-Bahn*) on weekdays 9 AM - 3 PM and after 6:30 PM, Saturdays after 9 AM and Sundays and holidays all day. You must purchase a half-price ticket for the bike before you get on, and you can only board a car that has a bicycle sign on it. On the U6 line, bikes are only allowed on newer cars (look for the blue-and-white bicycle symbol). On the commuter train (*Schnellbahn*), you can take your bike on any line that has a bicycle symbol on the train schedule. Hours are the same as above. Beyond Zone 100, a bicycle ticket, valid all day, must be purchased. On longer train rides, you can send your bike ahead as part of your baggage, or leave it at the major train stations (e.g., *Westbahnhof*, *Südbahnhof*).

Bike Rentals at Train Stations

If you arrive by train and show your train ticket for the same day, you can rent a bike for ATS 50 per day, otherwise the regular price is ATS 100 per day. You can rent for up to five days. You must show photo identification (e.g., passport), but you can return the bike to any train station during operating hours for a return fee of ATS 45.

WESTBAHNHOF
☎ 580 03 29-85
Daily, 4 AM - midnight

BAHNHOF WIEN NORD (PRATERSTERN)
☎ 580 03 48-17
Daily, 6:30 AM - midnight

BAHNHOF FLORIDSDORF
☎ 345 85 or ☎ 310 11
Daily, 6 AM - 7:30 PM

SÜDBAHNHOF
☎ 580 03 58-86
Daily, 6 AM - 8 PM

Bike Rentals

RADVERLEIH HOCHSCHAUBAHN
1020, Prater
(near roller coaster)
☎ 729 58 88
Mon - Fri 10 AM - dusk (March - Oct), Sat - Sun 9:30 AM - dusk

You need to bring a photo ID in order to rent a bike. English is spoken.

RADVERLEIH PEDAL POWER
1020, Ausstellungsstrasse 3
☎ 729 72 34
Daily, 8 AM - 8 PM (April - Oct)

There is a 10-percent discount with The Vienna Card. The store can bring the bike to you (including a lock). It also conducts a bike tour of Vienna daily at 10 AM. English is spoken.

For information about bike tours, see the Tours section of the Excursions chapter.

BILLIARDS *Billard*

Playing billiards (which is different from pool and snooker) is a popular activity for all ages here. At the following locations, you must buy drinks as well as rent a table. For other locations, see the Teens section of the Children chapter.

BILLARD-CAFÉ CARAMBOLAGE 3000
1100, Inzersdorferstrasse 8
☎ 604 15 15
Mon - Thurs, 9 AM - 1 AM,
Fri - Sat, 9 AM - 2 AM,
Sun, 9 AM - midnight

This café has seven tables.

VIENNESE BILLIARDS ASSOCIATION
Wiener Billard Assoziation
1150, Hackengasse 21
☎ 985 69 87
Daily, 10 AM - 10 PM

This place has 13 tables.

CAFÉ WEINGARTNER
1150, Goldschlagstrasse 6
☎ 982 43 99
Daily, 9 AM - midnight

This place has three tables.

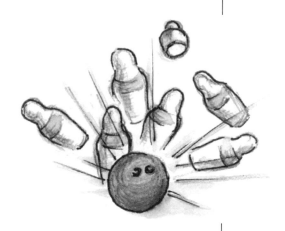

BOWLING *Bowling*

BRUNSWICK BOWLING
1020, Prater Hauptallee 124
☎ 728 07 09
Mon - Thurs, 10 AM - 1 AM,
Fri - Sat, 10 AM - 2 AM,
Sun, 9 AM - 1 AM

This bowling alley has 32 lanes.

BRUNSWICK BOWLING
1170, Schumanngasse 107
☎ 486 43 61
Mon - Thurs, 10 AM - 1 AM,
Fri - Sat, 10 AM - 2 AM,
Sun, 9 AM - 1 AM

This bowling alley has 32 lanes.

BOWLING CENTER FLORIDSDORF
1210, Pitkagasse 4
☎ 271 40 51
Daily, 10 AM - midnight

This bowling alley has 36 lanes.

For additional locations, look in the yellow pages under *"Bowling."* Austrian *Kegeln* is skittles, and differs considerably from bowling.

CRICKET *Cricket*

Cricket is not normally associated with Austria. There are, however, a number of clubs with members who are very serious about this game. The Vienna Cricket Club leased land in 1995 to build Vienna's only outdoor cricket grounds, with sightscreens and a pavilion to be added. Players come from many nations and there are even a few female players. There is no women's league, however. The European Cricket Federation governs cricket and is recognized by the ICC and MCC. Friendlies at all levels also take place and nonregistered teams are invited to play.

Indoor cricket is also very popular, with tournaments and championships held regularly. From Nov - March practice is on Saturday at 11 AM at the following location:

DOMINIK HOFFMAN HALLE
 1210, Dunantgasse 21

For more information on outdoor or indoor cricket, call:

AUSTRIAN CRICKET ASSOCIATION
 Andrew Simpson-Parker
 ☎ 985 70 70

 Pushy Ranawat
 ☎ 513 58 70

FISHING, ANGLING *Fischen, Angeln*

Austria offers many good locations for anglers, both in game fishing and course fishing. Strict government regulations on pollution ensure that fishing waters are kept pure. In the numerous lakes, there are trout, char, pike, catfish and pike perch. The mountain streams are good for fly fishing, where you can catch brown trout, rainbow trout and grayling.

FISHING PERMITS *Amtliche Fischerkarten*

All anglers must have an official fishing permit (*Amtliche Fischerkarte*), which is issued by the local district authorities and covers the whole of the particular province. You must also obtain permission from the owner of the fishing waters. Statutory minimum sizes and closed seasons vary from area to area. Visitor's permits are limited for some fishing grounds.

An excellent brochure on fly fishing, *"Fischwasser Österreich"* (in German), is available from the Austria Holiday Information office (see Info Offices appendix). For more specific permit information, call one of the following numbers:

AUSTRIAN FISHING SOCIETY
Österreichische Fischereigesellschaft (ÖFG)
  1010, Elisabethstrasse 22
  ☎ 586 52 48

LOWER AUSTRIAN HUNTING FEDERATION
Niederösterreichischer Landesjagdverband
  1080, Wickenburggasse 3
  ☎ 405 16 36

FEDERATION OF AUSTRIAN WORKER-FISHING ASSOCIATIONS
Verband der Österreichischen Arbeiter-Fischerei-Vereine (VÖAFV)
  1080, Lenaugasse 14
  ☎ 403 21 76

Also look for the magazine *Angeln in Österreich* (in German), which has information on fly-fishing sites, fish, gear, etc. The photographs are impressive.

FITNESS *Turnen*

Health/fitness clubs with various programs (e.g., aerobics, weight lifting, personal training) are becoming more prevalent in Vienna. Sports clubs with extended facilities (e.g., tennis courts, squash courts and swimming pools) are also available. For additional clubs, look in the yellow pages under *"Fitness."*

The following are some of the major health clubs in Vienna:

**BEER'S VIENNA
HEALTH & DANCE CLUB**
  1010, Neutorgasse 16
  ☎ 533 68 63
  Fax 535 12 34-5

This is a fairly new gym with employees who speak some English. It offers dance classes and personal trainers who can help you create a fitness routine. Exercise equipment and weight machines are available, as well as a sauna, solarium and massage services. Vienna Deli is next door. The club charges an entrance fee plus varying monthly fees, which depend on the package you choose.

JOHN HARRIS
  1010, Nibelungengasse 7
  ☎ 587 37 10

  1010, Parkring 16
  (Radisson SAS Palais)
  ☎ 587 37 10

The first location has recently been completely remodeled and furnished with all new equipment. The club now has an indoor pool and sauna. For both, there is an entrance fee plus a monthly fee. They are owned by an American, so some English is spoken.

PHAROS FITNESS
1020, Nordbahnstrasse 36
☎ 216 98 29
Here you'll find aerobics, body styling, fitness, massage and sauna facilities.

CLUB ALVAREZ
1130, Hietzinger Hauptstrasse 29
☎ 877 65 00
This club has aerobics, weights, a training center, outdoor pool, sauna and steam bath for a monthly fee.

PIKAL FITNESSCENTER
1080, Laudongasse 60
☎ 406 22 32

1110, Gudrunstrasse 115
☎ 602 71 82

1210, Prager Strasse 126A
☎ 270 67 80
These centers each have a gym, workout center, weight machines, sauna and solarium available for use at daily and monthly rates.

CITY CLUB VIENNA
2334 Vösendorf, Parkallee 2
☎ 699 00
This is a center for fitness, tennis, swimming, golf instruction and archery. Daily fees vary depending on when you visit. The tennis-court fee is extra.

TOP GYM
1190, Kreilplatz 1/3 Stock
(third floor behind Pam Pam)
☎ 37 49 41
Mon - Fri, 7 AM - 11 PM,
Sat - Sun, 9 AM - 9 PM
This large facility has free weights, weight machines, bikes and treadmills. Bodybuilding is its specialty. Rates vary according to the number of months you pay in advance. Massages and solarium use cost extra. Some English is spoken.

MANHATTAN SQUASH UND FITNESS CENTER
1190, Heiligenstädter Lände 17
☎ 368 73 11
Daily, 7 AM - midnight
This is Vienna's largest fitness center with aerobics, aqua aerobics, spinning (aerobic workout on stationary bikes), workout rooms (including a separate one for women), badminton and squash courts, an indoor running track, indoor golf, a swimming pool, sauna, steam bath, massage, restaurants and bars. Special sports medicine diagnostics for strength and cardiac programs are available. There is an entrance fee, which can be resold, plus a monthly or yearly fee. For more information, call the above number. Some employees speak English. Those interested in seeing the gym should come 10 AM - 7 PM.

CLUB DANUBE
1030, Franzosengraben
(Parkhaus U3)
☎ 798 84 00

1100, Laxenburger Strasse 66
☎ 603 35 80

1150, Geyschlagergasse
(in Lugner City)
☎ 982 57 71

1170, Geblergasse 73-75
☎ 486 51 81

1220, Wagramer Strasse 94
(in Donauzentrum)
☎ 203 78 80
Club Danube has many locations with fitness facilities, as well as squash, tennis and badminton courts, indoor golf and saunas. Call the above locations for information on specific facilities. Ask for a brochure with information on all the locations and their daily, monthly and yearly rates.

The Gymnastics Club (*Der Turnverein*) is a less expensive way to exercise and meet Austrians. You do need an intermediate understanding of German in order to follow the instructions. Classes are held at local schools in most districts in the late afternoon or evening. For more information, contact:

AUSTRIAN GYMNASTICS AND SPORTS UNION
Österreichische Turn- und Sportunion
   1010, Dominikanerbastei 6
   ☎ 512 74 63

Classes are held for children in different age groups, mothers and children, those older than 50 and singles. Volleyball and basketball are also available at some schools. You can get booklets with information on specific districts and the classes offered.

Frau & Sport in Wien is another program that offers different fitness activities for women. A brochure (in German) describes the various courses, which include body sculpting, gymnastics, swimming, Tai Chi and tennis. It's available at the City Information (*Stadtinformation*) office (see Info Offices appendix).

GO-CARTS

There are several indoor go-cart tracks with specific times allocated for different age groups. These tracks are supervised. Some have special times for children ages 10 to 16. Call for times and rates.

KART-O-MANIA
   1020, Ausstellungsstrasse
   Halle 23 (Haupteingang West)
   1070, Messegelände
   ☎ 726 15 75

   1230, Brunner Strasse 85
   ☎ 865 88 69

   Mon - Fri, 1 PM - 11 PM,
   Sat - Sun, 10 AM - 11 PM
Prices are lower before 5 PM.

DAYTONA RACEWAYS
   2103 Langenzersdorf bei Wien,
   Plantagenweg 2
   ☎ (02244) 305 60
   Daily, 11 AM - 2 AM

ÖMV DRIVE KART
   1210, Siemensstrasse 101
   ☎ 258 74 58
   Daily, 11 AM - 2 AM

This is a modern facility with a playground for younger children and a bistro.

GOLF *Golf*

Just like in the rest of the world, golf is gaining popularity in Austria. There are several golf courses within a short drive of Vienna. If you're an avid golfer, pick up the guide *Golf in Österreich*, which contains information on all of Austria's golf courses and is available at local golf shops. You will need to produce your current handicap (an official card from your local golf club) in order to be eligible to play on most courses. Beginners need to attend classes on the game and its etiquette and receive a course certificate (*Platzreife*) before being allowed to play. Some courses are open all year, some from April - Nov only.

The following are some nearby golf courses:

GOLF CLUB WIEN
1020, Freudenau 65A
☎ 728 95 64

You can only play here as a guest of a member. For a membership application, call the above number, though you may be on a waiting list for several years.

CITY & COUNTRY GOLF CLUB AM WIENERBERG (GOLF C & C)
1100, Gutheil-Schoder-Gasse 9
☎ 661 23-70 00

This club has a nine-hole course and offers golf lessons. It also has a floodlit driving range, badminton, squash and tennis courts, a restaurant and a club-house. You can play without being a member.

CLUB DANUBE GOLF-WIEN
1220, Weingartenallee 22
☎ 250 72
Fax 250 72-44

This club has an 18-hole course, putting green and driving range. If you're a Club Danube member, you can play.

GOLFCLUB SCHLOSS SCHÖNBORN
2013, Schönborn 4
☎ (02267) 2863

This club, which is close to the 18th and 19th districts, has 27 holes of golf during the season (March - Nov). It also rents clubs and golf carts, and has a restaurant on the premises.

GOLFCLUB SCHÖNFELD

2291 Schönfeld, Am Golfplatz 1
☎ (02213) 2063 or
☎ (02213) 2911

This club, which is located about 30 kilometers from Vienna, has an 18-hole course and is open year-round. You can rent clubs and golf carts, and there is a restaurant. A discount card for multiple visits is available at the pro shop.

GOLF & COUNTRY CLUB BRUNN AM GEBIRGE

2345 Brunn am Gebirge, Rennweg 50
☎ (02236) 315 72 or
☎ (02236) 337 11

This club, which is just south of Vienna, has an 18-hole course open year-round, as well as a restaurant.

GOLF-CLUB ENZESFELD

2551 Enzesfeld/NÖ
☎ (02256) 812 72

This 18-hole course is 30 kilometers from Vienna. The season is April - Oct. There is a clubhouse, restaurant and golf carts for hire.

For more information on golf clubs or tournaments, contact the following organization:

AUSTRIAN GOLF ASSOCIATION
Österreichischer Golfverband
1040, Prinz-Eugen-Strasse 12
☎ 505 32 45
Mon - Thurs, 9 AM - 5 PM,
Fri, 9 AM - 3:30 PM

This association has a booklet with information about golf clubs and green fees in Austria.

HIKING *Wandern*

Hiking is almost as popular with Austrians as skiing. A beautiful full-color brochure detailing Austria's national parks is available from the following office:

FEDERAL MINISTRY FOR ENVIRONMENT, YOUTH AND FAMILY AFFAIRS, DEPARTMENT 1/1
Bundesministerium für Umwelt, Jugend und Familie, Abt. 1/1
1010, Stubenbastei 5
☎ 515 22-1402
Fax 515 22-7402
www.bmu.gv.at
Mon - Fri, 9 AM - 4 PM

The newest national park, *Donau-Auen*, actually includes a part of Vienna as it stretches along the *Donau* toward the Slovakian border.

There are books published in English offering detailed advice and information, as well as daily itineraries for many hiking tours throughout the Austrian Alps. *Walking Austria's Alps*, by Jonathan Hurdle, and *Walking Easy in the Austrian Alps* are two to consider (see Books appendix). The Austrian Alpine Association (*Österreichischer Alpenverein/ÖAV*) publishes maps and a book called *Die Alpenvereinshütten* (*Alpine Association Huts* or *The Green Hut Book*), which provides addresses, telephone numbers, hut hours and other useful information. For more information on hiking and mountain climbing, contact the association:

AUSTRIAN ALPINE ASSOCIATION
Österreichischer Alpenverein
1010, Rotenturmstrasse 14
☎ 513 10 03
Mon - Wed, Fri 9 AM - 6 PM, Thurs 9 AM - 7 PM

The United Nations Hiking Club is a registered organization. Its members hike year-round, with a majority of outings in the spring. Accredited leaders supervise hikes that are graded from easy to strenuous, with some requiring special equipment.

Always check weather reports on the radio, TV, or look in the front of the A–H telephone directory for *"Offizieller Wetterdienst"* ("Official Weather Service") and call the listed number to receive current information (in German) for a specific region.

In Austria, traditional hiking clothing can be made from *Loden*, a heavy waterproof wool, or *Walken*, a fabric made of wool exposed to pressure, heat and moisture.

 If you hike regularly, you should also check your insurance coverage. In some areas, if you have an accident on a mountain trail and have to be rescued, there's a charge based on the number of hours spent searching for, rescuing and transporting you to the nearest hospital.

Hiking-Map Terms

Alm, Alpe Mountain pasture
Berg Mountain
Gasthaus, Gasthof Inn
Gipfel Peak, summit
Höhe Altitude, height
Klamm Gorge, ravine
Steig Steep trail, path
Spitze Peak, top
Wald Forest, woods
Weg Path, trail

HORSEBACK RIDING *Reiten*

If you'd like to go horseback riding, contact one of the following facilities:

REITCLUB DONAUHOF
1020, Hafenzufahrtsstrasse 63
☎ 728 36 46
Daily, 8 AM - 8 PM

This riding club has 80 horses available and can give riding lessons. You should call two days ahead to reserve a horse. English is spoken.

REITSTALL ST. LEOPOLD
3400 Klosterneuburg,
Strandbadgasse 4-6
☎ (02243) 374 92
Tue - Fri, 8 AM - noon,
3 PM - 8 PM,
Sat 8 AM - noon, 3 PM - 6 PM,
Sun 9 AM - noon

An English-speaking instructor can give riding lessons and take you on trails. A 10-percent discount is available to AWA members.

ICE HOCKEY & ICE-SKATING *Eishockey und Eislaufen*

The ice-skating season in Vienna begins in mid-October and ends in mid-March. Lessons and skate rentals are available for adults and children. Ask at the following ice rinks about hockey teams for all ages.

WIENER EISLAUFVEREIN
1030, Lothringerstrasse 22
(next to Hotel Inter-Continental)
☎ 713 63 53

EISRING SÜD
1100, Windtenstrasse 2
☎ 604 44 43

WIENER STADTHALLE
1150, Vogelweidplatz 14
☎ 981 00-0

KUNSTEISBAHN ENGELMANN
1170, Syringgasse 6-8
☎ 405 14 25

ALBERT-SCHULTZ EISHALLE
1220, Attemsgasse 1
☎ 204 85 80

This is the home of the Penguins hockey team and CE Vienna.

For more information on ice hockey, contact:

AUSTRIAN ICE HOCKEY FEDERATION
Österreichischer Eishockey-Verband
1040, Prinz-Eugen-Strasse 12
☎ 505 73 47

It has a book (in German) with information about ice hockey in Austria.

Rinks are not the only places for skating. Many lakes and ponds freeze sufficiently in winter for good skating. In Vienna, Austellungsstrasse in the second district and Osterleitengasse in the 19th district are two locations. *Hansel Teich* in the *Wienerwald* is a popular location because it's a pretty setting and there's a *Gasthaus* for coffee and snacks. *Alte Donau* is also a possibility, but take your own hot drinks if you go to *Donaukanal*. A little farther away is the pond at Laxenburg Palace (*Schloss Laxenburg*) and Neusiedlersee.

ROCK CLIMBING *Klettern*

If you're interested in climbing rock faces, call the following association for information:

AUSTRIAN ALPINE ASSOCIATION
Österreichischer Alpenverein
  1010, Rotenturmstrasse 14
  ☎ 513 10 03
  Mon - Fri, 9 AM - 9 PM

The climbing center is open to nonmembers (for double the fee).

ROLLERBLADING

Bike paths in Vienna can also be used for rollerblading. The paths in some parks and those along the *Donau, Donauinsel, Donaukanal* and *Prater Hauptallee* are also quite popular. You can rent inline skates at the U1 Donauinsel and U6 Floridsdorf stations or from the following facility:

SCHUH SKI
  1220, Donauinsel Reichsbrücke
  ☎ 236 518-57
  Daily, 9 AM - 6 PM

You need to bring a photo ID in order to rent skates, which must be returned by 4 PM. You can also rent bikes.

For indoor facilities, try the following locations:

AUSTRIAN INLINE SKATING ACADEMY
  1020, Messegelände Wien
  Halle 25
  ☎ 727 20-353
  Mon - Fri, noon - midnight, Sat - Sun 10 AM - midnight (Nov -Feb)

This facility has qualified skating instructors, a street rink, miniramp and two half-pipes. Street soccer and inline- hockey courts cater to team players. An admission ticket is good for all day, with prices varying by age group.

SKATELAB
  1020, Engerthstrasse & Walcherstrasse
  ☎ 214 95 65
  Mon, 5 PM - 10 PM (women only),
  Tues - Fri, 10 AM - 10 PM,
  Sat - Sun, 10 AM - 8 PM

This is an indoor inline-skating rink.

RUNNING *Laufen*

There are many running paths in the city, its parks and along the *Donau*. Also check the *"Die Wiener Stadtwanderwege"* brochure referred to in the Walking section.

The **Vienna City Marathon** is usually held in April or May, along with a variety of other runs and triathlons. You can find a free brochure (in English) with information on the marathon and other runs in Vienna at the City Information (*Stadtinformation*) office (see Info Offices appendix).

Each year around June, the **Frauenlauf,** an all-women's fun run, is held over 3.1 kilometers or 6.2 kilometers. The previously mentioned brochure has more details.

The **Hash House Harriers** is a group that meets weekly at different locations around the Vienna area for a noncompetitive run lasting about an hour, followed by a get-together with beer. For more information, call John Russell at ☎ 206 02 29-34 (work) or ☎ (02215) 3178 (home) or Tina Jeggo at ☎ 707 18 40 (home).

SAILING *Segeln*

In Vienna, you can sail on the *Alte Donau*, and in Burgenland, on the *Neusiedlersee*, a lake about 30 kilometers from Vienna. There are also two sailing schools:

FIRMA ING. WOLFGANG IRZL
    1220, Florian-Berndl-Gasse 33
    1220, Untere Alte Donau 29
    ☎ 203 67 43
    Daily, 10 AM - 8 PM

This place offers private sailing and windsurfing lessons in English. You can also rent sailboats, motorboats, rowboats, paddleboats and wind-surfers.

SCHULE HOFBAUER
    1220, An der
    oberen Alten Donau 185
    ☎ 204 34 35
    Daily, 8:30 AM - 5 PM

This school offers instruction in sailing and surfing for adults and children at its locations on the *Alte Donau* as well as at *Neusiedl am See*. An English-speaking group can be arranged if you call at least two weeks in advance. Boats are available to rent, provided you have some sailing experience.

For more sailing information, contact the following organization:

AUSTRIAN SAILING ASSOCIATION
Österreichischer Segelverband
   1040, Grosse Neugasse 8
   ☎ 587 86 88
   Daily, 11 AM - 1 PM, 2 PM - 5 PM

To check the weather before you go, listen to the radio or watch TV. You can also look in the front of the A–H telephone book under *"Offizieller Wetterdienst"* ("Official Weather Service") for a number to call for the latest weather information (in German) for a specific region.

SKIING *Schifahren*

Skiing in Austria is superb. Every winter thousands of visitors and local skiing enthusiasts flock to its many winter resorts. The ski runs are well-maintained and accessible via numerous cableways and ski lifts. Many resorts also have toboggan runs and ice rinks, and an increasing number even have enclosed swimming pools. There are also many trails for cross-country skiing *(Langlauf)*.

You can try summer skiing, known as glacier skiing *(Gletscher Schi)*, in regions of Tirol, Salzburg and Steiermark. Extensive skiing information in English is available from Austria Holiday Information and Austria Promotions (see Info Offices appendix). The German-only brochure *"Skitips des Österreichischen Schiverbandes"* ("Ski Tips from Austrian Ski Associations") explains the various signs for cross-country and alpine skiing.

You should reserve your accomodations well in advance, especially during the holiday season. The most reasonable are family-owned motels *(Pensionen)* with HP *(Halbpension* = breakfast and dinner) meal plans. Some hotels and *Pensionen* offer a visitor's card, which gives the bearer a discount on ski-lift tickets. Many places require a one-week minimum stay.

Daily Bus Ski Trips

Austrian travel agencies, sporting-goods stores and local newspapers have current information concerning daily bus trips to nearby ski resorts, such as Semmering, Stuhleck and Hochkarlackenhof. Schuh Ski Sports Clothing & Equipment sponsors its own bus ski trips. Check your telephone directory's white pages for store locations.

For local skiing, try the following resort·

SCHILIFT HOHE WAND WIESE
1140, Mauerbachstrasse 174
☎ 979 10 57

This is a great place for local skiing and can be reached via public transportation (bus 249 or 449 from the U4 Hütteldorf station). The area is floodlit and is covered with artificial snow so you can always ski. There's a charge for each run, or you can purchase a block of 10 tickets.

SOCCER *Fussball*

Soccer is a popular sport in Europe — many play it, but many more watch it. Games are played between Austrian and visiting international teams. These are held at the famous *Prater Stadion*. An annual indoor-soccer tournament is held in December in the *Stadthalle*. For individual clubs, look in the yellow pages under *"Sportverbände."*

SQUASH

U3 FITNESS & SQUASH CLUB
1150, Johnstrasse 65
☎ 985 38 90
Daily, 9 AM - 11 PM

This club has two courts and a sauna.

SQUASH CENTRE HERNALS
1170, Hernalser
Hauptstrasse 13
☎ 403 60 50
Mon, 1 PM - 11 PM,
Tues - Sun, 10 AM - 11 PM

This facility has four courts and a sauna.

SQUASH CLUB 19
1190, Heiligenstädter Strasse 86
☎ 37 21 72
Mon - Thurs, 9 AM - 11 PM,
Fri, Sun, 9 AM - 10 PM,
Sat, 9 AM - 8 PM

This club has six courts and a sauna.

MANHATTAN SQUASH UND FITNESS CENTER
1190, Heiligenstädter Lände 17
☎ 368 73 11
Daily, 7 AM - midnight

This club has 22 courts. See the Fitness section for more information.

Also ask other fitness centers if they have squash facilities.

SWIMMING *Schwimmen*

There are many outdoor and indoor public swimming pools in Vienna. Pools (*Bäder*) are supervised by lifeguards who have life-saving qualifications. Some of the older establishments are beautifully decorated (e.g., *Jörgerbad* in the 17th district), making it a treat to swim and admire these buildings.

City Information (*Stadtinformation*; see Info Offices appendix) has brochures listing pools in Vienna. For outdoor pools, get the brochure *"Wiens Sommerbäder"* ("Vienna's Summer Pools") for addresses, phone numbers and opening hours. For indoor pools (*Hallenbäder*), ask for the brochure *"Hallenbäder & Saunas"* ("Indoor Pools & Saunas"). You can also call the *Bäder* hotline at ☎ 1535 or the *Hallenbäder* information line at ☎ 601 12-8044. Some centers also have saunas and steam rooms.

The following is just a sampling of available pools:

Outdoor Pools

BUNDESBAD SCHÖNBRUNN
1120, Schlosspark
☎ 815 01 32

KRAPFENWALD BAD
1190, Krapfenwaldgasse 65-73
☎ 320 15 01

This *Bad* has a large outdoor recreation area. Parking is available, but you can also take bus 38A.

Indoor & Outdoor Pools

KURHALLE OBERLAA
1100, Kurbadstrasse 14
☎ 68 16 11

HALLENBAD DÖBLING
1190, Geweygasse 6
☎ 37 22 18 or ☎ 37 22 19

Indoor Pools

MARGARETENBAD
1050, Strobachgasse 7-9
☎ 587 08 44
Mon,Thurs 10 AM - 11 PM,
Tues, Wed, Fri, Sat 9 AM - 11PM,
Sun 8 AM - 10 PM

This facility is family-friendly with swimming classes, discounts for children and seniors, birthday parties for children over seven and saunas.

HALLENBAD HIETZING
1130, Atzgersdorfer Strasse 14
☎ 804 53 10 or ☎ 804 53 19

OTTAKRINGER BAD
1160, Johann-Staud-Strasse 11
☎ 914 81 06

CITY CLUB VIENNA
2334 Vösendorf, Parkallee 2
☎ 699 00

The *Stadionbad*, located at *Prater Krieau* in the second district, near the big stadium, has a wave pool, a big fun pool, two waterslides and playground areas.

Many pools also have entertainment and swimming classes July - Aug. Ask for the brochure *"Auf in die Bäder-Akademie"* ("In Swimming School") at the City Information (*Stadtinformation*) office (see Info Offices appendix).

There are also areas along both banks of *Neue Donau* suitable for swimming. These are marked on the brochure *"Freizeitparadies Donauinsel"* ("Leisure Paradise Danube Island"), available from City Information (*Stadtinformation*; see Info Offices appendix). Or take the U1 to *Donauinsel*, get off and walk until you see the crowds. Nude beaches are at the lower end of *Donauinsel*.

TAI CHI & QI GONG

If you're interested in learning ancient Chinese meditative movement and breathing techniques (good for relieving stress), contact the following facility:

YEEKUNG-ZENTRUM
1060, Mariahilfer Strasse 115
☎ 596 26 81
Fax 596 87 59
Class instructions can be translated into English.

TENNIS *Tennis*

For a newcomer to Vienna, finding tennis facilities like those available in the United States can be a frustrating experience. You just have to be persistent in your search. You can find tennis courts listed in the yellow pages under *"Tennisanlagen," "Tennishallen"* and *"Tennisplätze."*

Freiplätze are outdoor courts (usually with clay surfaces). These are usually only used in the summer, but many may be covered with a bubble tent for play during the winter. *Hallenplätze* are covered courts (usually with carpeted surfaces). Some have floodlights for late-evening games.

If you're interested in private lessons, contact the following school:

TENNIS SCHULE WITZ
2721 Bad Fischau-Brunn, Bruno Riedlgasse 24
☎ (02639) 2746
Fax (02639) 2680   Instruction is available in English.

Reserving Tennis Courts

If you intend to play regularly on one court, there are three possible options:

- **Season hour (*Saisonstunde*):** You rent a court for the same hour and day of the week throughout the season.
- **Rent hour (*Mietstunde*):** You rent a court for one hour that is convenient to you. Call a few days in advance to schedule.
- **Club member (*Clubmitglied*):** You become a club member, which is recommended for those who intend to stay in Vienna for a while because you can then enjoy all the advantages of club life. A waiting list is common, however.

For a complete list of tennis courts and trainers, as well as a tournament schedule, contact the following organization:

AUSTRIAN TENNIS ASSOCIATION
Österreichischer Tennisverband
1235, Häckelstrasse 33
☎ 865 45 06
Mon - Thurs, 8 AM - 4:30 PM,
Fri, 8 AM - 2 PM

The following are a few of the available tennis courts in Vienna:

TENNISPLÄTZE STADIONBAD
1020, Prater Hauptallee
☎ 720 20 70

This facility has seven outdoor courts.

TENNIS POINT VIENNA
1030, Baumgasse &
Nottendorfer Gasse
☎ 799 99 97

This facility has 10 indoor tennis courts, squash courts, a sauna, solarium and restaurant.

POSTSPORTSVEREIN
1170, Roggendorfgasse 2
☎ 486 23 23

This facility has 47 outdoor tennis courts available in the summer (April 18 - Oct 9), though some are reserved for members.

HOHE WARTE (Sportplatz Wien)
1190, Klabundgasse
☎ 368 35 72

This facility has 14 outdoor courts and seven indoor courts (only in winter).

TENNISCENTER LA VILLE
1230, Kirchfeldgasse 3-5
☎ 804 67 37

This facility has 10 indoor and 10 outdoor tennis courts, along with a swimming pool and sauna.

TENNIS EUROPAHALLE
1230, An den Steinfeldern 2A
☎ 869 86 63 or ☎ 869 01 15

This facility has 14 indoor tennis courts as well as badminton and squash courts and a sauna.

HAPPYLAND
3400 Klosterneuburg, In der Au
☎ (02243) 217 00

This facility has a tennis school, seven indoor and 11 outdoor tennis courts, a swimming pool, bowling alley, basketball courts, exercise rooms and a sauna.

Tennis package vacations are available through many travel agencies. Brochures on tennis vacations in Austria can be obtained from Austria Holiday Information (see Info Offices appendix).

WATERSKIING *Wasserschifahren*

There are few open-water areas for skiing because most are protected by environmental regulations. The following facility offers a unique way to practice the sport:

WASSERSKILIFT NEUE DONAU
1220, Am Wehr 1
☎ 22 53 75

In the summer, a special rectangular drag-lift structure over the water can pull you over a one-kilometer distance at a speed between 28 km - 58 km per hour.

WINDSURFING *Windsurfen*

The *Donau* and *Neusiedlersee* are two places to try windsurfing. For information on lessons and renting equipment, call the following facilities:

K. HOFBAUER (Vienna & Neusiedl am See)

1220, An der oberen
Alten Donau 185
☎ 204 34 35

You can ask about facilities in Vienna and *Neusiedl am See* at the above number.

FIRMA ING. WOLFGANG IRZL

1220,
Florian-Berndl-Gasse 33-34
☎ 203 67 43

This facility offers windsurfing lessons in English, as well as sailing lessons (see Sailing section).

Take a look around, and you'll see that the Viennese clearly love their pets—especially dogs. Just as humans have to adjust to a new environment and culture, so do their pets. This chapter points out some important laws and customs regulations of which you should be aware, as well as veterinary care and other animal services available in Vienna.

MOVING & TRAVELING WITH YOUR PETS

Although Austria does not impose a quarantine for dogs and cats, there are special regulations governing the import of animals. The import of birds, turtles, horses, rabbits and fish is strictly controlled according to policies regarding the international protection of endangered species. You should, therefore, contact the Austrian Embassy or Consulate in your home country PRIOR to your departure for Austria in order to find out about current restrictions. For more information here, call the Federal Chancellor's Office of Veterinary Administration (*Bundeskanzleramt-Veterinärverwaltung*) at ☎ 711 72-4813.

There are a few basic regulations concerning the import of cats and dogs. A dog or cat more than 12 weeks old must have a valid vaccination against rabies (*Tollwut*), which is certified by the pet's home veterinarian in an International Vaccination Certificate (*Internationaler Impfausweis*). The vaccination must be administered at least 30 days—but no more than one year—prior to entering Austria. You need the vaccination certificate in order to bring your pet into Austria (and it is also required in order to travel with your pet in Europe). A cat or dog less than 30 days old must have its age confirmed by a veterinarian.

DOG TAX *Hundesteuer*

Dogs above the age of one year living in Vienna are subject to a "dog tax" (*Hundesteuer*), which is paid annually to the city cashier (*Stadtkassa*) at your district police station or district office (*Bezirksamt*). You should pay this tax as soon as you establish residency here (i.e., apply for a *Meldezettel*; see Essentials chapter). This serves to register your dog. The tag you receive must be worn by the dog on its collar. The tax is about ATS 600, though the amount can vary depending on the number of dogs you're registering. Be sure to bring your pet's vaccination certificate.

LEASH & MUZZLE *Leine & Beisskorb*

The law requires that when you take your dog outside your home or on public transportation, it must be led on a leash and wear a muzzle (see end of chapter for a list of legal free-run areas). Be aware that there is an ATS 300 fine if your dog is found without a leash and muzzle, as well as a more severe penalty if your dog attacks someone. If your dog or cat bites a person, it must be tested for rabies immediately and then again 10 days later. A judge will decide the final punishment.

PETS ON PUBLIC TRANSPORTATION

In Vienna, you must buy a half-price ticket for a dog accompanying you on public transportation, unless you're carrying it the whole time (that's why you see small dogs in baskets or carpet bags). Remember, leashes and muzzles are still required.

PET INSURANCE

You can get pet insurance in Austria from companies such as Anglo-Elementar, so ask your insurance agent for details.

TRAVELING OUTSIDE OF AUSTRIA

If you plan to take your dog or cat outside of Austria, additional documentation or vaccinations may be required, depending on which country you're traveling to. In many cases, your pet will need a Certificate of Origin and Health (*Ursprungs- und Gesundheitszeugnis*). In Austria, only specially designated veterinarians, known as *Amtstierärzte*, can issue this certificate, which states, on behalf of the Republic of Austria, that the animal has been properly vaccinated and no contagious diseases exist in the area where the animal is living. You should see an *Amtstierarzt* at least eight days before your departure. Bring your pet, its existing valid vaccination certificate and ATS 90. Depending on which country you're visiting, the certificate—which is in German, English, French and Spanish—is good for one to three months, though only valid for one trip. *Amtstierärzte* are listed by district in the telephone directory's white pages under "*Veterinäramt der Stadt Wien.*" You can also call the main office for more information:

VETERINARY OFFICE OF VIENNA
(*Veterinäramt der Stadt Wien*)
   MA 59 (Dezernat III)
   1030, Henneberggasse 3
   ☎ 795 14 97-96
   Mon - Fri 8 AM - 9 AM, 2 PM - 3 PM

HOTELS

Many hotels and *Pensions* in Austria and other European countries will accept pets, but they may charge an extra fee. Check ahead to avoid problems and ask for the policy in writing when making reservations.

VETERINARIANS *TIERÄRZTE*

Veterinarians are listed by district in the yellow pages under *"Tierärzte."* In addition to their regular services, vets can also recommend a pet sitter (*Tierpension*) and grooming salon (*Hundesalon/Hundekosmetik*). The following are some English-speaking vets recommended by AWA members:

DR. MONIKA ANGERER & DIPL-TIERARZT MICHAELA FISCHER

1030, Stanislausgasse 2
☎ 718 48 47
Mon 9 AM - 11 AM, 5 PM - 8 PM
Tues - Fri 9 AM - 11 AM
5 PM - 7 PM, Sat 9 AM - 11 AM

This facility has an X-ray machine, EKG machine and laboratory, and offers neural therapy and homeopathy. An appointment isn't necessary for routine services.

TIERKLINIK NEULINGGASSE DR. DIPL-TIERARZT RENATE LORIN

1030, Neulinggasse 32
☎ 712 58 68
Mon, Tues, Thurs, Fri
8 AM - 10 AM,
4:30 PM - 6:30 PM

Dr. Lorin, who studied in the United States, doesn't require an appointment during regular office hours. Avalable 24 hours a day at (0663) 91 95 118.

DR. TAMARA GERES

1060, Mariahilfer Strasse 13/1/8
(entrance at Königsklostergasse 10/1/8)
☎ 586 10 93
Mon - Fri 9 AM - 11 AM,
2 PM - 5 PM

You should make an appointment to see the doctor, who also offers acupuncture and neurological therapy.

TIERKLINIK THERESIANUM DR. GERHARD VYTLACIL

1040, Theresianumgasse 9
☎ 505 35 74
Mobile ☎ (0676) 504 20 20
(for emergencies)
Mon - Wed 9 AM - 10 AM,
4 PM - 7 PM
Thurs 4 PM - 7 PM
Fri 9 AM - 10 AM, 4 PM - 7 PM
Sat noon - 1 PM

You don't need an appointment with this veterinary surgeon, who has the latest technology (including an ultrasound machine). He offers 24-hour emergency care and accepts credit cards and the Bankomat Card.

PROFESSOR KARL ZETTNER & DR. IRIS STEURER

1120, Tivoligasse 29
☎ 812 28 08
Mon 10 AM - 1 PM, 7 PM - 9 PM,
Tues - Fri 10 AM - 1 PM,
3 PM - 7 PM

Professer Zettner cleans pets' teeth (most other vets do, too).

DR. MICHAEL FISCHER

1130, Trazerberggasse 89/3/1
☎ 876 54 59

Dr. Fischer requires an appointment and offers such alternative therapy as homeopathy and acupuncture.

DR. JANOS SIPOS
1130, Lainzer Strasse 11
☎ 877 14 87
Mon - Fri 10 AM - noon,
5 PM - 7 PM, Sat 10 AM - noon

Dr. Sipos, who speaks German and Hungarian, does not require an appointment, and his wife speaks English.

TIERKLINIK DÖBLING
DR. HEIDI CORETH
1190, Peter-Jordan-Strasse 12
☎ 368 16 84
Mon - Sat 10 AM - 1 PM

M, T, Th, F 2 PM - 7 PM
(By Appoinment)

Tierklinik Döbling can be reached 24 hours a day, seven day a week. You should make an appointment to seethe doctor. Dog grooming is also available by appointment.

DR. SUSANNE BARTH
1230, Kaiser Franz Josef-Strasse 38
☎ 889 50 80
Mon, Tues, Thurs, Fri,
9 AM - 11PM, 5 PM - 7 PM,
Wed, Sat 9 AM - 11 AM

TIERKLINIK HOLLABRUNN
DR. GUNTER SCHWARZ
2020 Hollabrunn,
Ziegelofenweg 4
☎ (02952) 4949
Mon - Fri 10:30 AM - noon,
4 PM - 6:30 PM, Sat 9 AM - 11 AM

Dr. Schwarz specializes in major surgery, such as hip dysplasia and cruciate-ligament replacement.

EMERGENCY VETERINARY CARE

Emergency Veterinary Switchboard /   ☎ 531 16
Veterinarians Chamber
(Nottierarztvermittlung/Tierärztekammer)
This emergency service (available 24 hours a day, seven days a week) will give you the name and phone number of the on-call veterinarian in your district. If your dog is hit by a car or cannot be safely moved they can dispatch an animal ambulance. During the day, English speakers are available.

University of Vienna   ☎ 250 77-0
School of Veterinary Medicine
(Veterinärmedizinische Universität Wien)
1210, Josef-Baumann-Gasse 1
The school has an emergency animal clinic (where English is spoken), open 24 hours a day, seven days a week.

HOMEOPATHIC PHARMACIES
Homöopathische Apotheken

Homeopathy is becoming an increasingly popular treatment method among Austrian veterinarians. Ask your vet if he or she can personally administer alternative-medicine treatments before you go to one of the pharmacies listed below.

ZUM ROTHEN KREBS
1010, Lichtensteg 4
☎ 533 67 91 or ☎ 533 85 40
Mon - Fri 8 AM - 6 PM,
Sat 8 AM - noon

English is spoken.

ZUR KAISERKRONE
1070, Mariahilfer Strasse 110
☎ 526 26 46
Mon - Fri 8 AM - 6 PM,
Sat 8 AM - noon

This *Apotheke* also specializes in essential oils and fragrances. English is spoken.

ST. ANNA
1120,
Meidlinger Hauptstrasse 86
☎ 813 10 62
Mon - Fri 8 AM - 6 PM,
Sat 8 AM - 12:30 PM

This *Apotheke* specializes in homeopathic medicine for humans and pets. English is spoken.

PET STORES
Tierhandlung, Zoo

There are pet stores all over Vienna. Look in the yellow pages under *"Tierhandlung."* Drugstore chains such as DM, Bipa and Schlecker also sell pet food and supplies. Many American and British products are available at dog shows (show dates are listed in the Ö.K.V. magazine; see opposite page). Or try the following pet store:

BUDWEISER
1070, Neubaugasse 41
☎ 523 84 37
Mon - Fri 10 AM - 12:30 PM, 1:30 PM - 6 PM, Sat 9 AM - noon

This is a large, well-stocked store carrying all your pet needs.

PET CARE & BOARDING *Tierpension*

If you plan to travel, you can call the following facility to care for your pet in your absence. Also, ask your veterinarian or the Viennese Animal Protection Society (*Wiener Tierschutzverein*; see below) to recommend a pet sitter or kennel (some vets even have their own facilities).

VERONIKA PRETT

8282, Loipersdorf 159
☎ (03382) 84 44
Mobile ☎ (0664) 658 44 94
eMail doghouse@utanet.at

The dogs are kept in an old farmhouse living room (no cages) and they are able to run around 3 acres of land with a pool. French and English is spoken. Approximately one and half hours south of Vienna, but the special care and reasonable daily rates, make it worth the drive.

PET CLUBS & ORGANIZATIONS

There are many individual-breed dog clubs in Vienna, which usually meet regularly and have members who speak English. If you need information about these clubs, obedience classes or dogs in Austria, call the Ö.K.V., where some English is spoken. If you're looking for a pet, why not try the *Wiener Tierschutzverein* (the Viennese equivalent to an animal shelter or animal services)?

AUSTRIAN KENNEL CLUB
Österreichischer Kynologenverband/ÖKV
1230, Johann-Teufel-Gasse 8
☎ 888 70 92
Mon - Thurs 9 AM - 5 PM, Fri 9 AM - 2 PM

This organization, where English is spoken, can answer all questions concerning dogs. It can even help you find a puppy to adopt.

VIENNESE ANIMAL PROTECTION SOCIETY
Wiener Tierschutzverein
2331, Vösendorf, Triesterstrasse 368
☎ 699 24 50
Fax 699 24 50 97
Mon - Sat 1 PM - 6 PM, Sun 1:30 PM - 5 PM

This is the place to look for a lost pet or to adopt a new one. The costs are reasonable and the staff is friendly.

DOG ZONES/FREE-RUNNING AREAS
Hundezonen und Hundeauslaufplätze

Die Hundezonen und Hundeauslaufplätze

❶ 2., Prater	❿ 6., Linke Wienzeile	⓲ 10., Heubergstätten	⓬ 12., Flohberg	⓯ 15., Dudlerpark	㉑ 21., Floridsdorfer Aupark
❸ 3., Linke Bahngasse		(Alfred-Grünwald-Park)	⓬ 10., Humboldtpark	⓬ 12., Zanaschkagasse	⓰ 16., Kongelpark	㉒ 22., Hirschstetner-Badeteich
❸ 3., Kardinal-Nagl-Park	⓫ 6., Esterharypark	⓲ 10., Grünanlage	⓬ 12., Längenfeldgasse	⓱ 17., Lorenz-Bayer-Park	㉓ 23., Draschepark
❸ 3., Arenbergpark	⓫ 8., Schönbornpark		Wieselburgergasse	⓬ 12., Untermeidlinger Straße	⓲ 18., Währinger Park	㉓ 23., Grünfläche
❸ 3., Puntigamerwiese	⓰ 8., Hamerlingpark	⓲ 10., Amonsplatz	⓬ 12., Breitenfurter Straße	⓳ 19., Trautenauplatz	Theophil-Hansen-Gasse
❻ 5., Spengergasse	⓰ 8., Tigerpark	⓫ 11., Am Kanal	⓭ 13., Roter Berg	⓴ 20., Forsthauspark	㉓ 23., Zanaschkagasse
❺ 5., Klieberpark	❾ 9., Lichtenalerpark	⓬ 12., Korbergasse	⓭ 13., Napoleonwald	⓴ 20., Allerheiligenpark	
❺ 5., Willy-Frank-Park	⓾ 10., Eisenstadtplatz	⓬ 12., Grünfläche	⓮ 14., Matznergark	⓴ 20., Wehlistraße	
❺ 5., Einsiedlerpark	⓾ 10., Hebbelpark		Edelsinnstraße	⓯ 15., Vogelweidpark	㉑ 21., Grünfläche Illgasse	

Some of the locations listed above have specific areas designated for dogs, so look for signs. You can also try these other free-run areas, as provided by MA 42 (*Stadtgartenamt*):

1010, Stadtpark, Wienflusspromenade
1020, Max-Winter-Park
1030, Stadtpark, Wienflusspromenade and Kinderpark
1030, Schweizergarten
1050, Spengergasse, in front of Bacherpark
1050, Hartmannpark
1050, Margaretengürtel, in front of Haydnpark
1050, Mittersteigpark
1080, Schönbornpark
1090, Arne-Karlsonpark
1120, Theresienbadpark
1120, Steinbauerpark
1120, Dunklergasse/Harthausergasse
1120, Schlöglgasse

1120, Vierthalergasse 4
1120, Gaudenzdorfergürtel, in front of Haydnpark
1130, Hügelpark
1140, Ordeltpark
1140, Baumgartner-Casinopark
1150, Teithofferpark
1160, Richard-Wagner-Park
1190, Saarpark
1190, Hugo-Wolf-Park
1200, Durchlaufstrasse, between Hellwag- and Vorgartenstrasse
1220, Treustrasse, parking lot
1220, Nordwestbahnstrasse, from Waldmüllergasse to Pappenheimgasse
1230, Ölzeltpark, Gesslgasse

groß = big
klein = small
billig = cheap
teuer = expensive

L iving in a foreign country can be a rich educational experience for both you and your child. Learning a new language and making friends from different cultures will change your lives forever. While you may choose to send your child to one of the English-language schools listed in this chapter, you will find that continuing to learn German will broaden your foreign living experience, and help you to feel comfortable in dealing with everyday situations.

PRESCHOOLS & KINDERGARTENS

The following schools accept a certain number of students each year, but there may be vacancies any time, so call to find out.

INTERNATIONAL MONTESSORI PRE-SCHOOL
1010, Marc-Aurel-Strasse 5/16
☎ 533 20 24
eMail dekleva.montessori@netway.at

This preschool accepts about 50 students a year and offers half-day (8 AM - 12:30 PM) and full-day (8 AM - 3 PM) program. Children are accepted for the entire school year, September through August.

UNITED CHILDREN-INTERNATIONALER KINDERGARTEN
1060, Stumpergasse 49
☎ 597 00 06

The teachers speak English, French and German at this school, which has 20 spots for two- to six-year-olds.

AMERICAN INTERNATIONAL SCHOOL (AIS)
1190, Salmannsdorfer Strasse 47
☎ 401 32-0   www.ais.at
Fax 401 32-5   eMail info@ais.at

The pre-kindergarten school has one class (16 students) for four-year-olds, and the kindergarten has two classes (20 students each) for five-year-olds. See the Primary Schools section for more information.

THE CHILDRENS HOUSE (International Montessori *Kindergarten*)
1210, Kugelfanggasse 56

This school has 35 to 40 spots for two-and-a-half- to six-year-olds.

CHILDREN'S WORLD NURSERY SCHOOL
(International/British system)
1220 Erzherzog-Karl-Strasse 164
☎ 282 59 06
Fax 282 59 06

This school has Montessori qualifications and accepts about 25 students a year between the ages of two-and-a-half and six-and-a-half. Hot lunches are provided.

INTERNATIONALER KINDERGARTEN
D. WIENER KINDERFREUNDE (Montessori)
1220, Wagramer Strasse 55/1
☎ 203 78 08

This *Kindergarten* school accepts about 12 students a year.

For a listing of all Montessori schools in Vienna,
call ☎ 911 69 68.

VIENNA INTERNATIONAL SCHOOL (VIS)
1220, Strasse der Menschenrechte 1
☎ 203 55 95
Fax 203 03 66

This pre-primary school has four classes (25 students each) for three- to five-year-olds. See the Primary Schools section for more information.

PRIMARY
& SECONDARY SCHOOLS

DANUBE INTERNATIONAL SCHOOL (DIS)
1020, Josefgallgasse 2
☎ 017 203 110
Fax 017 203 110-40   eMail danube@chello.at
www.ecis.org/danubeschool/home.htm

DIS has just moved into new premises, and is an English-speaking, independent, nondenominational, coeducational day school with courses designed for students seeking an international education in Vienna. Students may enroll at five years of age, and may continue to complete the International Baccalaureate (IB). Mother-tongue instruction is extracurricualr. Total enrollment is about 300 students.

AMERICAN INTERNATIONAL SCHOOL (AIS)
1190, Salmannsdorfer Strasse 47
☎ 401 32-0
Fax 401 32-5

AIS offers an integrated program from kindergarten to 12th grade, with an optional 13th year for full Baccalaureate students. The curriculum and teaching methods follow the American educational system. Instruction is in English, with a comprehensive German curriculum in all grades and French introduced in middle school. Diplomas offered are: US High School Diploma, International Baccalaureate Diploma and Certificates, and Austrian *Matura*. Boarding is not available, but bus transportation and a hot-lunch program are offered. Total enrollment is about 780 students.

VIENNA CHRISTIAN SCHOOL (VCS)
1190, Kreilplatz 1/2
☎ 318 82 11
Fax 318 82 11-4   eMail 100337.1501@compuserve.com

VCS offers small classes from first through 12th grade. It is affiliated with the Network of International Christian Schools and offers a basic American curriculum in a nondenominational setting. Students are trained to develop high ethical standards based on biblical principles in an international environment. Total enrollment is about 130 students.

VIENNA INTERNATIONAL SCHOOL (VIS)
1220, Strasse der Menschenrechte 1
☎ 203 55 95   www.vis.ac.at
Fax 203 03 66   eMail info@vis.ac.at

VIS is an accredited international school approved by the Austrian Ministry of Education, with Primary to grade 12. Instruction is in English, with a comprehensive German program at each level. French and Spanish are language electives taught by native speakers. English as a Second Language (ESL) is offered. Mother-tongue courses are extracurricular. In the school enrollment of about 1,400 students, over 80 nationalities are represented. A full International Baccalaureate (IB), is offered, along with preparation for the Austrian Matura.

AUSTRIAN SCHOOLS

You may choose to enroll your child in an Austrian school. The quality of education is excellent, but you should be aware that the system is structured differently from international schools. (For example, a student's academic direction is determined at an early age, so your child's initial lack of language skills may preclude some opportunities. Also, teachers here are often less nurturing than those in the United States, and your German-language skills need to be adequate enough to communicate with teachers and school administrators.) For information (in German) about state or private Austrian schools, contact:

CITY SCHOOL INSPECTOR FOR VIENNA
(*Stadtschulrat für Wien*)
1010, Dr.-Karl-Renner-Ring 1
☎ 525 25-775 61
Fax 525 25-99 775 61

UNIVERSITY STUDIES

THE OPEN UNIVERSITY AND BUSINESS SCHOOL
1010, Fischerstiege 10/12
☎ 533 23 90
Fax 533 30 73   s

A complete English curriculum is offered in the humanities and social sci-
ences. The business school offers Masters degrees and postgraduate programs in management and business.

INSTITUTE OF EUROPEAN STUDIES
1010, Johannesgasse 7
☎ 512 26 01   www.ies.ac.at
Fax 512 90 60   eMail ies@ies.ac.at

The Institute offers a semester or academic year abroad for college juniors
and seniors. Most classes are taught in English with special concentrations
in East-West studies, humanities, German and international business. Affiliated with the University of Chicago and Robert Morris College in Illi-
nois. Total enrollment is about 100 students.

INTERNATIONAL UNIVERSITY

1030, Rennweg 1 (entrance on Traungasse)
☎ 718 506 813 www.iuvienna.edu
Fax 718 506 89 eMail info@iuvienna.edu

This university offers programs in marketing, management, accounting, economics, computers, English and German. Includes undergraduate and Masters degrees in Diplomatic Studies and Business Administration. Operates in partnership with Waynesburg College, Pennsylvania for its MBA program. Ninety nations are represented in the student enrollment.

OPEN UNIVERSITY (EURO STUDIES CENTER)

1080, Strozzigasse 2
☎ (0660) 7342 (toll-free/free phone call to United Kingdom)
☎ 404 74 15-0
Fax 404 74 248

UNIVERSITY OF MARYLAND

1090, Boltzmanngasse 16
☎ 313 39-2159

The European Division of the University of Maryland conducts five eight-week academic terms a year at the U.S. Embassy in Vienna. Tentative course offerings are publicized in local English newspapers. Call for a free catalog, brochures and course descriptions.

WEBSTER UNIVERSITY

1220, Berchtoldgasse 1
☎ 269 92 93-0
Fax 269 92 93-13
www.webster.ac.at
eMail info@webster.ac.at

Webster University—in St. Louis, Missouri—is a fully accredited American university recognized in Austria. BA, BS, MA and MBA programs are offered in English during the day and evening. Courses in international relations, management, computer science, psychology and other areas are taught in small-classroom settings. Student services such as academic advising, career workshops and internships are also available. The library focuses on areas related to Webster programs and is available to the general public for on-site use (call for times; see Reading section of Recreation chapter). U.S.-government financial aid is available to U.S. citizens and green-card holders.

Webster
UNIVERSITY

The American University in Austria

BA, BS, MA & International MBA Programs

Tel.: 269 92 93-0, Fax: 269 92 93-13
E-mail: info@webster.ac.at, Internet: www.webster.ac.at
Berchtoldgasse 1, 1220 Vienna

COLLEGE INTERNATIONAL, BUDAPEST

☎ (0036) 1 66 97 40
Fax (0036) 1 209 23 28

ENGLISH-TEACHING CERTIFICATE COURSE

INTERNATIONAL HOUSE VIENNA

1010, Schwedenplatz 2/6
☎ 535 57 46-0
Fax 535 57 46-17

This institute offers courses biannually to native-English speakers to qualify for the internationally recognized Certificate in English Language Teaching to Adults (CELTA), which is approved by Cambridge University.

LANGUAGE COURSES

ALPHA SPRACHINSTITUTE AUSTRIA

1010, Schwartzenbergpl. 16

☎ 503 69 69

www.alpha.at   eMail office@alpha.at

Alpha Sprachinstitut Austria is the specialist in teaching German as a foreign language in Vienna. Located in the city center it offers Intensive and Evening Courses, One-to-one Training, Business German and Company Training throughout the year. It is the Examination Centre for "The German Language Diploma" of the *Goethe-Institut* and for the "Austrian Language Diploma".

AUSTRO-AMERICAN SOCIETY
(*Österreichisch-amerikanische gesellschaft*)

1010, Schubertring 6

☎ 512 67 34-0

Fax 513 37 18-14

The society offers four-week, three-hour-a-day intensive German courses as well as twice-a-week evening classes and individual tutoring. Its curriculum follows *Goethe-Institut* guidelines and is authorized to hold *Goethe-Institut* examinations.

BERLITZ SCHOOL OF LANGUAGES

1010, Graben 13 (main office)

☎ 512 82 86

Fax 512 82 86-4

1060, Mariahilfer Strasse 27

☎ 586 56 93

Fax 587 99 25

1010, Rotenturmstrasse 1-3

☎ 535 61 20

Fax 535 61 22

1100, Troststrasse 50

☎ 604 39 11

Fax 604 39 11-20

Utilizing the "Berlitz" teaching method, this school offers individual, intensive and evening courses in various languages—including German—focusing on conversational skills.

EF INTERNATIONAL LANGUAGE SCHOOLS

1010, Annagasse 3

☎ 512 14 60

Fax 512 20 76

www.ef.com

eMail studienjahr.at@ef.com

This school is for high-school students and adults. Business English classes are available for professionals. English, French, Italian Chinese, Russian and Spanish are taught by immersion on a boarding basis in host countries.

CULTURA WIEN
1010, Bauernmarkt 18/4
☎ 533 24 93
Fax: 535 59 12
www.culturawien.at
eMail cultura@nextra.at

German courses
in Vienna

Call for all year round
and summer courses in the
centre of the city.

ULTURA WIEN
Sprach-und Kulturinstitut

Bauernmarkt 18/4 • A-1010 Wien • Austria
Tel. +43-1-533 24 93 • Fax +43-1-535 59 12
cultura@nextra.at • www.culturawien.at

Situated right in the center. Offers top quality German courses in the morning, in the afternoon and in the evening. One-to-one tuition at any time. Company-courses. Summer-camp for children. Examination-center for the "ÖSD-Diplom". Interesting activities and culture program.

INLINGUA SPRACHSCHULE
1010, Neuer Markt 1
☎ 512 22 25   www.inlingua.at
Fax 513 94 56   eMail wien@inlingua.at

This school offers four-hour-a-day intensive courses in various languages (including German) in sessions lasting two weeks or longer, as well as twice-a-week evening courses. Classes are limited to four to eight students and interactive videos are used.

INTERNATIONAL HOUSE VIENNA
1010, Schwedenplatz 2/6
☎ 535 57 46-0
Fax 535 57 46-17

This teaching-accreditation institute also offers tailor-made classes in conversational and business German for small groups or individuals.

INTERNATIONALES KULTURINSTITUT (IKI)
1010, Opernring 7
☎ 586 73 21   www.ikivienna.at
Fax 586 29 93   eMail iki@ikivienna.at

IKI Offers year-round intensive German courses to approximately 300 students of 50 nationalities in which all language skills (hearing, speaking, reading, writing) are taught. Instructors are well-qualified, with advanced degrees in the German language. Students work in pairs or small groups, in a relaxed, pleasant atmosphere. IKI is an examination center for the *Österreichisches Sprachdiplom* and is a member of the association of Austrian language schools CAMPUS AUSTRIA. Also offers an immersion course in cooperation with the University of Washington.

TALK PARTNERS (PART OF THE OPEN UNIVERSITY)
1010, Fischerstiege 10/16
☎ 535 96 95
Fax 533 30 73   eMail talk.partners@telecom.at

This group offers individually designed programs where students choose the content, time, place, duration and intensity of the language instruction.

UNIVERSITY OF VIENNA *UNIVERSITÄT WIEN (WIENER INTERNATIONALE HOCHSCHULKURSE)*
1010, Ebendorferstrasse 10/4
☎ 405 12 54
Fax 405 12 54-10

The university offers German courses for foreigners (at all levels) during the academic year for nine weeks (10 to 18 students per class) and 12 weeks (14 to 20 students per class), as well as during the summer from July to mid-September. A language lab is also available for use.

WIENER INTERNATIONALE HOCHSCHULKURS UNIVERSITY OF VIENNA
GERMAN COURSES
Summer Intensive Courses Courses during the Academic Year
For further details please contact: **Wiener Internationale Hochschulkurse** Ebendorferstraße 10/4, A-1010 Vienna Tel. 405 12 54-0, Fax 405 12 54-10 http://www.univie.ac.at/WIHOK E-mail: WIHOK@univie.ac.at

SUPER LANGUAGE LEARNING (SLL)
1080, Florianigasse 55/15
☎ 408 41 84
Fax 403 66 02
eMail pearl.nitsche@chello.at

This school offers intensive weekly year-round, weekend and summer course in six languages, including English and German, in small-group settings of seven to eight people.

ADULT EDUCATION PROGRAMS
Volkshochschulen

Volkshochschulen offer classes (in German) in such areas as foreign languages, art, music and dance. These are offered during the day and evening at reasonable costs. They are located in various districts, so look in the yellow pages under *"Volkshochschulen"*. (See Recreation chapter.)

A ustria is predominantly Roman Catholic. The City of Vienna provides many places of worship to cover the diversity of the city's international population. A yearly pamphlet is published titled "Grüs Gott!". You can find it in many of the vestibules of the different churches thoughout the city. This pamphlet includes lists of the different churches, locations, a map, phone numbers, times of worship, languages spoken, etc. If you can't find copy of the pamphlet, you can call the Pastoral Ministry for Tourism (Tourismuspastoral) ☎ 515 52 3375.

This chapter includes a few churches that provide worship services in English. Due to unexpected schedule changes, it is always best to call before attending. Times vary during the Summer months.

The following is a list of the major houses of worship offering services in English:

ROMAN CATHOLIC

MASSES IN ENGLISH AND LATIN

ST. STEPHAN'S CATHEDRAL (*STEPHANSDOM*)
1010, Stephansplatz 3   Sat 7:00 PM
☎ 515 52 35 30

VOTIVKIRCHE
1090, Rooseveltplatz 8 (at Schottentor)
☎ 402 18 30   Sunday 11:00 AM

VIENNA ENGLISH-SPEAKING ROMAN CATHOLIC COMMUNITY
American Deacon and English-speaking priest. Hours of operation vary, answering maching gives information. Religious Education Programs offered from September to June at the Church and at various English language schools. eMail vessc@aon.at

MASSES IN LATIN

ST. PETERS (PETERSKIRCHE)
Petersplatz 6   Sundays 11:15 AM   Monday - Saturday 11:00 AM

ST. STEPHANS
in the Crypt Church Sundays 11:15 AM

ST. ANNE'S - (ANNAKIRCHE)
Annagasse 3b   Sundays 11:15 AM

DOMINICAN CHURCH - (DOMINIKANERKIRCHE)
Postgasse 4a   Sundays Noon (Gregorian Chanted Mass)
For Sunday Masses, booklets with the prayers in Latin are provided. You may purchase booklets with the Mass in Latin and in German in the book rack at the back of St. Peters for ATS 25. Highly recommended as well if you plan to attend Mass in German.

CONFESSIONS IN ENGLISH - (BEICHTE UND MUSSPRACHE - SPRITUAL DIRECTION)

ST. STEPHANS
Two Confessionals - one to the right of the Maria Pocs Altar, the other to the left of the Altar and votive candles, on the other side of the railing - in front of the statue of St. Anthony. In front of the Confessionals you will find a listing of times and languages spoken by the priests. A large majority of Austrian priests speak some English and will hear your Confession.

ST. PETERS
Petersplatz 6   Held at lest 4 times per week before Masses. Check board as you enter the portico of the Church on the left hand side.
VOTIVEKIRCHE
Sundays 10:30-10:45 (before Mass) and any time by appointment ☎ 402 18 30

EXPOSITION OF THE BLESSED SACRAMENT – EUCHARISTISCHE ANBETUNG

ST. STEPHANS
As you enter, to the right of the Maria Pocs Altar, past the confessional, inside St. Eligius Chapel. Open daily, the same opening times as the Church (6 AM - 10 PM).

ST. ANNE'S
Annagasse 3b   Monday - Saturday 9:00 AM - 6:00 PM
Many churches have this devotion, and many on the First Friday of the month. Check with your local parishes.

HIGH MASSES WITH MUSIC – (HOCHAMT)
ST. STEPHANS
Sundays and High Feast Days: 10:15 AM. For Christmas Midnight Mass and Mass of Christmas Day, plan to arrive very early and scramble for a seat. The front pews are reserved for local parishioners. (July and August - High Mass is at 9:30).

MASSES WITH MUSIC – CHOIR AND ORCHESTRA
UNIVERSITY CHURCH (UNIVERSITATSKIRCHE)
Dr. Ignaz Seipelplatz 1   Sundays 10:00 AM
ST. AUGUSTIN (AUGUSTINERKIERCHE)
Augustinerstrasse 3   Sundays 11:00 AM
Plan to arrive at least one half hour before in order to get a good 'pew' (the Viennese love their music and the pews fill very quickly). No music during the Summer months. The season begins about the second week in September until the end of June.
HOFBURGKAPELLE
Sundays 9:15 AM. Tickets are required (better if purchased in advance). Sometimes you may be able to find last minute tickets near the entrance of the Church. This is where the Vienna Boys Choir accompany the Mass from mid September to the end of June. (Sadly, this is more a concert for tourists than a religious service.)

RESOURCES FOR SURVIVING MASS IN GERMAN

To acquire the Mass readings in English
via the Internet at: www.ewtn.com; click the Faith button, then Daily
Mass Readings. Also visit www.ignatius.com.

Magnificat Devotional
a wonderful monthly book with Mass prayers and readings, a meditation
on the Gospel of the day and daily devotionals. P.O. Box 91 Spencerville,
MD 20868; via Internet: www.magnificat.net; ☎ 301-853-6600.

The Ordinary of the Mass in Eight Languages
available from www.amazon.com and from www.catalog.litpress.org
ISBN # 0-8146-2125-2.

There is no shortage of Churches here. Vienna is a city of glorious Catholic Churches! Daily Masses abound in the First District Churches as well as
in the local parishes in the other districts. Many churches, like the
Franziskanerkirche, at Franziskanerplatz 4, have beautiful traditional Catholic
Devotions and celebrations. Most churches have First Fridays Sacred Heart
Devotions. Do not miss the beautiful Corpus Christi processions. A word
of caution - during the winter months, the churches in Vienna are freezing
cold, so please dress appropriately.

PILGRIMAGE SITES

Austria has many famous pilgrimage sites, as well as in the near by countries. Recommended reading **Catholic Shrines of Central and Eastern Europe** by Kevin J. Wright available from www.amazon.com. Austrias's
most famous place of pilgrimage is to Our Lady of Mariazell, the Great
Mother of Austria in the town of Mariazell about 80km southwest of Vienna.

St. Stephans
There among the treasures is the miraculous weeping Icon of Our Lady of
Mariapocs, immediately to the right in the back of the Church.

Karmelitenkonvent
1190, Silbergasse 35
Our Lady of the Bowed Head this miraculous picture was found in 1610.

Each year in May, the Tourismus Pastoral Office publishes a guide to the
services in the more famous Churches called **Grüss Gott**. This booklet is
supplemented by special publications during Advent and Lent (in English
and full of useful information). Avilable from the Tourism Office on
Maysedergasse or directly from the Tourismus Pastoral Office, Stephansplatz
6/6/70 ☎ 515 52 3375.

> **Don't forget the tradition-**
> **When visiting a Catholic Church for the first time, accord-
> ing to the Austrians, you make one wish and one Hail Mary.
> The Spanish tradition is three wishes and three Hail Marys.**

OTHER SURVIVAL INFORMATION

Live American Catholic Television via the Internet: www.ewtn.com

The Vatican TV at www.vatican.va

Live American Catholic Television - EWTN 24 hours a day on Satellite HOT BIRD.

Live American Catholic Radio - EWTN with your Astra Satelite Dish.

OTHER MINISTRIES

AIRPORT CHAPEL (open to all denominations)
Vienna International Airport (upper-level transit area)
☎ 7007 222 89   Prayer room is open 7 AM - 8:30 PM
                             Sunday 8 AM: Mass

ANGLICAN/EPISCOPALIAN

CHRIST CHURCH
    1030, Jaurèsgasse 17-19   Sunday 8 AM: Eucharist
    ☎ 720 79 73   Sunday 10 AM: Eucharist

BAPTIST

INTERNATIONAL BAPTIST CHURCH
    1100, Herndlgasse 6   Sunday 9:30 AM: Bible Study
    ☎ 804 92 59   Sunday 10:45 AM: Worship Service

BUDDHIST

BUDDHIST CENTER
    1010, Fleischmarkt 16   These are regular meditations
    ☎ 512 37 19   in most Buddhist traditions.

GREEK ORTHODOX

ZUM HL. GEORG (ST GEORGE)
    1010, Griechengasse 8
    ☎ 535 78 82

ZUM HL. DREIFALTIGKEIT
    1010, Fleischmarkt 13
    ☎ 533 29 65   Liturgies on alternating Sundays.

ISLAMIC

ISLAMIC CENTRE VIENNA (CULTURAL CENTER/LIBRARY)
    1210, Am Hubertusdamm 17-19   For more information,
    ☎ 263 21 20   call Mon - Thurs 9 AM - 4 PM.

JEWISH

CITY SYNAGOGUE (*STADTTEMPEL*)
1010, Seitenstettengasse 4   Mon - Fri 7 AM
☎ 531 04-0   Saturday 9 PM
In order to be admitted, you must bring your passport.   Call for weekly Sunday times.

JEWISH WELCOME SERVICE
1010, Stephansplatz 10
☎ 533 27 30 (for information)
☎ 533 88 91

OR CHADASCH (Liberal Jewish community in Vienna)
1020, Haidgasse 1   Friday 7 PM: Worship Service
☎ 02252 852 35
This community belongs to the WorldUnion of Progressive Judaism.First-time visitors must bring a photo ID card or passport.

METHODIST

UNITED METHODIST CHURCH
1150, Sechshauser Strasse 56
☎ 892 91 54   Sunday 11:15 AM: Worship Service

MORMON

CHURCH OF JESUS CHRIST OF LATTER DAY SAINTS
1020, Böcklinstrasse 55
☎ 728 10 55   Sunday 9:30 AM: Sacrament Meeting

NONDENOMINATIONAL CHRISTIAN

INTERNATIONAL CHAPEL OF VIENNA (EVANGELICAL)
1190, Kreilplatz 1   Sunday 9:30 AM: Worship Service
☎ 318 59 79   In Summer 10:00 AM

VIENNA CHRISTIAN CENTER
A CHURCH FOR ALL NATIONS
1030, Rennweg 74   Sunday 10 AM: Worship Service &
☎ 796 91 76   Sunday School
    Sunday 6 PM: Evening Celebration Service

VIENNA CHURCH OF CHRIST
1030, Rennweg 1   Sunday 10:30 AM: Worship Service
Entrance Traungasse
☎ 214 74 96
☎ 718 50 68-11

VIENNA COMMUNITY CHURCH (ECUMENICAL)
1010, Dorotheergasse 16
☎ 505 52 33   Sunday 11:30 AM: Worship Service

No matter where in the world you are, appearance is important. It is how you express yourself and your culture, and upon which others base their first impressions. Vienna is no different with its blend of old and new styles—from tailored *Loden* suits to baggy jeans and T-shirts. This chapter contains information to help you maintain your current style or try something new in the way of hairstyle, makeup or fashion.

HAIRSTYLISTS *Friseure*

Finding a hairstylist you like is not always easy, especially if you've just left your favorite one behind. Eventually, though, you should be able to find one here who can give you what you want. We've listed some salons recommended by AWA members; you can also ask friends and coworkers for their recommendations. And, remember, hair always grows out.

Hair salons are usually closed Sunday and Monday.

Giving a 10-percent tip to your hairstylist is customary. In some salons, "trainees" wash your hair and usually receive a tip of about ATS 10 to ATS 15. You don't generally tip the owner.

HAIR-SALON TERMS

Bangs *Stirnfransen*
Bleach *bleichen*
Blow dry *föhnen*
Bob *Bob*
Body only *Stützwelle*
Brush *bürsten*
Comb *kämmen*
Comb out *auskämmen*
Conditioner *Kurspülung, Conditioner*
Curl *Locken machen*
Curling iron *Lockenschere*
Curly *lockig*
Cut *schneiden*
Dye *färben*
Electrolysis *epilieren*
Eyebrow plucking *Augenbrauen zupfen*
Eyelash dyeing *Wimpern färben* (dye)
Facial *Gesichtsbehandlung*
Facial-hair removal *Gesichtshaar entfernen*
Frost *mäschen, Highlights*

Gel *Gel*
Hair spray *Haarspray*
Leg-hair removal *Beine harzen*
Long nails *Nagelverlängerung* (nail extensions)
Manicure *Handpflege*
Mousse *Schaum, Mousse*
Pedicure *Fusspflege*
Permanent *Dauerwelle*
Rollers *Lockenwickler*
Set *legen*
Setting lotion *Haarfestiger, Modellierschaum*
Shampoo *Shampoo*
  dry hair *trockenes Haar*
  normal hair *normales Haar*
  oily hair *fettiges Haar*
  hair with dandruff *gegen Schuppen*
Teasing *toupieren*
Tint, rinse *Tönung, Spülung*
Trim *Trim*
Wash *waschen*

HAIR SALONS IN VIENNA

HAIR-SALON KEY

Price for wash, cut & styling:

$ Inexpensive (less than ATS 500)
$$ Moderate (ATS 500 - ATS 750)
$$$ Expensive (more than ATS 750)

The following hair salons are conveniently located and have stylists who speak English. Also, look in the yellow pages under *"Friseure und Frisiersalons"* and ask neighbors, coworkers and friends for recommendations.

BUNDY BUNDY EXCLUSIV $$$

1010, Habsburgergasse 3/1
☎ 535 53 53
Mon 10 AM - 6 PM
Tues, Wed, Fri 9 AM - 7 PM,
Thurs 9: AM - 8 PM,
Sat 8 AM - 4 PM

1030, Schwarzenbergplatz 8
☎ 712 73 63
1130, Maxingstrasse 4A
☎ 877 71 60
1180, Salierigasse 30
☎ 479 89 47

STYLE IN BUNDY BUNDY $$

1070, Mariahilferstr. 38-40
☎ 522 50 40
Mon - Fri 9:30 AM - 7 PM,
Sat 9 AM - 3 PM
1020, Praterstr. 45
☎ 214 13 21
1210, Ignaz-Köck Str.1
☎ 271 58 88
1220, Wagramer Str. 5
☎ 263 60 60

COIFFEUR KRAMMER $

1010, Annagasse 11
☎ 512 24 50

1010, Freyung 2 (*Palais Ferstel*)
☎ 535 43 52
Mon - Fri 9 AM - 7 PM,
Sat 8 AM - 2 PM

The Krammers are both native-English speakers. Mention the AWA and receive a discount. Extremely friendly atmosphere.

GRUPPA L'ULTIMA $$

1010, Köllnerhofgasse 3
☎ 512 71 56
1090, Nussdorfer Strasse 29
☎ 317 45 80
1190, Sieveringer Strasse 4-10
☎ 320 69 39
Mon - Fri 9 AM - 5:30 PM,
Sat 8 AM - 2 PM

This salon has eight other locations in Vienna, so check the telephone directory's white pages.

Salon Rochat
English Hairdresser from London
for Ladies and Gents
1080 Wien, Josefstädter Strasse 70
Telephone 407 55 28

Open: Tue - Thu 8:30 - 17:30
Fri 8:30 - 19:30 · Sat 8:00 - 12:00

U-Bahn U6
Strassenbahn 33, 5, J

SALON ROCHAT $
1080, Josefstädterstrasse 70
☎ 407 55 28
Tues - Thurs 8:30 AM - 5:30 PM,
Fri 8:30 AM - 7 PM,
Sat 8 AM - noon

MIKE (Adult) $$
FRISEUR TEAM (Child) $
1010, Wildpretmarkt 2-4
☎ 535 84 87
Mon 1 PM - 6 PM,
Tues - Wed 9:30 AM - 6 PM,
Thurs - Fri 9:30 AM - 7:30 PM,
Sat 9 AM - 2 PM

This salon can take care of your whole family and is especially good with children.

GRECHT COMPANY P&K
GRECHT G.M.B.H. $$
1090, Spitalgasse 33
☎ 406 41 18 or
☎ 408 14 95
Mon 1 PM - 7 PM,
Tues - Wed 10 AM - 7 PM,
Thurs - Fri 9 AM - 7 PM,
Sat 9 AM - 3 PM

MARTHA STEFAN $
1190, Krottenbachstrasse 114
☎ 320 30 39
Mon, Sat 8 AM - 1 PM,
Tues - Fri 8 AM - 6 PM

You can also receive a manicure at this shop or go next door for facials at Studio Esteca ☎ 320 56 61.

ROBERT WELNER $$
1190, Döblinger Hauptstr. 4
☎ 369 53 00 (women and children)
☎ 369 53 01 (men)
Tues - Fri 8:30 AM - 6 PM,
Sat 8:00 AM - 2 PM

This is a family salon where French is also spoken. Women can just walk in, but you should make an appointment for men and children.

COIFFEUR WOLFGANG $$
1190, Gymnasiumstrasse 64
☎ 369 66 67
Tues, Fri 8:30 AM - 6 PM,
Thurs 8:30 AM - 7 PM,
Sat 8 AM - noon
You can have a cut and style, perm, color or conditioning based on your individual needs.

COIFFEUR BEA $

1220, Schüttaustrasse 4
☎ 263 62 62
Tues, Fri 8:30 AM - 8 PM,
Wed, Thurs 8:30 AM - 6 PM,
Sat 8 AM - noon

This is a family salon located near the Vienna International Centre. They will gladly make appointments at lunchtime. You can also have manicures, head massages, eyebrow/eyelash dyeing and natural coloring for hair. There is a 10-percent discount for seniors on Wednesday. It is best to call ahead so you can make appointments in English.

COSMETICS & BEAUTY CARE

You'll find cosmetics stores everywhere in Vienna, especially in major shopping areas like the first district and Mariahilfer Strasse in the seventh district. For listings, look in the yellow pages under *"Parfümerien."* Many carry both American and European brands. Drugstores (*Drogerien*) carry less expensive brands and hypoallergenic makeup (*Hypoallergenisches Makeup*), while department stores offer all the major international brands. Be aware, however, that even well-known brands may be formulated differently here, which may cause allergic reactions. If you want to pamper yourself, *Kosmetik Salons* offer specialized beauty care such as facials, manicures and pedicures, massages, tanning booths and saunas, but appointments are necessary. For a listing of such salons, look in the yellow pages under *"Kosmetikinstitute."* Below are some *Kosmetik Salons*:

DAGMAR SHANNON KOSMETIK

1010, Krugerstrasse 3
☎ 512 34 31
Tues - Fri 9 AM - 8 PM
This full-service salon offers pedicures, laser hair removal, leg waxing, permanent-makeup application and tattoos. English is spoken.

DAPHIN-VIENNE

1010, Neutorgasse 12
☎ 535 66 10
Mon - Thurs 8 AM - 8 PM,
Fri 10 AM - 5 PM
This salon sells French beauty products and performs facials and skin analysis. By appointment only.

BEAUTYLAND

2380, Perchtoldsdorf
Salitergasse 26
☎ & Fax 869 96 96
Mon - Sun, 10 AM - 7 PM
This salon, run by Elisabeth Ondrey is complete with facials, waxing, gel nails and tanning. The great service and good prices from an English-speaker makes it worth the short drive from the city. Plenty of parking available.

VIENNA BEAUTY KOSMETIK
1010, Plankengasse 1
☎ 512 01 24
Mon 2 PM - 8 PM,
Tues, Thurs, Fri 8:30 AM - 6 PM
This salon offers acne and skin-allergy treatments.

DANI-KOSMETIK
1040, Mozartgasse 7
☎ 505 44 10
Tues, Thurs, Sat 8 AM - 6 PM,
Wed 10 AM - 8 PM,
Fri 8 AM - 8 PM

The owner was trained in the United States. She does beauty treatments, facials, makeup lessons and hair removal. Hours can be adapted to meet customer needs; call for an appointment. Her husband is a masseur. Both speak English.

COLOR ME BEAUTIFUL
1090, Stroheckgasse 12/12
☎ 310 16 27

Image consultant Christine Pamphlett, who speaks English, offers image advice about coloring, styling, makeup and fashion. Consultations are by appointment only, so call in advance.

CARESSE COSMETIQUE INSTITUT
1190, Grinzinger Allee 3/2/7
☎ 328 95 34
Mon - Fri 9 AM - 8 PM
eMail caresse@netway.at

This salon is nicely decorated, very clean and offers monthly specials. Besides a variety of facials, they provide body treatments, manicures and pedicures. The proprietor is Claudia Semper and she speaks some English. By appointment only.

BEAUTY-PRODUCT TERMS

Astringent Astringierend
Blush Rouge
Combination skin Mischhaut
Deodorant Deodorant
Dry skin trockene Haut
Eyeliner Eyeliner
Eye-makeup remover Augenmakeup-Entferner
Face mask Gesichtsmaske
Facial cleanser Gesichtsreinigung
Facial scrub Rubbelcreme
Fragrance-free/ unscented geruchlos

Hypoallergenic Hypoallergenic
Lip liner Konturenstift
Lipstick Lippenstift
Moisturizer Feuchtigkeitscreme
Nail polish Nagellack
Nail-polish remover Nagellackentferner
Oily skin fette Haut
Sensitive skin empfindliche Haut
Transluscent powder transluscent Puder
Waterproof Wasserdicht

CRÈME DE LA MER

MOISTURIZATION IS ROCKET SCIENCE

Max Huber, aerospace physicist from NASA, suffered severe chemical burns on his face and eye area after working with fuels. He went through numerous medical treatments and therapeutic preparations during the course of his recovery. As a result, he became obsessed with skincare and built a laboratory in his own home. Six thousand experiments and twelve years later, he succeeded - Crème De La Mer was introduced in 1965.

CRÈME DE LA MER HAS NO "MIRACLE" INGREDIENTS: JUST SEA KELP, VITAMINS AND MINERALS

Sea kelp is the key ingredient in Crème De La Mer's recipe. Huber used minerals extracted from fresh sea kelp from the Pacific Ocean. He then combined other natural ingredients, including calcium, magnesium, potassium, iron, lecithin, Vitamins C, D, E, and B12 as well as extracts from citrus, eucalyptus, wheat germ, alfalfa and sunflower. When kelp and vitamins are united, they produce micronutrients that help energize the skin.

MORE TIME GOES INTO MAKING CRÈME DE LA MER THAN SELLING IT

Huber invented a bio-fermentation process that is so precise, each batch takes three to four months to make. He found that most skin care products were manufactured at high temperatures and pressures, diminishing the effectiveness of key ingredients - like over-cooked vegetables zapped of most of their nutritional value. Instead, his breakthrough low temperature "bio-fermentation" process preserves and strengthens the integrity of organic ingredients. The strong natural activity of the broth protects Crème De La Mer from bacteria with minimum preservatives. His technology is unparalled to anything else in the industry. Each jar is still hand-filled to keep his formula from being altered.

WHAT ARE THE BENEFITS OF CRÈME DE LA MER?

The Crème De La Mer delivery system secures moisture on the skin's surface by locking in skin's own water and providing continuous rehydration. It functions as a moisturizer, natural smoothing agent and eye cream. Crème De La Mer will also help calm even the most sensitive skin from outside irritants. It is compatible with all skin types and can be used in conjunction with all other skin products (if using a prescribed skincare medication, consult a physician). Just a small amount of Crème De La Mer will help skin gain a healthy balance, feel smoother, firmer and ultimately younger.

Today, Crème De La Mer is exclusively available at "Nägele & Strubell" (Vienna) and "Topsi" (Ringstraßen-Galerien, Vienna) and other selected perfumeries in Austria. Information: Tel (01) 534 20 33

CLOTHING *Kleidung*

To find clothing and department stores, look in the yellow pages under *"Bekleidung"* ("Clothing"), *"Damenmoden"* ("Women's Clothing"), *"Boutiquen"* ("Boutiques"), *"Herrenmoden"* ("Men's Clothing") and *"Kaufhäuser"* ("Department Stores"). Also, try shopping in the areas listed on the next page.

CLOTHING TERMS

Baseball cap *Baseballkappe*

Belt *Gürtel*

Blazer *Blazer*

Blouse *Bluse*

Boots *Stiefel*

Bra *BH* (say "Bay hah")

Cap *Kappe*

Coat *Mantel*

Dress *Kleid*

Gloves *Handschuhe*

Hat *Hut*

High heels/pumps *Stöckelschuhe*

Jacket *Jacke*

Jeans *Jeans*

Men's suit *Anzug*

Nightgown/nightshirt *Nachthemd*

Pajamas *Pyjama*

Panties *Schlüpfer*

Pants *Hose*

Pantyhose/tights *Strumphose*

Rain coat *Regenmantel*

Robe *Bademantel, Schlafrock*

Scarf *Schal*

Shirt *Hemd*

Shoes *Schuhe*

Shorts *Shorts*

Skirt *Rock*

Slip *Unterrock* (skirt-length), *Unterkleid* (full slip)

Socks *Socken*

Sport coat *Sakko*

Stockings *Strümpfe*

Sweater/jumper *Pullover*

Sweatshirt *Sweatshirt*

Tennis shoes *Tennisschuhe*

Tie *Krawatte*

Umbrella *Schirm*

Underwear *Unterwäsche*

Vest/waistcoat *Weste*

Women's suit *Kostüm*

MAJOR SHOPPING AREAS & MALLS

1010, Kärntner Strasse and the Graben
(U1, U3 Stephansplatz)

This area, swarming with tourists, has many high-end designer boutiques and some more affordable clothing and shoe stores.

1060 & 1070, Mariahilfer Strasse
(U3 Neubaugasse, Zieglergasse, Westbahnhof, U6 Westbahnhof)

This is a long street with a wide assortment of affordable shops and department stores.

1100, Favoritenstrasse (U1 Keplerplatz)

This is a pedestrian walkway with a variety of shops.

1220, Donauzentrum (U1 Kagran)

This two-floor mall offers clothing and shoe stores in abundance.

2334, Vösendorf Süd, Shopping City Süd (WLB-Badner Bahn)

Europe's largest shopping mall has a selection of clothing, shoe and sporting-goods stores that is hard to match.

7111, Parndorf, Designer Outlet Center (A4 south to exit 43 Neusiedl am See)

This factory-outlet store is about 40 minutes south of Vienna. It's open Mon - Fri 8:30 AM - 7:30 PM, Sat 8:30 AM - 5 PM. ☎ 02166 36 14 0

 If you're in a small clothing boutique, especially in the first district, ask the salesperson for help before you take anything off the rack, or at least look around to see what other customers are doing.

AMERICAN & EUROPEAN CLOTHING SIZES

(Proportions may vary and size conversions are approximate.)

WOMEN'S COATS, DRESSES, SKIRTS & SUITS

U.S.	6	8	10	12	14	16	18
AUSTRIA	36	38	40	42	44	46	48
BRITAIN	10	12	14	16	18	20	22
FRANCE	38	40	42	44	46	48	50
GERMANY	36	38	40	42	44	46	48
ITALY	40	42	44	46	48	50	52

MEN'S COATS & SUITS

U.S.	34	36	38	40	42	44	46	48
Europe	44	46	48	50	52	54	56	58

MEN'S PANTS

U.S.	30	32	34	36	38	40	42
Europe	40	42	44	46	48	50	52

MEN'S SHIRT SIZES (Neck Size *Halsweite*)

U.S.	$14\,^1/_2$	15	$15\,^1/_2$	16	$16\,^1/_2$	17	$17\,^1/_2$
Europe	37	38	39	40	41	42	43

HATS

U.S.	7	$7\,^1/_4$	$7\,^1/_2$	$7\,^3/_4$
Europe	56	58	60	62

MEN'S SHOES

U.S.	$8–8\,^1/_2$	$9–9\,^1/_2$	$10–10\,^1/_2$	$11–11\,^1/_2$	$12–12\,^1/_2$
Europe	41	43	44	45	46

WOMEN'S SHOES

U.S.	5	6	7	8	$8\,^1/_2$	9	$9\,^1/_2$
Europe	35	37	38	39	40	41	42

CHILDREN'S CLOTHING

U.S.	2	4	6	8	10	12	14	16
Europe	92	104	116	128	140	152	164	176

Loden-Plankl ®

MICHAELERPLATZ 6, 1010 WIEN
TEL. 01/533 80 32
FAX 01/535 49 20

Number 1 in Vienna for Loden and traditional Austrian clothing

TRACHTEN & DIRNDLS

The traditional Austrian folk costume is called *Trachten*, which includes the dress known as *Dirndl* and leather knickers (*Lederhosen*) and jackets made of *Loden*. You'll still see some Austrians wearing *Trachten* for special occasions. Here are some stores that specialize in this type of clothing:

LODEN-PLANKL
1010, Michaelerplatz 6
☎ 533 80 32
This shop has a large selection for the whole family.

RESI HAMMERER
1010, Kärntner Strasse 29–31
☎ 512 69 52
This store sells *Loden* and sports couture, but it's more modern than classical.

LANZ OF SALZBURG
1010, Kärntner Strasse 10
☎ 512 24 56
This store carries coats, jackets, *Dirndl*s and clothing for children.

LEBEN MIT TRADITION
1010, Seilergasse 10
☎ 512 22 41
This store carries clothing for women and men; they have only jackets for children.

KETTNER
1010, Seilergasse 12
☎ 513 22 39
This store sells Bogner, Geiger, Loden Frey and other name brands for men and women. Many employees speak English.

TRACHTEN TOSTMANN
1010, Schottengasse 3A
☎ 533 53 31

You can get fabric and custom-made *Trachten* here.

MÜHLBAUER
1010, Seilergasse 5
☎ 513 70 70

This store has *Trachten* for the entire family and carries Gössl of Salzburg.

SECONDHAND-CLOTHING STORES

Every fall there is a ski sale at both the American International School (AIS) and the Vienna International School (VIS) where used skis and winter sports equipment, shoes, children's clothes and many other items are sold (see Secondhand Shops & Flea Markets section of Home chapter). Flea markets are held at both schools in the fall and spring. You can call the schools (see Education chapter), watch for announcements in AWA's monthly *Highlights* for details. Look under *"Second-Hand-Shops"* in the yellow pages, too. Here are a few of the major secondhand stores in Vienna:

F.F. SECOND HAND
1010, Krugerstrasse 10
☎ 513 54 84
Mon - Fri 9 PM - 6 PM,
Sat 10 AM - 5 PM

TAUSCHZENTRALE FÜR KINDERARTIKEL
1060, Mariahilferstr. 1216
1070, Westbahnstrasse 27
☎ 523 93 94

This is Vienna's oldest and largest secondhand store selling clothing, furniture, sports equipment, toys, kitchen utensils, books, etc. When you want to browse in the adult section of the *Tauschzentrale*, check your bags and get a claim ticket. When you want to buy something, give it to a salesperson and show your number so your item can be held at the counter. You'll pick it up on your way out after you pay. The *Tauschzentrale* will also accept items to sell on consignment, but they must be contemporary, clean and have all their buttons and functioning zippers. You will receive a number and a receipt for each item. After something has been sold, you pick up your money at the cash window.

FIRST CLASS SECOND HAND
1130, Maxingstrasse 4
☎ 877 17 22
Mon - Fri 10 AM - 1 PM,
2 PM - 6 PM,
Sat 10 AM - 12:30 PM

BRIGITTE DAMEN SECOND HAND SHOP
1190, Döblinger Hauptstr. 31-33
☎ 369 88 61

BRIGITTE KINDER SECOND HAND SHOP
1190, Döblinger Hauptstr. 58
☎ 362 76 23

AMERICAN INTERNATIONAL SCHOOL NEARLY NEW SHOP
1190, Salmannsdorfer Str. 47
☎ 440 38 70
Tues, Thurs 8:30 AM - 3 PM

This store, sponsored by the PTF of AIS, buys and sells clothing on a consignment basis.

CLOTHING RENTALS
Kostüm- und Kleiderleihanstalten

If you're invited to a costume party or are attending a ball or formal event, you can try one of the following stores for costume and clothing rentals:

J.M. OBERNIGG–
MILITARY COLLECTION
1060, Mollaregasse 8
☎ 586 22 95-1
Fax 586 22 95-4

This store rents military uniforms as well as a large assortment of costumes from Hollywood. The staff speaks English.

BRAUT MODEN
1090 Porzellangasse 36
☎ 317 61 55

This store, where English is spoken, rents tuxedos (including white ties and tails), ball and bridal gowns, Carnival (*Fasching*) costumes and clothing for all occasions.

ANNI SCHEIDL
1100, Laxenburger Strasse 9
☎ 607 59 79
(Dec 1 - Feb 28)

This store specializes in animal-fur costumes.

LAMBERT HOFER
1110, Simmeringer
Hauptstrasse 28
☎ 740 90-0
Fax 740 90-66

This is one of the largest clothing-rental stores for men's wedding suits, ball gowns and theatrical costumes.

BALLET COSTUMES
Ballett Kostüme

If you or your child is taking ballet lessons, you can try the following stores for clothing and shoes:

JUMP IN
1070, Neubaugasse 49
☎ 523 13 36

This store carries leotards, swimsuits and ballet, tap and flamenco shoes. It can order fabric for dance costumes. English is spoken.

WILHELM SCHACHTNER
1180, Edelhofgasse 6
☎ 479 54 89

This store sells ballet shoes and clothing, as well as gymnastics and ice-skating costumes.

LINGERIE & SWIMSUITS
Wäschewaren und Badeanzüge

Palmers and Gazelle are two large chains with locations throughout Vienna, so look in the yellow pages under *"Wäschewaren,"* where shops are listed by district.

HOSIERY *Strümpfe, Strumpfhosen*

Pantyhose and stockings are sold in lingerie stores, shoe stores, clothing boutiques, department stores and supermarkets. Support stockings are *Stützstrumpfhose*.

GLOVES *Handschuhe*

For stores selling gloves, look in the yellow pages under *"Handschuhe."* You can also try department stores. Some ice-cream parlors (*Eissalons*) become glove, hat and scarf stores in the winter, too. You also can try the following store with English-speaking clerks:

M. GIBIAN
    1010, Weihburggasse 3   1060, Mariahilfer Strasse 113
    ☎ 513 51 20   ☎ 596 49 01

HATS *Hüte*

For hat stores, look under *"Hüte"* in the yellow pages. Nagy Hüte has several locations in Vienna:

NAGY HÜTE
    1010, Wollzeile 36
    1090, Nussdorfer Str. 16
    1220, Donauzentrum Top 175
    ☎ 405 66 29-0 (for all stores)

Check the white pages of the telephone directory for additional locations.

OBERWALDER & CO.
    1010, Kärntner Strasse 39
    ☎ 512 28 41

    1060, Mariahilfer Str. 61
    ☎ 587 22 11

These stores carry hats and souvenirs, and the staff speaks English.

COLLINS HÜTE UND HERRENMODE
    1010, Opernpassage 1
    ☎ 587 13 05

This store carries hats from its own factory as well as traditional Austrian clothing (including boiled-wool jackets and *Loden* coats) for both men and women. You can also have your winter hat cleaned and steamed. They speak English.

FURS *Pelze*

You will see fur coats worn everywhere here, from formal events to grocery stores. If you're interested in buying a fur coat for the winter, look under *"Pelze und Pelzwaren"* in the yellow pages or try one of the following locations:

LISKA, M & A
1010, Hoher Markt 8-9
☎ 533 22 11
Fax 533 17 34

Cleaning and storage is also done at this location.

1010, Kärntner Strasse 8
☎ 512 41 20

This location sells furs, but has no cleaning or storage.

ZIKOS PELZE FURS
1010, Graben 28/1. Stock (1st floor)
☎ 533 99 41
Fax 533 99 42

This establishment also does alterations, cleaning and summer storage.

P. VALEK PELZDESIGN VIENNA
1010, Seilerstätte 16
☎ 512 14 08

This fur designer also handles storage and does repairs and alterations. The employees speak English.

FUR TERMS

Alteration **Umarbeitung**

Cleaning **Reinigung**

Measurements **Masse**

Repair **Reparatur**

Storage **Aufbewahrung**

Vienna has more than 2,000 years of history with a rich traditional and cultural background. Ornate churches abound, with St. Stephan's Cathedral (*Stephansdom*) sitting nobly in the city center. Museums and galleries house great Austrian and European works. The architecture itself is art on public display. The music represents some of the best in the world. No matter what your interests, there are numerous opportunities in Vienna to entertain and enrich yourself.

WHERE TO GET CULTURAL INFORMATION

Vienna Tourist Information Offices (see Info Offices appendix) have many brochures, maps and schedules in English for current cultural events. (See both Publications and Books appendices for additional resources.) Make the tourist office one of your first stops—the information you will find there is invaluable. Be sure to ask specifically for these free magazines and brochures:

- *Vienna Scene,* a biannual magazine (available mid-March and mid-October) describing the city's cultural offerings. It includes dates, hours and addresses. It is available in many languages—take your pick!

- *Programm,* a monthly list of events including theater productions, symposia, concerts, exhibitions, music cafés, guided tours and walks, films and alternative-music options.

- **"Museums,"** a tri-fold pamphlet listing the locations and opening hours of all the city's museums. Ask for it in English.

- **"Architecture from *Fin de Siècle* to the Present Day,"** a folded pamphlet with maps giving locations of 136 buildings of architectural interest, their addresses, architects and dates of construction.

- **"The Spanish Riding School and the Vienna Boys' Choir,"** a folded pamphlet in multiple languages detailing the procedure for getting tickets and times of performances. It is updated yearly.

Also visit www.info.wien.at for more information.

MUSEUMS

For opening times, entrance fees and exact locations, you can get the "Museums" brochure in English from any Vienna Tourist Information Office (see Info Offices appendix). A comprehensive list of all Vienna's cultural offerings would require a small library, but the useful resource *A Guide to Vienna's Museums* (Penguin) is available in bookstores and some museums. If you are an avid museum fan, you might want to join the following organization:

SOCIETY OF MUSEUM OF FINE ARTS FRIENDS IN VIENNA
Verein der Museumsfreunde in Wien
1070, Museumplatz 1 Stg 3
☎ 524 77 34 or ☎ 524 77 35
Fax 524 77 36

You can apply for a calendar-year membership at the information desk located in the main hall of the Museum of Fine Arts (*Kunsthistorisches Museum*) or the Upper Belvedere (*Oberes Belvedere*; see separate listing), Tues - Sat 10 AM - 5 PM. This entitles you to a monthly newsletter (*Mitteilungen*) in German, which highlights upcoming events and tours. (Be aware that if you buy it in November, it's only valid until the end of December of that year.)

FREE MUSEUM ADMISSION

Federal museums offer free admission on World Museum Day, which is celebrated in May, and the Austrian National Holiday (*Nationalfeiertag*) on October 26.

THE VIENNA CARD

If you have visitors, consider buying The Vienna Card, which is available at most hotels and any Vienna Tourist Information Office. For about ATS 210, a cardholder is entitled to 72 hours of unlimited public-transportation use and discounts at many museums, guided tours, restaurants, and stores in Vienna. You'll receive a brochure with details and a list of participating establishments.

TIPPING MUSEUM GUIDES

It is customary to tip a museum tour guide ATS 10 per person at the end of a tour.

KUNSTHISTORISCHES MUSEUM

MUSEUM OF FINE ARTS *Kunsthistorisches Museum*
1010, Maria-Theresien-Platz (entrance)
☎ 525 24-0
Tues - Wed, Fri - Sun 10 AM - 6 PM, Thurs 10 AM -9 PM
Restaurant Tues - Sun 10 AM - 10 PM
Guided tours in English (for an extra fee) 11 AM & 3 PM
(except Nov 1 - Dec 15 & Jan 8 - Easter weekend)

On the Ring and facing the Natural History Museum (*Naturhistorisches Museum*), the *Kunsthistorisches Museum* contains the most famous collection of paintings in Austria. Once the private collection of the Habsburgs, there are works from Dutch, Flemish, French, German, Italian and Spanish artists. The Brueghel collection and Benvenuto Cellini's famous salt cellar are highlights. There are also Greek, Roman and Egyptian exhibits. For a small fee, you can buy a brochure in English, which includes the museum floor plan, from the information desk.

CAFÉ GERSTNER, in a corner on the first floor (in Europe, that's the one above the ground floor), offers cakes, snacks and drinks (Tues - Sun 10 AM - 5 PM). There is also a dinner buffet Thurs 6:30 PM - 9:30 PM, when the museum is open later. For reservations, call ☎ 512 49 63-40.

PALAIS HARRACH
1010, Freyung 3
☎ 523 17 53
Mon, Wed - Sun 10 AM - 6 PM

This is an extension of the *Kunsthistorisches Museum* containing arms, armor and hunting rooms. It also hosts special exhibits.

NATURAL HISTORY MUSEUM *Naturhistorisches Museum*
1010, Maria-Theresien-Platz (entrance)
☎ 521 77-0
Mon, Wed - Sun 9 AM - 6 PM

Facing the *Kunsthistorisches Museum*, this museum contains fine examples of taxidermy, fossils, meteorites, prehistoric objects, the Venus from Willendorf (circa 20,000 B.C. - 30,000 B.C.) and botanical and zoological exhibits.

THE HOFBURG

IMPERIAL PALACE *Hofburg*
   1010, Michaelerplatz (entrance at *Kaisertor*, inner courtyard)
   ☎ 533 75 70
   Fax 533 75 70-33
   Daily 9 AM - 4:30 PM

You can buy a combination ticket to visit both the Imperial Apartments and the Court Silver and Tableware Chamber (*Hofsilber- und Tafel-kammer*). The golden ceremonial centerpiece is the main attraction. Guided tours are in German only. In the gift shop, however, you can buy a guidebook in English that explains each room. There is also a café.

The Treasury (*Schatzkammer*) is open Mon, Wed - Sun 10 AM - 6 PM. Secular and ecclesiastical treasures collected over the centuries are on display, including the crown of the Holy Roman Empire and the crib of Napoleon's son. Audio-tape tours in English are available for a small fee. Enter via the palace's *Schweizerhof*.

The Ethnological Museum (*Museum für Völkerkunde*) is open Mon, Wed - Sun 10 AM - 4 PM. Considered one of the world's best ethnological museums, it houses collections from Argentina, Asia, Brazil, Mexico (Crown of Montezuma), North America, Peru, the South Seas and West Africa. Guided tours are available Sun at 11 AM. The entrance is on *Heldenplatz*.

For information on other *Hofburg* museums, such as the National Library (*Nationalbibliothek*), the Ephesos Museum, the Ancient Musical Instruments Museum and the Arms and Armory Collection, consult the "Museums" brochure, available at any Vienna Tourist Information Office (see Info Offices appendix).

SCHLOSS SCHÖNBRUNN

SCHÖNBRUNN PALACE *Schloss Schönbrunn*
   1130, Schönbrunner Schlossstrasse
   ☎ 811 13 (general information)
   ☎ 811 13 239 (to book guided tours)
   Fax 811 13 333
   Daily 8:30 AM - 5 PM (April - Oct),
   Daily 8:30 AM - 4:30 PM (Nov -March)
   www.schonbrunn.at

Completed in 1749 during the reign of Maria Theresia, *Schönbrunn* was the summer palace of the Habsburgs. The park (open daily 6 AM - dusk) contains artificial Roman ruins, an Egyptian obelisk and the

Neptune Fountain. The *Gloriette* (open daily Nov - Feb 9 AM - 7:30 PM, and March - Oct 8 AM - dusk) is a 100-meter-long colonnade situated on a hill overlooking the palace. It has recently been turned into a café and the view of Vienna is worth the climb. There are two guided tours available in English: the Grand Tour (40 state rooms) and the Imperial Tour (22 state rooms). Handsets with recordings in several languages, including English, allow for self-guided tours. The painted rooms (*Berglzimmer*) where Maria Theresia's many children used to play and escape the summer heat are accessible by special arrangement.

Other Schönbrunn Attractions

Each of the following has a separate admission fee. You can, however, purchase a combination card (*Kombikarte*) for the Schönbrunn Zoo and Palm House at a reduced rate. The *Kombikarte* is valid for one year (i.e., you don't have to visit them all on the same day).

IMPERIAL COACH MUSEUM *Wagenburg*
☎ 877 32 44
Daily 9 AM - 6 PM (April - Oct)
Tues - Sun 10 AM - 4 PM (Nov - March)

The varied means of transportation of the Habsburgs is all on display—from gilded coronation coaches to sedan chairs, to children's sleighs to funeral coaches. Empress Elisabeth's travel toilet is even here!

SCHÖNBRUNN ZOO *Schönbrunner Tiergarten*
Daily 9 AM - closing (varies 4:30 PM - 6:30 PM by season)

Europe's oldest zoo, founded by Maria Theresia's husband, Franz Stephan, in 1752, contrasts stately imperial gazebos with wild animals cared for with the latest technology.

PALM HOUSE *Palmenhaus*
Daily 9:30 AM - 5:30 PM (May - Sept)
Daily 9:30 AM - 4:30 PM (Oct - April)

Europe's largest glass-and-iron building houses plants from all over the world in three rooms. The first features plants from Australia and Asia, the second has those found in a tropical rain forest, and the third duplicates an African desert.

SCHLOSS BELVEDERE

BELVEDERE PALACE *Schloss Belvedere*

For guided tours and educational programs, call ☎ 795 57 0 or fax 798 43 37.

The City Palace of Prince Eugene of Savoy consists of a garden (open Tues - Sat 10 AM - 5 PM) with two buildings, Upper Belvedere and Lower Belvedere, both of which have art exhibits. The museums are only part of the magnificent Baroque palace, which the prince commissioned Johann Lukas von Hildebrant to build. The gardens of the palace offer a marvelous panorama of Vienna and are worth an afternoon stroll.

UPPER BELVEDERE *Oberes Belvedere*

Austrian Gallery *Österreichische Galerie*
    1030, Prinz-Eugen-Strasse 27
    ☎ 795 57-0
    Tues - Sun 10 AM - 5 PM

The upper floor of the palace contains Austrian and international art of the 19th and 20th centuries, including the works of Austrian artists such as Gustav Klimt, Egon Schiele and Oskar Kokoschka and of Europeans like Auguste Rodin and Vincent van Gogh. The collection begins with the *Biedermeier* period and ends with the *Secession*. Temporary exhibits also are included.

LOWER BELVEDERE *Unteres Belvedere*
Belvedere Baroque Museum *Barockmusuem Belvedere*
    1030, Rennweg 6
    ☎ 795 57 0
    Tues - Sun 10 AM - 5 PM
    www.belvdere.at

This museum can be reached from the Upper Belvedere through the palace gardens. It contains Austrian Baroque art from the 17th and 18th centuries, including the works of artists such as Georg Raphael Donner, Franz Anton Maulbertsch and Paul Troger. Its orangery is a museum of medieval Austrian art.

OTHER MUSEUMS

 For addresses, phone numbers and opening hours for the following locations, see the "Museums" brochure from the Vienna Tourist Information Office (see Info Offices appendix).

- The *Albertina* contains a world-renowned collection of graphic arts; especially valuable is its Dürer collection. Due to restoration projects from mid-1997 - 2000, its collections will be exhibited at the *Akademiehof* at 1010, Makartgasse 3.

- The **Museum for Applied Arts (*Museum für angewandte Kunst/MAK*)** is dedicated to the display of creatively designed objects of everyday life. It has collections of items such as Viennese porcelain, Venetian and old European glass, furniture, tapestries and carpets. Much of the museum's text is also in English. The MAK has a café/restaurant with a garden.

- The **Geymüller Summerhouse (*Geymüllerschlössl*)** is an extension of the MAK. It is the only fully furnished *Biedermeier* house in Austria open to the public.

- The **Museum of Modern Art (*Museum Moderner Kunst*)** in the Liechtenstein Palace and the **Museum of the 20th Century (*Museum des 20. Jahrhunderts*),** near *Südbahnhof*, both display modern art and host temporary exhibits.

- The **Museum Quarter (*Museumsquartier*)** formerly held the Court Stables that housed the horses and coaches for the Imperial Court in the early 18th century. It has recently reopened as a center for contemporary and performing arts. It accommodates the **Leopold Museum,** the **Austrian Archives of Photography** (a municipal hall of changing art exhibits and various cultural events), a **children's museum,** an **architectural center** and **media archives.** Eventually it will house the Museum of Modern Art/Ludwig Foundation, which is presently at Liechtenstein Palace.

- The **Museum of Military History (*Heeresgeschichtliches Museum*)** is located in the Armory. The building itself is interesting because of its architecture and marble halls. For centuries, the Imperial and Royal Army were the mainstay of both empire and dynasty. This museum is dedicated to the glory and tragedy of the emperor's soldiers and sailors. One of the many interesting artifacts on display is a Turkish tent from the siege of 1683. There is also a café.

- The **Academy of Fine Arts (*Akademie der bildenden Künste*)** was originally built and still functioning as a fine-arts academy; its collections include a famous Hieronymous Bosch triptych.

- The nearby **Historical Museum of the City of Vienna (*Historisches Museum der Stadt Wien*)** in Karlsplatz chronicles Vienna's history from early Neolithic times to the present. There are two 19th-century models of the city before and after the fortification walls came down.

- The **Jewish Museum of the City of Vienna (*Jüdisches Museum der Stadt Wien*)** documents the history of Jews in Vienna and hosts temporary exhibits as well.

- The Association of Visual Artists—the Vienna Secession—was founded in 1897 by 19 artists (among them were Gustav Klimt, Kolo Moser, Carl Moll and Josef Hoffmann). The *Secession* was built in 1898 and now hosts exhibitions of contemporary art. The 34-meter-long "Beethoven Frieze," by Gustav Klimt, is a special attraction. A brochure in German, English and French explains the significance of this monumental work.

- *Kunstforum Bank Austria,* a leader in private galleries, sponsors a variety of significant exhibits of 19th- and 20th-century international art.

- *KunstHausWien* is the black-and-white building with the uneven pavement around it. It houses the permanent exhibit of Viennese artist Friedensreich Hundertwasser's works and also hosts exhibits of major international artists.

- The modern frame of *Kunsthalle Wien* reflects the modern media of many contemporary art exhibits here. They have a website at www.kunsthallewien.at.

- The **Sigmund Freud Museum** is in what was his last apartment/office in Vienna. It contains photos, mementos and a video of him with family and friends.

- You can see hundreds of bears at the **Vienna Teddy Bear Museum (*Wiener Teddybären Museum*).**

- In the **Austrian Theater Museum (*Österreichisches Theatermuseum*),** located in the Baroque Palais Lobkowitz, you'll find costumes and set designs from Vienna's rich stage history. Younger visitors can go down a slide into the children's museum in the cellar.

ART GALLERIES

One of the more interesting aspects of Vienna's art scene is the city's many galleries, which exhibit and sell both older and contemporary works. In contrast to federally owned and sponsored museums, most of these galleries are privately owned. There are 155 listed in the yellow pages under *"Galerien."*

Entrance to galleries is free, and you can always ask to see some of their permanent stock. Exhibits change frequently, so look for listings in newspapers. A good reference is *"Schaufenster,"* a supplement in the Friday edition of the newspaper *Die Presse.* Other reputable newspapers may also have special sections on culture and art galleries. They are also listed in the monthly *Programm,* which is free from the Vienna Tourist Information Office (see Info Offices appendix). When visiting galleries, ask to have your name put on the mailing list so you can receive invitations to openings.

VIENNA'S ARCHITECTURE

Vienna is a city filled with architectural delights. Not only are the details intriguing, but the colors defy description. Although it's a treat just to walk through the city admiring buildings at random, those desiring a more directed view can pick up a free brochure (see beginning of this chapter). Buildings not to be missed include: **Secession, Kirche am Steinhof, Postsparkasse** (Old Post Office Building), **Looshaus** (the "house without eyebrows"), **Stadtbahn Pavillon Karlsplatz, Majolikahaus, Wohnhaus mit vergoldeten Medaillons von Kolo Moser** (House with Gold Medallions), **Vienna International Centre** (UNO-City), **Villa Wagner** (*Fuchs-Villa*), **Kirche Zur Heiligen Drei-faltigkeit** (*Wotruba-Kirche*) and the **Hundertwasser-Haus.** You can find details on many of these in *Vienna 1900: Architecture and Painting* (see Books appendix), which is sold in many museum shops.

MUSIC

Vienna is the capital of music. No other city in the world has been home to so many famous composers — **Mozart, Haydn, Beethoven, Schubert, Brahms, Bruckner, Mahler, Schönberg** and the **Strausses.** In Vienna, there is always a wide variety of performances to enjoy. The following are some of the more popular venues.

OPERA & OPERETTA

VIENNA STATE OPERA

VIENNA STATE OPERA *Wiener Staatsoper*
1010, Opernring 2
☎ 514 44 29-60

An Austrian state theater, this opera house rivals the greatest in the world, such as the New York Metropolitan, Milan's *La Scala* or London's Covent Garden. The season runs Sept - June with different performances every evening in the original language. You can get a yearly performance schedule (*Spielpläne*) just before the season begins in September from a Vienna Tourist Information Office (see Info Offices appendix) or the *Bundestheaterverband* (the *Volksoper* schedule is also included). Every New Year's Eve, the Vienna State Opera puts on a splendid production of Johann Strauss' famous operetta *Die Fledermaus*. At all performances, drinks and light snacks are available at intermission. Children's operas are performed at the tope of the opera in a specially designed theater.

VIENNA STATE OPERA TOURS

Forty-five-minute guided tours of the *Wiener Staatsoper* are offered on certain days in different languages. Because the schedule varies, call for information at ☎ 514 44 26-13 or ☎ 514 44 24-27.

OPERA APPRECIATION CLASSES

Study the story and music to great operas with your musical guide Prentiss Dunn, then go see them at the *Wiener Staatsoper*. Tickets for the opera studied are arranged for all class participants. Morning or evening classes are offered in informal apartment settings, usually with wine and cheese. No prior musical knowledge is necessary—many students started as total novices. For more information, call the AWA office at ☎ 320 14 95.

PEOPLE'S OPERA

PEOPLE'S OPERA *Volksoper*

1090, Währingerstrasse 78

Also an Austrian state theater, most of the *Volksoper*'s performances are operettas, with some musicals, light operas and ballets as well. Most performances are in German, although some are in Italian with German subtitles. You can book tickets for standing room the same day advance ticket sales start (see Getting Tickets section below). The box office opens one hour before the performance.

GETTING TICKETS

Tickets for Austrian State Theaters (*Wiener Staatsoper, Volksoper, Burgtheater, Akademietheater*) can be purchased at the theaters themselves or at the following locations:

FEDERAL THEATER ASSOCIATION/TICKET OFFICE
Bundestheaterverband/Bundestheaterkassen

1010, Goethegasse 1
☎ 514 44 29-60 or ☎ 514 44 29-59 (information)
Mon - Fri 8 AM - 6 PM
Sat, Sun, and holidays 9 AM - 12 PM
1st Saturday of the month 9 AM - 5 PM
☎ 513 15 13 (credit-card ticket reservations)
Mon - Fri 10 AM - 9 PM

You can buy tickets no earlier than one month before the performance until the performance date at the *Bundestheaterverband*. Those living in other Austrian provinces or overseas must send written ticket requests to the office no later than three weeks before the performance. You can also fax Statsoper at ☎ 514 44 29 69, and Volksoper at ☎ 51 444 36 69.

INFORMATION OFFICE IN THE ARCADES
WIENER STAATSOPER

1010, Kärntner Strasse 40
Mon - Fri 10 AM - one hour before performance, Sat 10 AM - 5 PM

You can buy advance tickets at this office and also get information on the *Wiener Staatsoper* and *Volksoper*.

WIEN TICKET PAVILLON

1010, Kärntner Strasse (outside *Staatsoper* gift shop)
Daily 10 AM - 7 PM

This office adds a six-percent service charge to the price of each ticket.

TICKETS BY TELEPHONE

☎ 513 15 13 or ☎ 514 44-0
Mon - Fri 10 AM - 6 PM, Sat, Sun 10 AM - noon

If you have a credit card (American Express, Diners Club, Eurocard/MasterCard, Visa and Air Plus), you can buy tickets by phone one month before the performance date. During the months of July and August they are closed, and you must order by fax (514 44 29-69).

Evening Box Offices

Box offices open one hour before the performance to sell any remaining tickets.

Ticket Agencies

Ticket agencies throughout the city also sell tickets, but at a 20-percent or more markup. It's a good idea to patronize the same agency in order to cultivate a relationship there. In Vienna, the cheapest seats are, of course, the hardest to get, so buy tickets as soon as they go on sale.

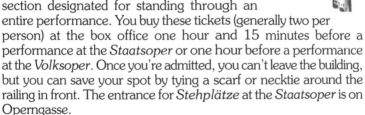

STANDING ROOM

No discussion of Vienna's musical scene would be complete without addressing the unique institution of standing room (*Stehplätze*), where you buy a ticket for ATS 20 or ATS 30 for a section designated for standing through an entire performance. You buy these tickets (generally two per person) at the box office one hour and 15 minutes before a performance at the *Staatsoper* or one hour before a performance at the *Volksoper*. Once you're admitted, you can't leave the building, but you can save your spot by tying a scarf or necktie around the railing in front. The entrance for *Stehplätze* at the *Staatsoper* is on Operngasse.

One constant rule is that the more famous the singer, the earlier you must arrive for tickets. In the summer, when a star is performing, the line can start forming the night before ticket sales. People bring sleeping bags and get to know other "cheap opera buffs." You can also get a *Stehplatz* at the *Raimundtheater* and the *Theater an der Wien*. Both have different procedures, so check before you go.

In the summer, the Roman Ruins in the Schönbrunn Palace gardens are transformed into a stage for open-air opera productions. For tickets and information, call the **Vienna Chamber Opera (*Wiener Kammeroper*)** at ☎ 513 60 72 or fax 512 01 00.

The **Marionette Theater at Schloss Schönbrunn (*Schönbrunner Schloss-Marionettentheater*)** performs *The Magic Flute* (*Die Zauberflöte*), *and other operas and operettas*. For more information, call ☎ 817 32 47 or visit their website at www.marionettentheater.at.

CONCERT HALLS

MUSIKVEREIN

MUSIC SOCIETY *Musikverein*
    1010, Bösendorferstrasse 12
    ☎ 505 81 90
    Cashier 1010, Karlsplatz 6
    ☎ 505 81 90
    Fax 505 81 90 94
    Mon - Fri 9 AM - 7:30 PM, Sat 9 AM - 5 PM

The beautiful and prestigious Main Hall (*Grosser Saal*) is familiar to international TV audiences because of the annual New Year's concert broadcasts. The *Brahms-Saal* hosts mainly chamber-music performances and *Lieder* recitals. Tickets are available one month in advance for members and three weeks in advance for everyone else at the cashier (*Kassa*), though you might consider buying a subscription series (*Abonnement*). A schedule for the season is available at the *Kassa*, or a monthly listing of concerts is in *Programm* (see beginning of chapter).

KONZERTHAUS

CONCERT HOUSE *Konzerthaus*
    1030, Lothringerstrasse 20
    ☎ 718 9 718 (information only)
    Mon - Fri 9 AM - 7:45 PM, Sat 9 AM - 1 PM
    Sat - Sun & Holidays 45 minutes before concert
    eMail ticket@konzerthaous.at
    www.konzerthaus.at

First-class musicians perform everything from classical to jazz in either the *Grosser Saal*, *Mozart-Saal* or *Schubert-Saal*. Tickets are available three weeks before from the *Konzerthaus* ticket office or from Tickets by Telephone (see Getting Tickets section).

TICKET TRANSPORTATION BONUS

Performance tickets stamped *"Fahrausweis Kernzone 100"* ("Travel ID Card for Zone 100") also can be used for public transportation, valid from two hours before the performance until six hours after the starting time.

Subscriptions (*Abonnements*) at the *Musikverein* and *Konzerthaus*

You can reserve tickets for a series of concerts well in advance by getting an *Abonnement*. The concerts are categorized in groups, each described as a cycle (*Zyklus*). Each *Zyklus* consists of a series of four to eight concerts (e.g., chamber concerts, *Oratorios*, *Lieder* concerts, major symphonies) spread throughout the year.

If concerts are your passion, consider becoming a member of the music society that promotes concerts, *Gesellschaft der Musikfreunde*, *Musikvereinsgebäude*. Membership, which costs ATS 960, entitles you to reduced ticket prices and a monthly program. You decide in advance which *Zyklus* interests you, then reserve your tickets and pick them up in person from the box office or have them mailed to you (see address and telephone numbers for the *Musikverein*). A season's schedule is available from the *Musikverein* cashier (*Kassa*).

Membership in the Wiener Konzerthausgesellschaft costs ATS 550 for adults, ATS 250 for youths. The season runs July 1 to June 30.

Vienna has numerous high-caliber solo musicians and musical groups offering concerts in various venues according to group and date. The most reliable source of information on all the available opportunities is the "Concerts" section of the monthly *Programm* (see beginning of this chapter).

AUSTRIAN ORCHESTRAS

VIENNA PHILHARMONIC ORCHESTRA *Wiener Philharmoniker*
1010, Bösendorferstrasse 12
☎ 505 65 25

Famous not only for its New Year's concert televised all over the world, the *Wiener Philharmoniker* is an institution. A concert subscription—let alone a ticket—is often hard to come by. The philharmonic performs in Vienna several times a year, giving a pair of concerts: the traditional Saturday-afternoon and Sunday-morning performances. These are held at the *Musikverein, Grosser Saal*. There are a few extra concerts each season that are not part of the subscription; call the *Musikverein* or the *Konzerthaus* for details. Don't despair if you can't get tickets because you can at least hear portions of the Sunday-morning performances on Austrian Radio 1 (92 FM or 87.8 FM).

Other notable groups offering performances in Vienna include the *Wiener Symphoniker*, the Vienna Radio Symphony Orchestra (*Radio Symphonieorchester Wien*), the Viennese Chamber Orchestra (*Wiener Kammerorchester*), the Lower Austria Orchestra (*Niederösterreichische Tonkünstler*), the *Wiener Hofburg Orchestra*, the *Wiener Mozart Orchestra* and the *Vienna Walzer Orchestra*. At the Operetta Gala in *Palais Ferstel*, you can hear famous Austrian music in a romantic setting. Check *Programm* for details.

JEUNESSE MUSICALE *Musikalische Jugend Österreichs*
☎ 505 63 56
Fax 505 82 77
Mon - Fri 12 AM - 7:30 PM

These concerts at the *Musikverein* are intended for people 26 and younger. If you're older (and a concert isn't sold out), you can buy tickets at a 50-percent markup at the box office.

THEATERS FOR MUSICALS

For the following theaters, bookings in person are recommended—at least until you become familiar with the theater layout.

RONACHER
1010, Seilerstätte 9
☎ 514 02
Performances Tues - Fri 7:30 PM, Sat 3 PM & 7:30 PM, Sun 5 PM

Seeing this beautifully renovated theater is almost as much of a treat as the performances here.

For both of the following theaters, call ☎ 588 85 for tickets. The operator answers, *"Vereinigte Bühnen Wien,"* which is an association of these two theaters. Don't be deterred, as this is the line for credit-card ticket reservations.

RAIMUNDTHEATER	THEATER AN DER WIEN
1060, Wallgasse 18-20	1060, Linke Wienzeile 6

CHURCH MUSIC *Kirchenmusik*

VIENNA BOYS' CHOIR *Wiener Sängerknaben*
1010, *Hofburg, Burgkapelle, Schweizerhof*
☎ 533 99 27
Performance 9:15 AM (in the *Burgkapelle*)
Ticket sales Fri 11 AM - 1 PM and 3 PM - 5 PM

The choir sings Mass every Sunday in the Imperial Chapel (*Burgkapelle*), accompanied by the Imperial Band (*Hofmusikkapelle*) and State Opera Orchestra and Men's Choir. Standing room is free, but you can buy tickets for seats the Friday before by standing in front of the Renaissance door at the *Burgkapelle*. However, because tickets are scarce, you'll have better luck booking through a ticket agent (expect a 22-percent markup). There are no performances July - Aug. Twice a year, May - June and Sept - Oct, the choir sings every Friday afternoon in the *Konzerthaus*. For tickets, contact the following travel agency:
REISEBÜRO MONDIAL
1040, Faulmanngasse 4
☎ 588 04-141
Fax 587 12 68
eMail: ticket@mondial.at

You can also hear Masses sung by other choirs at the St. Augustine Church (*Augustinerkirche*) on Sunday at 11 AM, at the University Church (*Universitätskirche*) on Sunday at 10 AM and at St. Stephan's Cathedral (*Stephansdom*) on Sunday at 11 AM.

CONCERT CAFÉS *Konzertcafés*

Vienna has many *Konzertcafés*, where a pianist, a pianist and a violinist or a trio plays. Check the monthly *Programm* for places and times.

HEURIGEN MUSIC *Schrammelmusik*

Visit any *Heurigen* (see *Heurigen* section of Dining chapter), and you'll probably hear the jovial tunes of this truly Viennese institution. *Schrammelmusik* usually consists of an accordion player and a violinist playing traditional songs and lively guests willing to sing along.

SPECIAL EVENTS

In addition to the following information, see the Holidays section of the Austria chapter.

Vienna Festival Weeks *Wiener Festwochen*

1010, Lehárgasse 11
☎ 589 22 0
Fax 589 22 49
www.festwochen.or.at

This arts festival takes place in late spring and includes art exhibitions and musical and theatrical performances. You can pick up a schedule from any Vienna Tourist Information Office (see Info Offices appendix) and order tickets directly as soon as the program comes out in December.

City Hall Film Festival *Rathaus-Filmfest*

1010, Rathausplatz
☎ 40 00 81-00
July - Aug

In midsummer a huge movie screen is set up in front of the *Rathaus* so people can watch free films of award-winning operas, concerts and ballets. Films begin at dusk, weather permitting. Several hundred seats are set up, which can be reserved by tying a scarf or laying a jacket on them.

International-Food Stalls

During the *Rathaus-Filmfest*, stalls sell international food and drinks. Take a look around and when you've decided what you want, pay the cashier for that stall, then stand in line to collect the food.

Vienna's New Year's Eve
Wiener Stadtsilvester

First district

On New Year's Eve, you can brush up on your waltzing in a heated tent in Vienna's *Neuer Markt* square 2 PM - 5 PM with the help of dance instructors. A New Year's Trail winds through the streets of the first district with stalls every few meters selling beer, wine, champagne (*Sekt*) and snacks. Viennese pubs (*Beisln*) also serve special New Year's Eve food and drinks. You can pick up a *Silvester* schedule from any Vienna Tourist Information Office (see Info Offices appendix).

Vienna Jazz Music Festival *Internationales Musikfest Jazz-Frühling*

JAZZ FEST WIEN
1090 Wien
Nußdorferstrasse 38
☎ 319 06 06
www.viennajazz.org

This jazz concert, which usually takes place in May at the *Wiener Konzerthaus*, hosts such famous jazz artists as Max Roach, Lionel Hampton and Sonny Rollins. You can get a schedule from the *Konzerthaus*.

Vienna Spring Festival
Wiener Frühlingsfestival
WIENER KONZERTHAUS
1037 Wien
Postfach 140
☎ 712 12 11
Fax 712 28 72
www.konzerthaus.at

Fast becoming a Viennese tradition, the *Wiener Konzerthaus* has held annual spring festival featuring classical-music concerts. This usually occurs May - June. You can pick up a schedule in early March and book the first concert at the *Konzerthaus* box office from March 20. Telephone booking begins March 21. Mailed ticket requests need to reach the *Konzerthaus* three weeks before the first concert.

ENGLISH-LANGUAGE THEATERS

Vienna's theaters offer a wide variety of performances, with the *Burgtheater* being one of the premier German-language theaters. However, if understanding a play in German is a problem, there are also three theaters here that perform works in English throughout the year.

VIENNA'S ENGLISH THEATRE
1080, Josefsgasse 12
☎ 402 12 60 or ☎ 402 82 84
Box office Mon - Fri 10 AM - 5 PM

This theater presents a minimum of five plays in English annually. Performances run Mon - Sat at 7:30 PM. Actors are from professional U.S. and U.K. companies. The theater also offers a discount on series subscriptions. Performance details are available at the theater and in newspapers and *Programm*. The box office will reserve tickets to be picked up before the performance, but they will not accept credit cards.

INTERNATIONAL THEATER
1090, Porzellangasse 8 (entrance on Müllnergasse)
☎ 319 62 72
Fax 310 89 97
Mon - Fri 11 AM - 3 PM

This is an American company that performs contemporary plays in English. It's a small theater, so you should reserve in advance (reservations accepted daily after 1 PM). Performances are usually Tues - Sat at 7:30 PM.

THE FUNDUS
1090, Müllnergasse 6A
☎ 319 62 72
Fax 310 89 97

This is a smaller theater affiliated with the International Theater. Performances are usually Tues - Sat at 7:30 PM.

CINEMAS/MOVIE THEATERS
Kinos

The phrase *"Film in Originalfassung mit deutschen Untertiteln"* means "movie in original format with German subtitles." Some newspaper listings print *"OV,"* which means "original version" or *"OMU,"* which means *"Original mit Untertiteln"* ("original with subtitles"). Consult your local *Kino* or newspaper listings for current movies and show times. If it is a new release or a popular movie, you should reserve tickets or buy them in advance. Your ticket is for a specific seat; the price varies according to the row (*Reihe*). The following are *Kinos* that feature movies in English or in their original language:

BURG-KINO
1010, Opernring 19
☎ 587 84 06

FILMMUSEUM
(famous old movies)
1010, Augustinerstrasse 1
☎ 533 70 54

STADTKINO
(German subtitles)
1030, Schwarzenbergplatz 7-8
☎ 712 62 76 0

FILMCASINO
1050, Margaretenstrasse 78
☎ 587 90 62

ENGLISH CINEMA HAYDN
1060, Mariahilfer Strasse 57
☎ 587 22 62
This *Kino* also offers discounted tickets on movies before 5 PM on weekdays.

FLOTTEN CENTER
1060, Mariahilfer Strasse 85-87
☎ 586 51 52

TOP KINO CENTER
1060, Rahlgasse 1
(near Mariahilfer Strasse)
☎ 587 55 57

FILMHAUS KINO
1070, Spittelberggasse 3
☎ 522 48 16

DE FRANCE
1090, Schottenring 7
☎ 317 52 36

VOTIV KINO
1090, Währinger Strasse 12
☎ 317 35 71

IMAX FILMTHEATER
1140, Mariahilfer Strasse 212
☎ 894 01 01

 DISCOUNT MOVIE TICKETS
Some *Kinos* offer reduced-rate tickets for full-length films on Monday nights.

The narration is in German, but the films are so visual that you don't need words to feel you're part of the action. The program varies, so pick up a brochure at any Vienna Tourist Information Office (see Info Offices appendix).

SPECIAL POINTS OF INTEREST

SPANISH RIDING SCHOOL
Spanische Reitschule

1010, Michaelerplatz 1
Training sessions
Tues - Sat 10 AM - noon
(no reservations)
Training with music
Sat 10 AM - 11 AM
(reservations necessary)
Performances
Sun 10:45 AM
(when they are in town)

Trained in an *haute école* unequaled in the world, the famous Lipizzaner horses are housed in one of Vienna's most elegant halls, the *Spanische Hofreitschule* in the *Hofburg*. The school maintains the classic and ceremonial riding traditions with riders still dressed in 17th-century-style Spanish costumes. The school's name, in fact, reflects the Habsburgs' respect for the riding style of and its relationship with the Spanish court during that period. They are frequently on tour, so check the brochure available at the Vienna Tourist Information Office (see Info Offices appendix) for exact dates, times and procedures.

You can mail or fax a written request for tickets in advance to the following:

SPANISCHE REITSCHULE
Hofburg
1010 Wien
Fax 535 01 86

You also can go to the ticket office at 1010, Michaelerplatz 1. It's extremely difficult to obtain tickets so make plans early. Reservations for weekday performances are only available from booking offices and travel agencies at a 25-percent markup.

URANIA OBSERVATORY
Urania-Sternwarte

1010, Uraniastrasse 1 (Urania building)
☎ 729 54 94 (recording in German with specific programs and viewings)
☎ 712 61 91-15 (to confirm viewing schedule)
Wed, Fri, Sat 8:30 PM (April - Sept 9 PM); closed August

Call the second number to arrange special programs. The cost for telescope viewing is nominal.

CENTRAL CEMETERY
Zentralfriedhof

1110, Simmeringer Hauptstrasse 234

There are many famous people buried or commemorated here, including Beethoven and Mozart. The time to visit is Nov 1 - 2 when graves are traditionally decorated for All Souls' Day. Enter through Door 2 (*Tor 2*).

MARXERFRIEDHOF
Mozart's Grave

A fabulously old cemetary on the way to the Central Cemetery on the last Strethof to Remnweg 1030, almost under the southeast tangent of the autobahn. Take the 71 streetcar from Schwarzenbergplatz.

One way to meet people who share common interests is through organizations. There are numerous opportunities for English speakers in Vienna to get together. Some groups focus on community service or professional issues, while others meet primarily for social reasons. Since the international community in Vienna is a fluid one, you should check with your embassy, school or church for additional information about new organizations.

The following is a list of organizations currently available for your participation or support.

THE AMERICAN WOMEN'S ASSOCIATION (AWA)

1190, Sieveringer Strasse 22A/1   www.awavienna.com
☎ 320 14 95   Mon - Thurs 9 AM - 3 PM
Fax 328 25 34   eMail awa@awavienna.com

The AWA of Vienna, which is a member of the Federation of American Women's Clubs Overseas (FAWCO), is a nonprofit organization founded to assist American women living in Vienna. Its purpose is to enable American and other English-speaking women to broaden their horizons while be-friending one another and to give them a better understanding of their host country. The AWA also actively raises funds for community and charitable organizations mainly in Austria.

Members receive a monthly magazine, *Highlights*, and are welcome to use AWA facilities. Many become involved in various activities (this book is the product of AWA volunteers). Others help organize events to raise funds (e.g., a holiday bazaar, the AWA Ball, a musical evening) for charities and groups that receive little or no government assistance. Women of all na-tionalities are welcome to join for an annual membership fee.

AWA Special-Interest Groups

AWA activity groups cover a wide range of interests, such as language and culture, parenting, health and sports, cooking and careers. The following are three special-interest groups.

DUAL CULTURAL PARTNERS

AWA Office   ☎ 320 14 95

Dual Cultural Partners addresses the needs of American and English-speak-ing women who are married to, or are dating, foreign nationals and are planning to primarily reside and raise their bilingual and bicultural children outside their home countries. Members vary in age and background. The group often invites guest speakers—including medical, financial and educa-tional professionals—to the monthly evening meetings to address issues of cross-cultural adaptation.

VIENNA HEALTH CARE PROFESSIONALS GROUP

AWA Office   ☎ 320 14 95

This group brings together expatriate health-care professionals such as doctors, registered nurses, pharmacists, dentists, physical therapists, speech therapists, social workers and health educators. Those who have lived in Austria longer can share experiences with newcomers. They also can help nonprofessionals with health-care questions. Monthly meetings held at the AWA office feature guest speakers who discuss health-care topics.

WOMEN'S CAREER NETWORK

AWA Office ☎ 320 14 95

The Women's Career Network serves as a resource and support network for women seeking to develop and expand their career opportunities. Monthly meetings are held at a hotel, and featured speakers address various topics pertaining to American and international women in the Austrian workplace.

OTHER ORGANIZATIONS

AFRO-ASIAN INSTITUTE
1090, Türkenstrasse 3
☎ 310 51 45
Mon - Fri 8:30 AM - 5 PM

The Institute sponsors cultural exchanges, support activities for Afro-Asian students in Vienna, cultural and educational programs and an art gallery at 1090, Schwarzspanierstrasse 15.

ANGLO-AUSTRIAN SOCIETY
1010, Stubenring 24
☎ 512 98 03-04

AUSTRALIAN WOMEN'S ASSOCIATION
Australian Embassy
1040, Mattiellistrasse 2-4
☎ 512 85 80

AUSTRIAN-AUSTRALIAN SOCIETY
1013, Postfach 2
☎ (02243) 817 13

AUSTRO-AMERICAN SOCIETY
1010, Stallburggasse 2
☎ 512 39 82
Mon - Thurs 9 AM - 5 PM,
Fri 9 AM - 3 PM

The society offers concerts, film screenings, lectures, German-language courses and guided tours.

AUSTRO-AMERICAN INSTITUTE OF EDUCATION
1010, Operngasse 4
☎ 512 77 20
eMail
amerika-institut@magnet.at
www.amerika-institut.at

This nonprofit organization promotes cultural interaction between the United States and Austria. Its activities include social gatherings, lectures, exhibits, film screenings and special seminars in English.

BIZEPS (*Zentrum für Selbstbestimmtes Leben*)
☎ 523 89 21-23
Fax 532 89 21-20
eMail bizeps@magnet.at

This is a complete resource for people dealing with a disability on a day-to-day basis. It is a support group for independent living run by and for people with disabilities. The staff is multilingual.

BRITISH COMMUNITY ASSOCIATION
British Embassy
1030, Jaurèsgasse 12
☎ 716 13 00

This is a social group of British passport holders offering various activities for all ages.

BEFRIENDERS
☎ 713 33 74

Befrienders is a confidential crisis-prevention hotline answered by English-speaking volunteers who try to help those going through a personal crisis or those at risk of taking their own lives. Callers can remain anonymous. Many who call do not have serious problems, but rather an accumulation of small troubles they need to get off their chests. Befrienders' volunteers do not counsel, give advice, solve problems or find jobs, money or friends for people. Rather, they offer the support and encouragement necessary to enable callers to make their own decisions.

Vienna's branch of Befrienders, in operation since 1977, has no political, philosophical or religious affiliation. Volunteers come from all countries and walks of life. It is a nonprofit organization financed by donations, sponsorships and fundraising events. The Vienna branch is a member of the London-based Befrienders International, an organization with more than 30,000 volunteers in more than 30 countries.

Trained volunteers are on duty daily, including holidays, 6:30 PM - 10 PM and Mon - Fri, 9:30 AM - 1 PM. Outside of these hours, you can leave a message on the answering machine and someone will get back to you.

BRUNO KREISKY FORUM FOR INTERNATIONAL DIALOGUE
1190, Armbrustergasse 15
☎ 318 82 60
email: kreiskyforum@kreisky.org
www.kreisky.org/kreiskyforum

The Kreisky Forum regularly invites internationally recognized politicians, business people and academics to participate in discussions, lectures and seminars. Call for more information about its open lectures.

CLUB INTERNATIONAL UNIVERSITAIRE (CIU)
1010, Schottengasse 1/ Mezzanine
☎ 533 65 33
Fax 533 65 33-9
Mon - Fri 9 AM - 8 PM

CIU is a focal point of international-student activity in Vienna, as well as a center of information on academic programs and scholarships. The organization sponsors lectures, debates, social events, courses and trips, which are advertised in local English-language newspapers (see Publications appendix). To receive the free monthly *CIU Bulletin*, call the number above.

CONTACT
☎ 714 67 20
Mon - Fri 9:30 AM - 1 PM, 6:30 PM - 10 PM

Contact is a community, or "good neighbor," group that helps newcomers settle in, sort out problems and meet other people who have similar interests. Though it's not an information service, Contact coordinators—who live in most districts and are familiar with Vienna and Austria—can help newcomers find the necessary information. Members are predominantly English speakers, but the group is intended for everyone in the international community. There is no membership fee.

ICH BIN O.K.
☎ 216 14 67

This is a cultural support organization integrating people with disabilities into theater, dance and other modes of expression. Although activities are conducted in German, there is usually someone who speaks English.

INTERNATIONAL INSTITUTE OF CONTEMPORARY MONTESSORI EDUCATION (IICME)
1010, Mahlerstrasse 9/13
☎ 512 87 33

This organization offers a Montessori teacher-training program.

INTERNATIONAL WOMEN'S COUNCIL
(formerly International Women's Center)
1190, Postfach 286

This organization has compiled a book entitled *Crisis in Vienna: A Resource Book to English-Language Services for Women and Children.*

JOY INTERNATIONAL
☎ 479 56 08

This group meets periodically for breakfast to help women find a meaningful life, a practical faith and a closer relationship with God. Meetings are presently held at the Hotel Modul, 1190, Peter-Jordan-Strasse 78.

LOLLIPOP PROJECT
Europa Schule
1200, Pöchlarnstrasse 12
☎ 330 31 52

This Vienna City School Board program recruits volunteers to help Austrian first- to fourth-graders learn English by introducing them to the rhythm, flow and sounds of English through songs, games and role playing.

TEACHERS OF ENGLISH IN AUSTRIA
1050, Kleine Neugasse 7/2A
Mon noon - 4 PM
Wed 2 PM - 4:30 PM

The membership fee covers subscriptions to two publications and selected discounts.

UNITED NATIONS WOMEN'S GUILD
1400, VIC, Postfach 400
Room F0919
☎ 2060 24276

The U.N. Women's Guild is an organization for women who want to help children in need and support mother/child-care programs throughout the world. It also allows women working for the United Nations or married to U.N. employees in Vienna to meet and share common interests.

U.S. CHAMBER OF COMMERCE
1090, Porzellangasse 35
☎ 319 57 51
Fax 319 51 51
eMail office@amcham.or.at
www.amcham.or.at

The Chamber of Commerce offers numerous publications, including the *U.S. List*, a directory of U.S. firms, subsidiaries, affiliates and licensees in Austria. The book is available to members for ATS 400 and to non-members for ATS 500. It is also available on CD-ROM to members for ATS 1.440 and to nonmembers for ATS 1.800.

ORGANIZATION OF LICENSED DENTAL HYGIENISTS IN AUSTRIA
(Verein der Diplomdentalhygienikerinnen in Österreich VDHÖ)
1190, Hutweidengasse 46/14/4
☎ 368 41 89

Hyacinth Logan is the contact person for this organization of registered dental hygienists.

VIENNA CHILDBIRTH TRUST
Janet Lacey
☎ 263 11 71

This organization offers information and support in pregnancy, childbirth and early parenthood to enable every parent to make informed choices. The VCT is affiliated with the United Kingdom-based National Childbirth Trust, Britain's leading organization concerned with prenatal and childbirth issues. The VCT provides a quarterly newsletter, monthly open meetings, weekly toddler activity sessions and breastfeeding information.

VIENNA TOASTMASTERS
Heidi Scheidl
☎ 817 04 97

This group works to develop better listening, thinking and speaking skills in an environment of team spirit and fun. This officially registered club of Toastmasters International presently meets at 7 PM every first and third Tuesday of the month at the Hotel Sofitel, 1030, Am Heumarkt 35-37.

VOLUNTEER OPPORTUNITIES

In addition to the organizations l⌐ earlier, the following English-lang⌐ schools accept volunteers to he⌐ the library, remedial-reading progr⌐ athletic programs and special activ⌐

INTERNATIONAL MONTESSORI PRE-SCHOO⌐
1010, Marc-Aurel-Strasse 5/16
☎ 533 20 24

DANUBE INTERNATIONAL SCHOOL (DIS)
1100, Gudrunstrasse 184
☎ 603 02 46

AMERICAN INTERNATIONA⌐ SCHOOL (AIS)
1190, Salmannsdorfer Strasse 4⌐
☎ 401 32-0

VIENNA CHRISTIAN SCHO⌐
1190, Kreilplatz 1/2
☎ 318 82 11

VIENNA INTERNATIONAL SCHOOL (VIS)
1220, Strasse der Menschenrech⌐
☎ 203 55 95

Vienna is wonderful to explore—part of the pleasure of living here is getting to know the city and its surrounding areas at your leisure. The first part of this chapter will help you find the information you need to travel and sightsee. Suggested excursions—some of which are not included in major guidebooks—are listed in the following section. These particular destinations were chosen because they embody Austria's richness and diversity and each sight has its own charm and unique attractions. Happy trails!

TOURIST INFORMATION

Vienna has many official tourist offices that provide information, maps, brochures and program guides for cultural events and festivals. The offices don't always have all the brochures on display, so if you want something you don't see, ask for it. You should also ask what information they have in English. (For addresses, see the Info Offices appendix, and for specific recommendations of brochures, see the Entertainment chapter.) In addition to these offices, many towns and villages in Austria have local tourist offices.

TRAIN EXCURSIONS

The **Train Station Travel Agency (*Reisebüro im Bahnhof*),** found at all Vienna's train stations, helps arrange train travel and accommodations (also tours, but these are in German). The train stations also have a variety of brochures (in German) on special train trips, including some on vintage trains and special ski trains during the winter. The **Austrian Train Timetable (*Fahrpläne Bahn Österreich*)** has all the train schedules for the year. It also has information on taking bikes on trains and stations that rent bikes and cars. There is a section in English on how to use the book. It's available every May for a fee at Vienna train stations.

WALKING TOURS

There are many different ways to get to know Vienna, both on organized tours and on your own. A map and a good guidebook (or two or three) are essential (see Books appendix). Vienna is a wonderful city to explore on foot. A number of the guidebooks provide walking- tour routes. Organized walking tours are available through the following two groups:

WALKS IN VIENNA (*Wiener Spaziergänge*)

A monthly multilanguage brochure called "Walks in Vienna" ("*Wiener Spaziergänge*") is available from any Vienna Tourist Information Office (see Info Offices appendix). There's no need to book in advance. Just show up at the designated meeting point (*Treffpunkt*) at the designated time (*Termine*). The brochure indicates which tours are also given in English, French or Italian. Tours last about one-and-a-half to two hours. Children under the age of 14 must be accompanied by an adult.

PERPEDES

☎ 544 96 68   Mobile 0664 301 76 05

This company offers walking tours for groups. Its brochure is available at Vienna Tourist Information Offices (see Info Offices appendix).

PRIVATE GUIDES

Vienna's tour guides are rightfully proud of their credentials, which result from a two-year intensive course leading to official certification. The following women are English-speaking guides who are knowledgeable, multilingual and enthusiastic:

HEBE JEFFREY
☎ 876 71 11
Fax & Handy 0676 402 33 30

SUSAN DE HEINRICH
☎ 877 37 24
Fax: 877 372 42
Mobile: 0676 317 29 02
eMail hit@aon.at

EDITH KUDLAK
☎ 319 07 76
Fax 319 07 76

IRENE JENKINS
☎ & Fax 877 13 19
eMail jenkins@netway.at

DR. CYNTHIA PROSSINGER
☎ & Fax 581 43 18

TOUR COMPANIES

A ride on tram (*Strassenbahn*) 1 or 2 around the Ring will introduce you to the first district, but if you'd like a more formal tour, ask at the Vienna Tourist Information Office (see Info Offices appendix) or call one of the following tour companies:

TYROLIAN TOURS
6372, Oberndorf, Tirol, PO Box 6
☎ 05352 631 34 or 05352 626 50, Fax 05352 653 90
Mon - Fri 9 AM - 5 pm · www.tyroliantours.com
TyrolianToursAustria@compuserve.com

Specialized in organizing winter/skiing holidays in the province of Tirol (Kitzbuehel area) for American citizens. Special offers for families, including nursery facilities, ski kindergarten, plus ski lessons from complete beginners to „experts". A variety of accomodations are available- from self catering apartments to excellent hotels with a meal plan. Within a radius of 15 miles, there are more than 200 lifts!

ELITE TOURS
　　1010, Operngasse 4
　　☎ 513 22 25
　　Fax 513 85 26
　　Mon - Sat 9 AM - 6 PM
You can also book tours with this company through ticket agents. They take credit cards.

VIENNA SIGHTSEEING TOURS
　　1030, Stelzhamergasse 4
　　☎ 712 46 83
　　Fax 714 11 41
　　Daily 6:30 AM - 7:30 PM
　　(April - Oct),
　　Mon, Wed, Thurs, Sun
　　6:30 AM - 4:30 PM
　　(Nov - March),
　　Tues, Fri, Sat
　　6:30 AM - 7:30 PM

CITYRAMA TOURS
　　1010, Börsegasse 1
　　☎ 534 13-0
　　Fax 534 13-16
　　Daily 6:30 AM - 8 PM

EUROPEAN TOURING PROGRAM RCV CAREY LIMOUSINE
　　1300 Flughafen Wien (arrival area), P.O. Box 158
　　☎ 7007 33 40
　　Fax 700 33 77
　　Mon - Sat 6 AM - 10 PM,
　　Sun 9 AM - 7 PM
This company offers deluxe city-tour packages and takes care of all the details for those interested in luxury travel. It accepts all credit cards.

BUS, CARRIAGE, BIKE, TRAM & BOAT TOURS

Bus-tour tickets can be purchased at any Austrian travel agency. The most conveniently located ones are in the *Oper-Karlsplatz* underground passage and in the ticket office next to the Vienna Tourist Information Office (see Info Offices appendix).

Horse-drawn carriages (*Fiaker*) stationed beside St. Stephen's Cathedral (*Stephansdom*), on Heldenplatz (at the *Hofburg*) and in front of the *Albertina* can also take you on a tour of the city. Be sure to agree on the route, price and duration before you leave.

Vienna Bike ☎ 319 12 58 provides a recording in German. (For details, you can fax to the same number using English) Offers guided city tours on bicycles.

Old-time tram rides, available Sat - Sun & Holidays, May - Oct, start at the *Otto Wagner Stadtbahn* pavilion at Karlsplatz and go along the Ringstrasse to the *Prater*. For times and information, call ☎ 790 94 49 03.

Boat tours on the Danube (*Donau*) start at Sweden Bridge (Schweden-brücke) on the Danube Canal (*Donaukanal*). DDSG (☎ 588 80, Fax 588 80 440, Mon - Fri, 9 AM - 6 PM) offers tours on the *Vindobona*, a boat designed by the late Viennese architect and artist Friendensreich Hundertwasser. Schedules are available at *Schwedenbrücke.* Donau Schiffahrt Pyringer-Zopper (☎ 715 15 25-18, -20, fax 715 15 25-17, Mon - Fri, 8 AM - 4 PM) offers three-and-a-half-hour tours along the *Donau* and the main channel of the *Donau* May - Oct.

A CASTLE CLOSE TO HOME

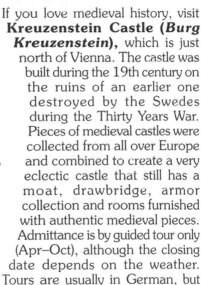

If you love medieval history, visit **Kreuzenstein Castle (*Burg Kreuzenstein*),** which is just north of Vienna. The castle was built during the 19th century on the ruins of an earlier one destroyed by the Swedes during the Thirty Years War. Pieces of medieval castles were collected from all over Europe and combined to create a very eclectic castle that still has a moat, drawbridge, armor collection and rooms furnished with authentic medieval pieces. Admittance is by guided tour only (Apr–Oct), although the closing date depends on the weather. Tours are usually in German, but some of the guides speak English. If you want to ensure a tour in English, call ☎ 02262 661 02 a week ahead to make arrangements. Private tours can also be arranged even after the winter closing date. The gates at the drawbridge are often closed between tour times, so you can either wait until they open or ring the bell to the left of the gate.

To get to **Burg Kreuzenstein,** follow the A-22 *Autobahn* to Korneu-burg and then follow the signs to Leobendorf. You can also get there on the *Schnellbahn* 3 from Landstrasse (*Wien Mitte*) to the Leobendorf station. Cross the tracks and follow the road and the signs to the castle. It's a 30- to 45-minute walk up the hill through vineyards and woods to the castle.

WOODS & VINEYARDS
SOUTH OF VIENNA

The area immediately south of Vienna is a combination of castles, an underground lake, vineyards and charming villages, which can be reached on the *Schnellbahn* 2 from *Südbahnhof*. There are also many walking paths between the villages and towns.

For an enjoyable driving tour, take the A-2 in the direction of Graz and then take the right fork toward Linz-St. Pölten (A-21). Take the Giesshübl exit and turn left, following the signs to **Liechtenstein Castle (Burg Liechtenstein),** built in the early 1800s by the Liechtenstein family.

For an impressive photo, walk through the meadow, instead of the path, toward the castle, which is open daily, from March 27th to October, 9:30 AM - 5 PM. The exterior was used in the 1990 Disney movie remake of *The Three Musketeers*. The chapel dates back to 1065 and the basic foundation to the 1400s. Be sure to check out the chaplain's private privy (toilet), the only one on the premises. It hangs out over the wall and can be seen from the outside once you've located it inside.

You can tour the castle on your own or arrange in advance for a paid guided tour in English by calling ☎ 02236 442 94; eMail: info@burgliechtenstein.com. Plans are under way to offer a self-guided audio tour in German and English. Also on the grounds are several ruins that were built that way in the early 1800s, a playground with a lot of open area and several kilometers of paths. There are also a restaurant in the *Schloss* and a *Burg-Buffet*, which is open on weekends.

As you leave Burg Liechtenstein, turn left on Johannesstrasse and follow the signs to reach **Lake Grotto (Seegrotte),** which began as a gypsum mine in 1848 but was eventually closed due to flooding. For one year during World War II (1944 - 1945), it was pumped dry in order for concentration-camp prisoners to build jet-fighter fuselages. The Germans destroyed the factory, but renovation has taken it back to its old mining days. Open year-round, the lake can only be seen in organized tours, which are offered daily in English. For more information, call ☎ 02236 263 64. The tour of Europe's largest underground lake is chilly (9° C), even in the summer, so bring jackets (or rent blankets). As part of the tour, you'll ride on the lake and see some leftovers (a dragon-headed boat and dungeon cells) from the filming of *The Three Musketeers*. There is a little café at the entrance.

From the Seegrotte, take the Hauptstrasse-Brühler Strasse through the gorge along the Mödling brook. On the hill to your right is **Mödling Castle (*Burg Mödling*)** and on the left is **Black Tower (*Schwarzer Turm*),** which is one of the ruins built on the *Burg Liechtenstein* grounds in the early 1800s. At the intersection of Spitalmühlgasse and Neusiedlerstrasse, turn right in the direction of Gumpoldskirchen for a beautiful drive through the vineyards on Weinbergstrasse. Stop in **Gumpoldskirchen** to sample some of its famous wine at a new-wine tavern (*Heurigen*) and stroll through the quaint village center. The arcaded Renaissance town hall is surrounded by buildings dating back to the 16th century.

Continue to and through Baden by taking Dammgasse to its dead end on Zubringerstrasse. Turn right on Zubringerstrasse, left on Vöslauerstrasse (toward Sooss), then right on Hauptstrasse, which is the main street of **Sooss.** Visit one of the many *Heurigen* for some good red wines produced here. The main street is only one house deep on both sides, and the village is surrounded by vineyards.

Head back to Zubringerstrasse, turn left and follow signs to Helenental. Keep your eyes on the castle ruin of **Rauhenstein** on the right **(Rauheneck** is on the left). When you're below the ruin, park and follow Rauhensteingasse up a well-marked, short path (about 15 minutes) to the ruin, which is fun for children, with lots of rooms, holes and windows to climb through and a staircase leading up inside the tower. Keep your eyes and hands on any rambunctious group members, as the castle is built on a cliff.

Continue your drive into **Helenental,** with the **Schwechat River** on your left. There are numerous restaurants, most with outdoor seating, all along the drive. There are also places to park and take a walk across the river. You're now heading in the direction of **Mayerling,** site of the famous dramatic death of Crown Prince Rudolph and his lover, Baroness Mary Vetsera. To get back to Vienna, follow the *Autobahn* signs bringing you back to the A-21. If you follow the signs to Wien, it will take you to the A-2, or you can follow the signs to Linz as far as Steinhaus and then signs for Wien, which will put you on the A-1.

VIENNA'S NEAREST MOUNTAINS

RAXALPE

Accessible all year, but particularly enjoyable in warmer weather, the **Raxalpe,** 2,007 meters high, is worth a trip. This is a favorite fresh-air destination of the Viennese, with meadows carpeted by alpine flowers in spring and summer. The eight-minute cable-car (*Seilbahn*) ride goes to the Berggasthof Raxalpe (1,547 meters), from which you can stroll, hike or climb. The Berggasthof (1,664 meters) and the Karl-Ludwig Haus (1,804 meters) are open for meals all year, while the Ottohaus (1,644 meters) is closed in winter. There are numerous other small restaurants and *Schutzhütten* (literally "shelters," but they usually serve food) throughout the area. You can spend the night at several spots up here. For more information (English is spoken), call ☎ 02666 28 65 50 (Mon, Wed, Fri, 9 AM - noon, 3 PM - 5 PM), fax 02666 42 66 or check with Lower Austria Tourist Information (see Info Offices appendix).

When you get off the cable car at the top, note the little stamping machine. Although you can walk down (or up), if you've bought a two-way ticket (*Berg- und Talfahrt*), stamp your ticket when you're ready to leave, as this helps space out return rides on busy days. The cable car usually runs every 30 minutes but often runs more frequently if needed.

To get to the **Rax Seilbahn** by car, take the A-2 to Gloggnitz, then drive through Payerbach, Reichenau and Hirschwang, and park at the cable-car station. Or take the train to Payerbach and then either a bus to the *Seilbahn* station in **Hirschwang** or a taxi. Call ☎ 02666 28 65 to confirm the sporadic bus times or call a taxi at ☎ 02666 36 80 for the six-kilometer ride. The taxi has a fixed price (at time of publication ATS 120) for up to eight people. You can also make arrangements for the taxi to return you to the train.

For a uniquely Austrian experience, take the **Schneeberg Cog-Wheel Railway (*Schneeberg Zahnradbahn*)** from **Puchberg** up to **Schneeberg,** the highest mountain in Lower Austria (2,075 meters). For information, call ☎ 02666 52497. The 10-kilometer ride lasts nearly one-and-a-half hours and ends at the highest train station in Austria. When the train stops after an hour for water at the **Baumgartner** station (1,397 meters), join the flood of passengers into the small station to indulge in *Buchteln*, which are sweet buns filled with plum jam (*Powidlbuchtel*) or cream cheese (*Topfenbuchtel*). If you have a window seat, close the window as you approach the tunnels or your car will fill up with soot. The train then enters an alpine region of dwarf pine trees.

The **Elisabeth Chapel (*Elisabethkapelle*)**—built in 1900 in memory of Empress Elisabeth's murder in Geneva in 1898—is across from the end station and offers panoramic views. There are many kilometers of marked paths and several choices for a meal or drink close to **Fisherman's Hut (*Fischerhütte*),** which can be seen out on its perch from the **Rax.** Buy a good hiking map (available at the Puchberg station) if you plan to do extensive walking. No matter how nice a day, bring a backpack with a jacket and rain poncho, wear sturdy shoes—and don't pick the flowers!

You should reserve tickets in advance, particularly on weekends, because the trains are frequently sold out. If you plan to take the train back to **Puchberg**—rather than walk—be sure to book a time for your return. There are no reserved seats going up or down and parking can be difficult, so arrive at the Puchberg station before your scheduled time. If you arrive early, visit the park with a pond, playground and miniature golf course, which is a short walk from the station. The **Szabo Café-Konditorei** is Austria's largest handmade-marzipan producer, with a permanent marzipan and chocolate exhibit. Trains to Puchberg depart from *Südbahnhof* and the Meidling station. There is a special *Schneeberg-Wanderticket*, with reduced prices for departures from Vienna (late April–early Nov) and lunch at one of six places on Schneeberg. For times, prices and information, call ☎ 02636 22 25-0, or make reservations at one of Vienna's train stations. To drive, take the A-2 south, exit Wiener Neustadt or Neunkirchen and follow signs to Puchberg am Schneeberg.

SEMMERING

Just over an hour from Vienna, Maria Schutz and Schottwien in the **Semmering** region are great for a day of dramatic scenery and interesting history. Leave Vienna on the *Südautobahn* (A-2) in the direction of Graz as far as the Semmering exit. Continue toward Semmering and, as you cross the bridge, look for the castle ruin of **Klamm** on your right. Before reaching the town of Semmering, take a left to **Maria Schutz** and park near the imposing **Pilgrimage**

Church (*Wallfahrtskirche*), which was built in 1728. The original Baroque roof was destroyed by fire in 1826 and replaced with a simple pyramid style, but the original onion domes were not replaced until 1995. Walk behind the altar (except during Mass) to see the fountain fed by spring water. The water is not holy water, as it has not been blessed, but stories of its miraculous properties date back to the time of the Plague. There are plastic bottles sold at the rear of the church to collect water, or you can bring your own or drink from your hands. There is a well-stocked tourist shop next door and several restaurants nearby. The **Sonnwendstein** chair lift, about a block from the church, is open year-round. The view is spectacular, and you can ride or walk back down (or ski down in winter).

Continue along the same road, following signs to **Schottwien.** Until 1854, when the first European mountain railway was completed over the Semmering, Schottwien was an important way station where horses were changed (*Fuhrwerksort*). Goods and passengers arrived in Schottwien by wagon and, after staying overnight, the drivers hired extra horses to take them over the Semmering and often on to the harbor in Trieste. This was also the staging area for wealthy Viennese on their way to vacations in Italy. The town was filled with breweries, restaurants and stables. Many important visitors stayed in Schottwien, including Austrian rulers, Pope Pius VI (in 1782) and Napoleon. On both ends of town, you can see the remnants of the town gates, which were built in 1254 to facilitate toll collecting.

The lovely **St. Vitus Church (*Vituskirche*)** was built in 955 and destroyed by flooding in 1266. The Gothic church, rebuilt in the 14th century, still stands, with numerous and extensive restorations, including ones funded by the Liechtensteins in the late 1800s. Look for the Schottwien coat of arms around town. It's red with a blue roof and the letters AEIOU, motto of Friedrich III. You will find various interpretations in Latin and German, like *"Austria Est Imperare Orbi Universo"* and *"Alle Erde Ist Österreich Untertan,"* which roughly means "all the Earth is Austria's subject."

For a stunning view, drive to the **Castle Ruin of Klamm (*Burgruine Klamm*).** Follow signs to Kreuzberg and then **Klamm.** With a population of 177, it's only on detailed maps, although it has its own train station. Park at the church and take the narrow path along the right side of the ruin to reach an outcropping with a fabulous view of the entire area. Keep an iron grip on children, as the path is along a very high cliff.

The ruin is privately owned, so the interior is closed to the public. The balls you see implanted in the castle wall, and one in the house across the street from the church, are remnants of Turkish invasions. In the churchyard is a memorial to the more than 1,000 workers who died while building the Semmering railway. Most of the deaths were due to disease, not accidents. There was fierce fighting in this area during the last days of World War II, taking a heavy toll on the local population. The German army fought to keep the Russians south of the Semmering so they could surrender to the Americans and go to their POW camps.

Drive back down into **Schottwien** and stop at **Brettner's Bräuerl,** ☎ 02663 88 73, open daily, 5 PM - midnight. It is the smallest, privately owned brewery in Austria. Ask for Brettner's *Fuhrmannsgold*, very pale and delicate, or a *Brettner's Malzerl*, somewhat darker, with a light malt flavor. Both are all-natural, unfiltered and have about an eight-week shelf life. The brewery is behind the bar, which is separately owned. Herr Brettner sells his beer to the bar owner and pipes it in directly from the brewery to the bar. You can take a tour of the brewery and the furniture exhibit upstairs (just ask for the key). The bar serves snacks, beer and some nonalcoholic beverages.

If you have time, drive to Semmering through Adlitzgraben, a romantic 12-kilometer ride along a brook **(Haidbach)** sandwiched between cliffs. Follow the signs from Schottwien. The entire area is filled with well-marked walking paths, which you should explore in the spring and summer. Call the Schottwien Municipal Office (*Gemeindeamt Schottwien*) at ☎ 02663 213 and ask for a walking tours brochure, which is in German but is very visual.

Another fabulous way to see more of this area is to take a train walking path (*Bahnwanderweg*). Take the train to Semmering, get off and walk back toward Vienna one or several stops along the marked paths and reboard at the station of your choice. The **"Bahnwanderweg-Historische Ghega-Semmeringbahn"** brochure, available from Lower Austria Tourist Information (see Info Offices appendix), details paths, distances, train stations and restaurants.

The entire Semmering area is criss-crossed with marked hiking paths for warm-weather activities and excellent skiing in the winter. For more information, call Tourism Region Lower Austria South (*Tourismusregion NÖ-Süd*) at ☎ 02664 25 39. They have no brochures in English.

WEINVIERTEL & WALDVIERTEL

The loose geographic area of the **Wine Quarter (*Weinviertel*)** is in the northeast, and the **Forest Quarter (*Waldviertel*)** is in the northwest section of **Lower Austria (*Niederösterreich*). Langenlois,** the largest wine village in Austria, is actually in the Waldviertel. Parts of the Weinviertel, like most of Austria, are forested. The following excursions are in the westernmost part of the Weinviertel and the Waldviertel.

RETZER LAND IN THE WEINVIERTEL

Leave Vienna on the *Autobahn* in the direction of Prague (*Prag/Praha*) and follow the signs to Stockerau, then Hollabrunn and Retz. You'll see increasingly greater numbers of small buildings, sometimes little more than doors, built into the hillsides. These are cellars for storing wine, and the streets they're located on are known as cellar lanes (*Kellergassen*).

Retz is the center of the loosely organized group of villages coming to be known as **Retzer Land.** It has one of the most spacious and imposing town squares in Austria. Most of the buildings date back to the second half of the 1600s or later. The Swedes occupied Retz for a year (1645 - 1646) during the Thirty Years War (1618 - 1648) and destroyed all but 28 buildings. Several of the buildings are particularly interesting: *Sgraffito* building, 1576, painted with Greek fables and biblical themes; *Verderberhaus,* 1583, with a pewter roof; Dominican Church, 1295; and City Hall (*Rathaus*), 1569. The old city wall dates back to about 1300 and is surrounded by a moat.

Underground **Retz** is a fascinating labyrinth of tunnels and cellars, some dating from the 13th century, which are used by the local vintners. The tunnels cover a distance of 16 to 25 kilometers and may be as deep as 20 meters underground to ensure a constant temperature. The exact total length has never been measured, as the vintners simply dig out a little more when they need more space. Excavated out of a deep sand layer, which can actually be dug by hand, some of these tunnels are still used. Many of the cellars have been lined with brick in the past two centuries (mostly as a sign of wealth), though the original sand tunnels and cellars were perfectly safe. The ground level is covered with air shafts. Stop at the information center or at the Rathaus to buy tickets for a tour or for information about the cellars. For more information, call or see Ofice of the Tourist Association, 2070 Retz, Hauptplatz 30, ☎ 02942 27 00.

There is an operational windmill just north of town at **Kalvarienberg.** It's the town symbol and was used in *The Three Musketeers*. Also outside the town are marked walking paths through the vineyards (*Weinwanderung*) with information signs and a large copper statue of *Reblaus*, the aphid-like pest (*phylloxera*) that destroyed Austria's (and much of Europe's) vineyards in the late 19th and early 20th centuries. (The solution to this pest was to graft European vines onto American root stock.) On the road between **Unterretzbach** and **Klein-haugsdorf** is a monument built during the Iron Curtain era, which Austrians used to climb to see what was then Czechoslovakia.

Every October one of the villages in **Retzer Land** hosts a two-day **Pumpkin Festival (*Kürbisfest*).** There are literally thousands of jack-o'-lanterns, a pumpkin patch, folk-art and crafts booths, and dozens of pumpkin-based products, from punch to waffles. Call the Retzer Land Tourist Bureau at ☎ 02942 200 10 for the exact location and weekend.

WALDVIERTEL

For a real change from city life, you can't beat a day or weekend in the scenic **Waldviertel.** The area offers excellent wine, falconry exhibits and beautiful castles. The first stop is **Langenlois,** just north of Krems. Take the A-2 to St. Pölten and go north, or take the A-22 toward Stockerau in the direction of Krems and then to Langenlois, the largest wine-growing town in Austria with 6,000 acres of vineyards.

The main square is lovely, and the surrounding lanes lend themselves to a leisurely stroll, especially along the brook (the **Loisbach**—hence the name Langenlois, which means "the long town along the Lois"). Park in the free short-term parking (*Kurzparkzone*), but be sure to first get a cardboard parking clock (*Parkuhr*) at the nearby *Tabak-Trafik*. Set it for the time you arrive, and return before the posted time limit has expired.

Be sure to visit the **Ursin-Haus** at Kornplatz 5/Kamptalstrasse 3, which is open Mon - Fri, 10 AM - noon, 1 PM - 6 PM, Sat - Sun, 10 AM - 6 PM. One of the best local tourist offices around, it has a *Vinothek* where you can sample local wines, sparkling wines, brandies and liqueurs (at a reasonable price per sample), and then buy any if you wish. They will also provide tours, wine seminars, wine-cellar visits and wine tastings in English if you make arrangements in advance. For more information, call ☎ 02734 20 00, Mon - Fri, 8 AM - noon, 2 PM - 6 PM, or ☎ 02734 20 17 before noon.

At this point, you have a choice; you can drive southwest to Krems and Melk, or up the Kamp River. From Krems, it is a short and scenic drive to Melk. The 900-year-old abbey (*Stift*), built high above the Danube at Melk, is widely acclaimed as containing the loveliest Baroque buildings in Austria, or even Europe. Today it serves primarily as a secondary school and museum. Its extensive library contains about 100,000 volumes, including 1,200 from the ninth through the fifteenth centuries, and several early manuscripts are on display. Ceiling frescos painted by Paul Tröger in 1731-32 can be seen in many of the magnificent rooms. A restaurant and snack bar are on the premises, or one can visit the charming town of Melk, which rests at the foot of the abbey.

Alternatively, you can head north along the **Kamp River** to **Gars am Kamp** and follow signs to Thunau and then to the **Gars Castle Ruin (*Burgruine Gars*).** This is really a ruin—with no souvenir shop or tours. Just put a donation in the box on the wall and wander around. Construction began in 1075 and it was inhabited until 1773. Restaurant Pfiffig is on the premises, and it is open year-round Wed - Sun, 11 AM - 2 PM, 6 PM - midnight. For reservations, call ☎ 02985 305 00. A very popular open-air opera is staged here annually late July - Aug. For information and tickets, call ☎ 02985 26 80 (Mon - Fri, 8 AM - noon).

Just north of Gars, you come to **Rosenburg,** which is open from the beginning of April - mid-Nov. You can tour the museum and renovated castle, which dates back to the 12th century. There are falconry shows daily with participants in medieval garb. For more information (in German only), call ☎ 02982 29 11 or ☎ 02982 23 03.

The drive west along the Kamp River and several reservoirs (*Stausee*) brings you to **Zwettl,** the geographic center of the Waldviertel. The recent renovation of the main street and square, and the 1994 addition of a Hundertwasser-designed fountain, make this a charming place to visit. Parts of the old town wall and defense towers still stand. Just less than three kilometers west of Zwettl is the famous **Stift Zwettl,** a Cistercian abbey, founded in 1138. Guided tours are offered regularly. The abbey has its own boys' choir, the *Zwettler Sängerknaben*.

Southwest of Zwettl on Route 38 is the picturesque castle of ***Rappottenstein.*** Call ☎ 02828 250 to arrange tours in English (May - Sept). Go northwest to **Gmünd,** at the Czech border, where you'll find two painted houses (*Sgraffito*). Follow signs to the *Naturpark Blockheide Eibenstein* on the edge of town. It's open all year, although the way is tough to negotiate in snow. It has an observation tower and kilometers of paths, but the big attraction is the enormous granite boulders that you can climb. A narrow-gauge steam train runs May-Oct from **Gmünd** to **Gross Gerungs,** 43 kilometers to the south. The ride is about two hours, and you can get on and off at any number of stations. The times are limited, and reservations are suggested. For information in German, call the *Gmünd Bahnhof* at ☎ 02852 525 88 33-0.

If you're interested in the ornate painted houses (*Sgraffito*) of this area, a detour to **Weitra,** southwest on Route 41, will be worth your time. Otherwise, drive northeast to **Heidenreichstein**, ☎ 02862 522 68, which is considered Austria's best-preserved moated castle. This massive castle, completed in 1160, was never captured. You can only see the castle on tours, which are given daily on the hour, except Monday, mid-Apri - mid-Oct. Although they are only in German, there is information in English that you can read during the tour. The castle closes for lunch, noon - 2 PM.

Just south of Heidenreichstein is the **Naturpark Hochmoor,** an area of natural moors. To round out an educational experience, there is a prize-winning **Peat and Bog Museum (*Torf-und-Moormuseum*)** in town, which is open weekend and holiday afternoons 2 PM - 4 PM (April - Oct). For more information, call ☎ 02862 525 06.

Head back to Vienna via Waidhofen-Horn-Stockerau or Horn-Krems-St. Pölten and the A-1, or leisurely wind your way back and see more of the many castles and villages of the Waldviertel.

CARNUNTUM

Carnuntum, the site of extensive Roman ruins, is less than an hour east of Vienna. The largest Roman garrison on the Amber Road, which stretched south from the Baltic Sea, at one point had a population of 30,000. The ruins include two amphitheaters and the *Heidentor*, an enormous gate standing in the middle of a field. There is an information center at **Petronell** with an extensive site behind it, including a reconstruction of a temple to Diana. The museum in **Bad Deutsch-Altenburg** houses many of the artifacts found in the area. Watch for signs to the various sights. A family ticket (two parents and up to four children) gets you into both the ruins at Petronell (April - Oct) and the museum in Bad Deutsch-Altenburg (mid-Jan to mid-Dec, Tues - Sun, 9 AM - 5 PM). For information, call ☎ 02163 33 77.

To reach Carnuntum, take the A-4 from Vienna and then turn onto Route 9 toward Hainburg. You can also get to Petronell-Caruntum on the *Schnellbahn* 7 from the *Wien Nord* or *Wien Mitte* (Landstrasse) station. You can take bikes on the train or rent them at the station.

NEUSIEDLER SEE

Neusiedler Lake (*Neusiedler See*), 52 kilometers southeast of Vienna and straddling the Hungarian border, is Europe's largest steppe lake, where you can bird-watch, tour villages, sail and enjoy water sports. Take the A-4 from Vienna to **Neusiedl am See.** A road going all the way around the lake passes into Hungary at the southern end. There are also bike paths around the lake. This area can be easily reached by train from *Südbahnhof* (see Austrian National Railway section of Transportation chapter) or bus from *Wien Mitte.*

Thirty-five kilometers long and up to 15 kilometers wide, Neusiedler See is only about two meters deep. Surrounded by vast reed beds and marshlands, it's a waterfowl haven. At Neusiedl am See, you can go either east or west. The east side of the lake is best for bird-watching. Much of the **Seewinkel National Park** is a wildlife sanctuary, with marshlands and small lakes and ponds. At **Illmitz,** there is a nature trail that takes you through the reed beds to the lake.

On the west side of the lake, **Rust** is the most popular and perhaps the prettiest village. The town square is full of well-preserved Renaissance and Baroque houses and is the stork capital of Burgenland, because storks spend the summer here after wintering in Africa. Look for their nests on top of chimneys. Rust is also an important wine center. Follow the signs to the beach **(*Seebad*)** and boat landing. You can take tours on the lake, rent a boat for an hour or the day and swim.

EXCURSIONS FOR THE DISABLED

Call the Austria Holiday Information (*Österreich-Urlaubsinformation*) at ☎ 587 20 00 for information for people with disabilities. *Niederösterreich, Oberösterreich, Burgenland, Steiermark* and *Vorarlberg* have some brochures in English describing accessible hotels, excursions, etc.

Reisebüro Egnatia Tours arranges international vacations for customers in wheelchairs. For more information about Mobility Tours, ☎ 405 53 46 (German only).

EUROPE KEY
Euroschlüssel

If you're disabled, you are eligible to receive a registered key that opens accessible toilets in Austria, Germany, France, Luxembourg, Liechtenstein, Spain, Switzerland and Turkey. (Great Britain and Sweden have their own systems.) To get a key and a list of accessible WCs, you must send proof of immobility (from a doctor or government source), your name and address to the following location:

AUSTRIAN WORK ASSOCIATION FOR REHABILITA-TION *Österreichische Arbeitsgemeinschaft für Rehabilitation /ÖAR*
   1010, Stubenring 2
   ☎ 513 15 33

You will then receive a bill for ATS 220. You can also request a key on behalf of a friend or relative who's planning to visit you here. You must send the same information, but you can use your local address for payment. If you have questions, call the above number, where they have some multilingual speakers.

Auf Wiedersehen

Y ou finally feel at home here—you've figured out the "hows" and "wheres" of living in Vienna and have even made some good friends along the way—when it's time to say goodbye. Regardless of whether you're going back to your home country or another foreign land, the moving process is the same: Pack up, clean up, close up and say, *"Auf Wiedersehen."* The following advice and checklist, however, should help make the transition a little easier.

CHECKLIST FOR LEAVING VIENNA

YOUR HOME

- **Notify your landlord that you will be vacating the property.** Three months' notice is standard; with less, you may still have to pay the three months' rent. If you notify the owner by telephone, follow up with a registered letter.
- **Ask what you're required to do before you move out.** Usually cleaning is expected, but you also may have to repaint. This should all be stipulated in your rental contract.
- **Cancel renter's or homeowner's insurance.**
- **Collect all door keys because you must return all those that were issued to you.**
- **Decide if you're leaving anything behind.** You could give things to friends or sell or donate them (see Donations section of Home chapter). Make notices for bulletin boards or ads for school newspapers (or *Bazar*; see Publications appendix).

UTILITIES & SERVICES

- **Arrange to have the utility company (*Wiener Stadtwerke*) read your meters.** Keep in mind that someone must come *after* you've moved out.
- **Cancel telephone service (*Abmeldung*).** Ask the landlord about leaving it connected for the next tenants.
- **Arrange to have your mail forwarded by filling out both a form and card at the post office.** This service is free for the first three months; beyond that, you can prepay graduated fees for up to one year's worth of forwarding.
- **Cancel your TV and radio registration at the post office where you registered.** Don't forget your car radio.
- **If you have a cable-TV connection, call *Telekabel* to cancel it.**

CAR INSURANCE

- **Cancel your car insurance.** (You can "freeze" it if you're coming back, which maintains any good-driver discount or other reductions you've earned.) If you're moving to Germany, it is transferable.

- **You may only be able to cancel car insurance at one time of the year (the date may be stipulated in your policy).** You may also be required to give three months' notice. If you have questions, ask your insurance agent.
- **If you sell your car, you must cancel your registration and turn in the license plates.** Your insurance company can handle the details for you.

MONEY MATTERS

- **Plan ahead for banking provisions.** It is best to contact an Account Representative at your bank to discuss your leaving and banking needs at the time of departure. You may want to consider leaving some money in your account to cover any automatic withdrawals that may come in after you leave, such as the last payment for services (phone, utilities, etc.). There are many options available to you and that's why it is best to contact the bank personally to find out what options there are and what best suits you.
- **If you pay church taxes (*Kirchenbeitrag*), cancel them.**
- **You may have to pay taxes on any alcohol you're importing.** Check with your destination country (and state, where applicable) for details.
- **If you are moving to a non-EU country (other than the US) you can purchase items VAT free.**

PERSONAL & PETS

- **Collect medical, dental and ophthalmological records (including prescriptions and X-rays) to hand-carry with your other important papers and documents.**
- **Notify the school of your children's withdrawal date so records can be prepared.** Collect them before going or leave a forwarding address to have them mailed to you.
- **Allow time for goodbyes.** Everyone needs enough time to detach.
- **Often pets must have a valid rabies shot, which must be administered at least one month prior to entry into another country (see Pets chapter).** You may need a certificate of health issued by your vet within the last 10 days of residence here (check destination requirements). If possible, avoid traveling through Great Britain because it has strict quarantine requirements.

MOVING TIME

- **Make appointments with moving/removal companies.** Your or your spouse's firm may require estimates from more than one company.

- **For insurance and customs purposes, you may be required to provide a detailed inventory with replacement prices.** Check in advance because it's much easier to compile this list before everything's packed up in sealed boxes.

- **Set a date for packing and loading.** European packers are generally very careful with your possessions, which, as a result, may take longer than you anticipate (usually several days to pack and at least a day to load the truck). Be aware of the season (e.g., extreme heat or freezing) your goods will be in transit and plan accordingly.

- **Tipping the movers is at your discretion, but the standard is ATS 100 per mover per day.** You should give the money at the end of each day to the crew leader, who will give it out. You may have a different team of packers each day.

- **Your goods could be in transit for up to eight weeks, so make arrangements for the interim.**

MOVING/REMOVAL COMPANIES

The following companies specialize in packing and moving international customers and have English speakers available:

A. KÜHNER & SOHN
　1190, Muthgasse 19
　FBF Heiligenstadt
　☎ 369 16 01
　Fax 368 29 49

INTERDEAN
INTERNATIONAL MOVERS
　1232, Eitnergasse 5
　☎ 865 47 06
　Fax 865 47 08
　eMail
　vienna.office@interdean.at

EXPEDITORS SPEDITION
  Air Freight:
  1300, Wien Flughafen
  Object 250 Room F261
  ☎ 7007 358 92
  Ocean:
  Industriestr. 15 Object 6 2431
  Entzersdorf/FISCHA
  ☎ 2230 20 52-0

SOBOLAK
INTERNATIONAL REMOVALS
  2100 Leobendorf,
  Stockerauer Strasse 161
  ☎ 201 30-0 or 02262 691-0
  Fax 204 82 50 or
  02262 691 44

LEGALITIES

- **Cancel police registration (*abmelden*) within three days of your departure.** Take copies of every family member's *Meldezettel* to your district police station, which will keep one copy and give one back to you for your records.

- **Find out the customs regulations for your destination country.** For those moving to the United States, you are, technically, required to claim for customs purposes goods purchased in the 12 months prior to entering the country; however, U.S. Customs recognizes that you will have obtained articles in the course of normal living. Use your common sense. Most expatriates claim a small number of items. The moving company will provide the necessary forms.

- **You are subject to the same value limitations as anyone else entering the country on items carried on the plane with you.**

- **If you're an Austrian male under the age of 55, you need to notify the military that you're leaving the country.**

AUF WIEDERSEHEN

The goodbyes have been said and you go for one last walk around *Stephansplatz*. It has been an exhilarating, challenging sojourn, but it will be nice to get "home" again. Home—your home country where people instantly understand you, where you know what to say and do in every situation, where family and friends are, where everything is easy.

> "It is a strange thing to come home. While yet on the journey, you cannot at all realize how strange it will be."
>
> Selma Lagerlöf,
> Nobel Prize–winning Swedish writer

At first, you are too busy unpacking and getting situated to notice much of anything. Nevertheless, things sneak up on you. You notice that you're ready to fork the hand of the waiter who tries to whisk your dinner away before you've had time to finish. Remember all those comparisons you used to make with "home"? Where you used to complain (in Europe) about missing your favorite foods and services, now you find that you're missing fresh dark bread, daily walks, visually exciting architecture, fresh flower stands and the nice lady at the bakery. You see home through different eyes, more aware of its strengths and weaknesses. You question the hectic pace of society and are a bit taken aback by all the changes. On the other hand, you appreciate knowing exactly what your rights are and what you can do to defend them.

Then a month or so after your move, when the boxes are unpacked and your schedule has some semblance of normality, you realize you are depressed. What's the story? After all, you're home. This is a piece of cake—or should be. After all, you moved to another country and functioned—possibly even thrived—what is the problem now?

Be aware that culture shock—that phenomenon you and your family dealt with when you moved abroad—will probably hit again when you return home. But this time, you're not looking for it, so it's harder to deal with. And the support system that helped you adapt to another culture may not be available to you at home to help you readapt.

Re-entry shock is a combination of what you've gained by living overseas plus what you've missed by not living in your home country. You may feel like a foreigner in your own land. A common human characteristic is to remember things as being better than they actually were. The disappointment can be as intense as you think, but this is HOME—if we can't be happy here, then where? The home that you envision is not waiting for you, even if you go back to your same house, because "home" is a concept consisting of habits and activity patterns. It must be reconstructed. One major point to keep in mind is that a move is a move. Any transition is inherently unsettling. A move to another city within your home country would be unsettling—maybe even physically and emotionally painful. Don't blame all problems on having been away or having lived in another country.

What has happened? Nothing that is obvious to you. But you are diffe-rent. Your perspective has changed in ways you may not have anticipated. You've lived with the stimulation of an overseas experience, and the associated difficulties created an emotional or intellectual intensity that is suddenly lacking. You have broader interests. You're used to functioning with more independence. Perhaps you've developed a more mature outlook. Abroad, you had to discover or uncover clues to living and, in the process, probably learned a bit more about yourself. The thrill of discovery is energizing and exhilarating—and now it's gone. You've developed your capacity to cope, be flexible and be patient. You are probably more tolerant and understanding. You are more worldly both in knowledge and in your thinking. Now there's no place to practice your hard-won skills of language development and market bargaining. There are not as many opportunities to meet different people. You find that the people at home are more interested in local rather than international issues. You are now ordinary—no longer an object of curiosity, no longer given the behavioral excuse of being "foreign."

Changes have occurred at home. What you left is not what you should expect to come back to. You think that because you've read *Time, Newsweek* or *The International Herald Tribune* that you understand what's going on in your home country. Actually, you may know much more, in a factual sense, than your friends. But publications don't provide the experience of living through these trends you've read about. (Can you really get a feel for an election without being bombarded with TV commercials, office debates and all the rigmarole that goes with the election process?) Although many of us have spent time back home, even these visits are a step removed from reality—we rush around seeing friends and family. During those trips we live in snapshots.

Friends may find it hard to believe that coming home takes getting used to, so they may be a little short on sympathy for you. They may actually have viewed your temporary relocation as an extended vacation. Sometimes, the many adventures you've had can cause jealousy. Beware of sharing too much with others—they're more interested in telling YOU what happened to THEM. People may ask about your experiences, but their attention span is often limited; you find that just as you're getting to the good part, they interrupt with local sports scores or Aunt Minnie's latest health crisis (which they're equally certain you're interested in). You need to rediscover a common ground.

Family who stayed behind expect you to be the same person you were before you left. They think that, of course, their daughter/sister/son/brother will act and think the same way as when she/he left. But because, for you, the experience of living in another culture was significant and emotional, you feel a bit cheated. By the same token, you expect everything to be the same. You want to just pick up where you left off. Things have changed in the interim—and even frequent phone calls, e-mail, letters and visits cannot provide the same connections as if you had been there.

Moving can also be lonely. You feel disconnected. Remember that even if you return to a known location, others have gone on with their lives and may not realize you're back as they plan their activities, or they may already have the right number of couples for their bridge group. Overseas, you expected to be out of place; at home, you expect to fit right back in. Your family will probably be more dependent on one another, which means you all need to communicate and try to be understanding.

There is a lot more dependency on the wife/mother, who is supposed to be the new home base, even as that home base is in the process of being established. The children are now different from their peers. They may be out of sync with their classmates socially or academically. It's possible that other children will ignore them or taunt them as they struggle to find their niche. There is the possibility of regression.

Job readjustment is another aspect of re-entry. Often an overseas post requires more autonomy, more creative problem-solving and more authority. Reintegration into an established home-country office may mean readjustment into a group, becoming part of a team again. Colleagues and superiors may lack appreciation for international experience or view it as irrelevant.

All this can cause marital stress. There may be a financial strain when overseas allowances are gone. Your social status may be lower and your standard of living reduced. The cost of buying a house (or refurbishing the one you rented out during your absence), new appliances, a car—ARGH! Family members may resist helping with jobs performed by household help while overseas.

"Here I am, safely returned over those peaks from a journey far more beautiful and strange than anything I had hoped for or imagined—how is it that this safe return brings such regret?"

P. Matthieson, American writer

Sound like more than you can handle? Not really—you've already done it at least once! Use the same coping technique as when you went overseas—realize that there will be differences and withhold judgment. Discuss your expectations with your family: What do you think it will be like to go back? What is ahead of us? You knew it would be different when you moved abroad, so accept that moving back will also be different. One source recommends slotting a small vacation between moving out and starting again in a new location, saying it puts distance where needed and refreshes you between stressful situations. (Maybe use some of the time before your sea shipment arrives to do that last bit of touring the continent.)

Even if you're going back to a house you left, think of it as a new location. That way, easy things will be pleasant surprises and hard things can be taken in stride. Play foreigner in your own land. Ask questions and seek advice. Listen to others. Accept people on their own terms. Find places and people with international experience. Search out opportunities with foreign nationals that will allow you to speak the language(s) you learned. Colleges and universities have foreign students or international programs. Try hosting an exchange student.

From those who have been there, we wish you a smooth transition. Before you know it, you will be back in the swing of things. Being aware of what CAN happen can help you acknowledge and overcome it on your way to enjoying all the good things your home country has to offer!

Fire Department (*Feuerwehr*)   ☎ **122**

Police (*Polizei*)   ☎ **133**

Ambulance (*Rettung*)   ☎ **144**

Poison Antidote Service
(*Vergiftungsinformationszentrale*)   ☎ **406 43 43**

Vienna Medical Association
Service Department for Foreign Patients
                    Daily 8 AM - 4 PM   ☎ **515 01-213**
                    Daily 4 PM - 8 AM   ☎ **404 44**

Medical Specialists
Fachärzte Lugeck   ☎ **512 18 18**

This is a group of doctors and an English-speaking nurse on call seven days a week, 24 hours a day, for adults.

Pharmacy Information
Apotheken-Bereitschaftsdienst   ☎ **1550**

This is a tape recording in German listing pharmacies by district that are open after normal business hours and on weekends.

Medicine Delivery Service
Medikamentenzustelldienst   ☎ **891 44**

This 24-hour service will pick up and deliver your medicine from a pharmacy for a fee of about ÖS 170.

Women's Emergency Center
Frauen Notruf der Stadt Wien   ☎ **717 19**

If you have been raped, call this service, where an English speaker may be available to help you.

House for Threatened & Battered Women
(Frauenhaus)　　☎ **512 38 48** (1st district)
　　　　　　　　　☎ **545 48 00** (5th district)
　　　　　　　　　☎ **485 30 30** (16th district)
　　　　　　　　　☎ **408 38 80** (18th district)
　　　　　　　　　☎ **202 55 00** (22nd district)

These shelters, where you should be able to find an English speaker, answer calls 24 hours a day.

Befrienders
Crisis Intervention　　　　　　　　☎ **713 33 74**

This hotline is answered by English speakers Mon - Fri 9:30 AM - 1 PM, Daily 6:30 PM - 10 PM.

Viennese Animal Protection Society Animal Rescue
(Wiener Tierschutzverein
Tierrettung)　　　　　　　　　☎ **699 24 50**

HOUSEHOLD EMERGENCIES
(Basic German required)

Gas Leaks *(Gasgebrechen)*　　　　☎ **128**

Emergency Plumbing Repair Service
(Installateur-Notdienst)　　　　☎ **586 37 30**

This service directs you to private plumbers and electricians available for emergencies. On weekends, a recording gives the same information by district.

Telephone Out of Order
(Ortsnetz Wien)　　　　　　　　☎ **111 +**
　　　　　　　　　　　　　　first three digits
　　　　　　　　　　　　　　of nonworking
　　　　　　　　　　　　　　phone number

LOST OR STOLEN CREDIT CARDS

Bankomat Card — Call your bank directly

Credit Cards (English speakers available)

American Express
(Weekdays 8 AM–6:30 PM)   ☎ 515 51 1
24-hour Customer Service
(toll-free)   ☎ 0800 20 85 66

Diners Club   ☎ 501 35-0

Eurocard/MasterCard   ☎ 717 01-0

Japanese Credit Bureau (JCB)   ☎ 587 76 25

Visa   ☎ 711 11-770

EMERGENCY ROAD SERVICE & TOWING

Austrian automobile clubs (some English is spoken) that provide free service to members (though you can join on the spot):

ÖAMTC   ☎ 120
(Österreichischer Automobil-,
Motorrad- und Touring Club)

ARBÖ   ☎ 123
(Auto-, Motor- und
Radfahrerbund Österreichs)

TELEPHONE DIRECTORY ASSISTANCE

(Ask for an English speaker)

Within Austria
(Auskunft Inland)   ☎ **118 11**

Germany *(Deutschland)*   ☎ **118 12**

All other European countries   ☎ **118 13**

All non-European countries   ☎ **118 14**

Long-distance operator
(Fernamt)   ☎ **118 16**
(for assistance placing a call)

TRANSPORTATION INFORMATION

Airport Information   ☎ **7007 2231**
(Flughafen Auskunft)   ☎ **7007 2232**
www.vie.co.at   ☎ **7007 2233**

Airport Taxi   ☎ **1731**
(Flughafen Taxi)   ☎ **31 300**
     ☎ **40 100**

Train-Schedule Information
(ÖBB Zugauskunft)   ☎ **1717**
www.oebb.at

Train Reservations
(ÖBB Zugreservierung)   ☎ **1700**

AUSTRIA & VIENNA INFORMATION OFFICES

VIENNA TOURIST INFORMATION OFFICE

1010, Albertina Platz
☎ 211 14-0
Daily 9 AM - 7 PM
http://info.wien.at

This is the main tourist information office in Vienna with brochures in English on cultural events, sights, stores, hotels and restaurants. Other offices are located in the arrival area of the Vienna International Airport and train stations.

CITY INFORMATION AT CITY HALL
(Stadtinformation Rathaus)

1010, Friedrich-Schmidt-Platz 1
(Rathaus)
☎ 525 50-0
Mon - Fri 8 AM - 6 PM,
Sat - Sun (phone 8 AM - 4 PM)

Located inside City Hall, this isn't a tourist-information office, but it does have some maps and brochures in English. You're better off calling the number above for upcoming opera performances and ticket sales, as well as museum hours. You'll hear a recorded message in German first, then in English, giving updated information on daily events.

AUSTRIA HOLIDAY INFORMATION (Österreich-Urlaubsinformation)

1040, Margaretenstrasse 1
(corner of Wiedner Hauptstrasse)
☎ 587 20 00
Mon - Wed, Fri 10 AM - 5 PM,
Thurs 10 AM - 6 PM

This center has some brochures in English on Austrian vacation destinations.

AUSTRIA PROMOTIONS (Österreich Werbung)

1040 Margaretenstrasse 1
☎ 588 66-0

This agency has information on travel and tourism in Austria (e.g., where you can ski in April).

LOWER AUSTRIA TOURIST INFORMATION (Niederösterreich-Touristik Information)

1010, Walfischgasse 6
☎ 513 80 22
Fax 513 80 22-30
Mon - Fri 9 AM - 6 PM

This center has a number of brochures in English on trips to Lower Austria.

Information Offices

CONSUMER INFORMATION

If you want to file a consumer complaint or have questions about your rights as a consumer, contact the following organization:

CONSUMER INFORMATION ASSOCIATION
(*Verein für Konsumenteninformation*)

> 1060, Mariahilfer Strasse 81
> ☎ 588 77-0

This number has a recording in German, then an information operator answers (ask for an English speaker).

INFORMATION FOR THE DISABLED

FEDERAL MINISTRY FOR SOCIAL AFFAIRS
(*Bundesministerium in Sozialen Angelegenheiten*)

> ☎ 711 00-5493

This is Austria's federal agency to help people with disabilities. It has information about finding accessible housing or transportation.

SOCIAL AND DISABILITY DEPARTMENT OF VIENNA
(*Sozial- und Behindertenreferat Stadt Wien*)

> *Magistratsabteilung* (MA) 12
> 1010, Schottenring 24/1
> ☎ 531 14-853 74
> Mon, Thurs 3:30 PM - 6:30 PM

If you have a residence permit (*Aufenthaltsbewilligung*), you can receive information from this city agency on accessible transportation, worker's protection and schools.

LANDESJUGENDREFERAT DER MAGISTRATSABTEILUNG (MA) 13

> ☎ 40 00-843 55

Behindertenatlas "Ämter, Soziales" is a binder full of information in German about social services and government agencies that serve people with disabilities. *Behindertenatlas "Kultur und Freizeit für Jugendliche"* (*Disabled Atlas on "Culture and Leisure for Young People"*) provides an extensive list in German of accessible cultural buildings, such as museums and theaters. You can order both for ATS 100 each by calling the above number (where English is spoken).

PUBLIC-TRANSPORTATION INFORMATION

Information offices in some *U-Bahn* stations provide pamphlets (some of which are in English) about Vienna's public-transportation system, its tickets and travel routes. Or you can visit them online at www.wienerlinien.co.at. The following are major *U-Bahn* stations with information offices:

KARLSPLATZ, STEPHANSPLATZ AND WESTBAHNHOF
    Mon - Fri 6:30 AM - 6:30 PM, Sat - Sun & Holidays 8:30 AM - 4:30 PM

LANDSTRASSE (WIEN MITTE), VOLKSTHEATER, PRATERSTERN AND PHILADELPHIABRÜCKE
    Mon - Fri 7 AM - 6:30 PM

STUDENT COMMUTER PASSES
Schülerstreckenkarten

Your child's school will provide you with the appropriate forms for a *Schülerstreckenkarte*. The Vienna Line's Customer Service Center also offers information in German, but an English speaker should be available.

VIENNA LINE'S CUSTOMER SERVICE CENTER
(*Das Kundenzentrum der Wiener Linien*)
    1030, Erdbergstrasse 202 (U3 Erdberg station)
    ☎ 790 91 20
    Mon - Fri 8 AM - 3 PM

TRAVEL INFORMATION OFFICES
Eastern Europe

The following tourist-information centers and travel agency have some brochures in English:

Czech Republic

TSCHECHISCHES ZENTRUM
    1010, Herrengasse 17
    ☎ 35 23 61
    Mon - Fri 10 AM - noon,
    1 PM - 6 PM

Hungary

UNGARISCHES ZENTRUM
    1010, Opernring 3-5
    ☎ 585 20 12
    Mon - Thurs 9 AM - 5 PM,
    Fri 9 AM - 2 PM

Slovakia

**SCK SLOWAKISCHES
REISEBÜRO**
   1010, Parkring 12
   ☎ 512 01 99
   Mon - Fri 9 AM - 5 PM

Slovenia

**SLOWENISCHES
FREMDENVERKEHRSAMT**
   1030, Am Stadtpark (Vienna
   Hilton), Room 261
   ☎ 715 40 10
   Mon - Fri 9 AM - 5 PM

The following are national & religious holidays, during which stores and other businesses close. (For more information, see the Austrian Holidays section of the Austria chapter.)

New Year's Day	*Neujahr*	**January 1**
Epiphany	*Heilige Drei Könige*	**January 6**
Easter Monday	*Ostermontag*	**Day after Easter Sunday**
Labor Day	*Tag der Arbeit*	**May 1**
Ascension	*Christi Himmelfahrt*	**Nine days before Pentecost**
Monday after Pentecost/Whitsun	*Pfingstmontag*	**50 days after Easter Sunday**
Corpus Christi	*Fronleichnam*	**Second Thursday after Pentecost**
Assumption Day	*Mariä Himmelfahrt*	**August 15**
Austrian National Day	*Nationalfeiertag*	**October 26**
All Saints' Day	*Allerheiligen*	**November 1**
Immaculate Conception	*Mariä Empfängnis*	**December 8**
Christmas Eve	*Heiliger Abend/ Weihnachten*	**December 24** (stores usually open half the day)
Christmas	*Christtag*	**December 25**
St. Stephen's Day	*Stefanitag*	**December 26**
New Year's Eve	*Silvester*	**December 31** (stores usually open half the day)

Here in Vienna, your country's embassy or consulate can perform many vital functions for you:

- Provide information on Austria's foreign-residency requirements.
- Renew an expired passport or replace a lost or stolen one (be sure to report the loss to the Austrian police first).
- Report a birth in Austria to your home country.
- Provide guidelines for getting married in Austria.
- Help make arrangements in the case of a death here.
- Assist in voter registration and obtaining absentee ballots.
- Register its citizens residing in Austria (in case of an emergency).

You should also be aware that non-Austrian citizens living in Austria are subject to Austrian laws. Therefore, private disputes here must be settled through the Austrian legal system, and diplomatic or consular officials are not authorized to practice law or to act as attorneys or agents in private matters. They can, however, provide names of local attorneys who can legally represent you.

HOW TO REACH AN EMBASSY IN AN EMERGENCY

If you have an emergency situation and need immediate help from your embassy or consulate after normal business hours, call the regular number, but stay on the line even after the recording has finished in order to hear the emergency phone number.

The following is a list of the embassies and consulates of the major English-speaking countries represented in Austria. Other embassies are listed under *"Botschaft"* and consulates are under *"Konsulat"* in the white pages of the telephone directory.

UNITED STATES OF AMERICA

EMBASSY
1090, Boltzmanngasse 16
☎ 313 39
Fax 310 06 82
www.usembassy-vienna.at

CONSULATE
1010, Gartenbaupromenade 2
(side entrance of Marriott Hotel)
☎ 313 39
Fax 513 43 51 or 512 58 35
Hours vary by function, so call beforehand.

U.S. Tax Information

Standard IRS tax forms are available beginning in early February of each year. If you have not received forms by March 1, call ☎ 313 39-7538 or send a request with a stamped, self-addressed envelope to the U.S. Consulate. If you have questions about filing taxes overseas, you can call Philadelphia at ☎ 001 (215) 516-2000 or Germany at ☎ 0049 (228) 339 21 19 (Mon - Fri, 9 AM - 4 PM). Or visit the Internet site www.irs.ustreas.gov.

AUSTRALIA

1040, Mattiellistrasse 2-4
☎ 512 85 80-0
Fax 513 16 56
(for consulate matters)
Mon - Thurs 9 AM - 1 PM,
2 PM - 5 PM, Fri 9 AM - 1 PM

CANADA

1010, Laurenzerberg 2
☎ 531 38 30-00
Fax 531 38 39-05
(for consulate matters)
Fax 531 38 39-11
(for visa applications)
Mon - Fri 8:30 AM - 12:30 PM,
1:30 PM - 3:30 PM

GREAT BRITAIN

EMBASSY
1030, Jaurèsgasse 12
☎ 716 13-0
Mon - Fri 8:30 AM - 6 PM

CONSULATE
1030, Jaurèsgasse 10
☎ 716 13-5338
Fax 716 13-5900
Mon - Fri 9:15 AM - noon,
2 PM - 4 PM (British passport
holders only in afternoon)

INDIA

1015, Kärntner Ring 2
☎ 505 86 66
Fax 505 92 19
Mon - Fri 9 AM - noon

IRELAND

1030, Landstrasser Hauptstrasse 2
(Hilton Center 16th floor)
☎ 715 42 46-0
Fax 713 60 04
Mon - Fri 9:30 AM - 11:30 AM,
1:30 PM - 4 PM

NEW ZEALAND

Call the British Embassy.

SOUTH AFRICA

1190, Sandgasse 33
☎ 32 64 93-0
Fax 32 64 93-18
(for consulate matters)
Mon - Fri 8:30 AM - noon

GLOSSARY OF OFFICIAL GERMAN TERMS (Words You Will Find on Forms)

Österreich Austria

Wien Vienna

Abmeldung (abgemeldet am) Registration of departure (date departure registered)

Akad. Grad (Akademischer Grad) Academic title

Anderer Staat Other country

Ankreuzen Cross, tick, check (a choice)

Anmeldung (angemeldet am) Registration of arrival (date arrival registered)

Anschrift Address

Art Type, kind

Ausgabe Edition, issue, version, printout

Ausland Abroad, foreign

Ausstellende Behörde Issuing authority

Ausstellungsdatum Date of issuance

Bestätigung Confirmation

Bezieher Recipient of benefits

Bisher, bisheriger Previous, until now

Blockschrift Capital letters

Bundesland Federal state

Ehe Marriage

Einsendeschluss Reply date, closing date

Erziehungsberechtigter Legal guardian

Familienname Family name

Familienname vor der ersten Eheschliessung Maiden name

Gebührenpflichtig Subject to a charge or fee

Geburtsdatum Date of birth

Geburtsort laut Reisedokument Place of birth, as in travel document

Geltungsbereich Area of validity

Geltungszeitraum Period of validity

Geschieden (gesch.) Divorced

Geschlecht Gender

Gültig bis, gültig für Good/valid until, good/valid for

Hauptwohnsitz Primary residence

Haus Nr. (Hausnummer) House number, street address

Kinder Children

Ledig Single

Männlich Male

Meldezettel Registration form

Minderjährig Minor (child)

Name Name

Nummer Number

Ort, Ortsgemeinde City or township

Document Terms

Personalausweis
Personal ID card

Postleitzahl Postal code

Raum für behördliche Vermerke Place for official remarks (i.e., for official use only)

Reisedokument bei Fremden Travel document, if a foreigner

Reisepass Passport

Religionsbekenntnis Religious affiliation

Richtigkeit Correctness

Staat Country, state

Staatsangehörigkeit Nationality

Stiege Staircase

Strasse/Platz Street/Place

Tür Nr. (Tür Nummer) Door/apartment number

Unterkunft Accommodation

Unterkunftgeber Landlord

Unterschrift Signature

Unterschrift des Meldepflichtigen Signature of person responsible for registration

Verheiratet Married

Verwitwet Widowed

Verzogen nach Moved to

Vorname First name

Weiblich Female

zB (zum Beispiel) For example

BOOKS ON AUSTRIA & VIENNA IN ENGLISH

Books

The Austrian Mind:
An Intellectual and Social History
1848 - 1938

by William M. Johnston. 1972 University of California Press, Berkeley. Winner of the 1971 Austrian History Award, this book evaluates the contributions of Austro-Hungarian intellectuals to economic, legal and social theory, to the arts, philosophy, literature and criticism, and to medicine. Notes, a bibliography and an index are included.

BildAtlas Vienna:
English Edition

by Günter K. Kodek. 1985 HB-Verlags- und Vertriebs-Ges.m.b.H., Hamburg. Detailed maps, pictures and accompanying information make this paperback atlas a treasure. Places of interest are listed by area of the city.

A Brief Survey
of Austrian History

by Richard Rickett. 1996 Georg Prachner Verlag, Vienna. This book is written in easy-to-understand chronological order.

Danube: A Journey Through the
Landscape, History, and Culture
of Central Europe

by Claudio Magris. 1989 William Collins Sons & Co. Ltd., New York. This book not only focuses on the river itself but also the history, literature, mythology and culture through which it has flowed.

Festivals and Traditions
in Austria

by Werner Schneider. 1985 Pinguin-Verlag, Innsbruck. Although customs of specific regions are described, there is, unfortunately, no explanation of the holidays themselves. Also, many common Austrian holidays that are new to foreigners are overlooked.

Fin de Siècle Vienna

by Carl Schorske. 1979 Alfred A. Knopf, Inc., New York. This book covers turn-of-the-century Vienna's politics and culture.

The Habsburgs

by Andrew Wheatcroft. 1995 Viking, London. Twenty years' worth of study and research went into this thorough book chronicling the 500-year history of the Habsburg royal family. Color illustrations, notes, bibliography and index are included.

In Mozart's Footsteps:
A Travel Guide
for Music Lovers

by Harrison James Wignall. 1991 Paragon House, New York. This book provides an alphabetical listing of sites—by country and city—associated with Mozart, with appropriate biographical, historical and sightseeing details. There are also a chronology of Mozart's travels, notes and a bibliography.

Introducing Austria

by Lonnie Johnson. 1987 Österreich. Bundesverlag, Vienna. This easy-to-read book offers historical and contemporary insights into what Vienna is and why. A bibliography and index are included.

The Kreisky Era in Austria: Contemporary Austrian Studies, Vol. 2

edited by Günter Bischof and Anton Pelinka. 1994 Transaction Publishers, New Brunswick, New Jersey. This is a collection of essays that shed light on the Socialist movement and its impact on Austria and the world. Biographical data is included.

Mucha: The Triumph of Art Nouveau

by Arthur Ellridge. 1992 Terrail, Paris. Alfonse Mucha profoundly influenced the visual world, not only with his posters and illustrations, but also with his typefaces and fashions. This Bohemian Austrian is synonymous with *Jugendstil/Art Nouveau*, an important part of Vienna's artistic heritage.

A Nervous Splendor

by F. Morton. 1979 Penguin Books, New York. This easy-to-read history provides fascinating insights into events and characters that preceded the fall of the Habsburg empire.

Thunder at Twilight: Vienna 1913/1914

by Frederic Morton. 1989 Macmillan Publishing Company, New York. This book looks into the turbulent times leading up to World War I and the intellectually charged activities in Vienna at that time. References, bibliography and index are included.

Vienna: Art and History

by Delia Meth-Cohn. 1993 Flow East Limited, Prague. This book is filled with color photos that spotlight Vienna's architectural achievements, while it also provides artistic and historical insight. A chronology and restaurant, coffeehouse and museum guide are included.

Vienna: Legend and Reality

by Ilsa Barea. 1992 Pimlico, London. This book separates the legend from the reality of Vienna's geography, history and contributions of its people, which ultimately merge to make it the complex city that it is today. Notes, bibliography and index are included.

Vienna 1900

by Hans Bisanz. 1995 Berghaus Verlag, Kirchdorf, Germany. This is a beautifully illustrated volume detailing the blossoming of art and science in Vienna at the turn of the century.

Vienna: A Travellers' Companion

edited by John Lehmann and Richard Bassett. 1988 Constable and Company, Ltd., London. This is a collection of eyewitness accounts from various periods in Vienna's long and fascinating history. A bibliography and index are included.

Viennese Design and the Wiener Werkstätte

by Jane Kallir. 1986 Galerie St. Etienne, New York. This book discusses the impact of the architects and craftsmen associated with these studios and workshops, where they combined classical elegance with streamlined functionality. Their works are still visible throughout Vienna and remain an inspiration to artists today.

Viennese: Splendor, Twilight, and Exile

by Paul Hofmann. 1988 Doubleday, New York. An excellent attempt at explaining what makes Vienna and the Viennese the way they are. Notes and an index are included.

Wiener Werkstätte 1903–1932

by Gabriele Fahr-Becker. 1995 Taschen, Cologne, Germany. This beautifully illustrated book celebrates the history and works of Vienna's artisans and artists who changed the face of the city.

Wittgenstein's Vienna

by Allan Janik and Stephen Toulmin. 1973 Simon & Schuster, New York. In order to explain native-Viennese Ludwig Wittgenstein's philosophy, the authors have placed him in the context of his times. Notes, a selected bibliography and an index accompany this work.

AUSTRIAN BIOGRAPHIES IN ENGLISH

The Cambridge Companion to Freud

edited by Jerome Neu. 1991 Cambridge University Press. This is a biography with specially commissioned essays written by an international team of scholars. It may be intended to be a reference book, but it also provides a straightforward explanation of Freud's work. Notes, bibliography and index are included.

Freud: A Life for Our Time

by Peter Gay. 1989 Anchor Books, New York. Although mainly a biography placing him in the context of his time, this book offers a succinct analysis of many of Freud's complex ideas. Notes, bibliography and index are included.

Maria Theresa

by Edward Crankshaw. 1983 Constable and Company, London. This is a biography of the leader who saved the Habsburg Empire and reared much of Europe's royalty. A bibliography and index are included.

Mozart in Vienna

by Volkmar Braunbehrens. 1991 Oxford University Press. This book chronicles the last 10 years of Mozart's life, challenging the myths about him and the prejudices against his wife. Notes, bibliography and index are included.

Mozart: The Real Amadeus

by Michel Parouty. 1993 Thames and Hudson, London. This is a well-documented, easy-to-read book full of anecdotes and color pictures. Documents, chronology and index are included.

The Reluctant Empress: A Biography of Empress Elisabeth of Austria

by Brigitte Hamann. 1986 Alfred A. Knopf, Inc., New York. This is a well-documented, unsentimental biography about Austria's beautiful but elusive empress. Notes, index and family tree are included.

Sissi: The Tragic Empress: The Story of Elisabeth of Austria

by Ludwig Merkle. 1996 F. Bruckmann KG, Munich, Germany. This is 112 pages of pictures (many in color) and text explaining the enigma who was Sissi. A bibliography is included.

GUIDEBOOKS ON AUSTRIA & VIENNA IN ENGLISH

Blue Guide to Austria
by Ian Robertson. 1992 A. & C. Black, London.

Charming Small Hotel Guides: Austria
by Paul Wade and Kathy Arnold. 1993 Duncan Petersen Publishing, Ltd., London.

Eating Out in Austria
by Gretel Beer. 1992 Robert Hall, London.

Fodor's Austria
Fodor's Travel Publications, Inc., New York. Published by the leader in travel guidebooks, this annually updated book is filled with useful information for all of Austria.

Frommer's Comprehensive Travel Guide Austria
by Darwin Porter. 1993 Prentice Hall, New York. Updated regularly.

Innocents Abroad: Traveling with Kids in Europe
by Valerie Wolf Deutsch and Laura Sutherland. 1991 Plume, New York.

Insight City Guides, Vienna
APA Publications. 1990 Höfer Press Pte. Ltd., Singapore. As its name implies, this guide taps into local resources to provide insights into what makes Vienna distinctive.

Karen Brown's Austria: Charming Inns & Itineraries
by Karen Brown. 1996 Travel Press, San Mateo, California.

Let's Go: The Budget Guide to Austria & Switzerland
edited by Sucharita Mulpuru. 1995 Macmillan, London. This guide is updated annually and aimed mainly at students, but it has loads of practical information.

Lonely Planet City Guide Vienna
by Mark Honan. 1995 Lonely Planet Publications, Hawthorn, Victoria, Australia. This pocket-sized guide has all the information you'll ever need as a tourist in Vienna.

Vienna (Eyewitness Travel Guides)
by Stephen Brook. 1994 Dorling Kindersley, New York. This is an indispensable guide with its easy-to-find information, color photos and detailed illustrations.

Vienna (Knopf Guides)
1994 Alfred A. Knopf, Inc., New York. This invaluable guide (very similar to the one by Eyewitness, but with slightly different information and pictures) was originally produced by the prestigious French publishing house Gallimard of Paris.

Vienna A to Z
edited by Wolfgang J. Kraus. 1995 Vienna Tourist Board, Vienna. This pocket-sized book—available in English, French, Italian and Japanese—is great for self-guided tours. It provides explanations for Vienna's more than 200 historical landmarks displaying a white sign surmounted by red-and-white pennants.

Vienna 1900: Architecture and Painting
by Christian M. Nebehay. 1991 Verlag Christian Brandstätter, Vienna. This guide to art and architecture by Viennese artists includes short biographies, pictures and maps to show specific locations where the works can be found.

Vienna Walks
by J. Sydney Jones. 1994 Henry Holt, New York. This book offers four walking tours of Vienna's most historic areas. Details given are both interesting and enlightening. It also contains a list of restaurants, cafés and shops, a bibliography and an index.

The Visitor's Guide to Austria
by Ken Allan. 1988 Moorland Publishing Co. Ltd., Ashbourne, England.

Walking Easy in the Austrian Alps
by Chet and Carolee Lipton. 1994 Gateway Books, Oakland, California. This book includes a section on different outings in Vienna. It is a good one to hand to visitors when you need to send them out the door on their own.

Xenophobe's Guide to the Austrians
by Louis James. 1994 Ravette Books Ltd., London. This thin book takes a whimsical but telling look at the history and habits of Austrians.

BOOKS ON CULTURAL ADJUSTMENT IN ENGLISH

The Art of Crossing Cultures
by Craig Storti. 1990 Intercultural Press, Inc., Yarmouth, Maine.

Do's and Taboos Around the World
edited by Roger E. Axtell; compiled by The Parker Pen Company. 1993 John Wiley & Sons, Inc., New York.

Moving Abroad: A Guide to International Living
by Virginia McKay. 1989 VLM Enterprises, Wilmington, Delaware.

Survival Kit for Overseas Living: For Americans Planning to Live and Work Abroad, Second Edition
by L. Robert Kohls. 1984 Intercultural Press, Inc., Yarmouth, Maine.

The Teenager's Survival Guide to Moving
by Patricia Cooney Nida, PhD, and Wendy M. Heller. 1985 Collier Books, New York.

MAGAZINE ARTICLES IN ENGLISH

"The Romance of Vienna"
National Geographic Traveler "Discover Europe" (Collector's Edition), 1996.

"Vienna"
National Geographic Traveler, December 1994.

BOOKS ON AUSTRIA & VIENNA IN GERMAN

Beisln und Altwiener Gaststätten

by Berndt Anwander. 1993 Falter Verlag, Vienna. This is a guide to and history of 180 old Viennese pubs and inns. Because these places were chosen for their atmosphere and good food, you can use this book just for the addresses and business hours (and the occasional recipe).

Feste feiern in Wien

1994 Falter Verlag, Vienna. This is a valuable handbook on where to find supplies and facilities—from banquet rooms to swimming pools, caterers to rentable glassware, bands to costumes—for a party or other festive occasion. Businesses, with their addresses and phone numbers (and sometimes business hours), are listed by category, making this a handy book for even those with minimal German skills (or with a good dictionary).

Handbuch WienKultur

1996 Falter Verlag, Vienna. Museums and performing-arts locations are only the tip of the iceberg in this listing of galleries, magazine publishers, festival sponsors, institutes and archives. You only need basic German to get the who, what, where, when and how.

Städteatlas Grossraum Wien

Freytag & Berndt, Vienna. This is an invaluable bookmap of Vienna and its surrounding areas with all public-transportation routes outlined and a street index in the back.

Wien, wie es ißt ...

Falter Verlag, Vienna. This book (released yearly in December) is a guide to Vienna's 4,000 restaurants, cafés, pastry shops (*Konditoreien*), ice-cream shops (*Eissalons*), new-wine taverns (*Heurigen*), bars and sausage stands (*Würtelstände*), which are listed by district. With minimal German and a dictionary, you can peruse such categories as "Eat on Sunday" (*"Essen am Sonntag"*), "Eat in the Green" (*"Essen im Grünen"*), "Live Music" (*"Live-Programm"*) and "Eat After Midnight" (*"Essen nach Mitternacht"*). Each establishment is listed with its business hours, average meal prices, specialties and credit-card policy.

Die Wiener Märkte

by Werner T. Bauer. 1996 Falter Verlag, Vienna. This guide covers 100 markets—from the famous *Naschmarkt* to flea and seasonal markets. Although their histories and descriptions are in German, the beginner can still find locations and basic information.

Wiener Heurigenführer

by Rudolf Steurer and Klaus Egle. 1996 Ueberreuter, Vienna. Though this guide to Vienna's *Heurigen* requires moderate German comprehension, you can easily decipher the locations, business hours, wines and specialties.

E nglish-language publications are commonly found at newsstands in the city center, some bookstores and the Vienna International Centre. Morawa Buch und Presse is the main foreign-periodicals distributor in Vienna, so look for the Morawa sign at newsstands. For English-language bookstores, see the Recreation chapter.

ENGLISH-LANGUAGE NEWSPAPERS
Zeitungen

Daily Mail

The Daily Telegraph

The Express

The Financial Times

The Guardian

The Independent

The International Herald Tribune

The Jerusalem Post

The Mirror

The Telegraph

The Times

USA Today

The Wall Street Journal Europe

ENGLISH-LANGUAGE NEWS SERVICE

Daily News Service
1020, Heinestrasse 1/20
☎ 216 86 00
This news service provides summaries in English of Austrian newspaper articles, which are faxed or e-mailed every Friday to subscribers.

Austrosearch
www.austrosearch.at/austrianews

Provides the top news headlines, weather forcast and more. In German and English.

VIENNA'S ENGLISH-LANGUAGE NEWSPAPERS

Austria Today

This weekly national newspaper covers business, culture, sports, politics and Austrian and international news.

AUSTRIAN NEWSPAPERS *Zeitungen*

If you can read German, the following Austrian papers are respected sources of business, political and cultural news:

Kronen Zeitung

Kurier

Die Presse

Salzburger Nachrichten
(national newspaper)

Standard

Bazar is a Viennese newspaper for classifieds. You can place ads for free, but you must pay for the paper itself. Each day is devoted to special editions, such as for real estate (good for finding an apartment) on Wednesday and used cars on Friday. You can read the ads with a little German knowledge or a good dictionary, but you'll have to be able to communicate with the sellers themselves.

All Viennese newspapers cover daily events, but they also have Friday supplements listing the following week's cultural events in and around Vienna. Thursday's *Die Presse* comes with a magazine, *Schaufenster*, which provides the following week's radio and TV listings; Friday's *Schaufenster* lists current gallery and museum exhibitions, tours, readings, concerts, festivals, plays and activities for children. Even if you don't know much German, you can decipher these supplements.

See the warning about subscription extensions in the Post section of the Communications chapter.

ENGLISH-LANGUAGE MAGAZINES *Zeitschriften*

These magazines are available at many city-center newsstands:

Barron's

Business Central Europe

The Economist

Fortune

Life

Newsweek

Time

A variety of science, travel, art, computer, fashion, literary, business and craft magazines are available in English at Morawa Buch & Presse, 1010, Wollzeile 11. There is an entire periodicals department in the back of the store. Their outlets at Westbahnhof and the Vienna International Airport also stock many international magazines and newspapers.

MAGAZINES ABOUT VIENNA

FALTER'S BEST OF VIENNA

This special edition of the weekly magazine *Falter* is published every spring and fall (in German). It offers a collection of tips from readers on their favorite shops, restaurants, hairstylists, etc. There are entries for everything from "Best Chinese Restaurant" to "Best Place to Cool Down on a Hot Summer Day."

HALLO WIEN

GEZA Verlag
1010, Biberstrasse 10
☎ 513 31 52

This monthly guide contains information on cultural events, maps, important phone numbers, a restaurant guide, shopping tips and ads. It is available at most four- and five-star hotels or by yearly subscription.

UNO MAGAZIN & SOCIETY

1140, Hüttelbergstrasse 23A
☎ 914 77 44-0
Fax 914 77 44-8

Members of the *Österreichische Liga für die Vereinten Nationen* can receive this magazine written in English, which covers United Nations, diplomatic, social-welfare and cultural topics.

WHAT'S ON IN VIENNA?

Available at *Tabak-Trafiks* at the beginning of each month, this magazine (in German) offers highlights of cultural events. Six- or 12-month subscriptions are also available.

WHERE VIENNA

2380 Perchtoldsdorf,
Brunnerfeldstrasse 45
☎ (0222) 863 31-0

Available at most newsstands or by subscription (six issues a year), this bimonthly magazine includes maps, guides to shopping, dining and the arts, and features on local culture.

WIEN PROGRAMM

You can pick up this events booklet from the Vienna Tourist Information Office anytime after the 20th of each month for the following month. It contains detailed information about operas, plays, concerts, museum exhibitions and special events.

GOVERNMENT PUBLICATION

AUSTRIA: FACTS AND FIGURES

Federal Press Service, Vienna. Published annually in English, this slim government-produced handbook is vital for newcomers because it provides an introduction to Austria—from its history and politics, economy and resources to culture and the media. Ask the Austrian Consulate in your home country for a copy.

WEIGHTS & MEASURES

U.S.		Metric
Length		
1 inch (in)		2.54 centimeters (cm)
12 in	1 foot (ft)	0.31 meter (m)
3 ft	1 yard (yd)	0.91 m
1,760 yd	1 mile (mi)	1.61 kilometers (km)
Area		
1 square inch (sq in)		6.45 sq cm
144 sq in	1 square foot (sq ft)	929.03 sq cm
9 sq ft	1 square yard (sq yd)	0.84 sq m
4,840 sq yd	1 acre	4,047 sq m
640 acres	1 square mile (sq mi)	2,590 sq km
Volume/Capacity		
8 fl ounces (oz)	1 cup	0.237 liter (l)
16 fl oz	1 pint (pt)	0.473 l
2 pt	1 quart (qt)	0.95 l
4 qt	1 gallon (gal)	3.79 l
Weight		
1 grain		0.07 gram (g)
27.34 grains	1 dram	1.77 g
16 drams	1 oz	28.35 g
16 oz	1 pound (lb)	453.6 g
14 lb	1 stone (British)	6.35 kilograms (kg)
28 lb	1 quarter (British)	12.7 kg
2,000 lb	1 ton (short) (T)	0.91 metric ton (mT)

Measurements

Metric		U.S.

Length
Längenmasse

1 millimeter (mm)		0.04 inch (in)
10 mm	1 centimeter (cm)	0.40 in
10 cm	1 decimeter (dm)	3.94 in
100 cm	1 meter (m)	39.37 in
1,000 m	1 kilometer (km)	0.621 mile (mi)

Area
Flächenmasse

	1 sq cm (or cm^2)	0.155 sq in
10,000 sq cm	1 sq m (or m^2)	10.76 sq ft
10,000 sq m	1 hectare (ha)	2.47 acres

Volume
Raummasse

1 cubic cm (or cm^3)		0.061 cu in
1,000 cu cm	1 cu dm (or dm^3)	61.02 cu in
1,000 cu dm	1 cu m (or m^3)	1.308 cu yd

Volume (Liquid)
Hohlmasse

1 liter	1.06 quarts (qt)	
10 l	1 dekaliter (dal)	2.64 gal

Weight
Gewichte

1 gram (g)	0.04 ounces	
1,000 g	1 kilogram (kg)	2.20 pounds
1,000 kg	1 metric ton (mT)	1.10 short tons

U.S. & BRITISH EQUIVALENTS

Liquid Volume

U.S.	Imperial
1 1/4 U.S. teaspoon (tsp)	1 Imperial tsp
1 1/4 U.S. tablespoon (TBSP)	1 Imperial TBSP
1 U.S. fluid ounce (fl oz)	**1 Imperial fl oz**
Scant 1/4 U.S. cup (c)	3 Imperial TBSP
1/2 U.S. c	6 Imperial TBSP (scant 1/4 Imperial pint)
2/3 U.S. c	1/4 Imperial pint (pt)
1 U.S. c (8 U.S. fl oz)	Scant 1/2 Imperial pt
1 1/4 U.S. c	1/2 Imperial pt (10 Imperial fl oz)
Scant 2 U.S. c	3/4 Imperial pt (15 Imperial fl oz)
1 U.S. pt (16 U.S. fl oz)	Generous 3/4 Imperial pt (16 Imperial fl oz)
2 1/2 U.S. c	1 Imperial pt (20 Imperial fl oz)

CONVERSION OF AVOIRDUPOIS & METRIC UNITS

1 oz = 28.35 g	15 oz = 425.25 g	11 g = 0.39 oz
2 oz = 56.7 g	16 oz = 453.59 g	12 g = 0.42 oz
3 oz = 85.05 g	1 lb = 0.454 kg	13 g = 0.46 oz
4 oz = 113.4 g		14 g = 0.49 oz
5 oz = 141.75 g	1 g = 0.04 oz	15 g = 0.53 oz
6 oz = 170.1 g	2 g = 0.07 oz	16 g = 0.56 oz
7 oz = 198.45 g	3 g = 0.11 oz	50 g = 1.75 oz
8 oz = 226.8 g	4 g = 0.14 oz	100 g = 3.5 oz
9 oz = 253.15 g	5 g = 0.18 oz	250 g = 9 oz
10 oz = 283.5 g	6 g = 0.21 oz	500 g = 17.5 oz
11 oz = 311.85 g	7 g = 0.25 oz	1,000 g = 1 kg =
12 oz = 340.2 g	8 g = 0.28 oz	35.5 oz
13 oz = 368.55 g	9 g = 0.32 oz	
14 oz = 396.9 g	10 g = 0.35 oz	

You can buy a Pyrex measuring cup (*Messbecher*) that has markings in pints and liters.

LIQUID MEASURES

~ means "approximately equal to"

$^1/_2$ tsp ~ 2.5 milliliters (ml)
1 tsp ~ 5 ml
1 TBSP ~ 15 ml
$^1/_2$ cup ~ 100 ml
1 cup ~ 225 ml
2 cups ~ 450 ml
4 cups = 1 quart ~ $^9/_{10}$ liter = 900 ml
4 $^1/_3$ cups ~ 1 liter

For some common equivalencies, see the Foods chapter.

1 gram = 100 centigrams = 1,000 milligrams
1 milligram (mg) = 0.001 g
1 centigram (cg) = 0.01 g
1 decigram (dg) = 0.1 g
1 decagram (dag) = 10 g
1 hectogram (hg) = 100 g
1 kilogram (kg) = 1,000 g

TEMPERATURE CONVERSION

Fahrenheit	Celsius	Fahrenheit	Celsius
Weather		**Human**	
-4° F	-20° C	95° F	35° C
5° F	-15° C	98° F	36.7° C
14° F	-10° C	**98.6° F**	**37° C**
23° F	-5° C	99° F	37.2° C
32° F	**0° C**	100° F	37.8° C
41° F	5° C	104° F	40° C
50° F	10° C		
58° F	15° C		
68° F	20° C		
77° F	25° C		
86° F	30° C		

OVEN TEMPERATURES

Fahrenheit	Celsius		
122° F	50° C		
140° F	60° C		
150° F	**65.5° C**		
158° F	70° C		
167° F	75° C		
176° F	80° C		
185° F	85° C		
194° F	90° C		
200° F	**93° C**		
203° F	95° C		
212° F	100° C		
230° F	110° C		
248° F	120° C		
250° F	**121° C**		
266° F	130° C		
275° F	**135° C**	Gas mark 1	Very slow
284° F	140° C		
300° F	**149° C**	Gas mark 2	Slow
302° F	150° C	Gas mark 2	Slow
320° F	160° C	Gas mark 2	Slow
325° F	**163° C**	Gas mark 2	Slow
338° F	170° C		
350° F	**177° C**	Gas mark 3–4	Moderate
356° F	180° C	Gas mark 3–4	Moderate
375° F	**190° C**	Gas mark 3–4	Moderate
392° F	200° C		
400° F	**204° C**	Gas mark 5–6	Hot
410° F	210° C	Gas mark 5–6	Hot
425° F	**218° C**	Gas mark 5–6	Hot
450° F	**232° C**	Gas mark 7	Very hot
482° F	250° C		
572° F	300° C		

Fahrenheit to Celsius:
Subtract 32 and multiply by $5/9$.
Celsius to Fahrenheit:
Multiply by $9/5$ and add 32.

D

G

H